KICK-ASS

MARK MILLAR
WRITER

JOHN ROMITA JR.
PENCILS

PETER STEIGERWALD
DIGITAL INKS AND COLORS

JOHN WORKMAN
LETTERER

MEGAN SHIRK
DIGITAL INK ASSISTANT

BETH SOTELO
COLORS ASSISTANT (ISSUES #3-6)

JAXEN DE NOBRIGA
DIGITAL INK ASSISTANT (ISSUE #6)

MELINA MIKULIC
DESIGN AND PRODUCTION

RACHAEL FULTON
EDITOR

IMAGE COMICS, INC.
IMAGECOMICS.COM

HIT-GIRL and **KICK-ASS** created by **MARK MILLAR** and **JOHN ROMITA JR.**

Robert Kirkman – Chief Operating Officer • **Erik Larsen** – Chief Financial Officer • **Todd McFarlane** – President • **Marc Silvestri** – Chief Executive Officer • **Jim Valentino** – Vice President
Eric Stephenson – Publisher / Chief Creative Officer • **Corey Hart** – Director of Sales • **Jeff Boison** – Director of Publishing Planning & Book Trade Sales • **Chris Ross** – Director of Digital Sales
Jeff Stang – Director of Specialty Sales • **Kat Salazar** – Director of PR & Marketing • **Drew Gill** – Art Director • **Heather Doornink** – Production Director • **Nicole Lapalme** – Controller

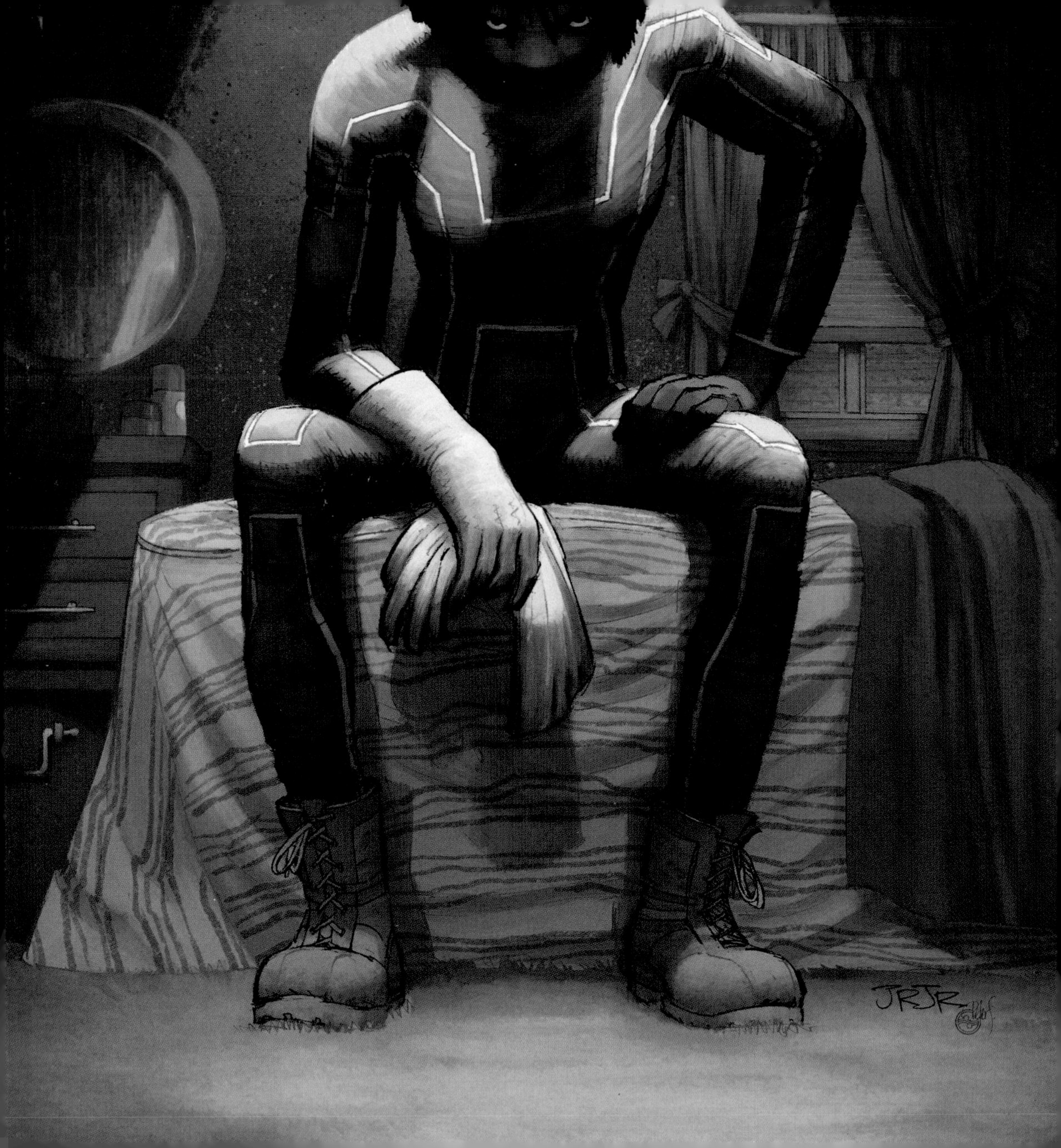
JRJR

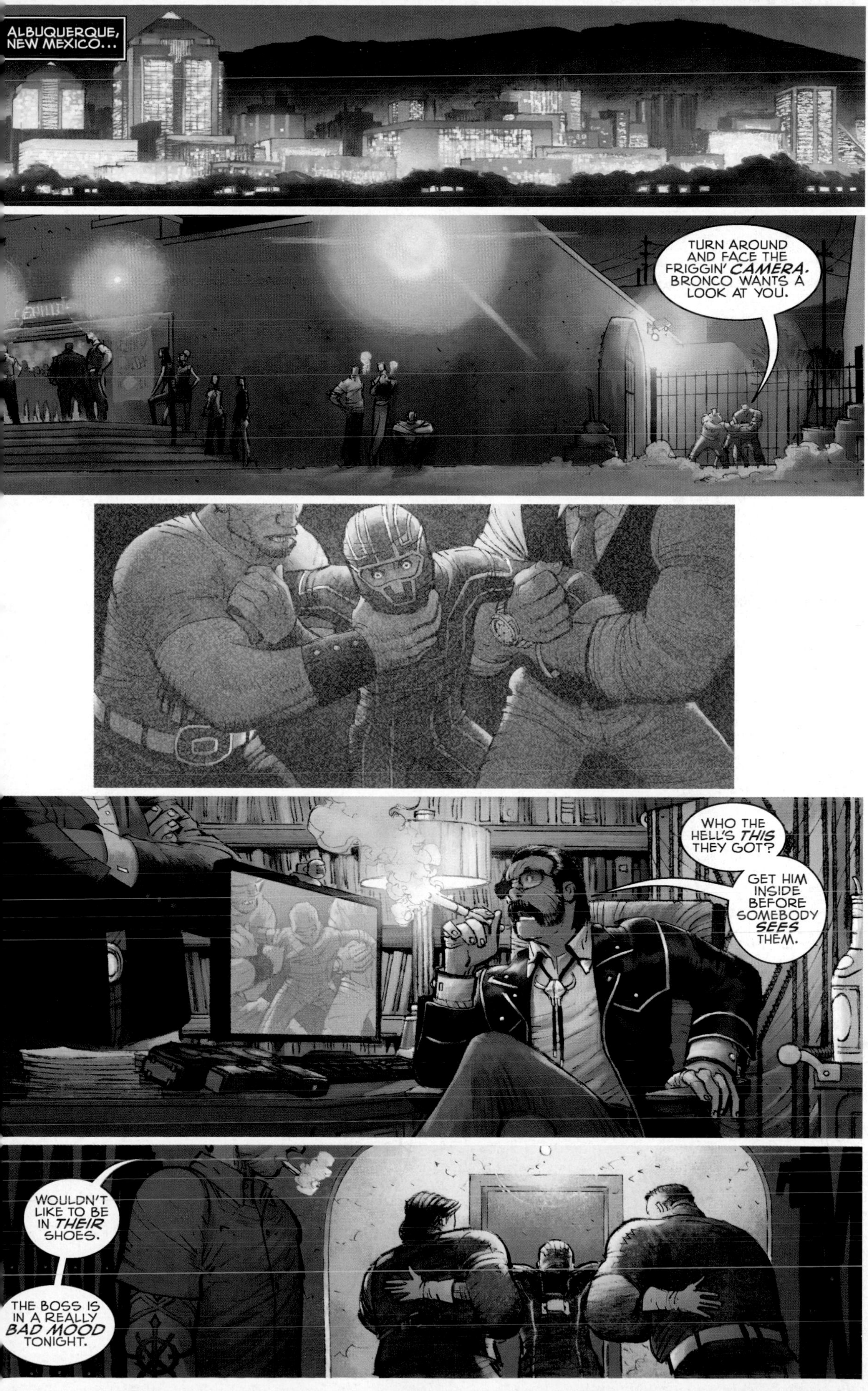
ALBUQUERQUE, NEW MEXICO...
TURN AROUND AND FACE THE FRIGGIN' CAMERA. BRONCO WANTS A LOOK AT YOU.
WHO THE HELL'S THIS THEY GOT?
GET HIM INSIDE BEFORE SOMEBODY SEES THEM.
WOULDN'T LIKE TO BE IN THEIR SHOES.
THE BOSS IS IN A REALLY BAD MOOD TONIGHT.

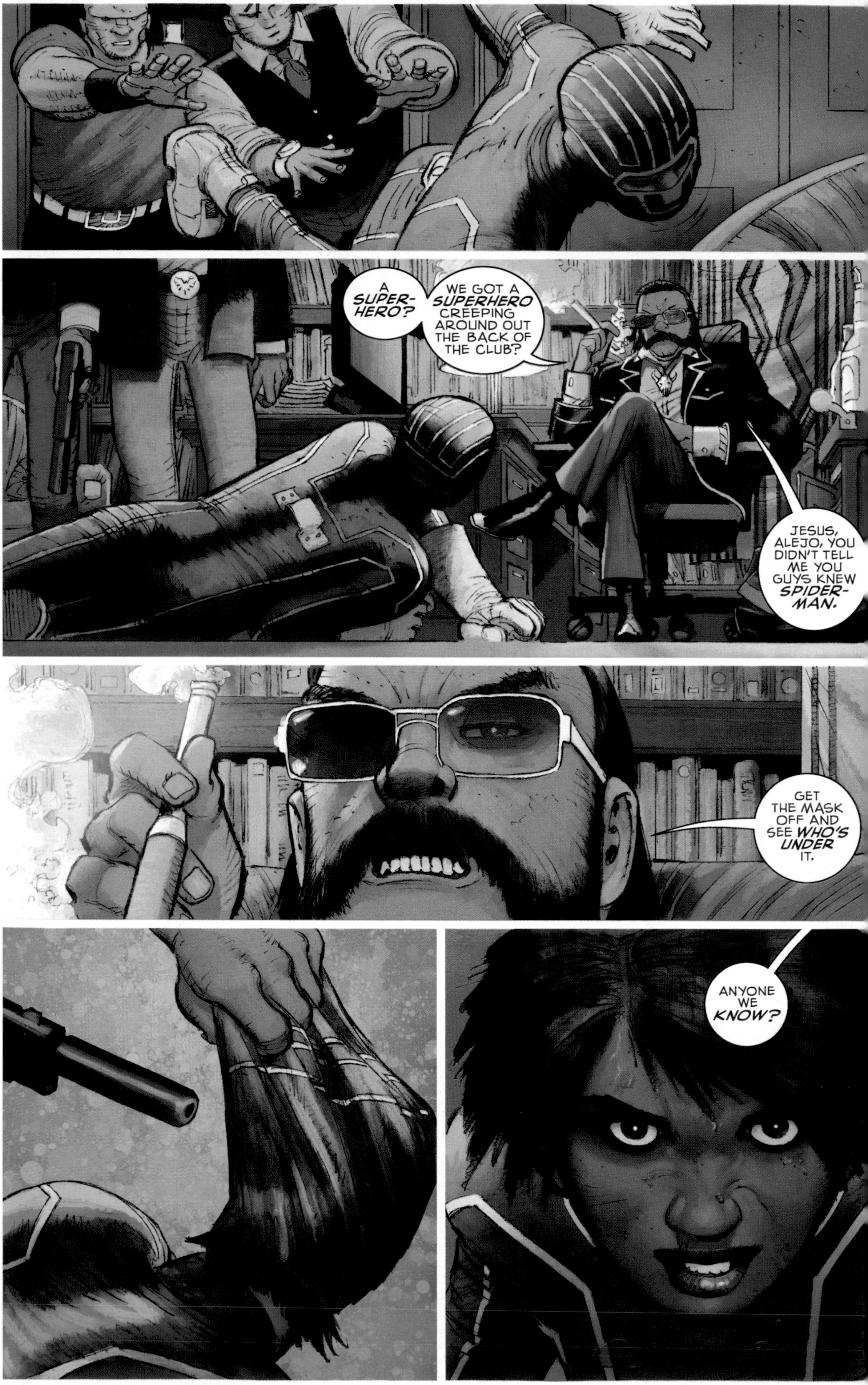
A SUPER-HERO?
WE GOT A SUPERHERO CREEPING AROUND OUT THE BACK OF THE CLUB?
JESUS, ALEJO, YOU DIDN'T TELL ME YOU GUYS KNEW SPIDER-MAN.
GET THE MASK OFF AND SEE WHO'S UNDER IT.
ANYONE WE KNOW?

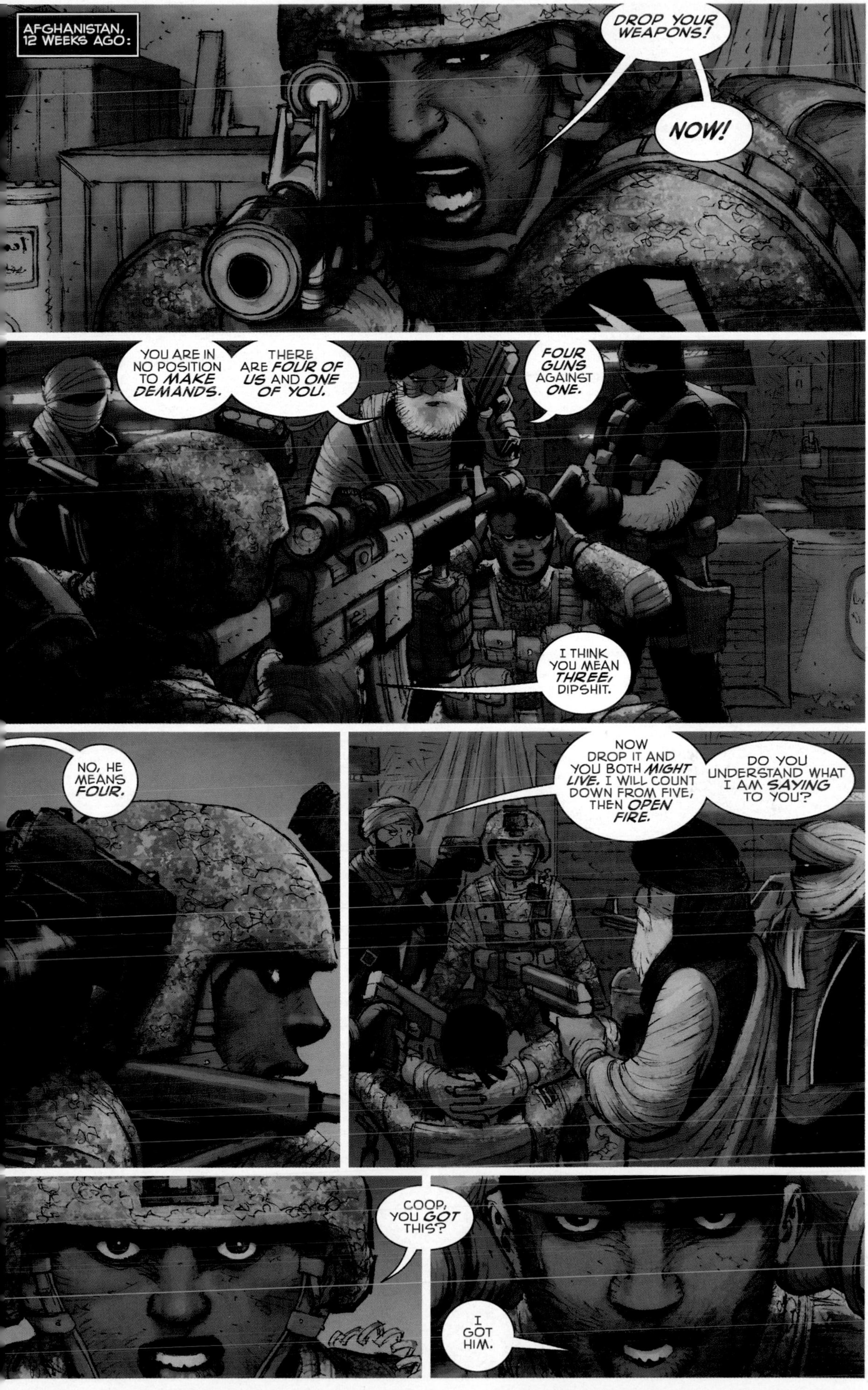
AFGHANISTAN, 12 WEEKS AGO:
DROP YOUR WEAPONS!
NOW!
YOU ARE IN NO POSITION TO MAKE DEMANDS.
THERE ARE FOUR OF US AND ONE OF YOU.
FOUR GUNS AGAINST ONE.
I THINK YOU MEAN THREE, DIPSHIT.
NO, HE MEANS FOUR.
NOW DROP IT AND YOU BOTH MIGHT LIVE. I WILL COUNT DOWN FROM FIVE, THEN OPEN FIRE.
DO YOU UNDERSTAND WHAT I AM SAYING TO YOU?
COOP, YOU GOT THIS?
I GOT HIM.

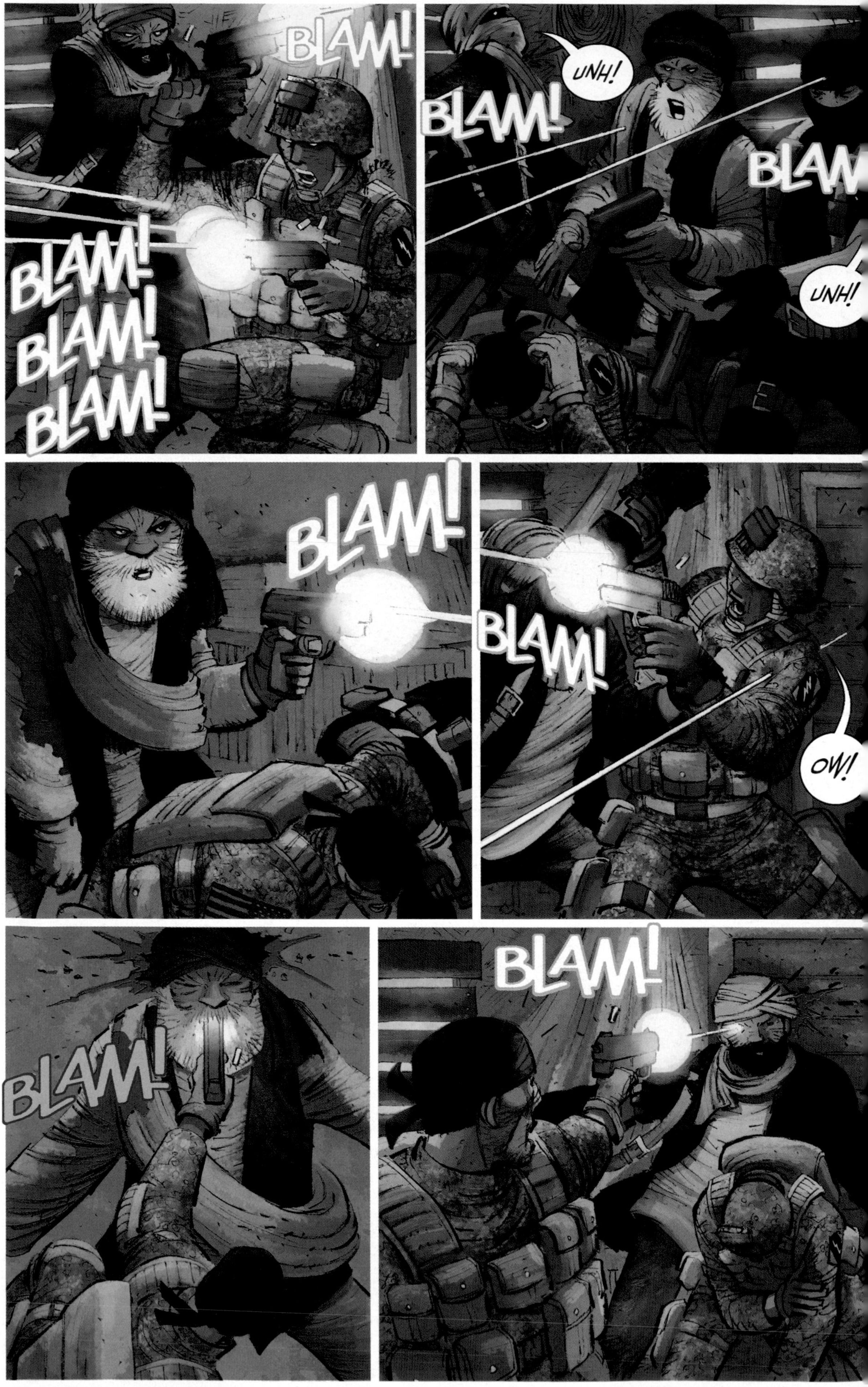
BLAM!
BLAM!
BLAM!
BLAM!
UNH!
BLAM!
UNH!
BLAM!
BLAM!
OW!
BLAM!
BLAM!

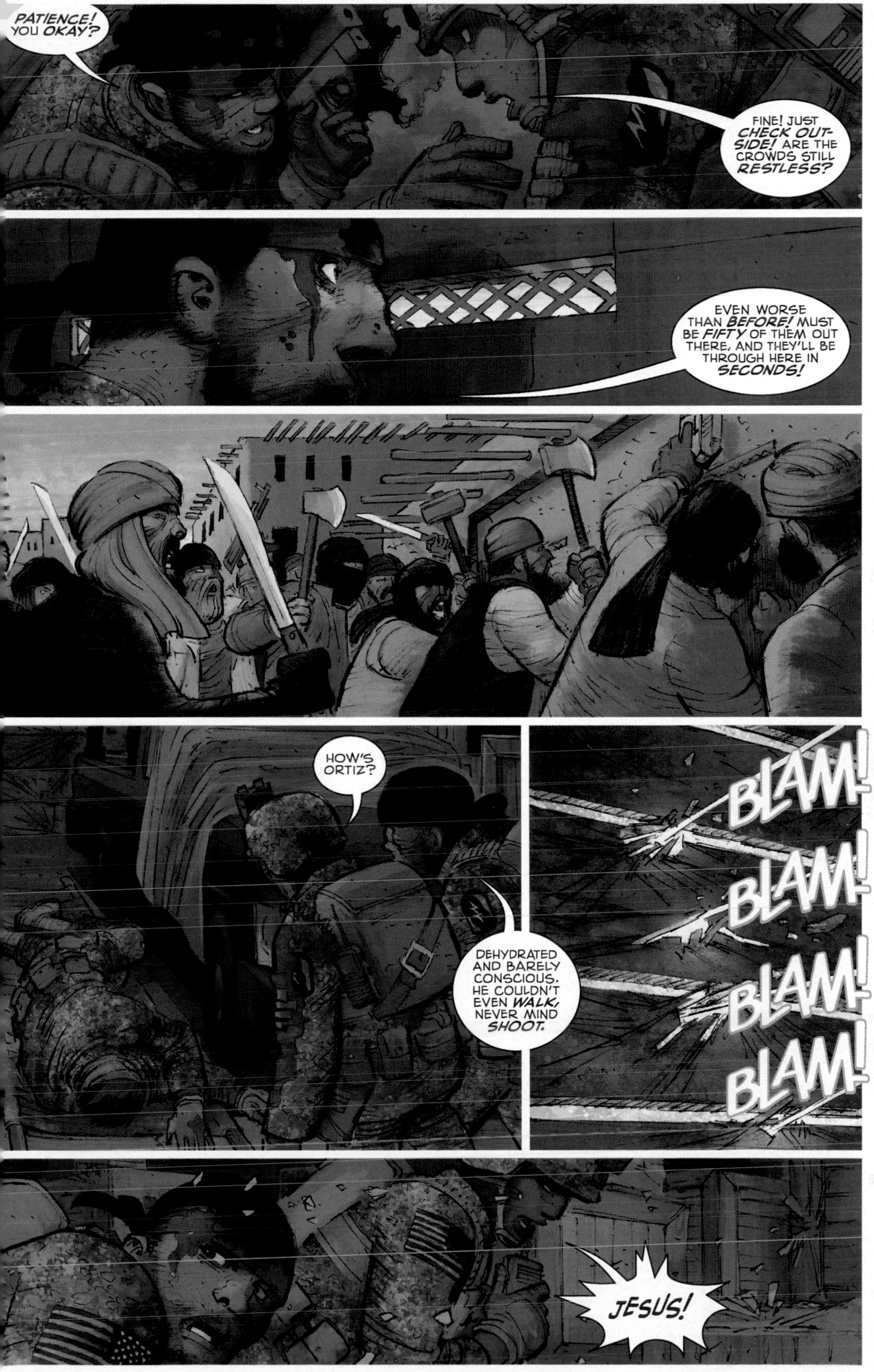
PATIENCE! YOU OKAY?
FINE! JUST CHECK OUT-SIDE! ARE THE CROWDS STILL RESTLESS?
EVEN WORSE THAN BEFORE! MUST BE FIFTY OF THEM OUT THERE, AND THEY'LL BE THROUGH HERE IN SECONDS!
HOW'S ORTIZ?
DEHYDRATED AND BARELY CONSCIOUS. HE COULDN'T EVEN WALK, NEVER MIND SHOOT.
BLAM! BLAM! BLAM! BLAM!
JESUS!

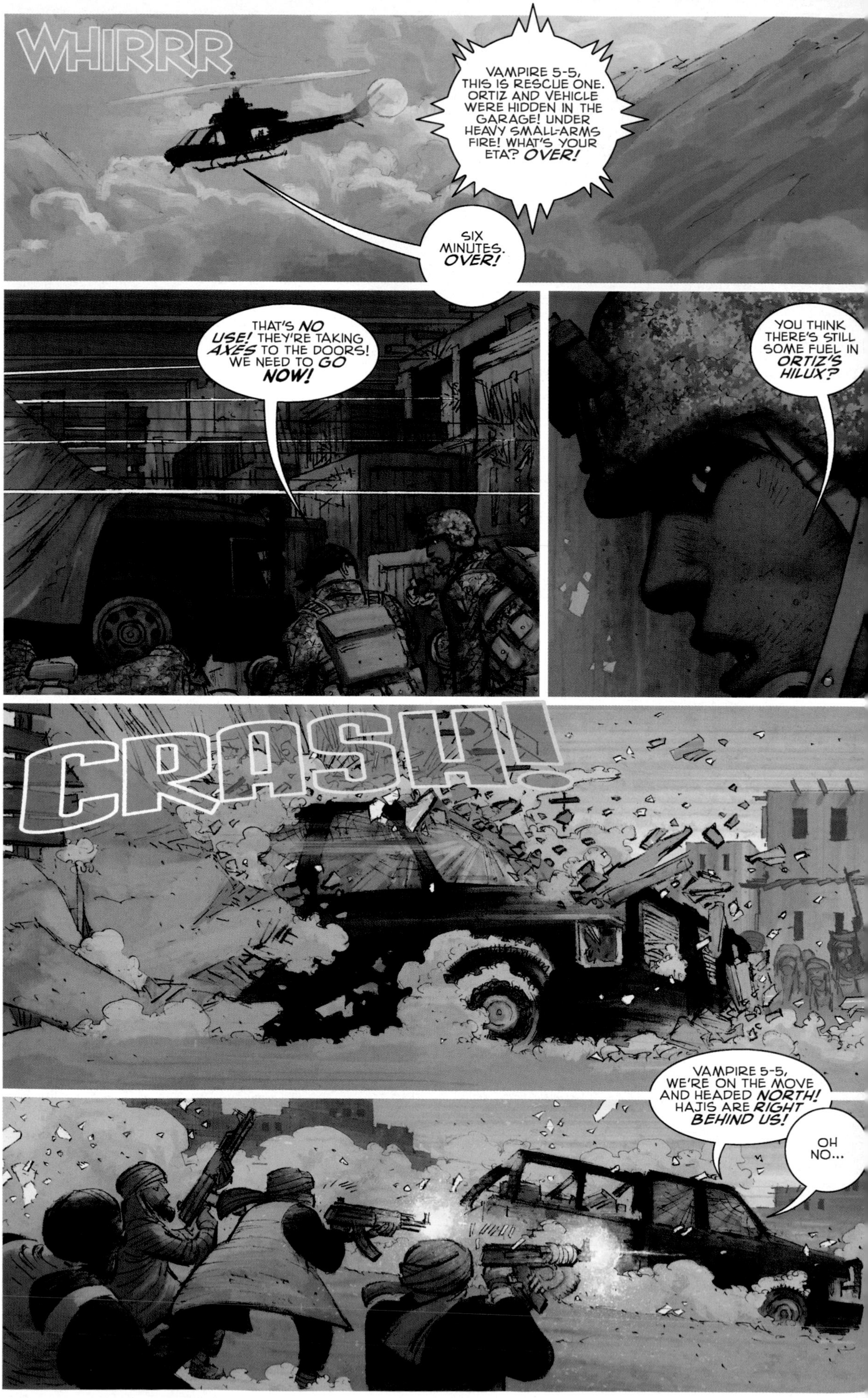
WHIRRR
VAMPIRE 5-5, THIS IS RESCUE ONE. ORTIZ AND VEHICLE WERE HIDDEN IN THE GARAGE! UNDER HEAVY SMALL-ARMS FIRE! WHAT'S YOUR ETA? OVER!
SIX MINUTES. OVER!
THAT'S NO USE! THEY'RE TAKING AXES TO THE DOORS! WE NEED TO GO NOW!
YOU THINK THERE'S STILL SOME FUEL IN ORTIZ'S HILUX?
CRASH!
VAMPIRE 5-5, WE'RE ON THE MOVE AND HEADED NORTH! HAJIS ARE RIGHT BEHIND US!
OH NO...

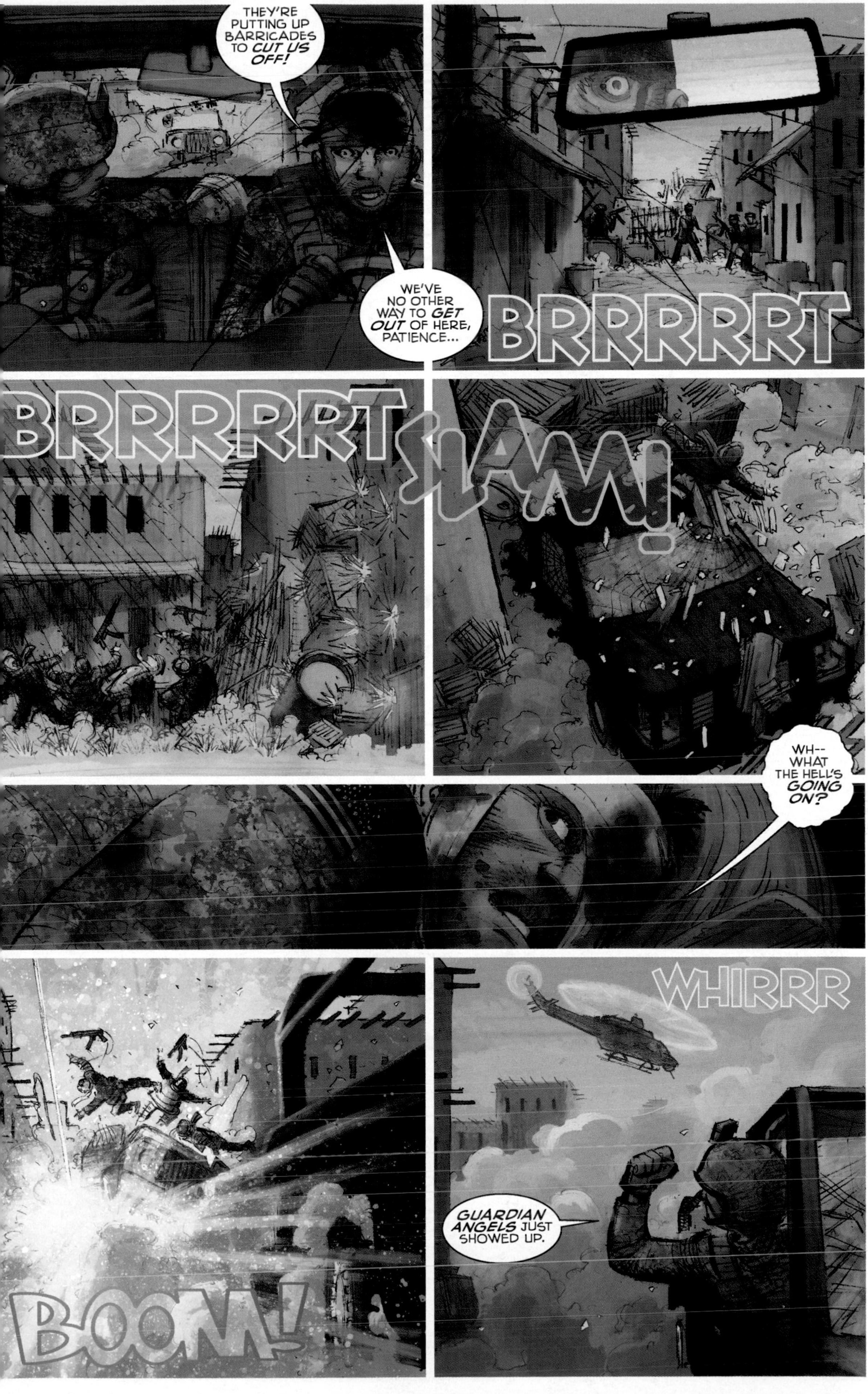
THEY'RE PUTTING UP BARRICADES TO CUT US OFF!
WE'VE NO OTHER WAY TO GET OUT OF HERE, PATIENCE...
BRRRRRT
BRRRRRT
SLAM!
WH-- WHAT THE HELL'S GOING ON?
BOOM!
WHIRRR
GUARDIAN ANGELS JUST SHOWED UP.

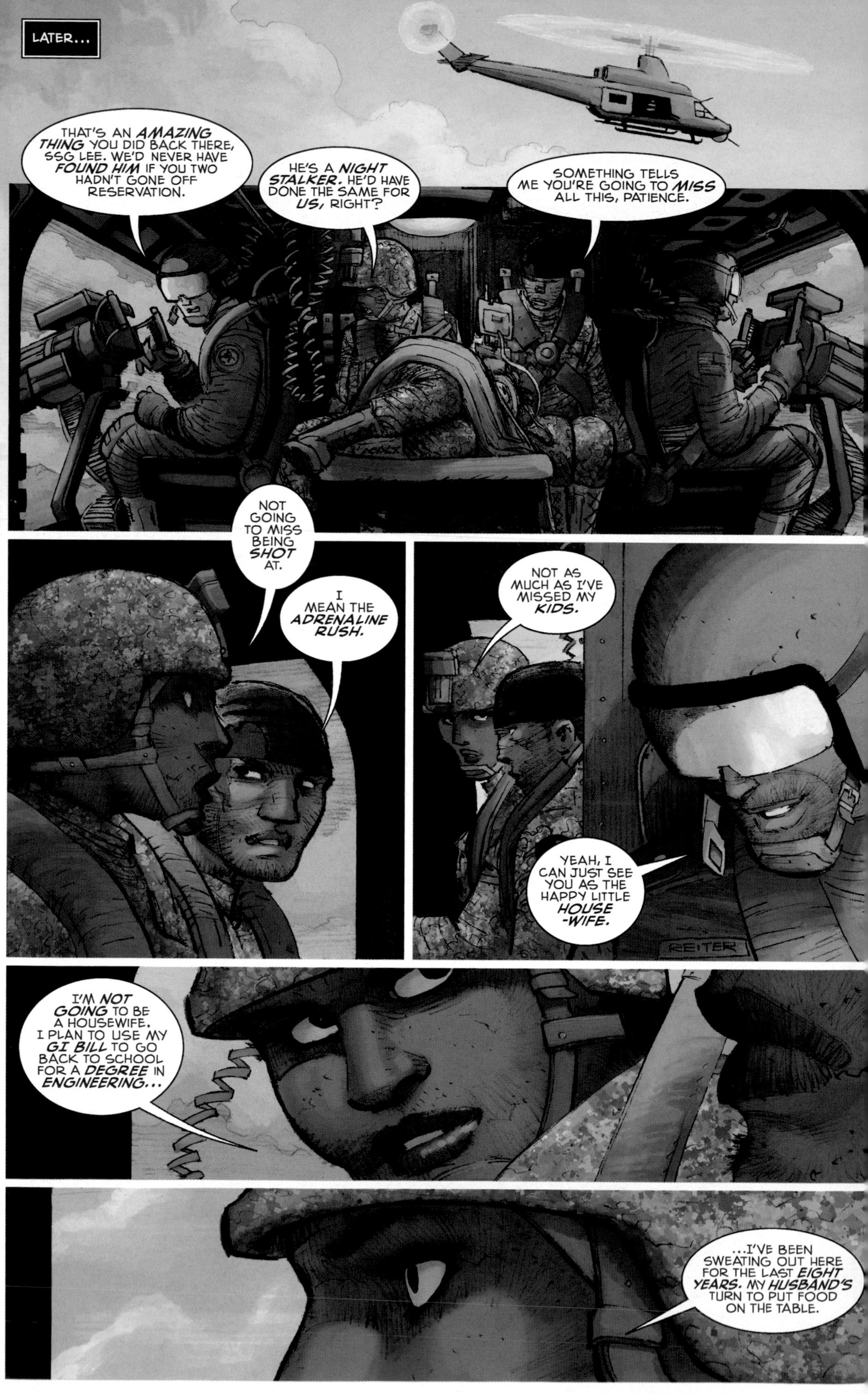
LATER...
THAT'S AN AMAZING THING YOU DID BACK THERE, SSG LEE. WE'D NEVER HAVE FOUND HIM IF YOU TWO HADN'T GONE OFF RESERVATION.
HE'S A NIGHT STALKER. HE'D HAVE DONE THE SAME FOR US, RIGHT?
SOMETHING TELLS ME YOU'RE GOING TO MISS ALL THIS, PATIENCE.
NOT GOING TO MISS BEING SHOT AT.
I MEAN THE ADRENALINE RUSH.
NOT AS MUCH AS I'VE MISSED MY KIDS.
YEAH, I CAN JUST SEE YOU AS THE HAPPY LITTLE HOUSE-WIFE.
REITER
I'M NOT GOING TO BE A HOUSEWIFE. I PLAN TO USE MY GI BILL TO GO BACK TO SCHOOL FOR A DEGREE IN ENGINEERING...
...I'VE BEEN SWEATING OUT HERE FOR THE LAST EIGHT YEARS. MY HUSBAND'S TURN TO PUT FOOD ON THE TABLE.

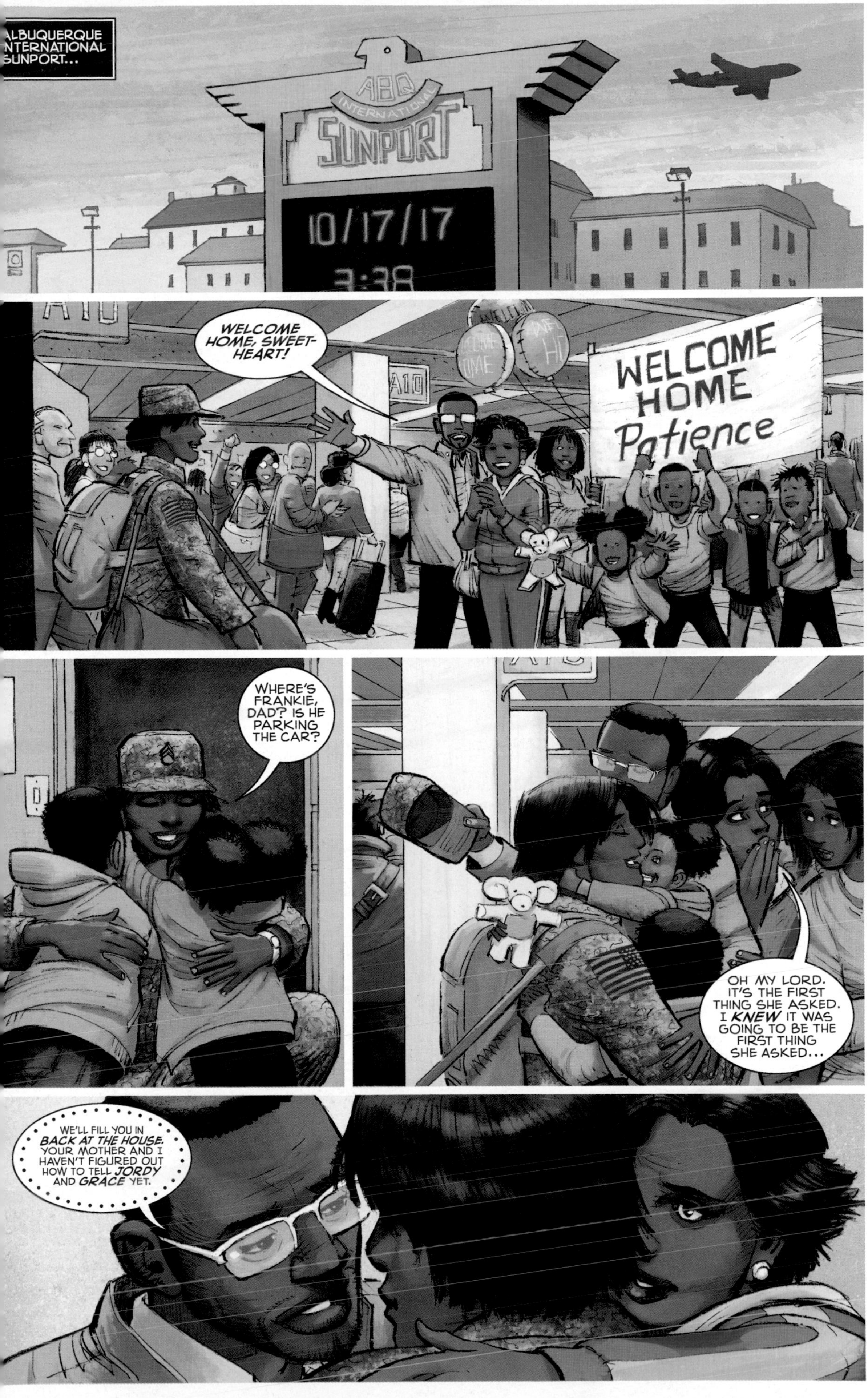
ALBUQUERQUE INTERNATIONAL SUNPORT...
ABQ INTERNATIONAL SUNPORT
10/17/17
WELCOME HOME, SWEET-HEART!
A10
WELCOME HOME Patience
WHERE'S FRANKIE, DAD? IS HE PARKING THE CAR?
OH MY LORD. IT'S THE FIRST THING SHE ASKED. I *KNEW* IT WAS GOING TO BE THE FIRST THING SHE ASKED...
WE'LL FILL YOU IN *BACK AT THE HOUSE.* YOUR MOTHER AND I HAVEN'T FIGURED OUT HOW TO TELL *JORDY* AND *GRACE* YET.

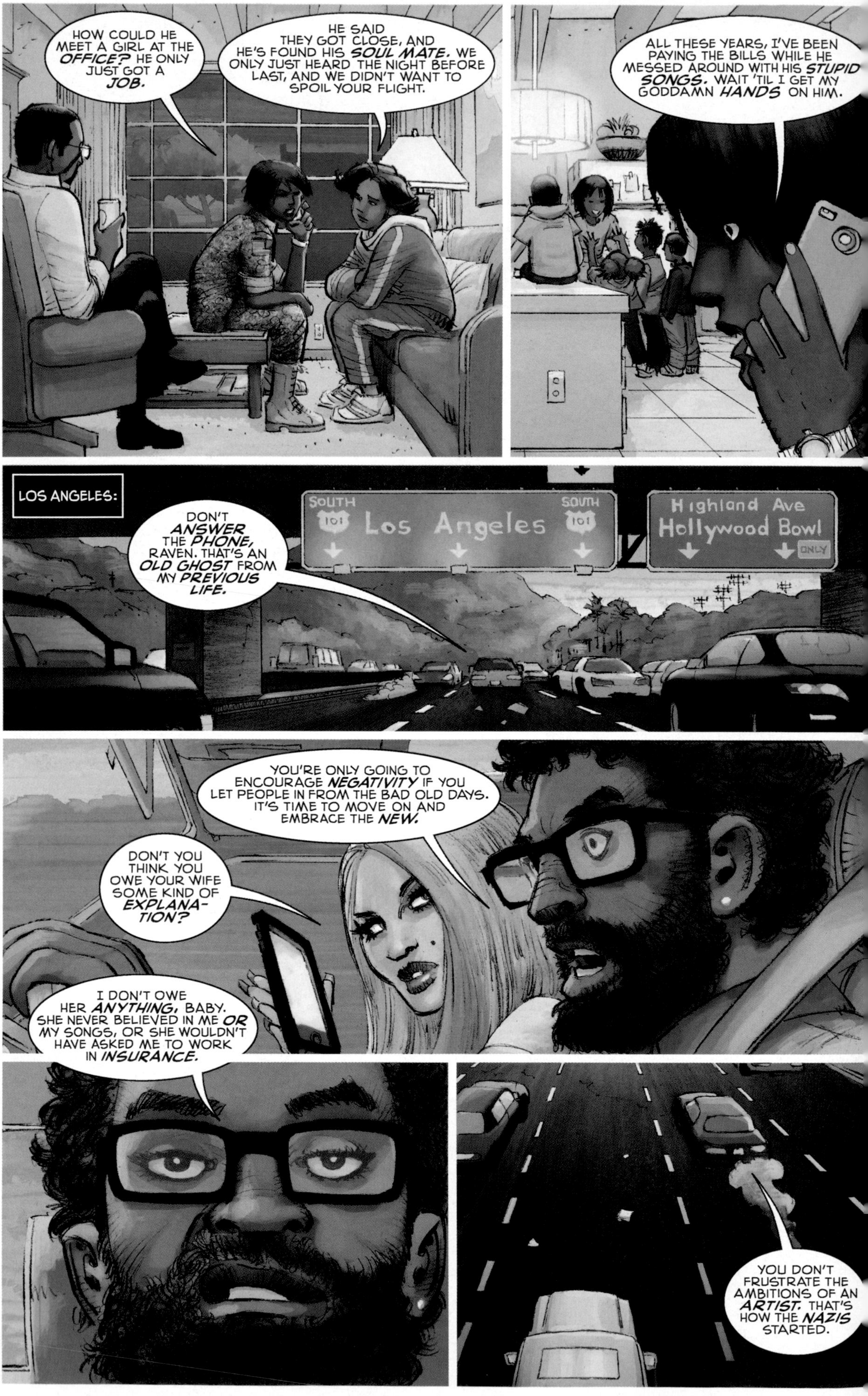
HOW COULD HE MEET A GIRL AT THE OFFICE? HE ONLY JUST GOT A JOB.
HE SAID THEY GOT CLOSE, AND HE'S FOUND HIS SOUL MATE. WE ONLY JUST HEARD THE NIGHT BEFORE LAST, AND WE DIDN'T WANT TO SPOIL YOUR FLIGHT.
ALL THESE YEARS, I'VE BEEN PAYING THE BILLS WHILE HE MESSED AROUND WITH HIS STUPID SONGS. WAIT 'TIL I GET MY GODDAMN HANDS ON HIM.
LOS ANGELES:
SOUTH 101 Los Angeles SOUTH 101
Highland Ave Hollywood Bowl ONLY
DON'T ANSWER THE PHONE, RAVEN. THAT'S AN OLD GHOST FROM MY PREVIOUS LIFE.
YOU'RE ONLY GOING TO ENCOURAGE NEGATIVITY IF YOU LET PEOPLE IN FROM THE BAD OLD DAYS. IT'S TIME TO MOVE ON AND EMBRACE THE NEW.
DON'T YOU THINK YOU OWE YOUR WIFE SOME KIND OF EXPLANATION?
I DON'T OWE HER ANYTHING, BABY. SHE NEVER BELIEVED IN ME OR MY SONGS, OR SHE WOULDN'T HAVE ASKED ME TO WORK IN INSURANCE.
YOU DON'T FRUSTRATE THE AMBITIONS OF AN ARTIST. THAT'S HOW THE NAZIS STARTED.

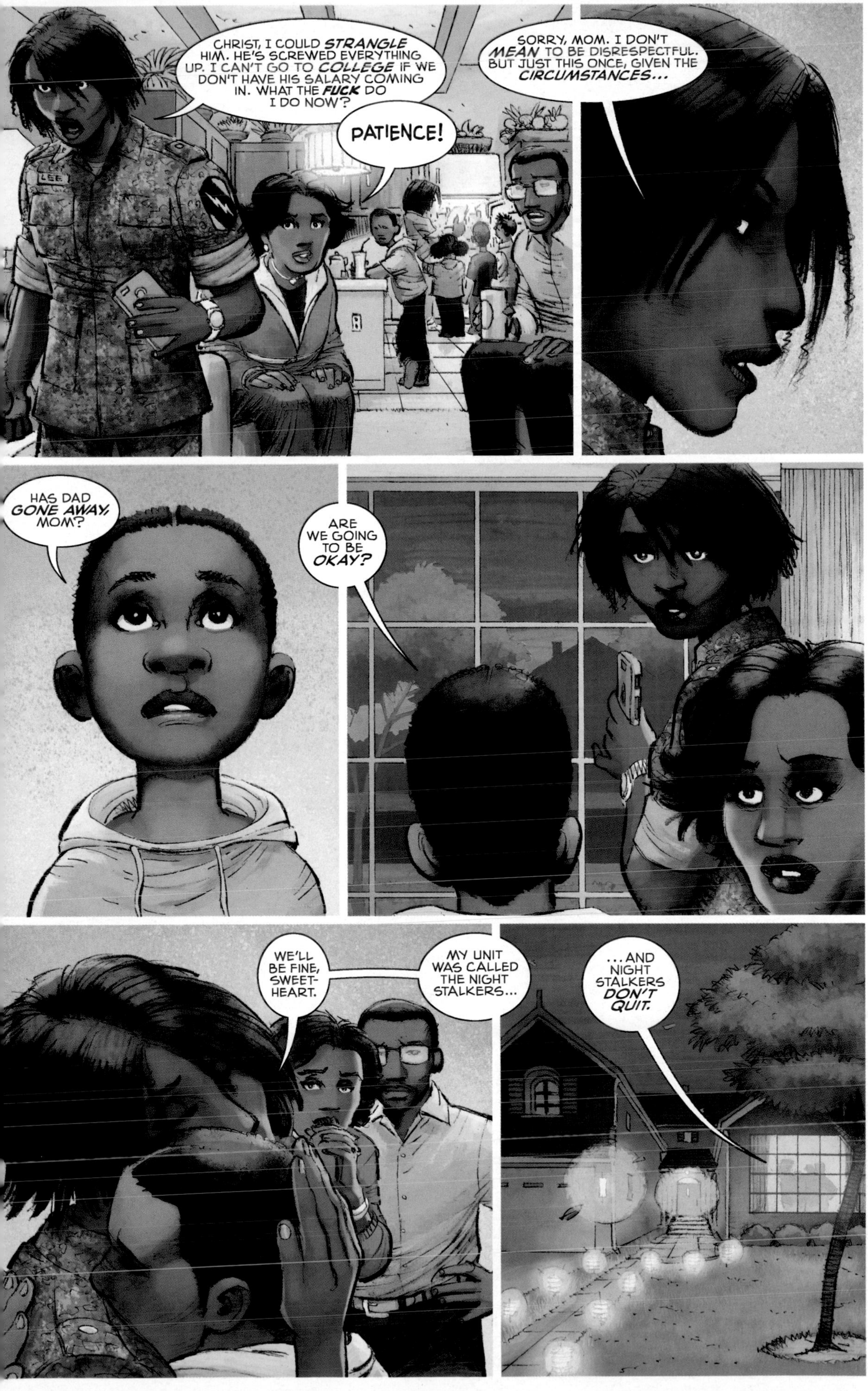
CHRIST, I COULD STRANGLE HIM. HE'S SCREWED EVERYTHING UP. I CAN'T GO TO COLLEGE IF WE DON'T HAVE HIS SALARY COMING IN. WHAT THE FUCK DO I DO NOW?
PATIENCE!
SORRY, MOM. I DON'T MEAN TO BE DISRESPECTFUL. BUT JUST THIS ONCE, GIVEN THE CIRCUMSTANCES...
HAS DAD GONE AWAY, MOM?
ARE WE GOING TO BE OKAY?
WE'LL BE FINE, SWEET-HEART.
MY UNIT WAS CALLED THE NIGHT STALKERS...
...AND NIGHT STALKERS DON'T QUIT.

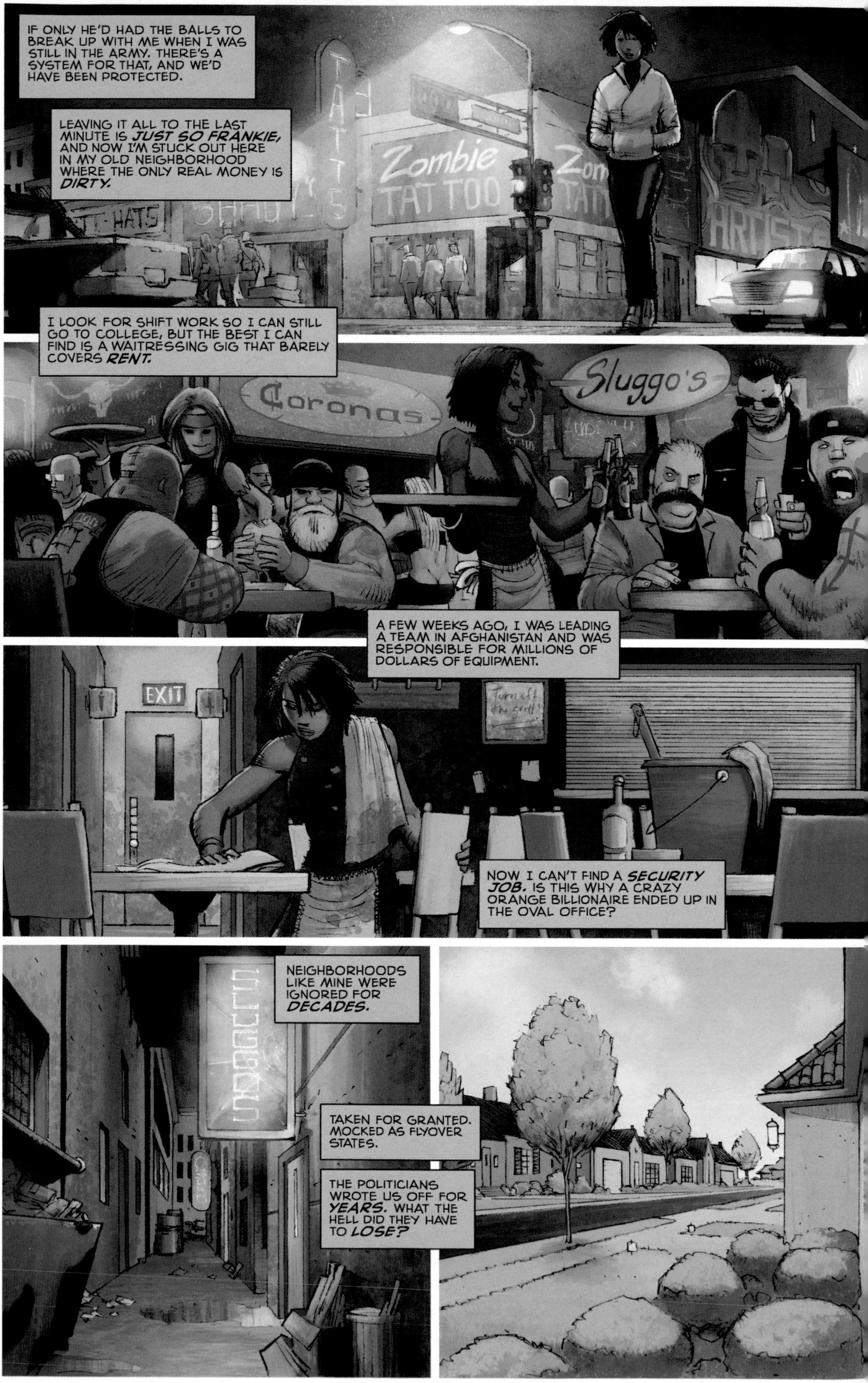
IF ONLY HE'D HAD THE BALLS TO BREAK UP WITH ME WHEN I WAS STILL IN THE ARMY. THERE'S A SYSTEM FOR THAT, AND WE'D HAVE BEEN PROTECTED.
LEAVING IT ALL TO THE LAST MINUTE IS JUST SO FRANKIE, AND NOW I'M STUCK OUT HERE IN MY OLD NEIGHBORHOOD WHERE THE ONLY REAL MONEY IS DIRTY.
TATTS
Zombie TATTOO
I LOOK FOR SHIFT WORK SO I CAN STILL GO TO COLLEGE, BUT THE BEST I CAN FIND IS A WAITRESSING GIG THAT BARELY COVERS RENT.
Coronas
Sluggo's
A FEW WEEKS AGO, I WAS LEADING A TEAM IN AFGHANISTAN AND WAS RESPONSIBLE FOR MILLIONS OF DOLLARS OF EQUIPMENT.
EXIT
NOW I CAN'T FIND A SECURITY JOB. IS THIS WHY A CRAZY ORANGE BILLIONAIRE ENDED UP IN THE OVAL OFFICE?
NEIGHBORHOODS LIKE MINE WERE IGNORED FOR DECADES.
TAKEN FOR GRANTED. MOCKED AS FLYOVER STATES.
THE POLITICIANS WROTE US OFF FOR YEARS. WHAT THE HELL DID THEY HAVE TO LOSE?

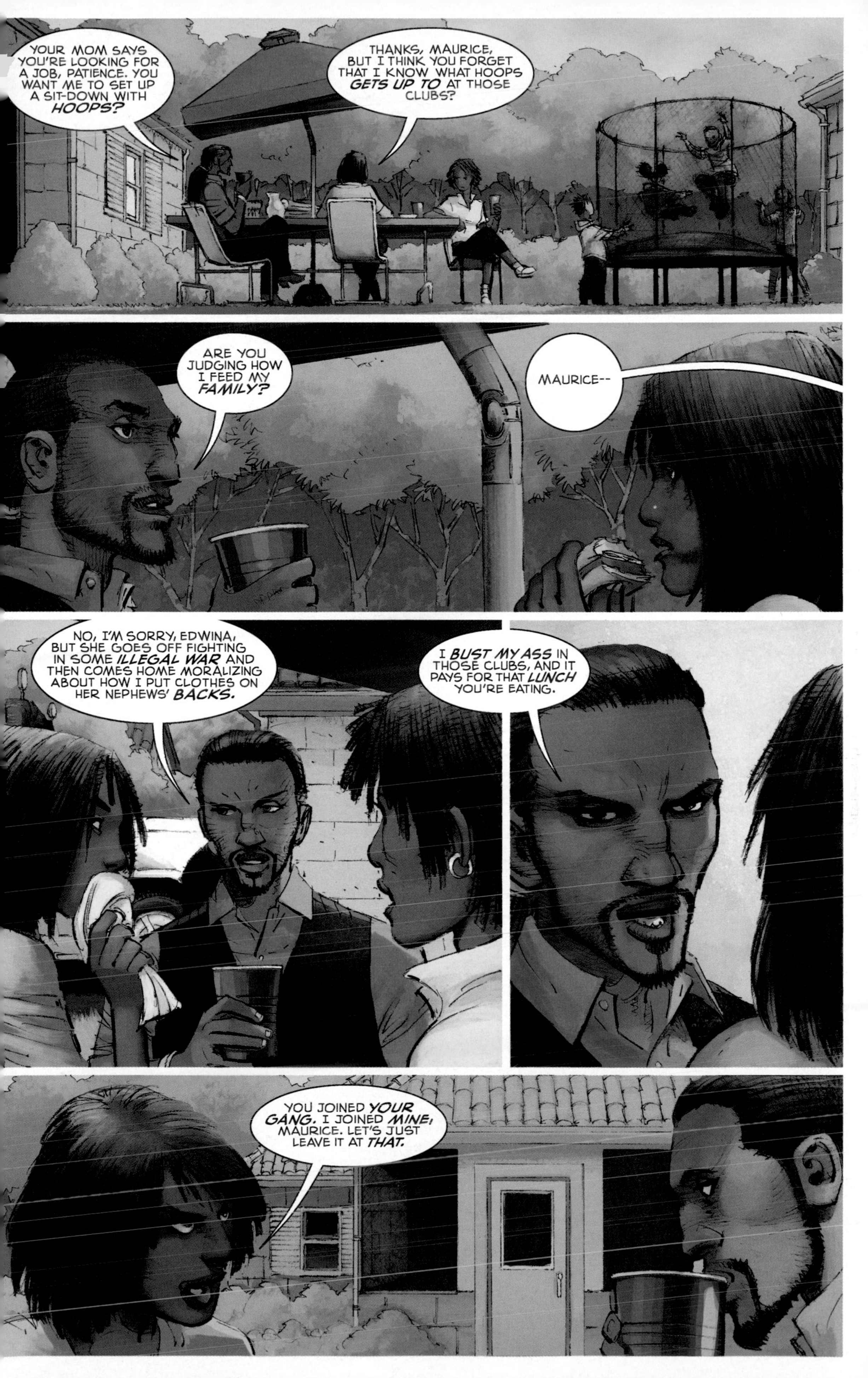
YOUR MOM SAYS YOU'RE LOOKING FOR A JOB, PATIENCE. YOU WANT ME TO SET UP A SIT-DOWN WITH HOOPS?
THANKS, MAURICE, BUT I THINK YOU FORGET THAT I KNOW WHAT HOOPS GETS UP TO AT THOSE CLUBS?
ARE YOU JUDGING HOW I FEED MY FAMILY?
MAURICE--
NO, I'M SORRY, EDWINA, BUT SHE GOES OFF FIGHTING IN SOME ILLEGAL WAR AND THEN COMES HOME MORALIZING ABOUT HOW I PUT CLOTHES ON HER NEPHEWS' BACKS.
I BUST MY ASS IN THOSE CLUBS, AND IT PAYS FOR THAT LUNCH YOU'RE EATING.
YOU JOINED YOUR GANG. I JOINED MINE, MAURICE. LET'S JUST LEAVE IT AT THAT.

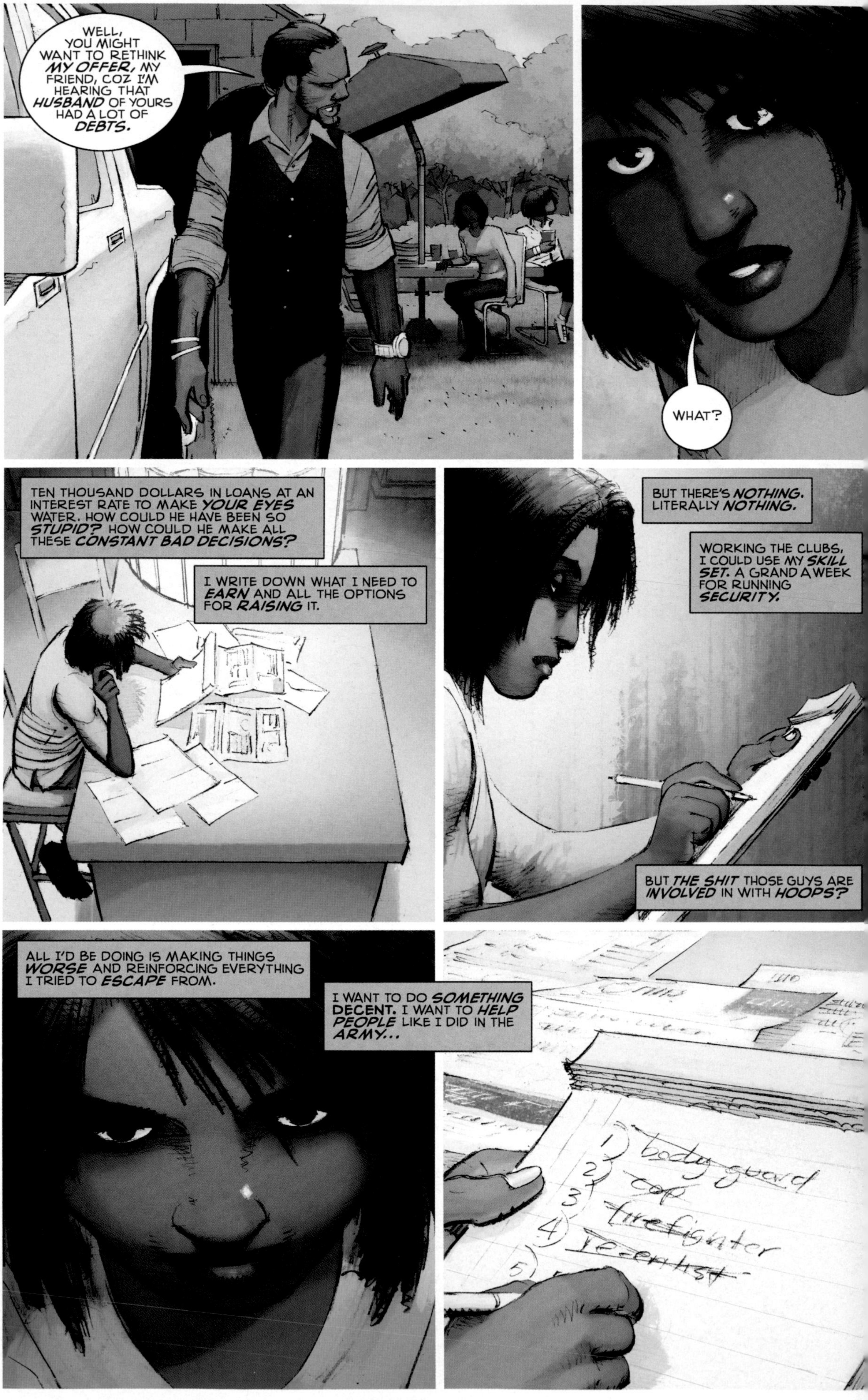
WELL, YOU MIGHT WANT TO RETHINK MY OFFER, MY FRIEND, COZ I'M HEARING THAT HUSBAND OF YOURS HAD A LOT OF DEBTS.
WHAT?
TEN THOUSAND DOLLARS IN LOANS AT AN INTEREST RATE TO MAKE YOUR EYES WATER. HOW COULD HE HAVE BEEN SO STUPID? HOW COULD HE MAKE ALL THESE CONSTANT BAD DECISIONS?
I WRITE DOWN WHAT I NEED TO EARN AND ALL THE OPTIONS FOR RAISING IT.
BUT THERE'S NOTHING. LITERALLY NOTHING.
WORKING THE CLUBS, I COULD USE MY SKILL SET. A GRAND A WEEK FOR RUNNING SECURITY.
BUT THE SHIT THOSE GUYS ARE INVOLVED IN WITH HOOPS?
ALL I'D BE DOING IS MAKING THINGS WORSE AND REINFORCING EVERYTHING I TRIED TO ESCAPE FROM.
I WANT TO DO SOMETHING DECENT. I WANT TO HELP PEOPLE LIKE I DID IN THE ARMY...
1) body guard
2) cop
3) firefighter
4)
5)

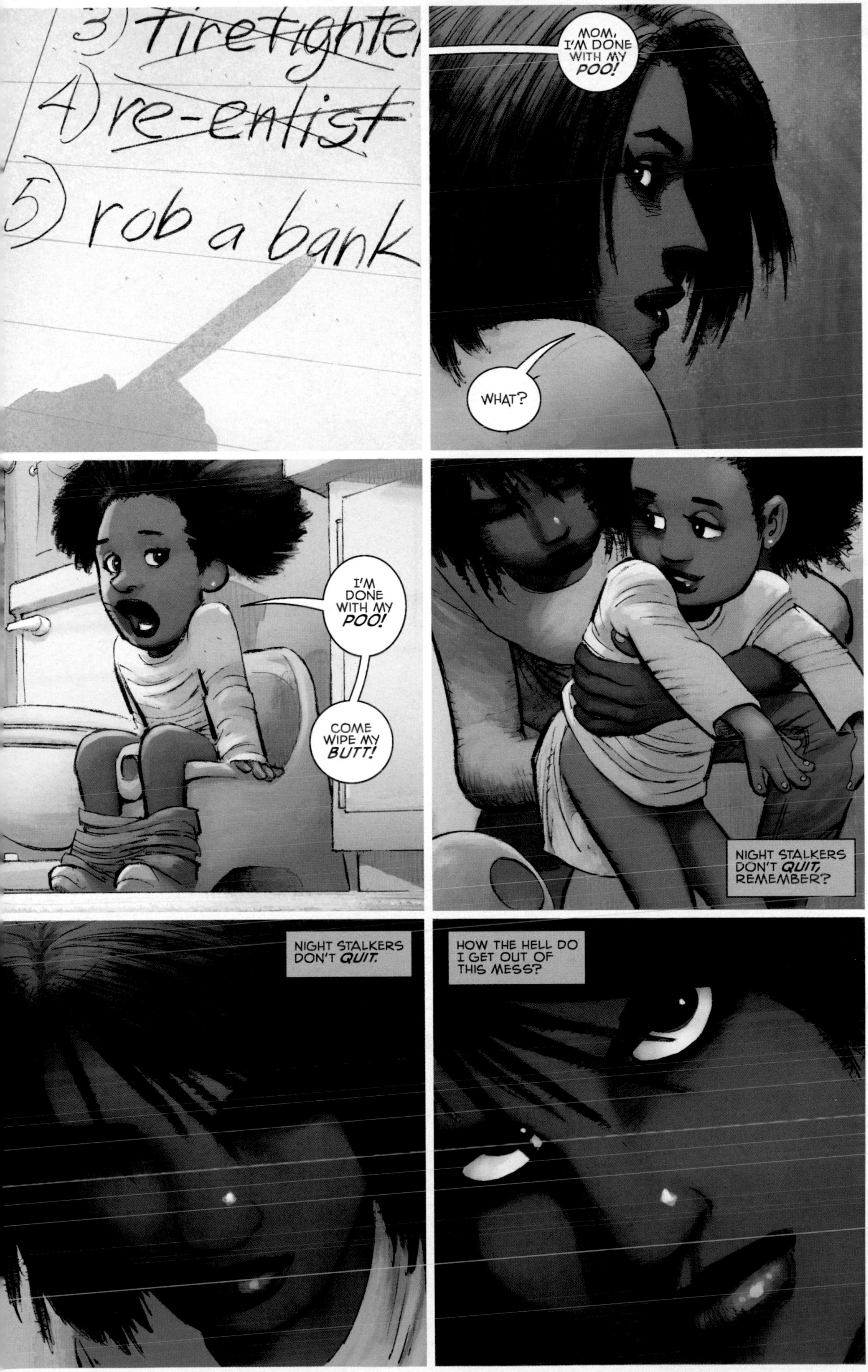
3) firefighter
4) re-enlist
5) rob a bank
MOM, I'M DONE WITH MY POO!
WHAT?
I'M DONE WITH MY POO!
COME WIPE MY BUTT!
NIGHT STALKERS DON'T QUIT, REMEMBER?
NIGHT STALKERS DON'T QUIT.
HOW THE HELL DO I GET OUT OF THIS MESS?

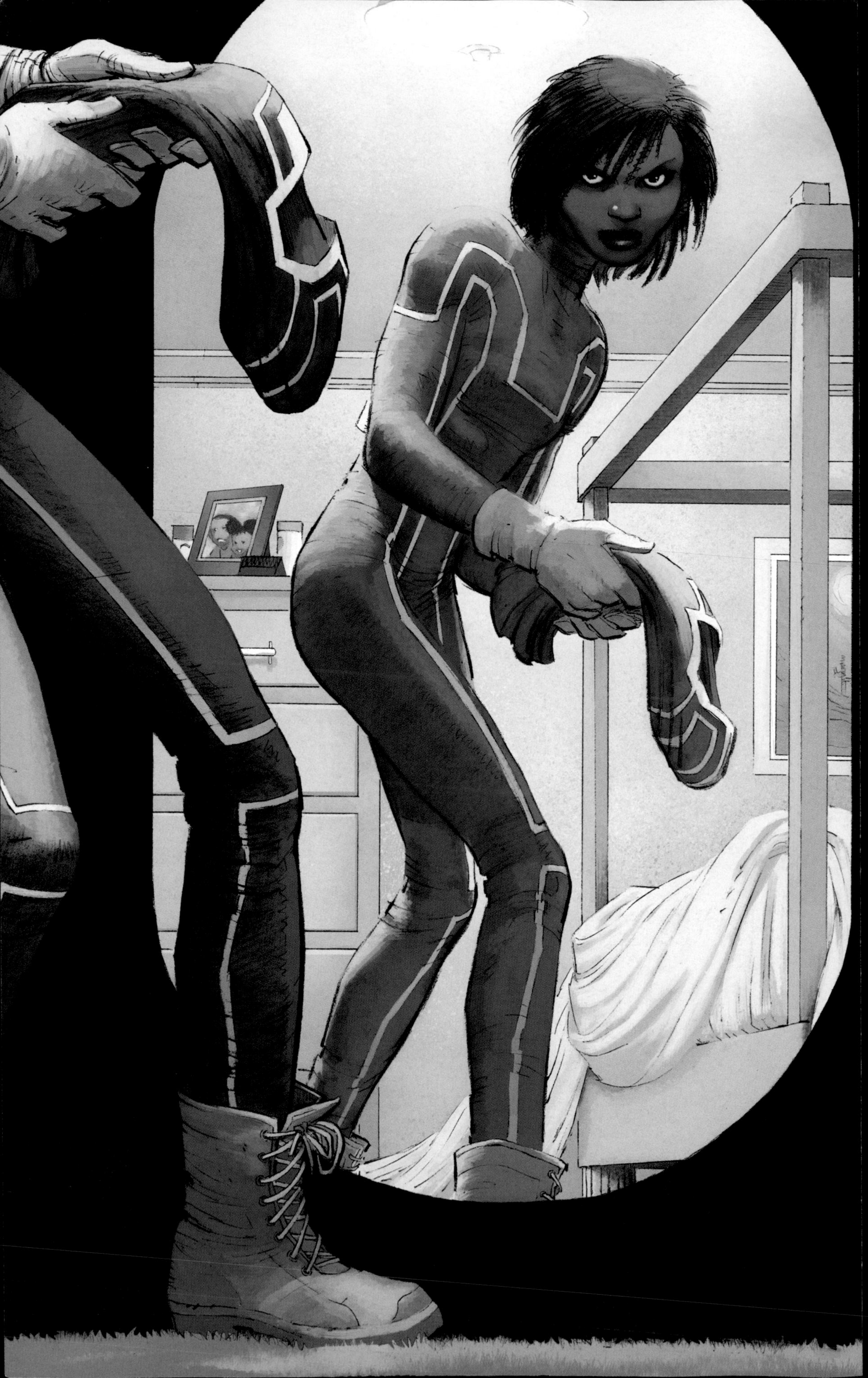

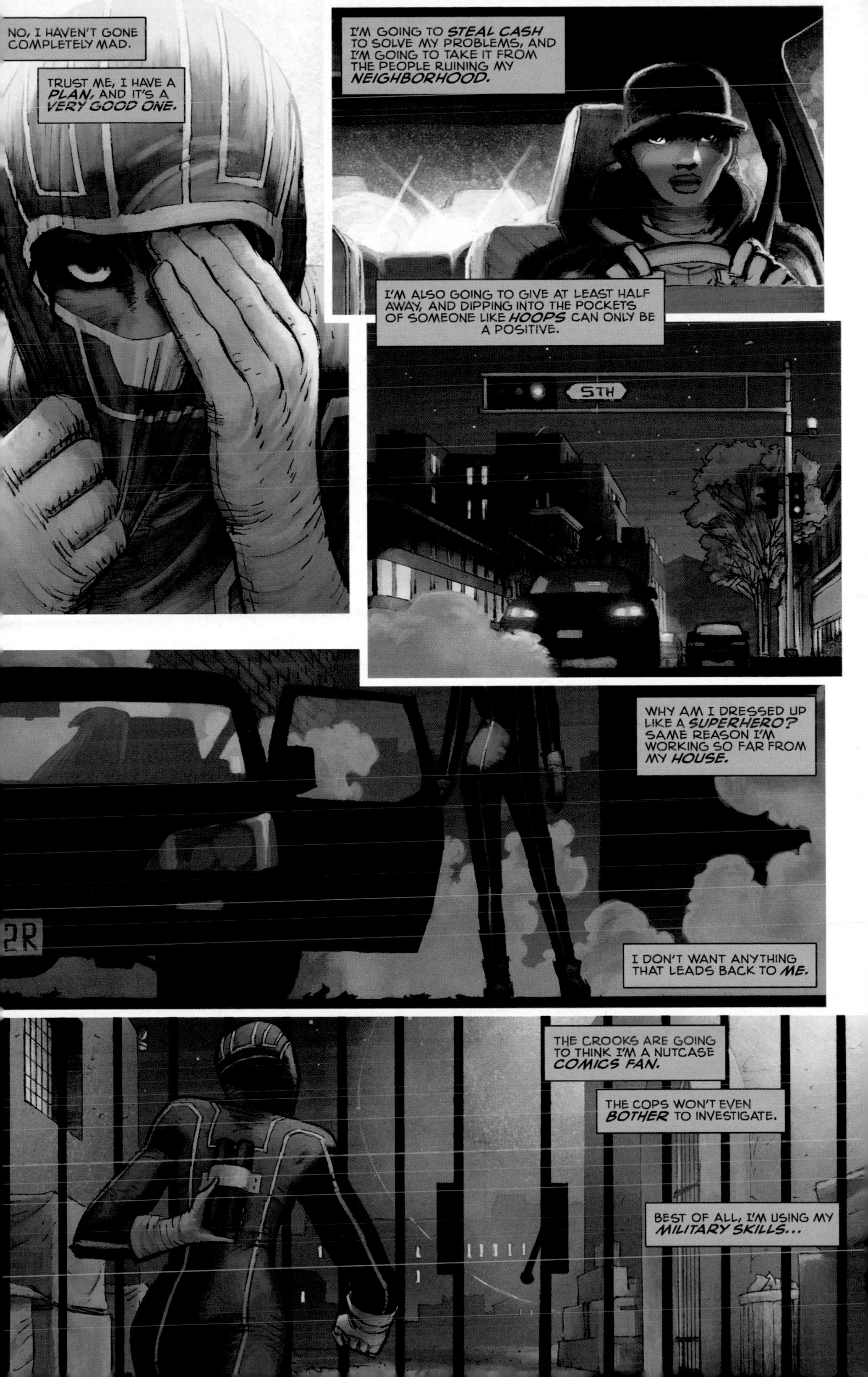
NO, I HAVEN'T GONE COMPLETELY MAD.
TRUST ME, I HAVE A PLAN, AND IT'S A VERY GOOD ONE.
I'M GOING TO STEAL CASH TO SOLVE MY PROBLEMS, AND I'M GOING TO TAKE IT FROM THE PEOPLE RUINING MY NEIGHBORHOOD.
I'M ALSO GOING TO GIVE AT LEAST HALF AWAY, AND DIPPING INTO THE POCKETS OF SOMEONE LIKE HOOPS CAN ONLY BE A POSITIVE.
5TH
WHY AM I DRESSED UP LIKE A SUPERHERO? SAME REASON I'M WORKING SO FAR FROM MY HOUSE.
I DON'T WANT ANYTHING THAT LEADS BACK TO ME.
THE CROOKS ARE GOING TO THINK I'M A NUTCASE COMICS FAN.
THE COPS WON'T EVEN BOTHER TO INVESTIGATE.
BEST OF ALL, I'M USING MY MILITARY SKILLS...

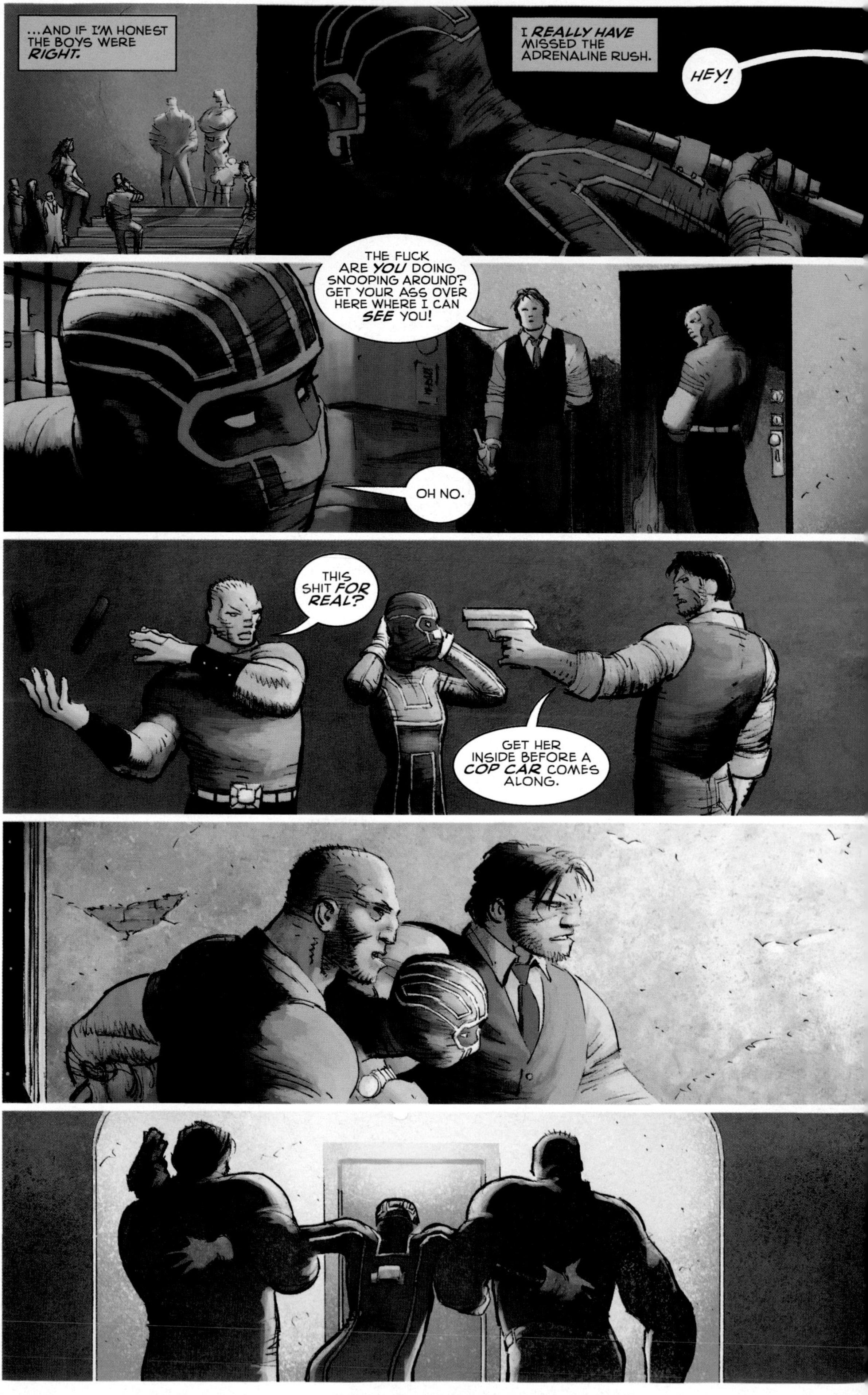
...AND IF I'M HONEST THE BOYS WERE RIGHT.
I REALLY HAVE MISSED THE ADRENALINE RUSH.
HEY!
THE FUCK ARE YOU DOING SNOOPING AROUND? GET YOUR ASS OVER HERE WHERE I CAN SEE YOU!
OH NO.
THIS SHIT FOR REAL?
GET HER INSIDE BEFORE A COP CAR COMES ALONG.

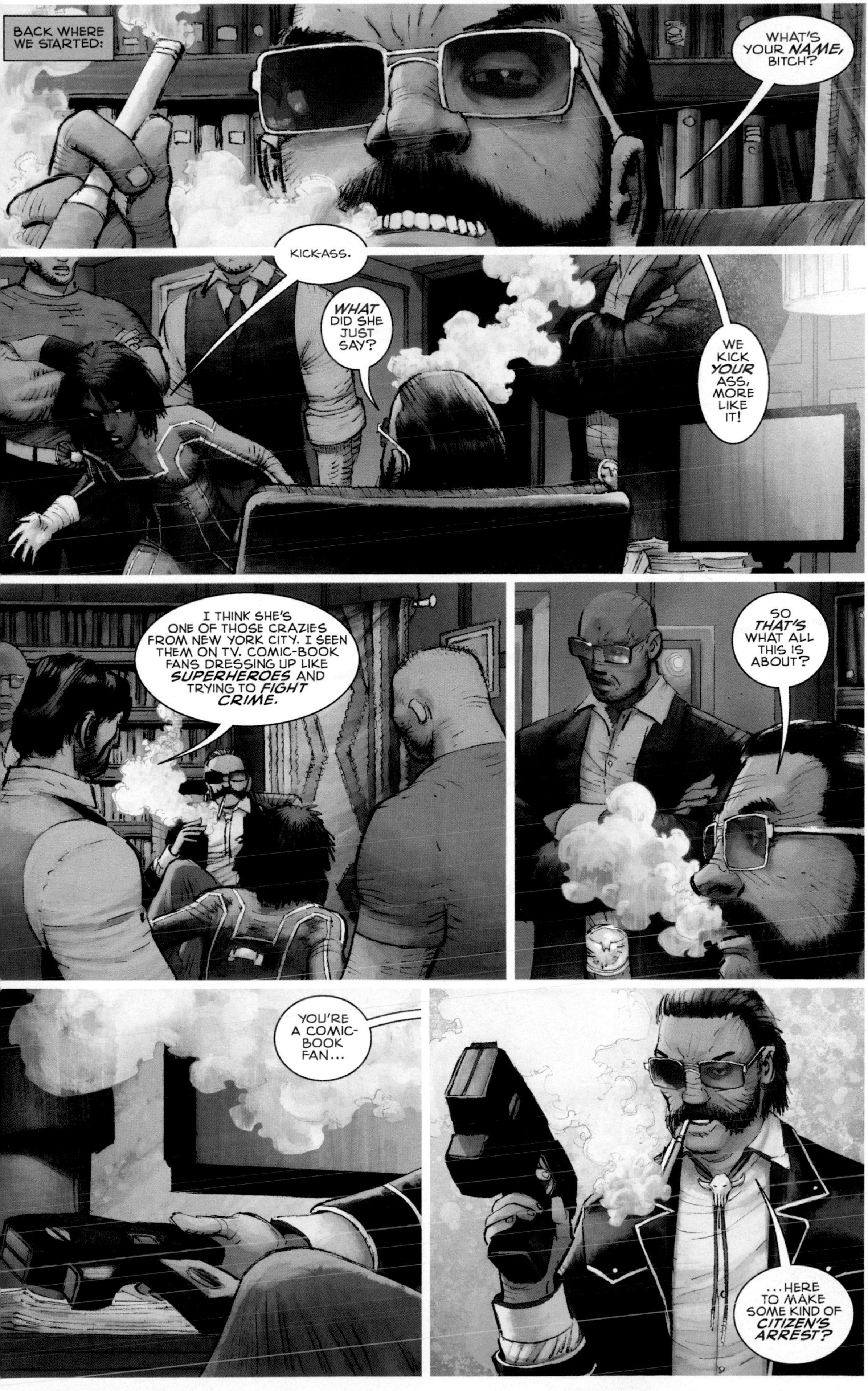
BACK WHERE WE STARTED:
WHAT'S YOUR NAME, BITCH?
KICK-ASS.
WHAT DID SHE JUST SAY?
WE KICK YOUR ASS, MORE LIKE IT!
I THINK SHE'S ONE OF THOSE CRAZIES FROM NEW YORK CITY. I SEEN THEM ON TV. COMIC-BOOK FANS DRESSING UP LIKE SUPERHEROES AND TRYING TO FIGHT CRIME.
SO THAT'S WHAT ALL THIS IS ABOUT?
YOU'RE A COMIC-BOOK FAN...
...HERE TO MAKE SOME KIND OF CITIZEN'S ARREST?

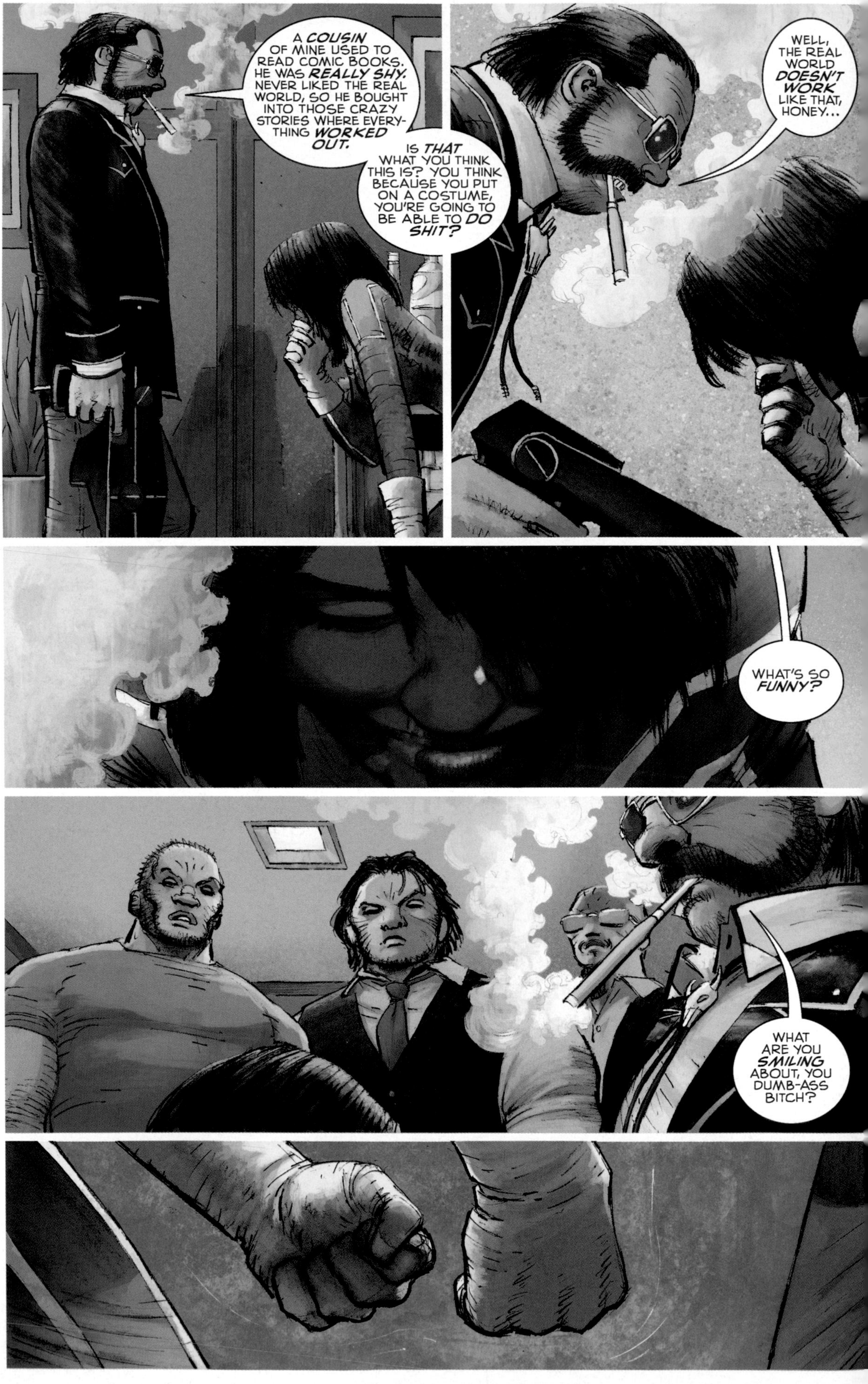
A COUSIN OF MINE USED TO READ COMIC BOOKS. HE WAS REALLY SHY. NEVER LIKED THE REAL WORLD, SO HE BOUGHT INTO THOSE CRAZY STORIES WHERE EVERY-THING WORKED OUT.
IS THAT WHAT YOU THINK THIS IS? YOU THINK BECAUSE YOU PUT ON A COSTUME, YOU'RE GOING TO BE ABLE TO DO SHIT?
WELL, THE REAL WORLD DOESN'T WORK LIKE THAT, HONEY...
WHAT'S SO FUNNY?
WHAT ARE YOU SMILING ABOUT, YOU DUMB-ASS BITCH?

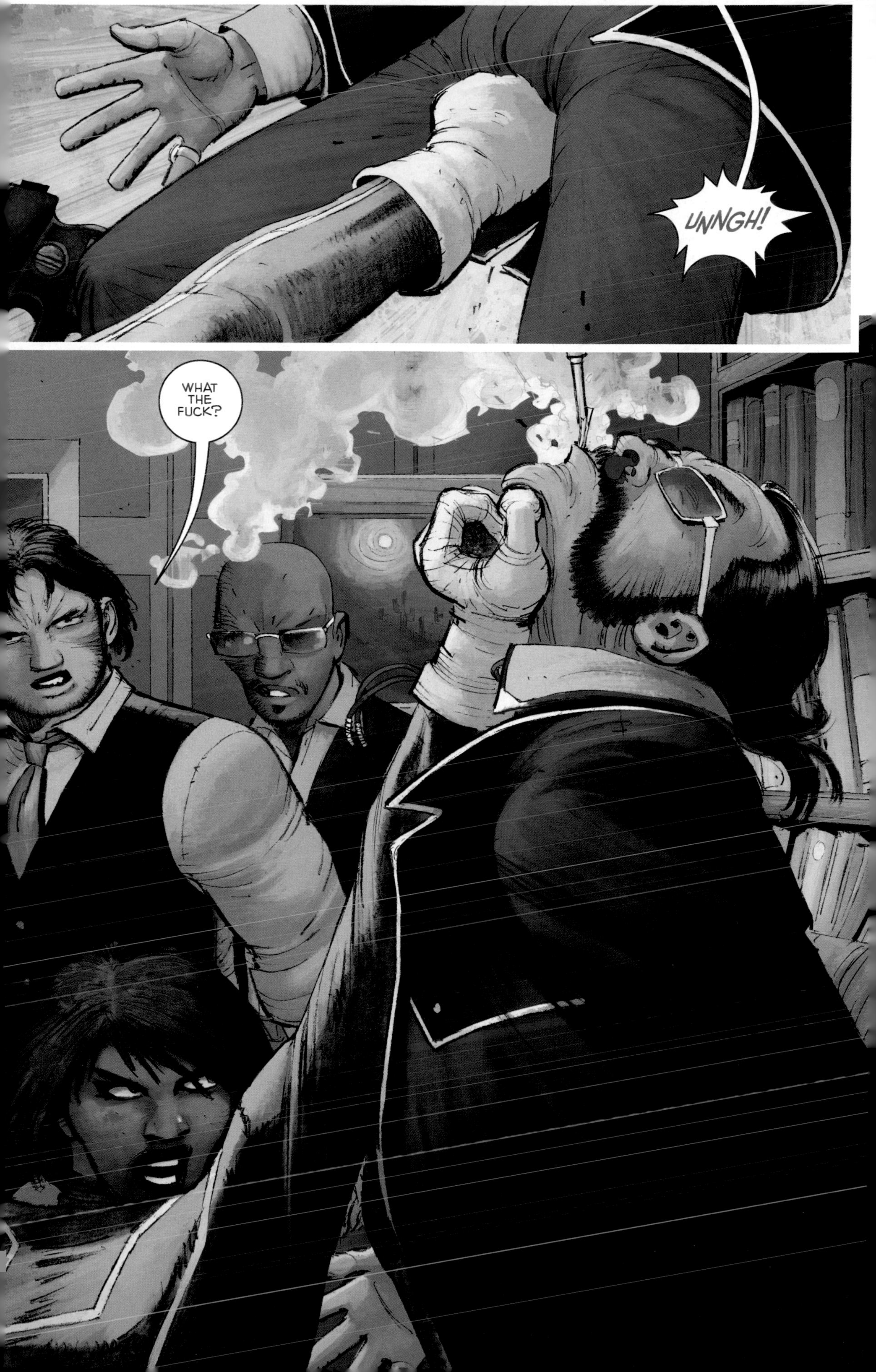
UNNGH!
WHAT THE FUCK?

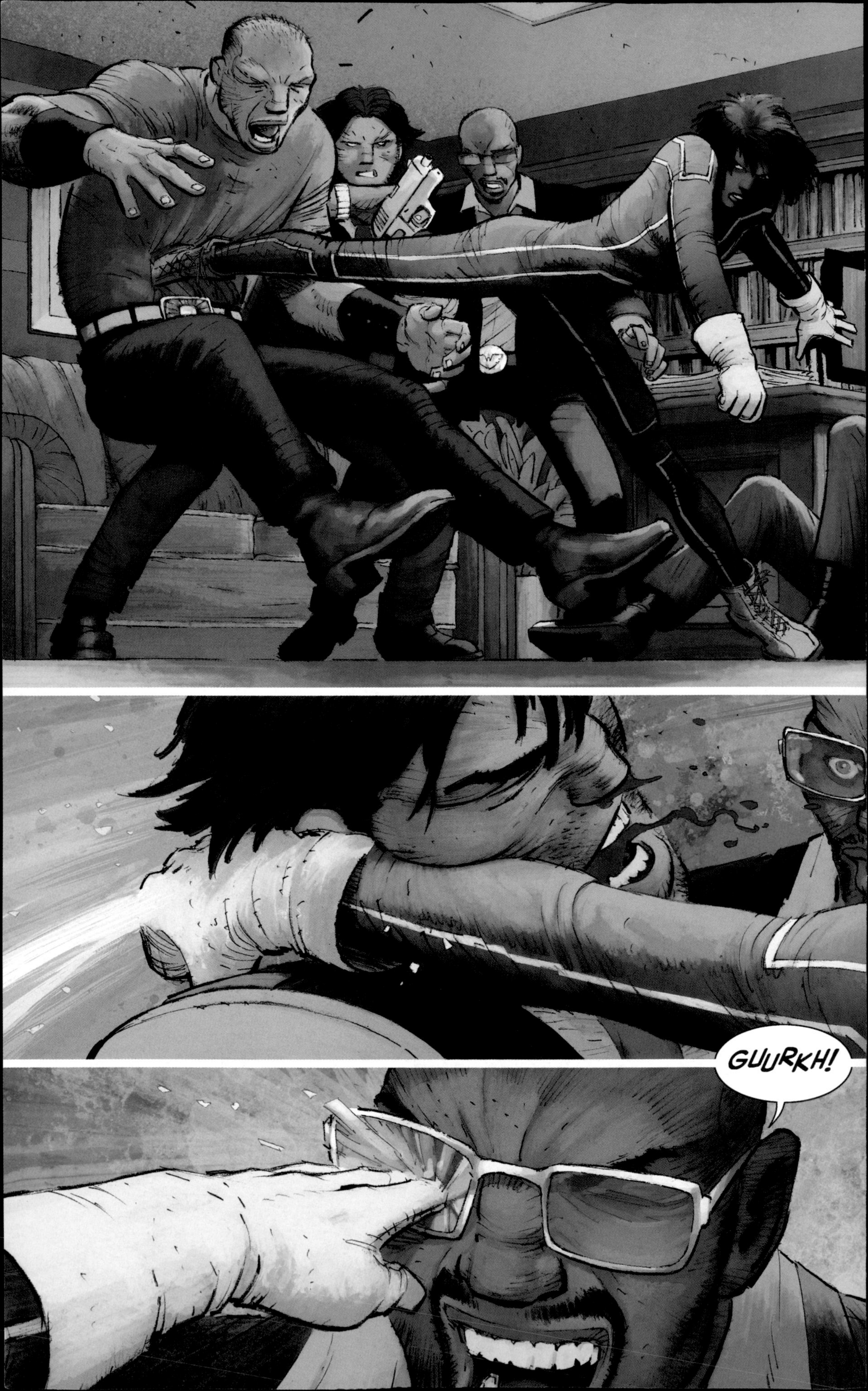
GUURKH!

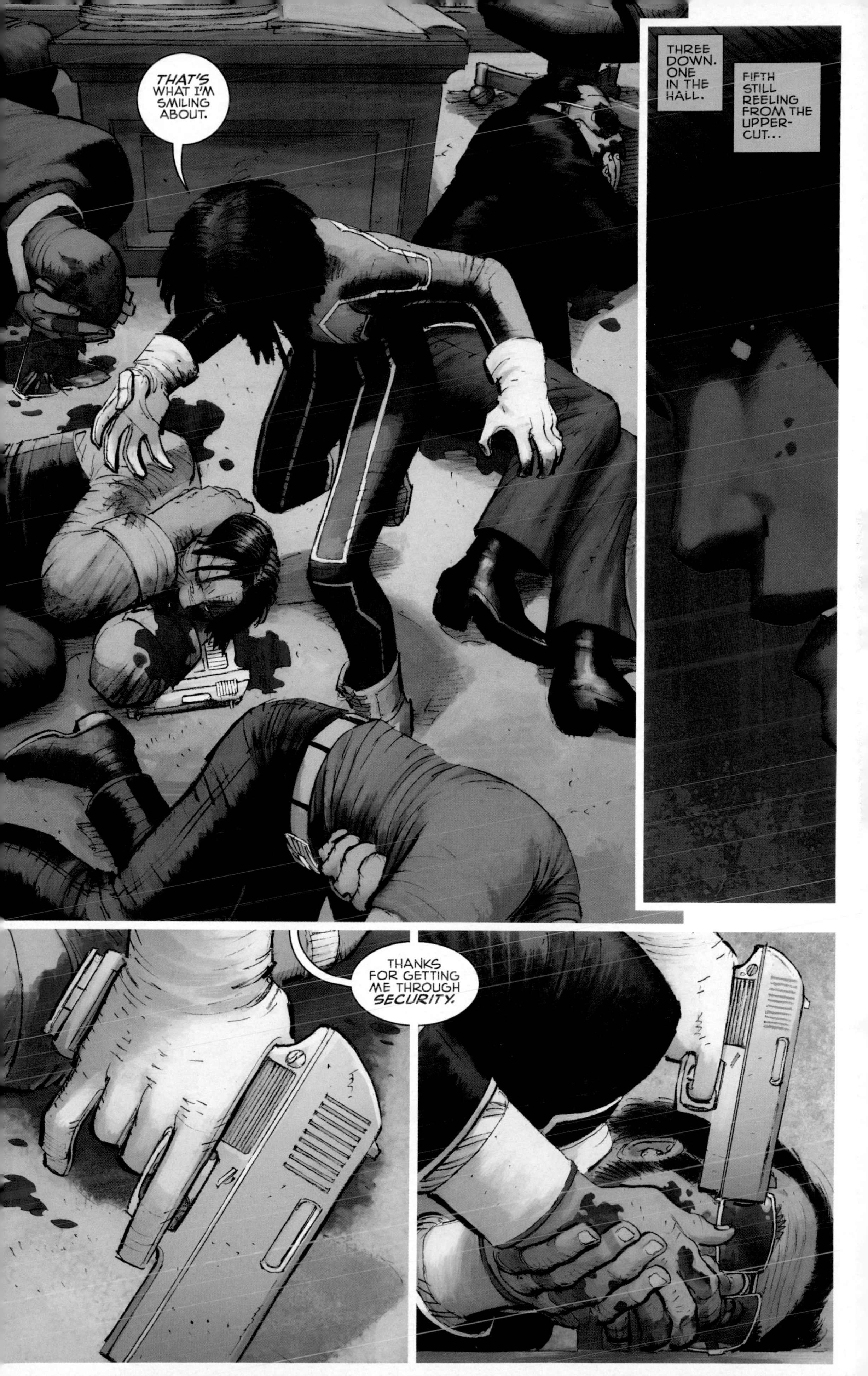
THAT'S WHAT I'M SMILING ABOUT.
THREE DOWN. ONE IN THE HALL.
FIFTH STILL REELING FROM THE UPPER-CUT...
THANKS FOR GETTING ME THROUGH SECURITY.

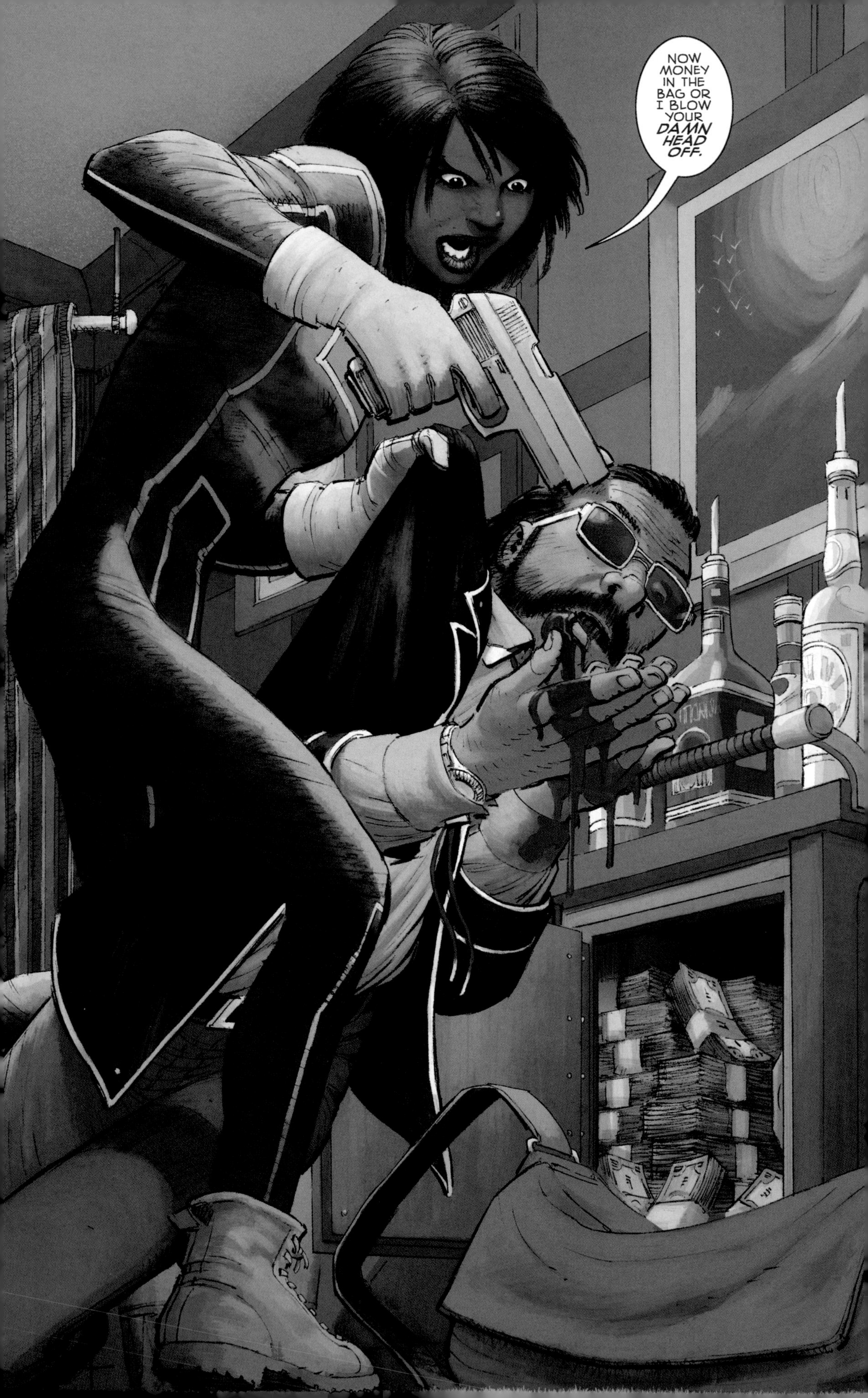
NOW MONEY IN THE BAG OR I BLOW YOUR *DAMN HEAD OFF.*

TWO

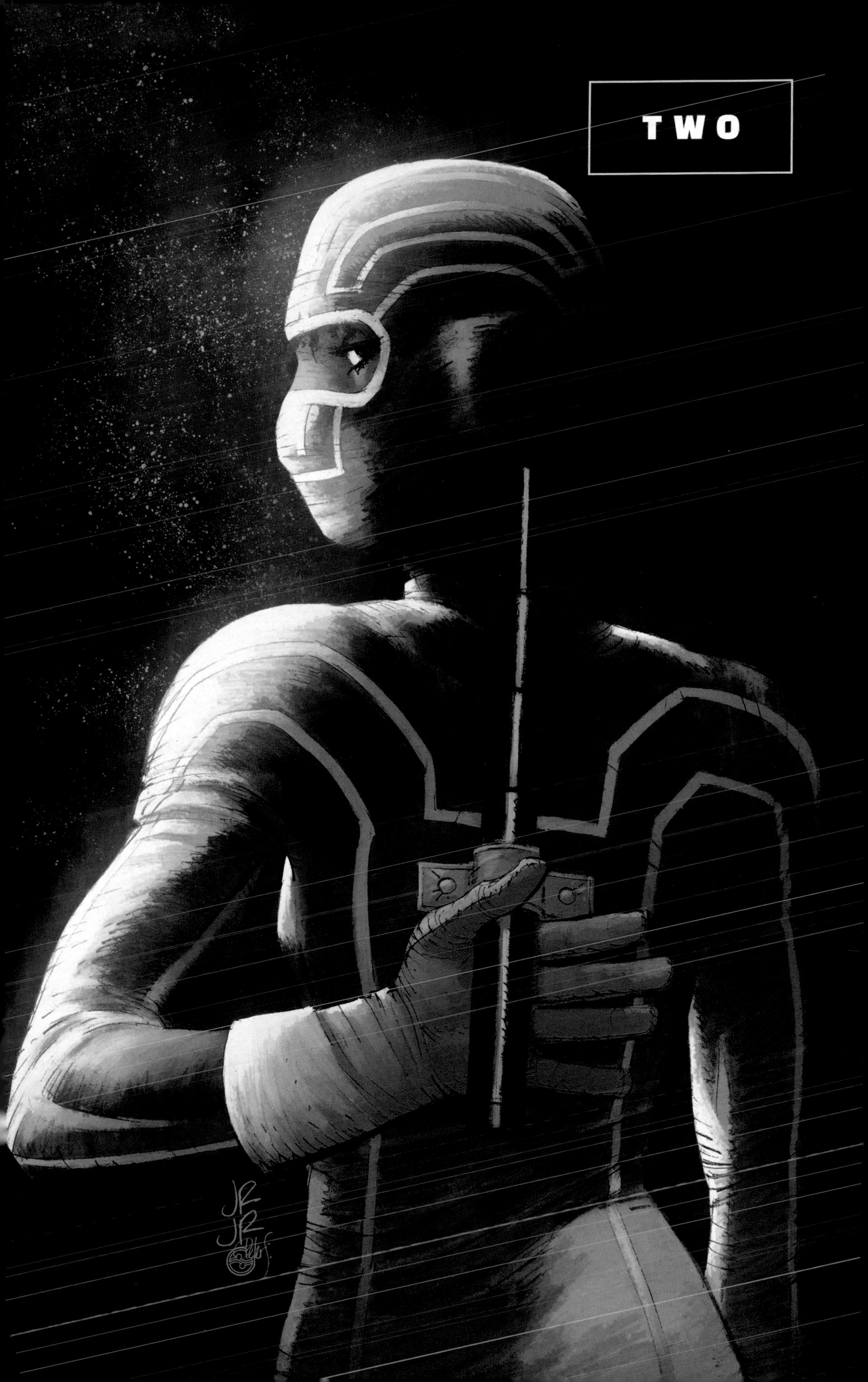

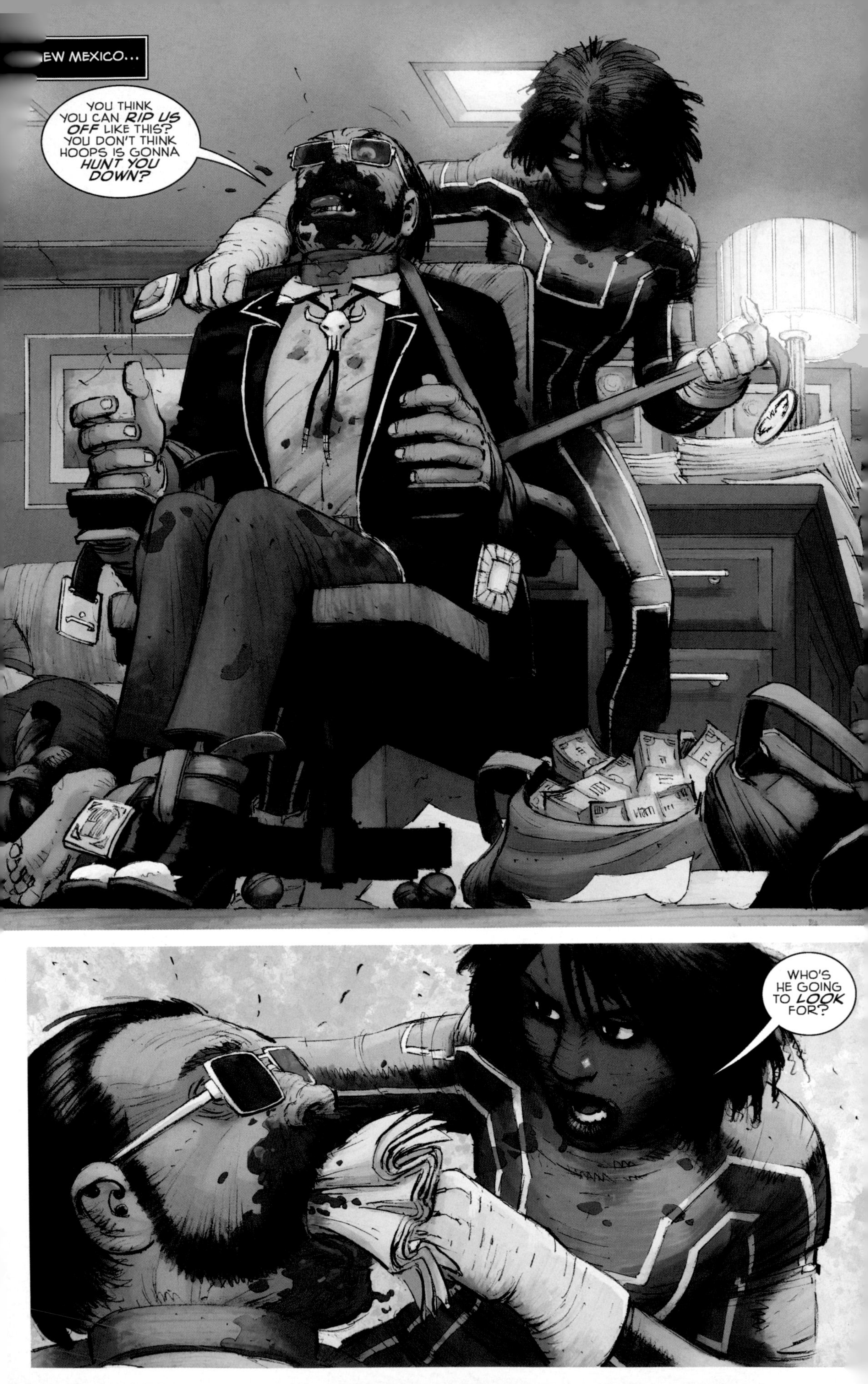
EW MEXICO...
YOU THINK YOU CAN RIP US OFF LIKE THIS? YOU DON'T THINK HOOPS IS GONNA HUNT YOU DOWN?
WHO'S HE GOING TO LOOK FOR?

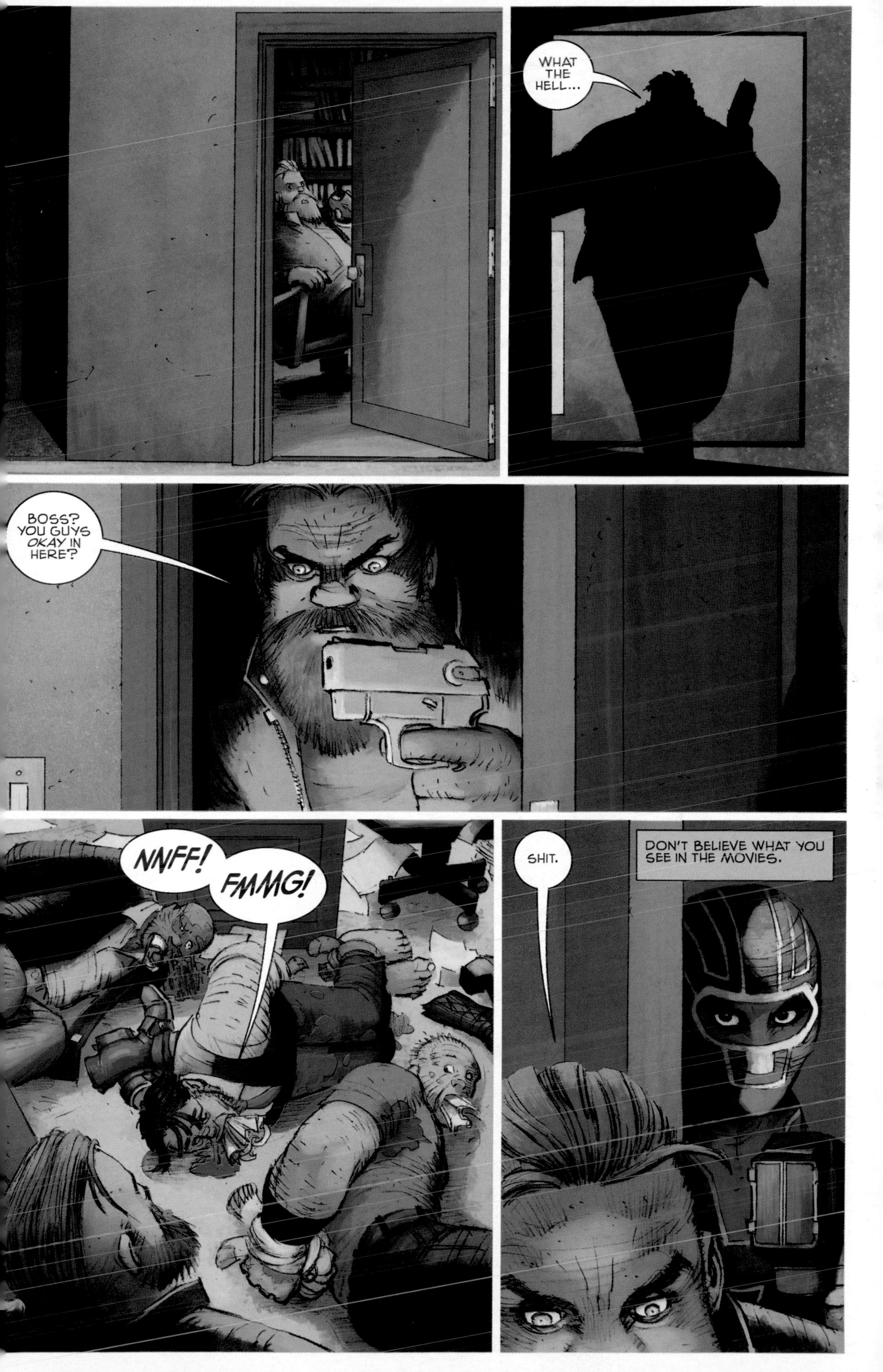
WHAT THE HELL...
BOSS? YOU GUYS OKAY IN HERE?
NNFF!
FMMG!
SHIT.
DON'T BELIEVE WHAT YOU SEE IN THE MOVIES.

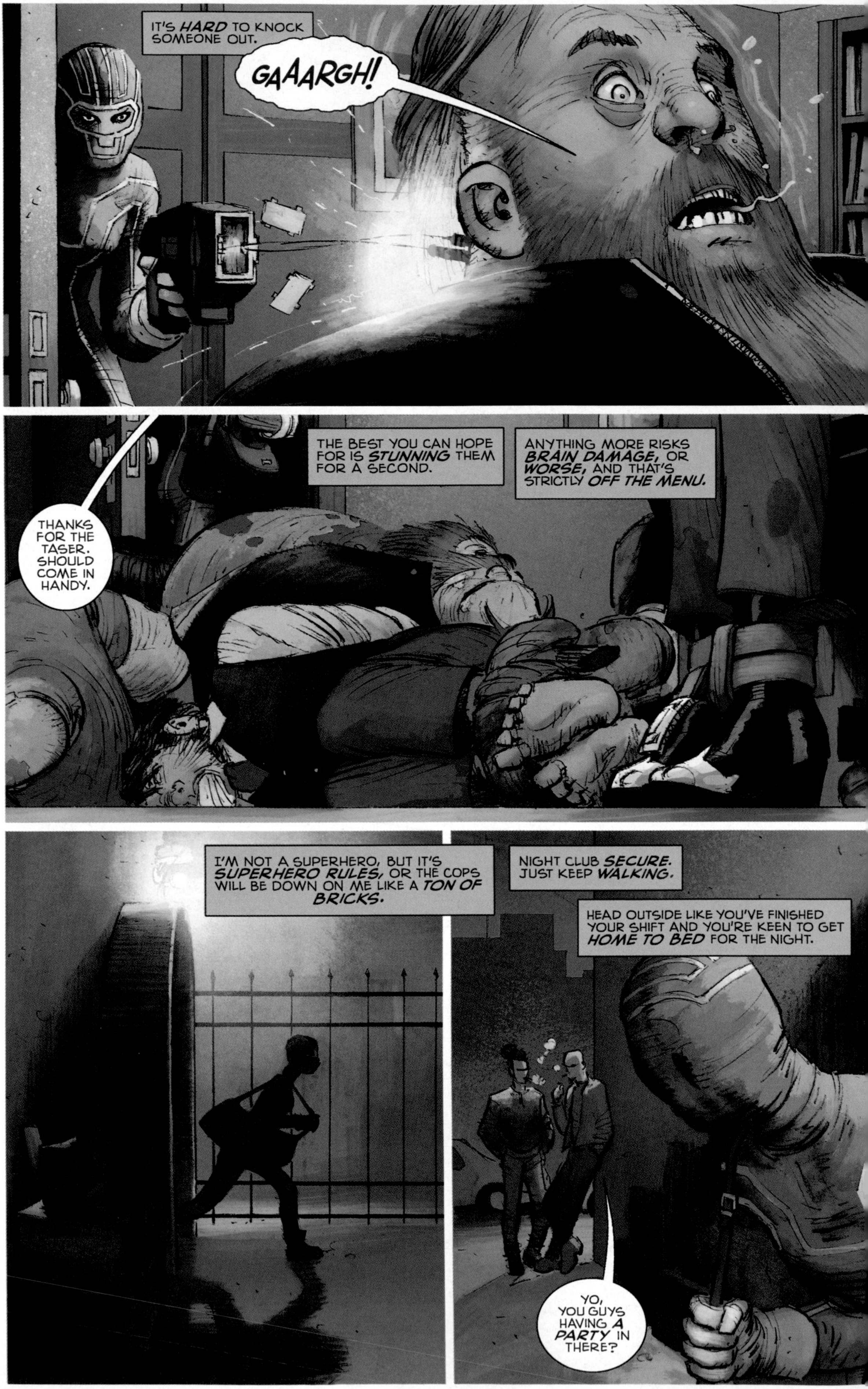
IT'S HARD TO KNOCK SOMEONE OUT.
GAAARGH!
THANKS FOR THE TASER. SHOULD COME IN HANDY.
THE BEST YOU CAN HOPE FOR IS STUNNING THEM FOR A SECOND.
ANYTHING MORE RISKS BRAIN DAMAGE, OR WORSE, AND THAT'S STRICTLY OFF THE MENU.
I'M NOT A SUPERHERO, BUT IT'S SUPERHERO RULES, OR THE COPS WILL BE DOWN ON ME LIKE A TON OF BRICKS.
NIGHT CLUB SECURE. JUST KEEP WALKING.
HEAD OUTSIDE LIKE YOU'VE FINISHED YOUR SHIFT AND YOU'RE KEEN TO GET HOME TO BED FOR THE NIGHT.
YO, YOU GUYS HAVING A PARTY IN THERE?

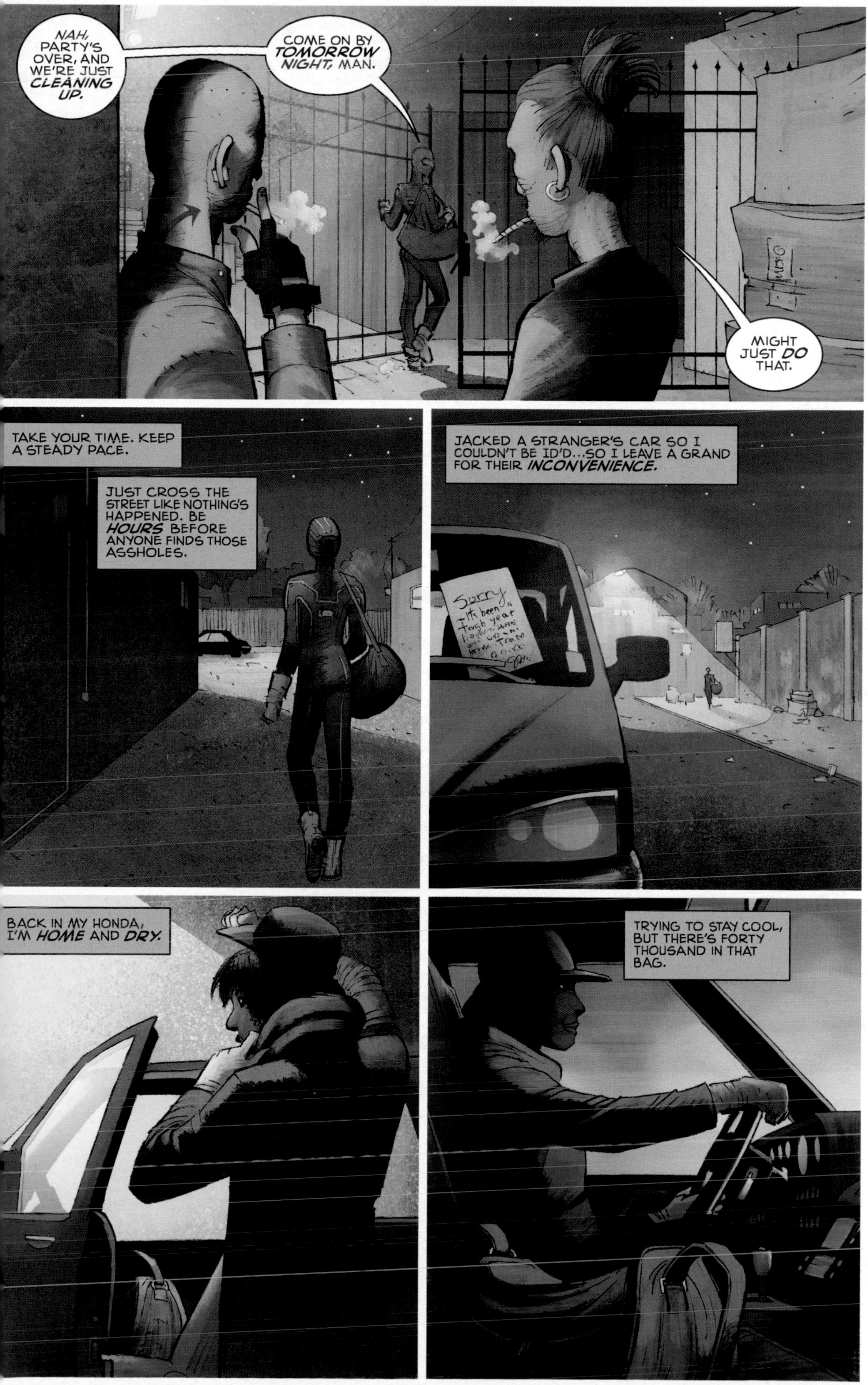
NAH, PARTY'S OVER, AND WE'RE JUST *CLEANING UP.*
COME ON BY *TOMORROW NIGHT,* MAN.
MIGHT JUST *DO* THAT.
TAKE YOUR TIME. KEEP A STEADY PACE.
JUST CROSS THE STREET LIKE NOTHING'S HAPPENED. BE *HOURS* BEFORE ANYONE FINDS THOSE ASSHOLES.
JACKED A STRANGER'S CAR SO I COULDN'T BE ID'D...SO I LEAVE A GRAND FOR THEIR *INCONVENIENCE.*
Sorry
BACK IN MY HONDA, I'M *HOME* AND *DRY.*
TRYING TO STAY COOL, BUT THERE'S FORTY THOUSAND IN THAT BAG.

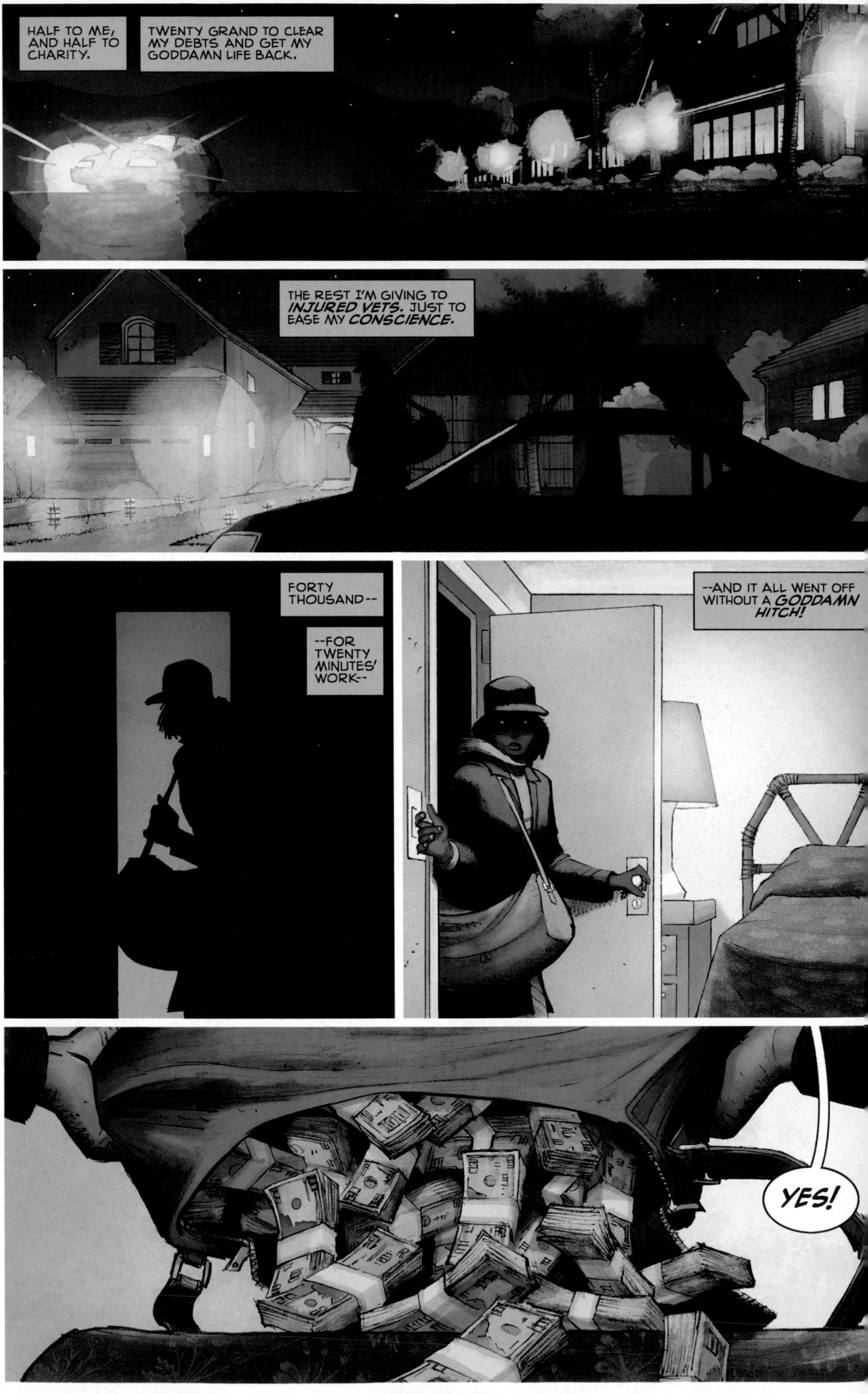

HALF TO ME, AND HALF TO CHARITY.
TWENTY GRAND TO CLEAR MY DEBTS AND GET MY GODDAMN LIFE BACK.
THE REST I'M GIVING TO *INJURED VETS.* JUST TO EASE MY *CONSCIENCE.*
FORTY THOUSAND--
--FOR TWENTY MINUTES' WORK--
--AND IT ALL WENT OFF WITHOUT A *GODDAMN HITCH!*
YES!

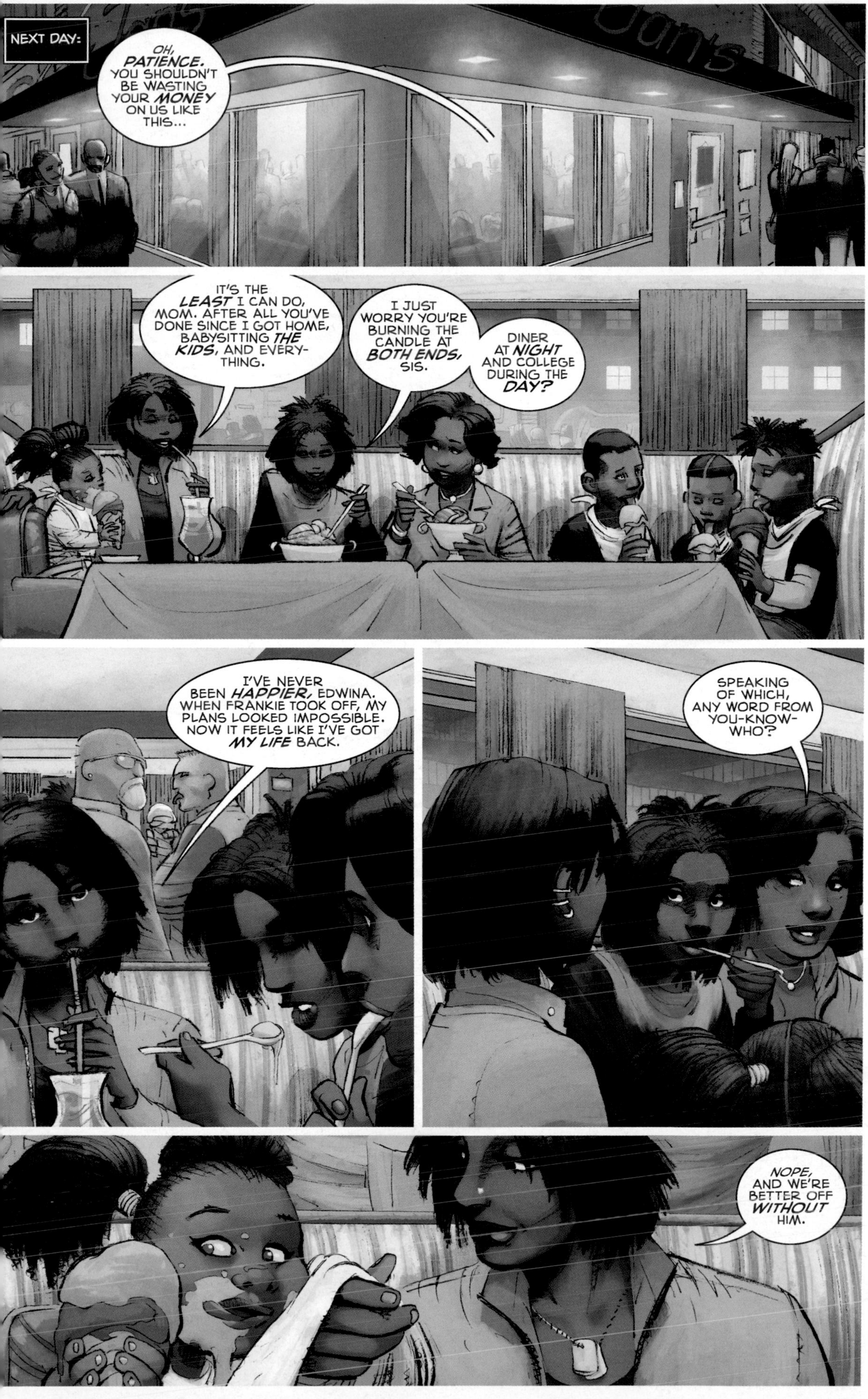
NEXT DAY:
OH, PATIENCE. YOU SHOULDN'T BE WASTING YOUR MONEY ON US LIKE THIS...
IT'S THE LEAST I CAN DO, MOM. AFTER ALL YOU'VE DONE SINCE I GOT HOME, BABYSITTING THE KIDS, AND EVERY-THING.
I JUST WORRY YOU'RE BURNING THE CANDLE AT BOTH ENDS, SIS.
DINER AT NIGHT AND COLLEGE DURING THE DAY?
I'VE NEVER BEEN HAPPIER, EDWINA. WHEN FRANKIE TOOK OFF, MY PLANS LOOKED IMPOSSIBLE. NOW IT FEELS LIKE I'VE GOT MY LIFE BACK.
SPEAKING OF WHICH, ANY WORD FROM YOU-KNOW-WHO?
NOPE, AND WE'RE BETTER OFF WITHOUT HIM.

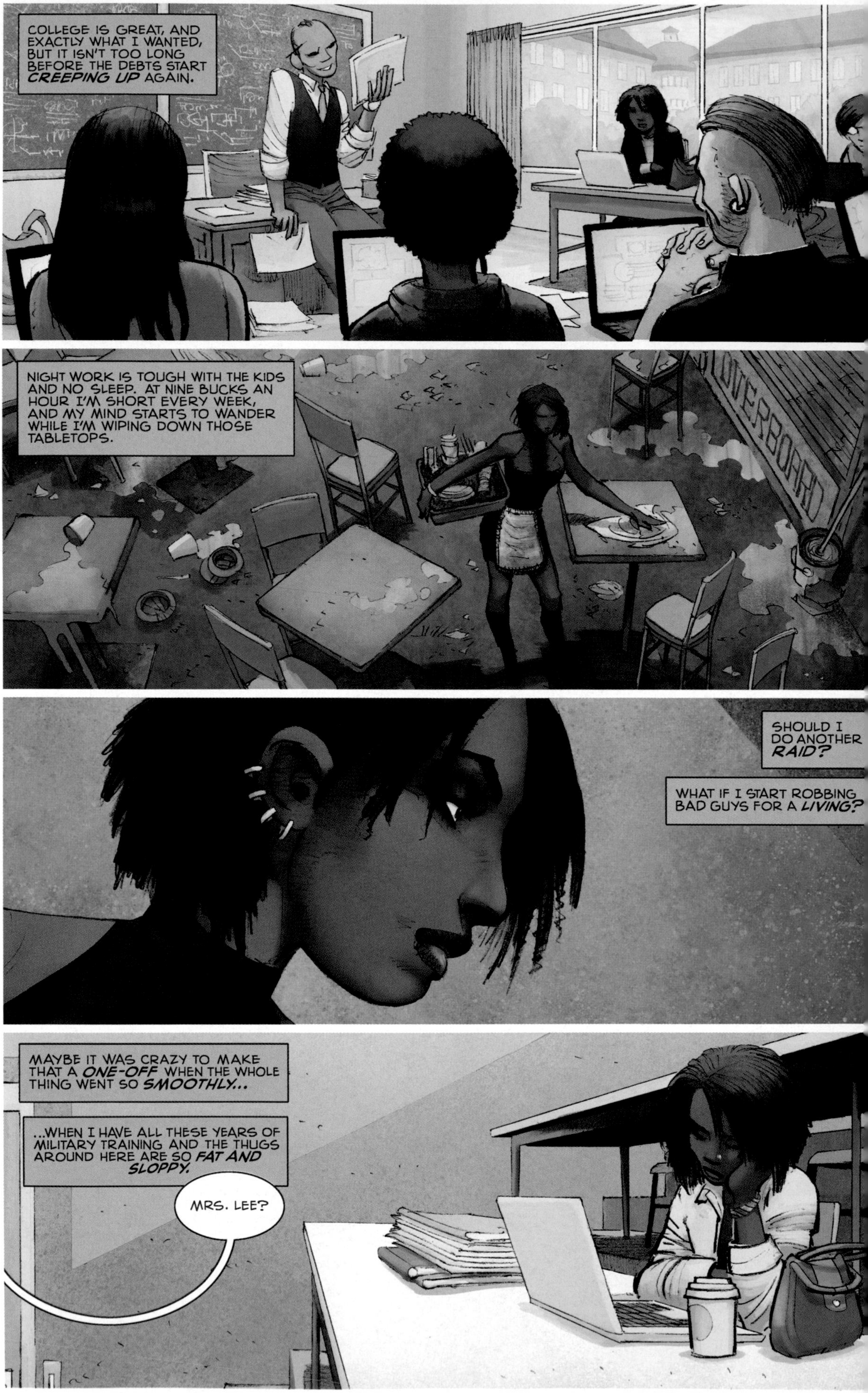
COLLEGE IS GREAT, AND EXACTLY WHAT I WANTED, BUT IT ISN'T TOO LONG BEFORE THE DEBTS START CREEPING UP AGAIN.
NIGHT WORK IS TOUGH WITH THE KIDS AND NO SLEEP. AT NINE BUCKS AN HOUR I'M SHORT EVERY WEEK, AND MY MIND STARTS TO WANDER WHILE I'M WIPING DOWN THOSE TABLETOPS.
OVERBOARD
SHOULD I DO ANOTHER RAID?
WHAT IF I START ROBBING BAD GUYS FOR A LIVING?
MAYBE IT WAS CRAZY TO MAKE THAT A ONE-OFF WHEN THE WHOLE THING WENT SO SMOOTHLY...
...WHEN I HAVE ALL THESE YEARS OF MILITARY TRAINING AND THE THUGS AROUND HERE ARE SO FAT AND SLOPPY.
MRS. LEE?

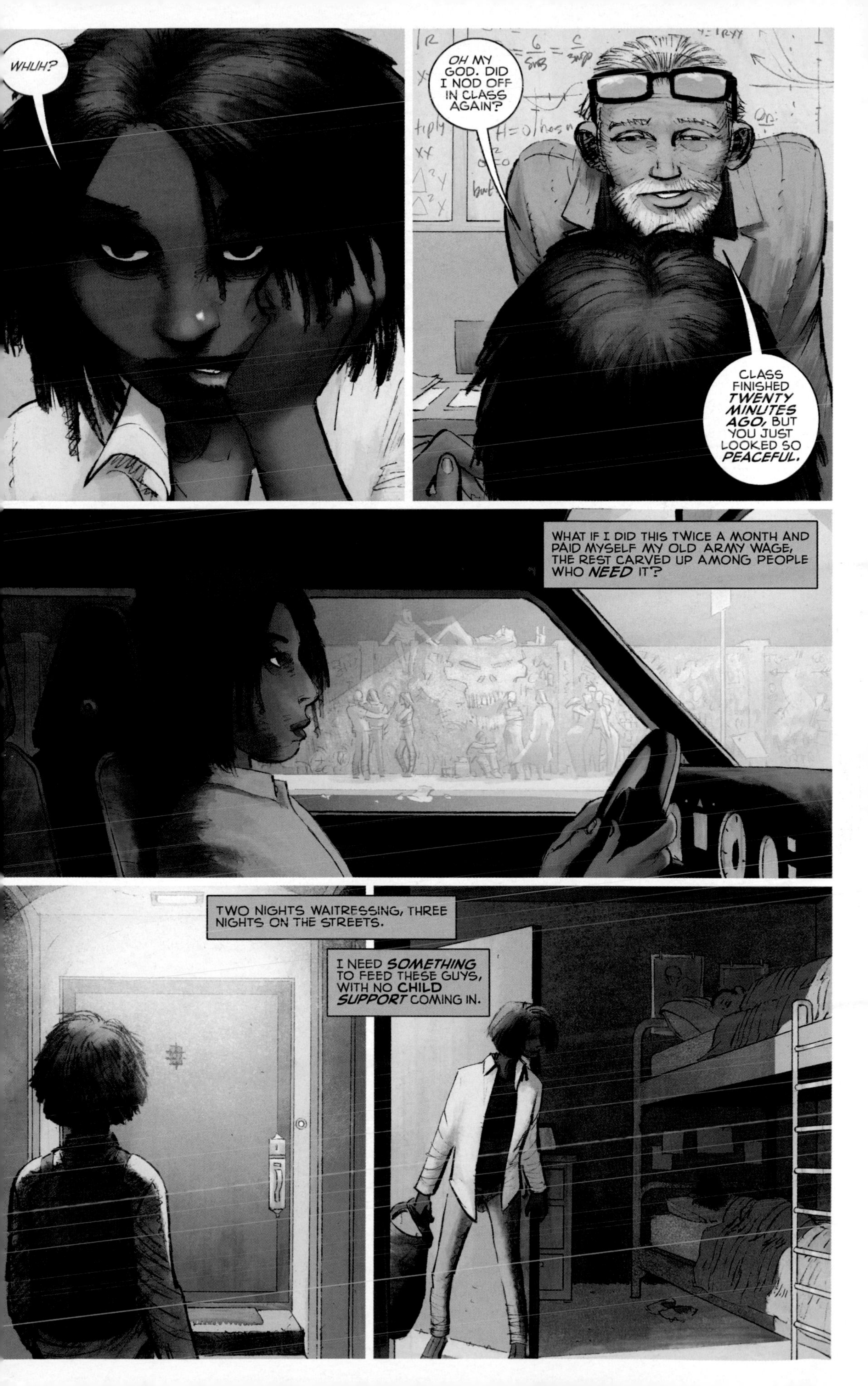
WHUH?
OH MY GOD. DID I NOD OFF IN CLASS AGAIN?
CLASS FINISHED TWENTY MINUTES AGO, BUT YOU JUST LOOKED SO PEACEFUL.
WHAT IF I DID THIS TWICE A MONTH AND PAID MYSELF MY OLD ARMY WAGE, THE REST CARVED UP AMONG PEOPLE WHO NEED IT?
TWO NIGHTS WAITRESSING, THREE NIGHTS ON THE STREETS.
I NEED SOMETHING TO FEED THESE GUYS, WITH NO CHILD SUPPORT COMING IN.

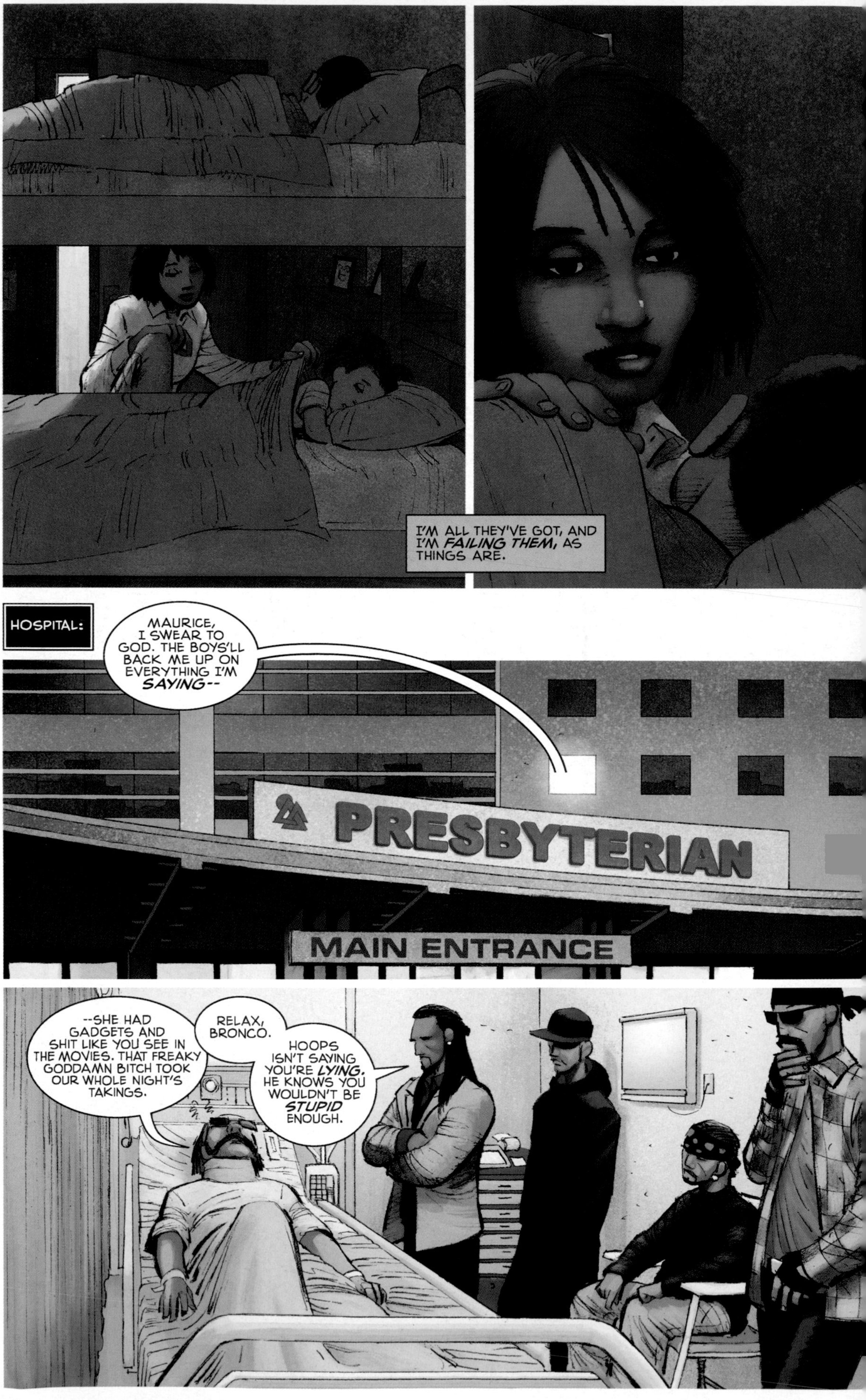
I'M ALL THEY'VE GOT, AND I'M FAILING THEM, AS THINGS ARE.
HOSPITAL:
MAURICE, I SWEAR TO GOD. THE BOYS'LL BACK ME UP ON EVERYTHING I'M SAYING--
PRESBYTERIAN
MAIN ENTRANCE
--SHE HAD GADGETS AND SHIT LIKE YOU SEE IN THE MOVIES. THAT FREAKY GODDAMN BITCH TOOK OUR WHOLE NIGHT'S TAKINGS.
RELAX, BRONCO.
HOOPS ISN'T SAYING YOU'RE LYING. HE KNOWS YOU WOULDN'T BE STUPID ENOUGH.

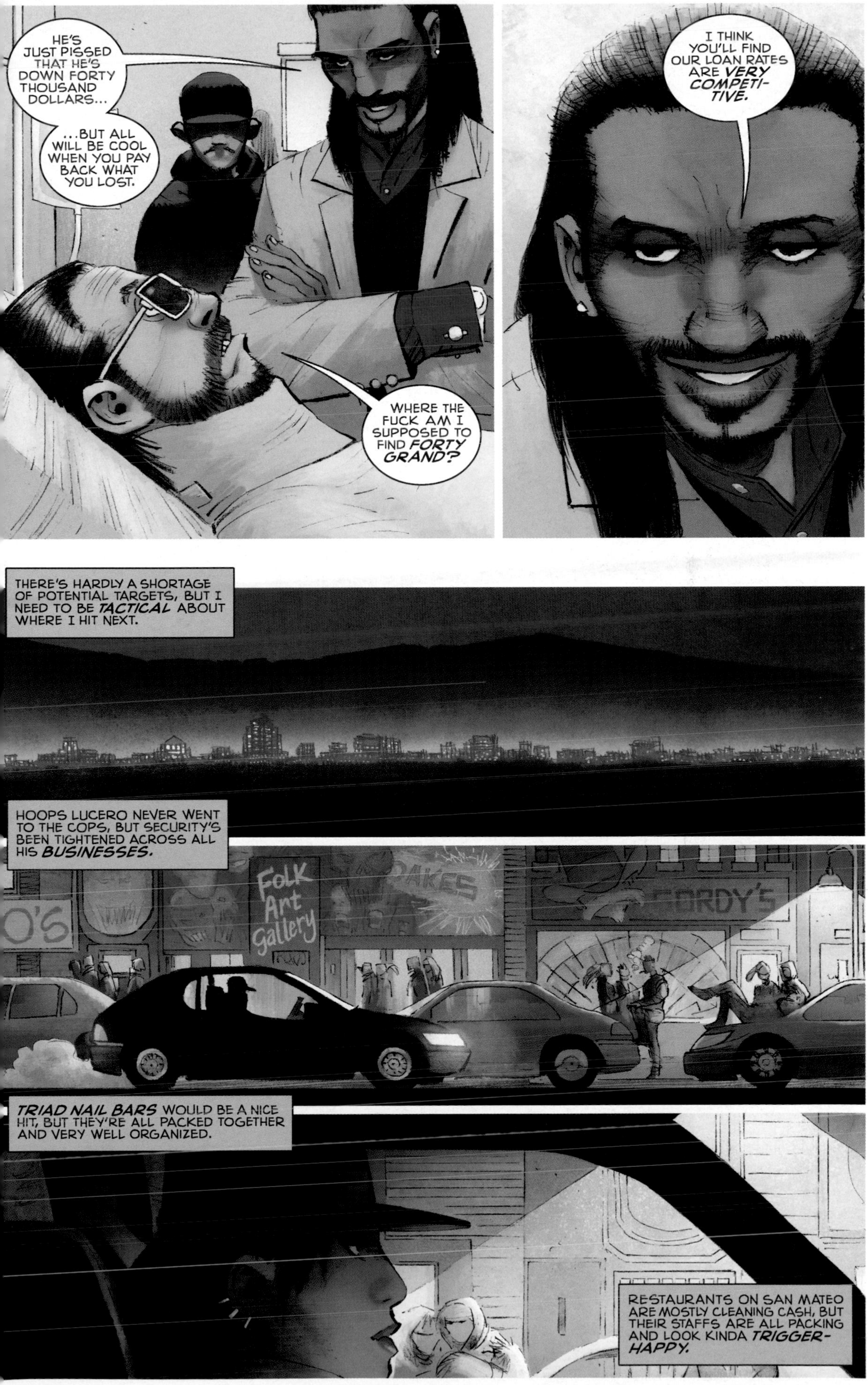
HE'S JUST PISSED THAT HE'S DOWN FORTY THOUSAND DOLLARS...
...BUT ALL WILL BE COOL WHEN YOU PAY BACK WHAT YOU LOST.
WHERE THE FUCK AM I SUPPOSED TO FIND FORTY GRAND?
I THINK YOU'LL FIND OUR LOAN RATES ARE VERY COMPETITIVE.
THERE'S HARDLY A SHORTAGE OF POTENTIAL TARGETS, BUT I NEED TO BE TACTICAL ABOUT WHERE I HIT NEXT.
HOOPS LUCERO NEVER WENT TO THE COPS, BUT SECURITY'S BEEN TIGHTENED ACROSS ALL HIS BUSINESSES.
Folk Art Gallery
GORDY'S
TRIAD NAIL BARS WOULD BE A NICE HIT, BUT THEY'RE ALL PACKED TOGETHER AND VERY WELL ORGANIZED.
RESTAURANTS ON SAN MATEO ARE MOSTLY CLEANING CASH, BUT THEIR STAFFS ARE ALL PACKING AND LOOK KINDA TRIGGER-HAPPY.

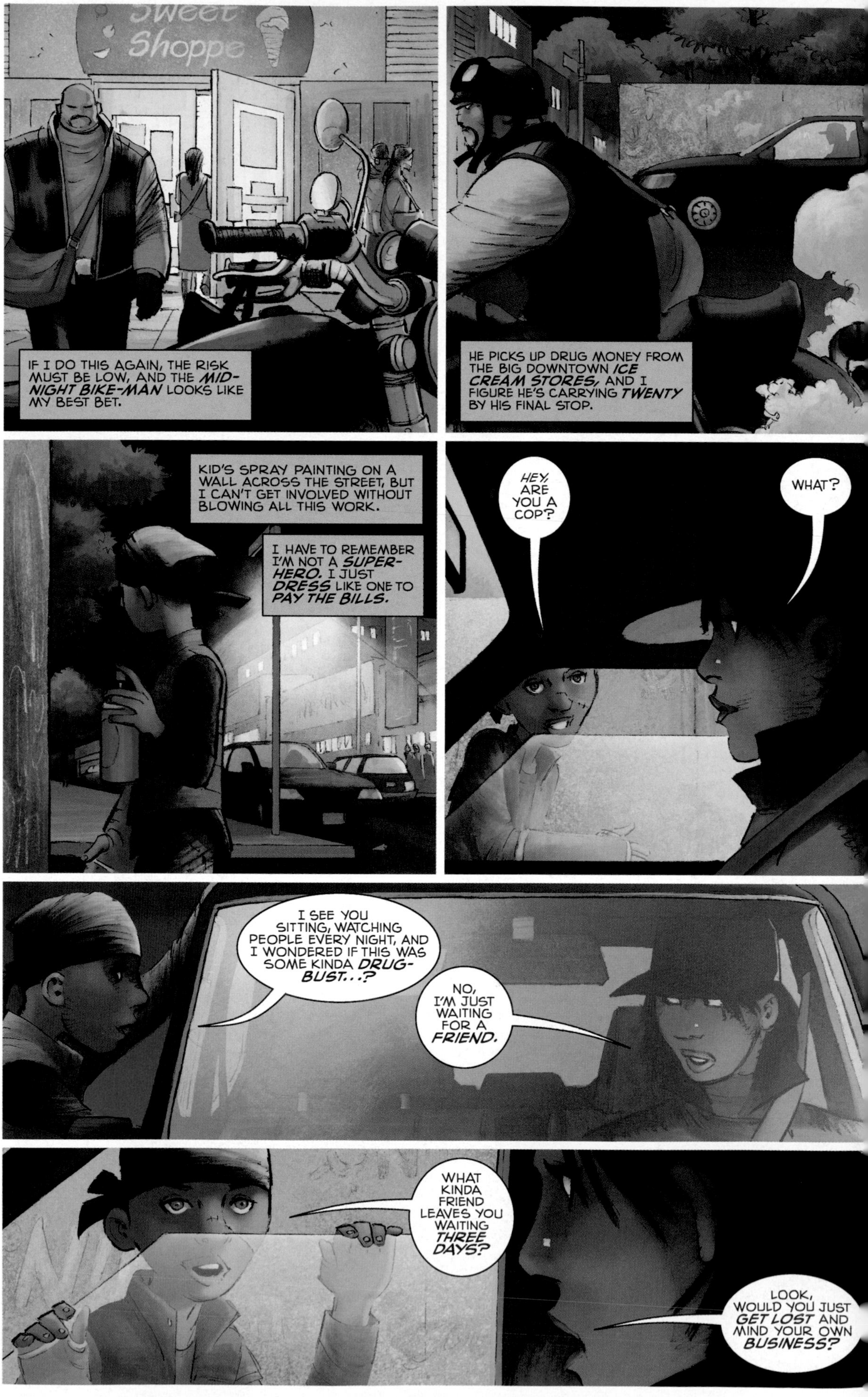
Sweet Shoppe
IF I DO THIS AGAIN, THE RISK MUST BE LOW, AND THE MID-NIGHT BIKE-MAN LOOKS LIKE MY BEST BET.
HE PICKS UP DRUG MONEY FROM THE BIG DOWNTOWN ICE CREAM STORES, AND I FIGURE HE'S CARRYING TWENTY BY HIS FINAL STOP.
KID'S SPRAY PAINTING ON A WALL ACROSS THE STREET, BUT I CAN'T GET INVOLVED WITHOUT BLOWING ALL THIS WORK.
I HAVE TO REMEMBER I'M NOT A SUPER-HERO. I JUST DRESS LIKE ONE TO PAY THE BILLS.
HEY, ARE YOU A COP?
WHAT?
I SEE YOU SITTING, WATCHING PEOPLE EVERY NIGHT, AND I WONDERED IF THIS WAS SOME KINDA DRUG-BUST...?
NO, I'M JUST WAITING FOR A FRIEND.
WHAT KINDA FRIEND LEAVES YOU WAITING THREE DAYS?
LOOK, WOULD YOU JUST GET LOST AND MIND YOUR OWN BUSINESS?

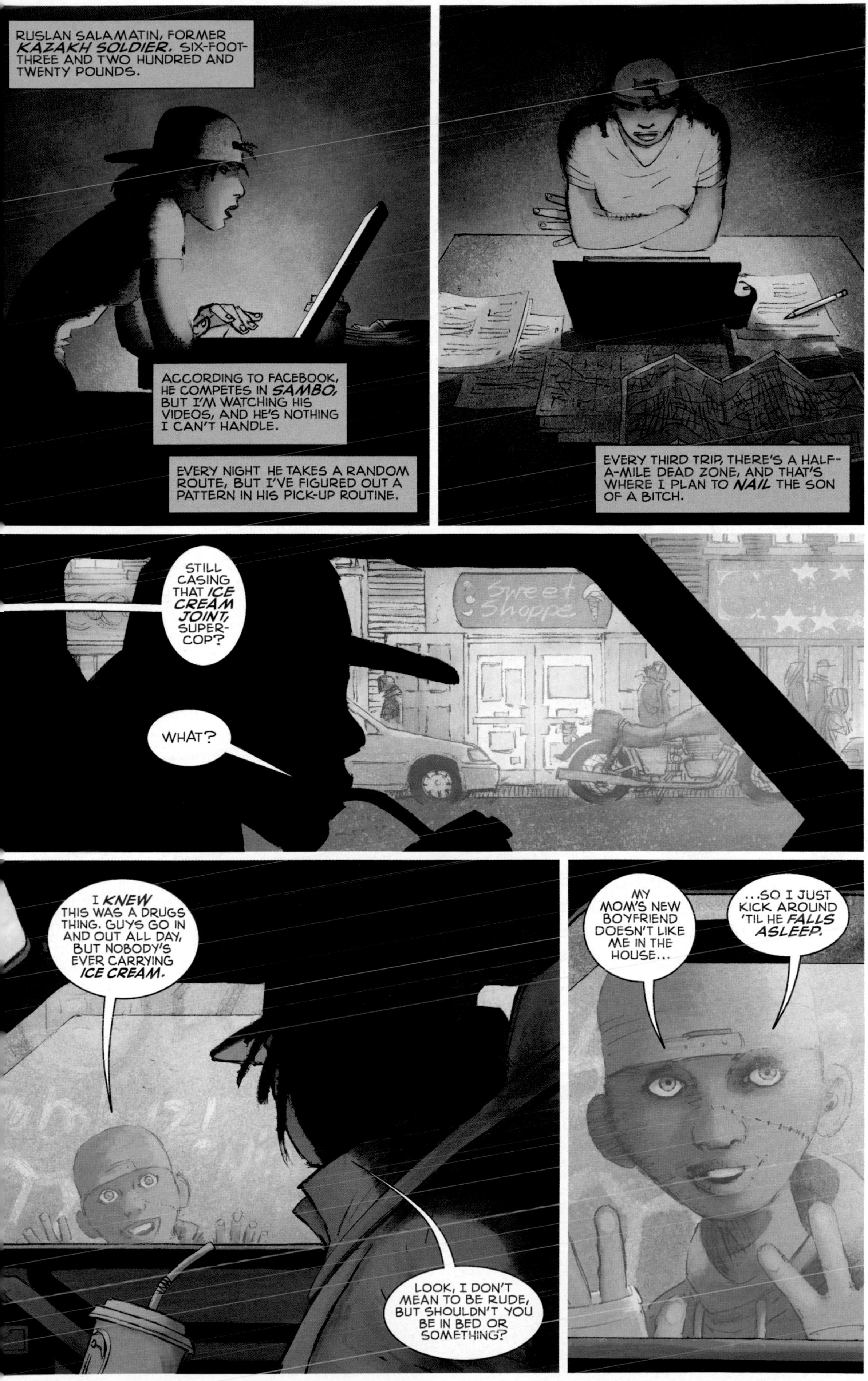
RUSLAN SALAMATIN, FORMER KAZAKH SOLDIER. SIX-FOOT-THREE AND TWO HUNDRED AND TWENTY POUNDS.
ACCORDING TO FACEBOOK, HE COMPETES IN SAMBO, BUT I'M WATCHING HIS VIDEOS, AND HE'S NOTHING I CAN'T HANDLE.
EVERY NIGHT HE TAKES A RANDOM ROUTE, BUT I'VE FIGURED OUT A PATTERN IN HIS PICK-UP ROUTINE.
EVERY THIRD TRIP, THERE'S A HALF-A-MILE DEAD ZONE, AND THAT'S WHERE I PLAN TO NAIL THE SON OF A BITCH.
STILL CASING THAT ICE CREAM JOINT, SUPER-COP?
Sweet Shoppe
WHAT?
I KNEW THIS WAS A DRUGS THING. GUYS GO IN AND OUT ALL DAY, BUT NOBODY'S EVER CARRYING ICE CREAM.
LOOK, I DON'T MEAN TO BE RUDE, BUT SHOULDN'T YOU BE IN BED OR SOMETHING?
MY MOM'S NEW BOYFRIEND DOESN'T LIKE ME IN THE HOUSE...
...SO I JUST KICK AROUND 'TIL HE FALLS ASLEEP.

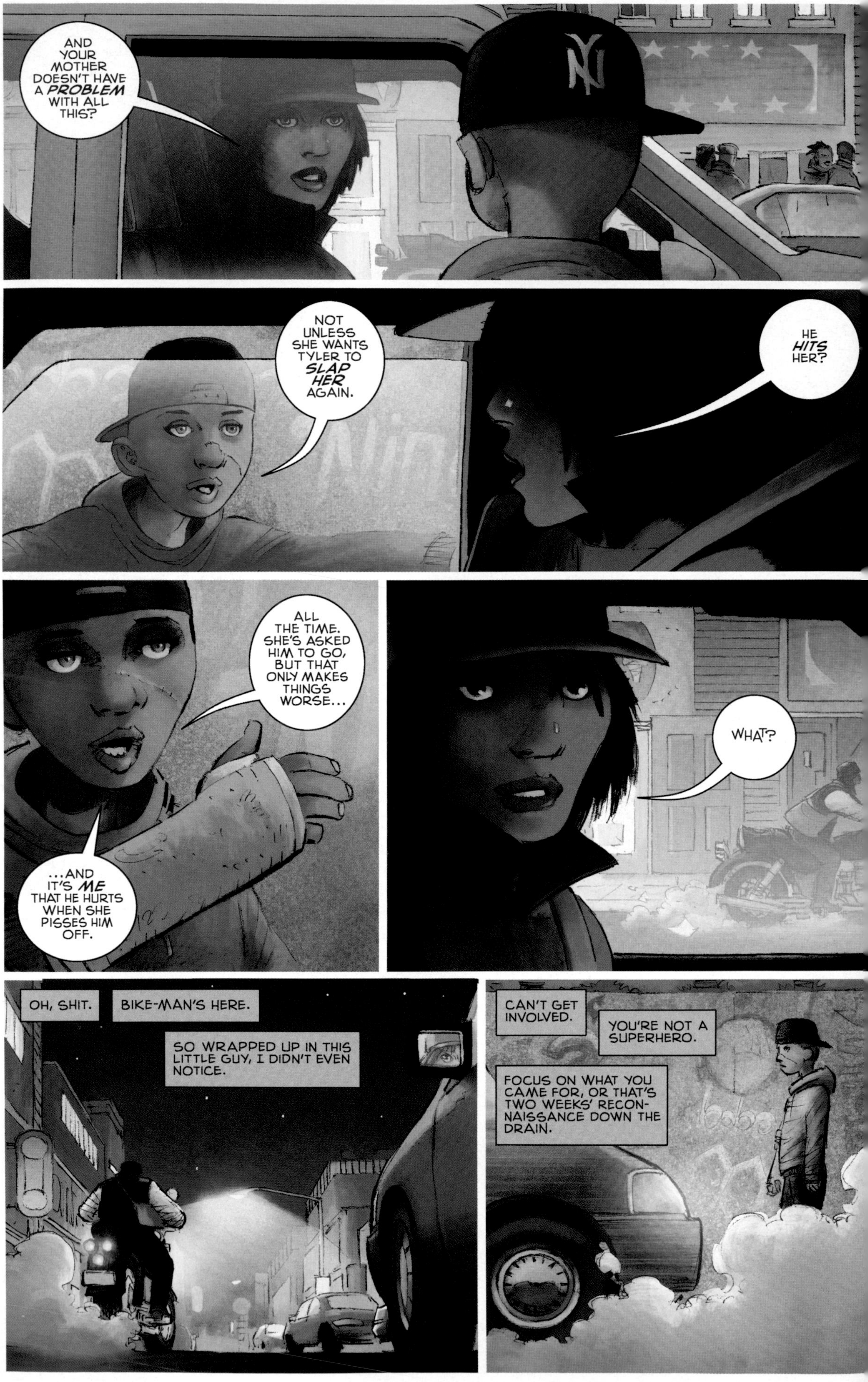
AND YOUR MOTHER DOESN'T HAVE A *PROBLEM* WITH ALL THIS?
NOT UNLESS SHE WANTS TYLER TO *SLAP HER* AGAIN.
HE *HITS* HER?
ALL THE TIME. SHE'S ASKED HIM TO GO, BUT THAT ONLY MAKES THINGS WORSE...
...AND IT'S *ME* THAT HE HURTS WHEN SHE PISSES HIM OFF.
WHAT?
OH, SHIT.
BIKE-MAN'S HERE.
SO WRAPPED UP IN THIS LITTLE GUY, I DIDN'T EVEN NOTICE.
CAN'T GET INVOLVED.
YOU'RE NOT A SUPERHERO.
FOCUS ON WHAT YOU CAME FOR, OR THAT'S TWO WEEKS' RECONNAISSANCE DOWN THE DRAIN.

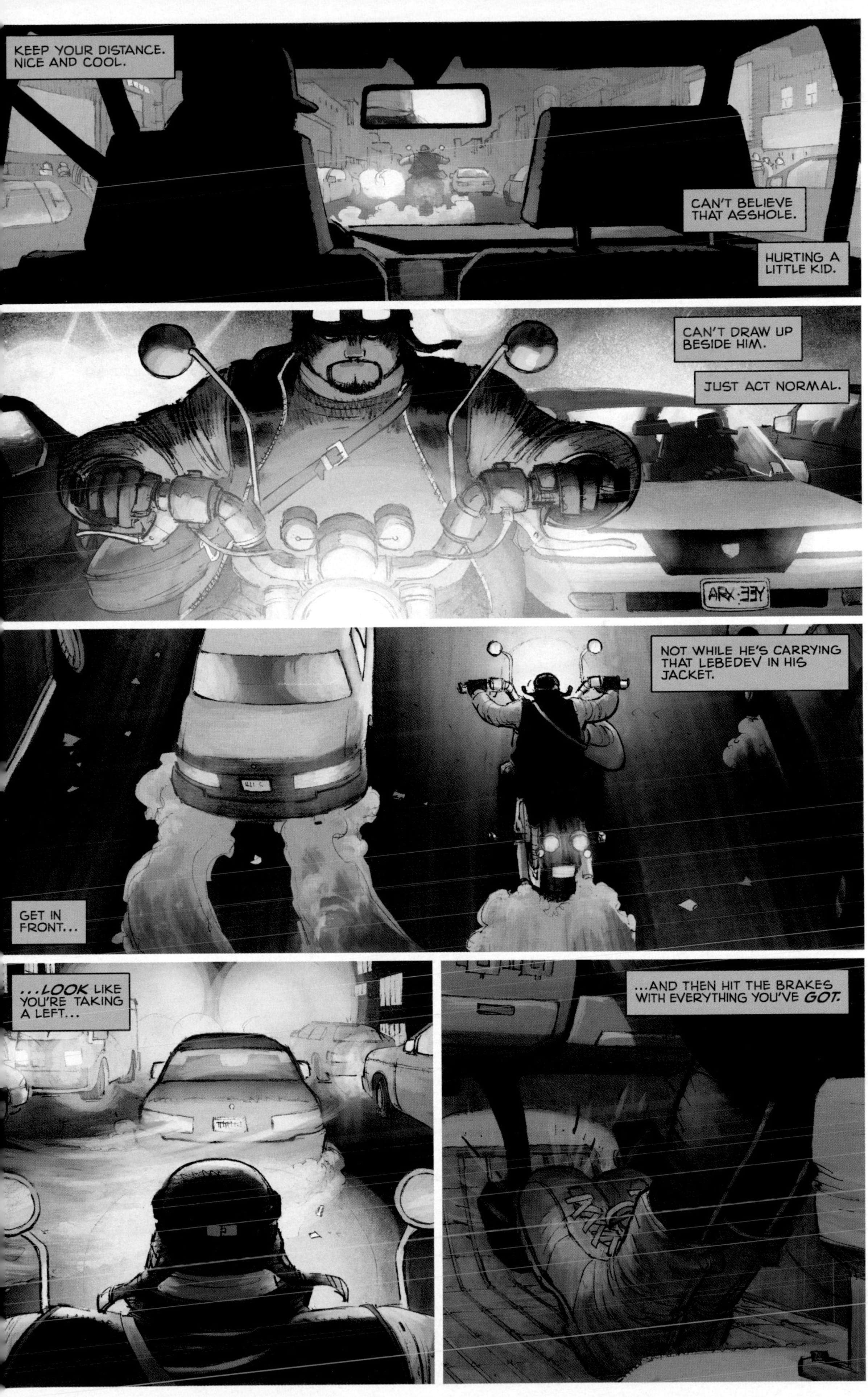
KEEP YOUR DISTANCE. NICE AND COOL.
CAN'T BELIEVE THAT ASSHOLE.
HURTING A LITTLE KID.
CAN'T DRAW UP BESIDE HIM.
JUST ACT NORMAL.
ARX·33Y
NOT WHILE HE'S CARRYING THAT LEBEDEV IN HIS JACKET.
GET IN FRONT...
...LOOK LIKE YOU'RE TAKING A LEFT...
...AND THEN HIT THE BRAKES WITH EVERYTHING YOU'VE GOT.

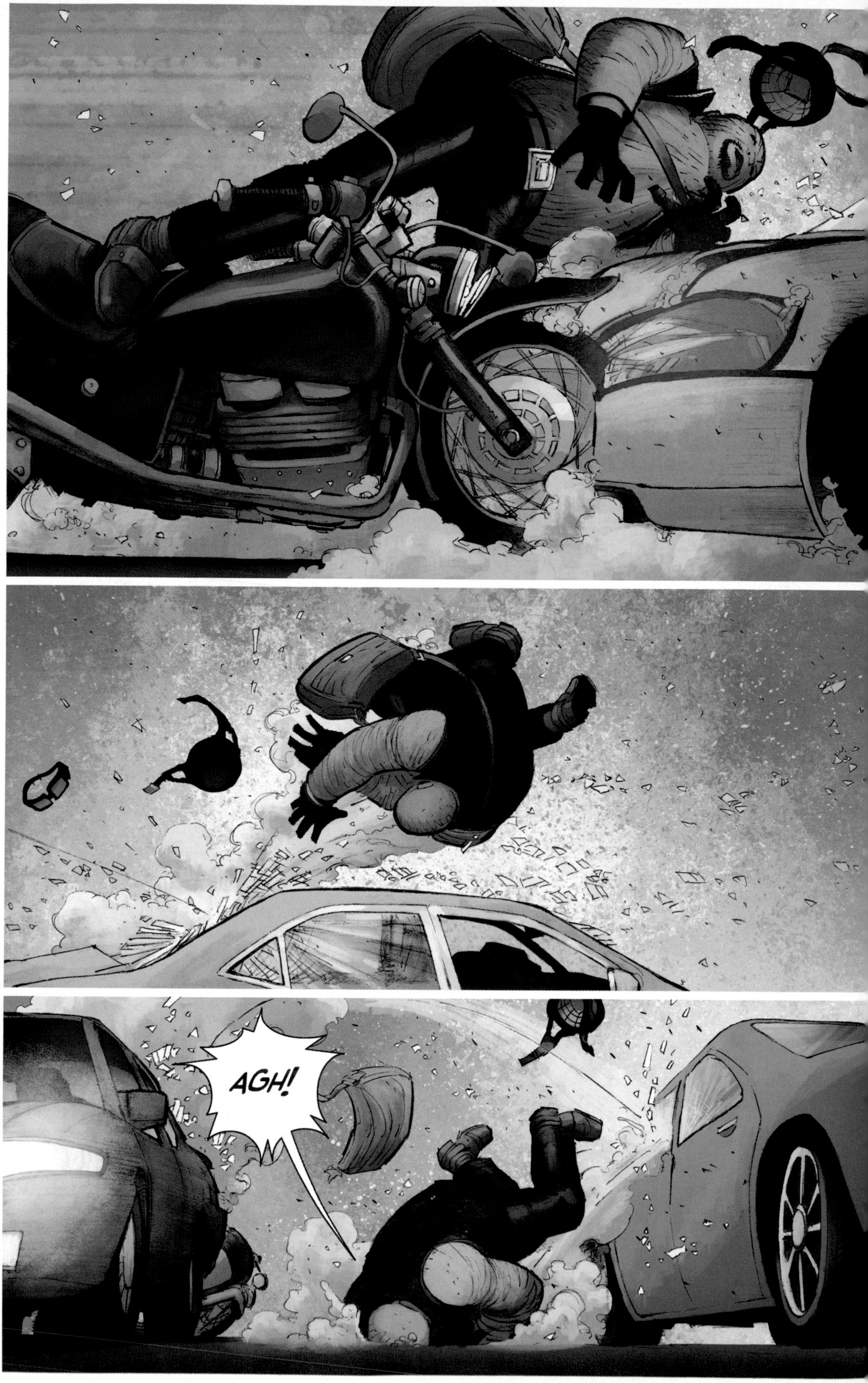
AGH!

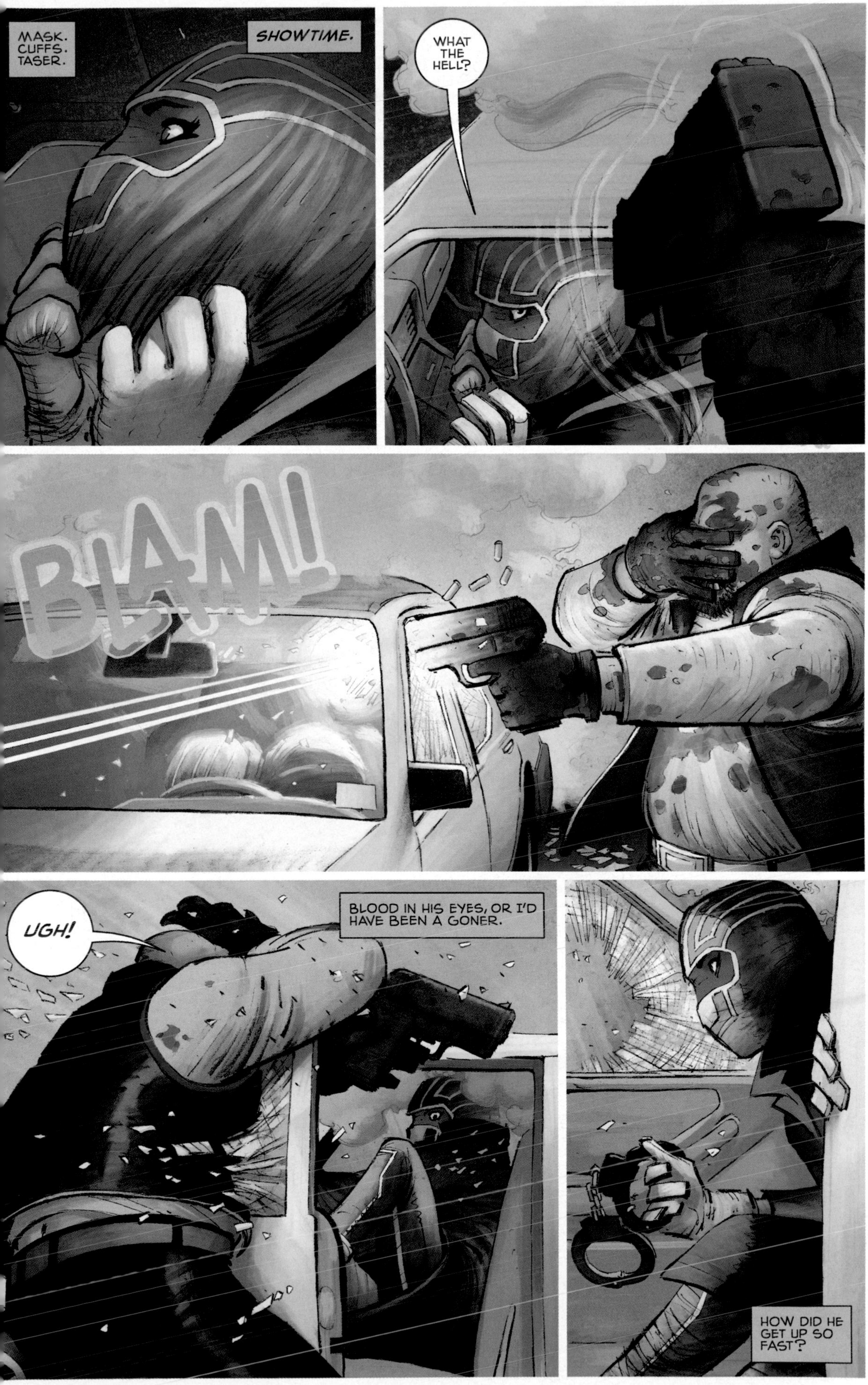
MASK. CUFFS. TASER.
SHOWTIME.
WHAT THE HELL?
BLAM!
UGH!
BLOOD IN HIS EYES, OR I'D HAVE BEEN A GONER.
HOW DID HE GET UP SO FAST?

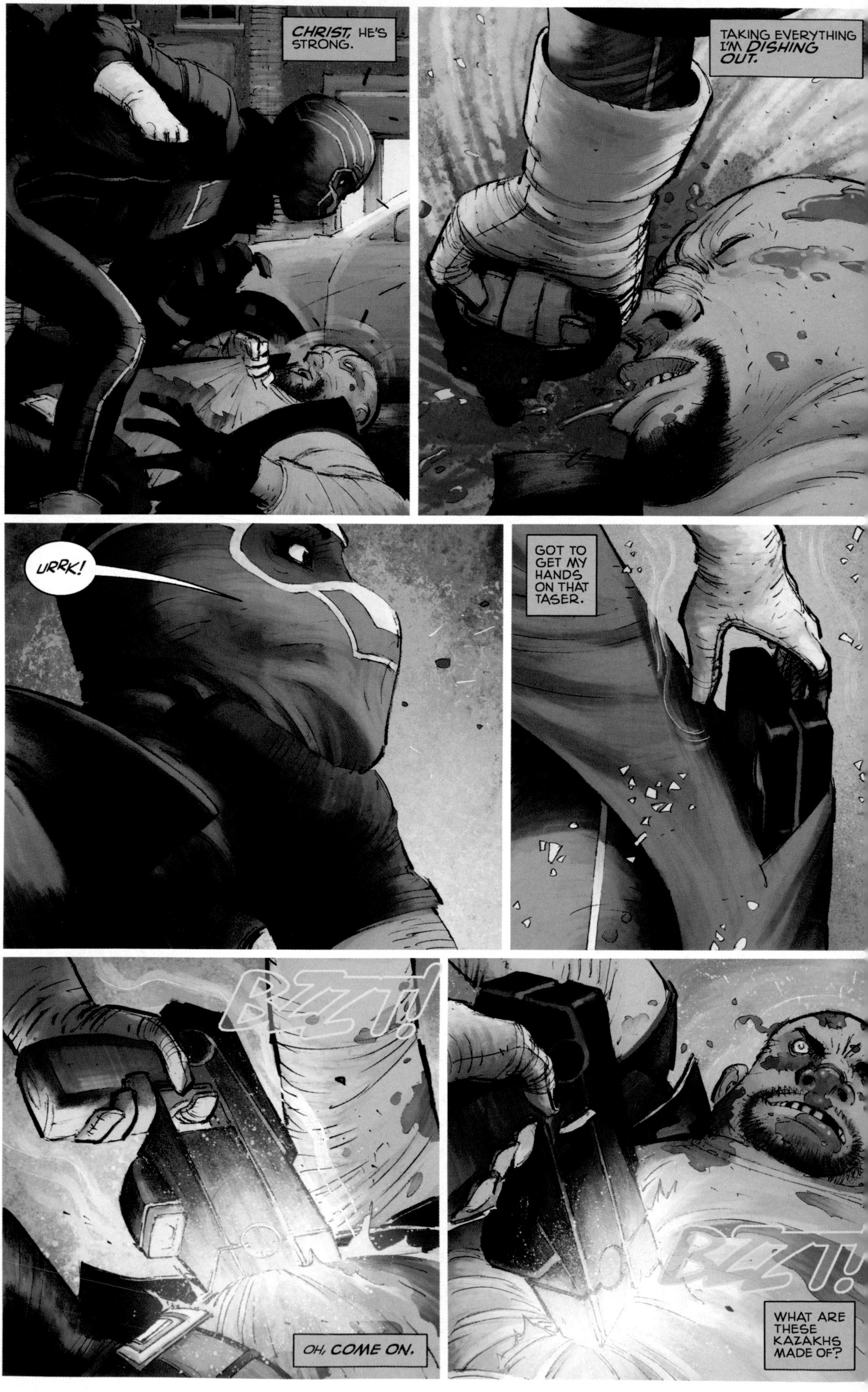
CHRIST, HE'S STRONG.
TAKING EVERYTHING I'M DISHING OUT.
URRK!
GOT TO GET MY HANDS ON THAT TASER.
BZZT!
OH, COME ON.
BZZT!
WHAT ARE THESE KAZAKHS MADE OF?

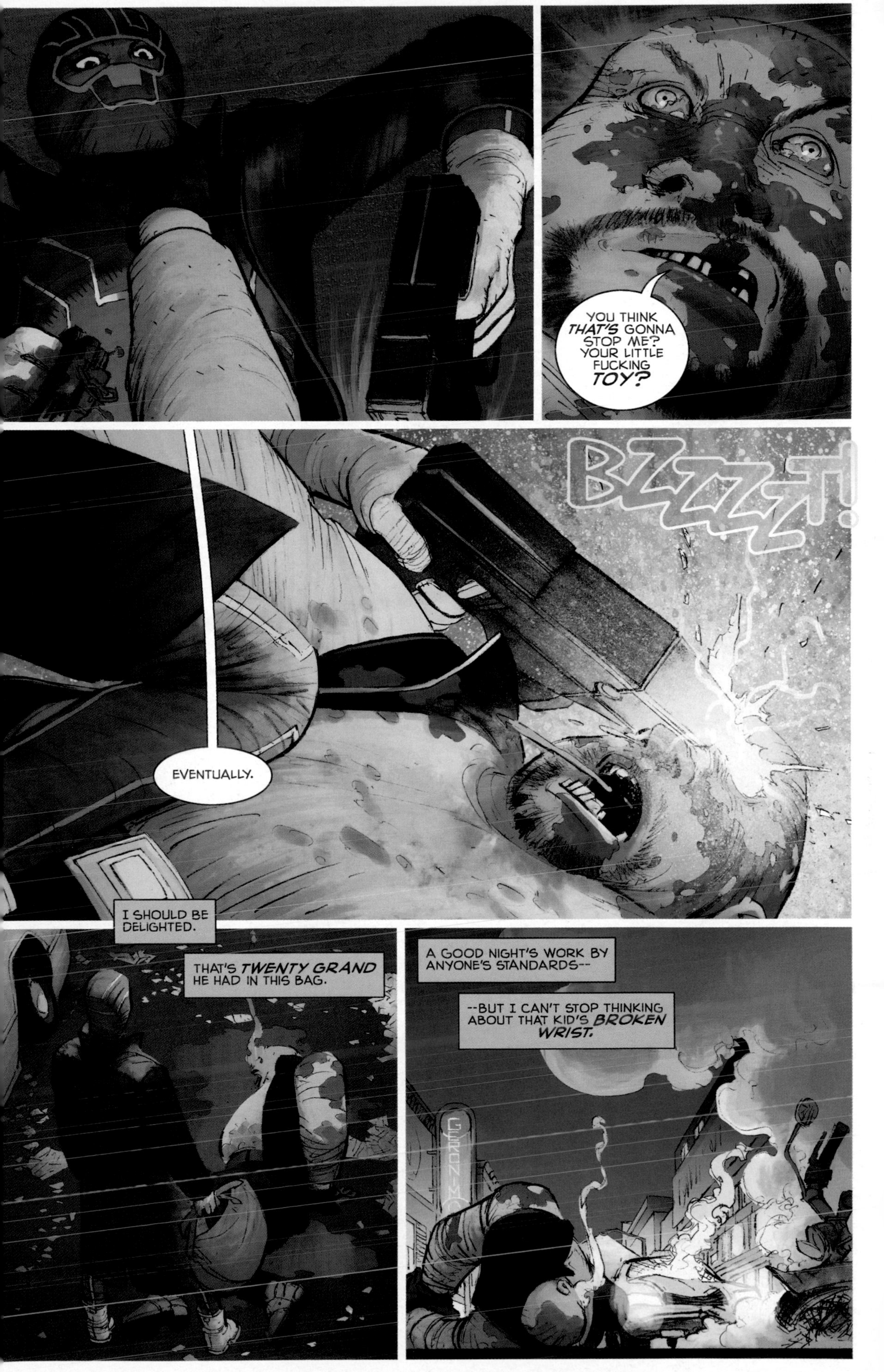
YOU THINK THAT'S GONNA STOP ME? YOUR LITTLE FUCKING TOY?
BZZZZT!
EVENTUALLY.
I SHOULD BE DELIGHTED.
THAT'S TWENTY GRAND HE HAD IN THIS BAG.
A GOOD NIGHT'S WORK BY ANYONE'S STANDARDS--
--BUT I CAN'T STOP THINKING ABOUT THAT KID'S BROKEN WRIST.

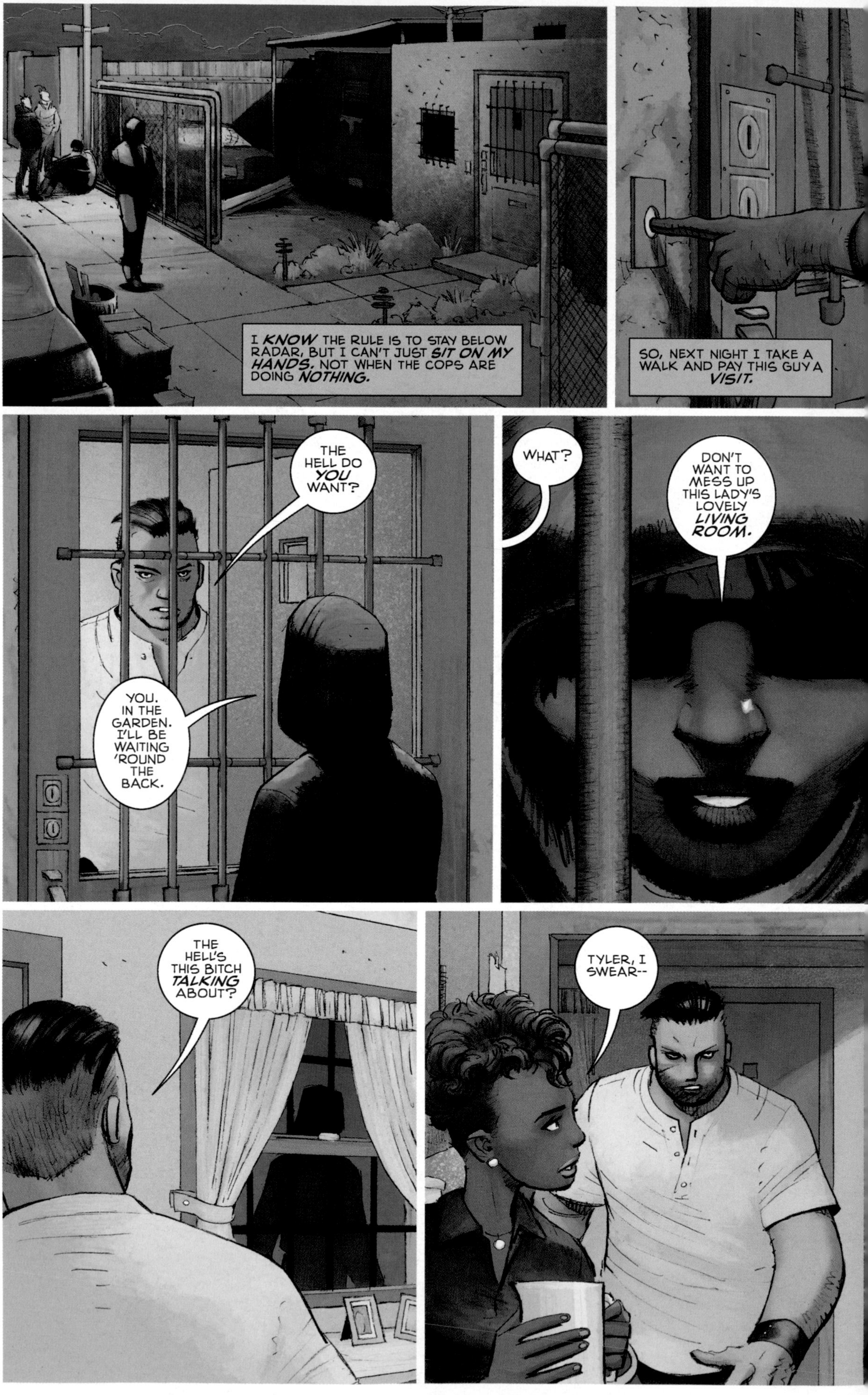
I KNOW THE RULE IS TO STAY BELOW RADAR, BUT I CAN'T JUST SIT ON MY HANDS. NOT WHEN THE COPS ARE DOING NOTHING.
SO, NEXT NIGHT I TAKE A WALK AND PAY THIS GUY A VISIT.
THE HELL DO YOU WANT?
YOU. IN THE GARDEN. I'LL BE WAITING 'ROUND THE BACK.
WHAT?
DON'T WANT TO MESS UP THIS LADY'S LOVELY LIVING ROOM.
THE HELL'S THIS BITCH TALKING ABOUT?
TYLER, I SWEAR--

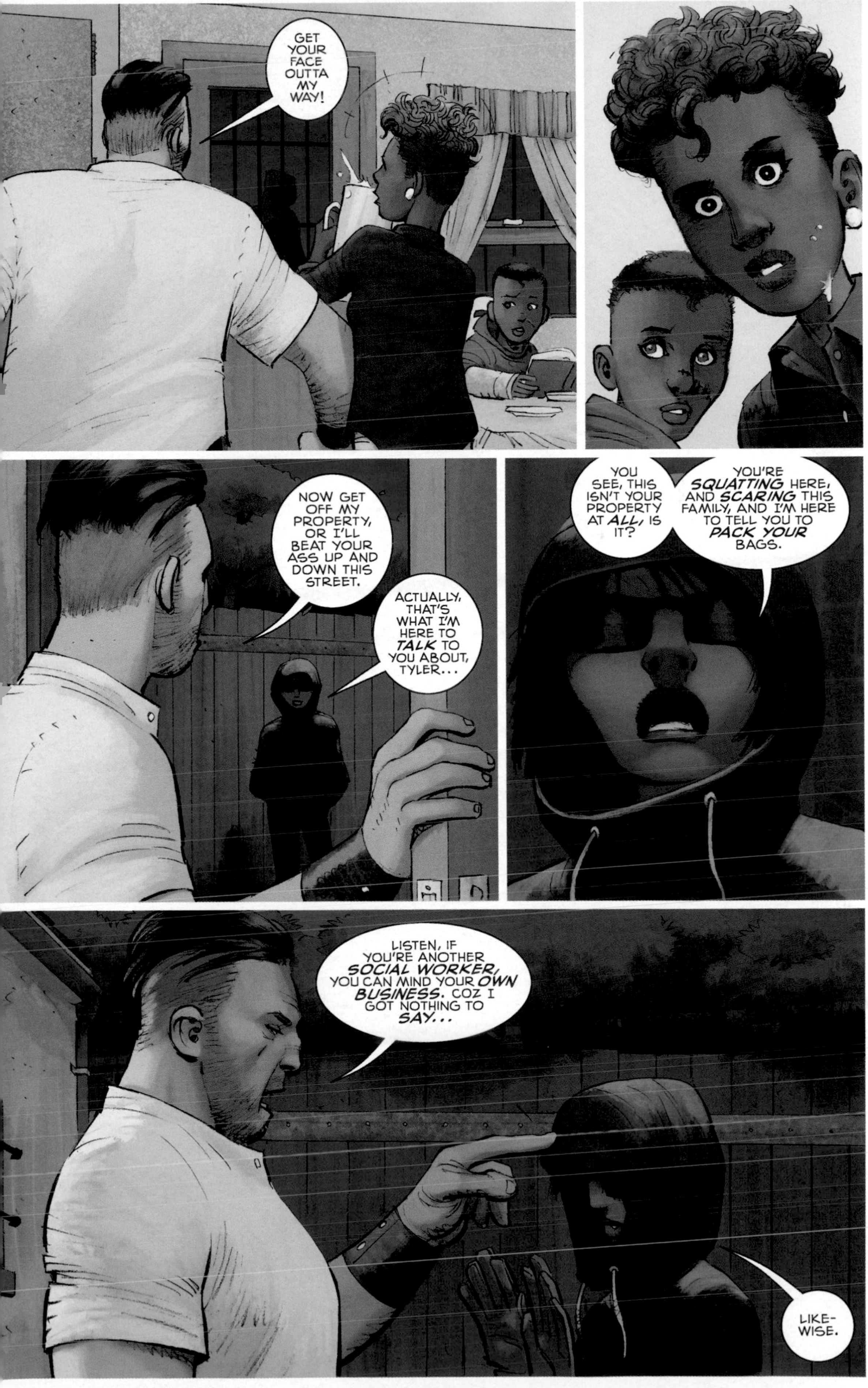

GET YOUR FACE OUTTA MY WAY!
NOW GET OFF MY PROPERTY, OR I'LL BEAT YOUR ASS UP AND DOWN THIS STREET.
ACTUALLY, THAT'S WHAT I'M HERE TO TALK TO YOU ABOUT, TYLER...
YOU SEE, THIS ISN'T YOUR PROPERTY AT ALL, IS IT?
YOU'RE SQUATTING HERE, AND SCARING THIS FAMILY, AND I'M HERE TO TELL YOU TO PACK YOUR BAGS.
LISTEN, IF YOU'RE ANOTHER SOCIAL WORKER, YOU CAN MIND YOUR OWN BUSINESS. COZ I GOT NOTHING TO SAY...
LIKE-WISE.

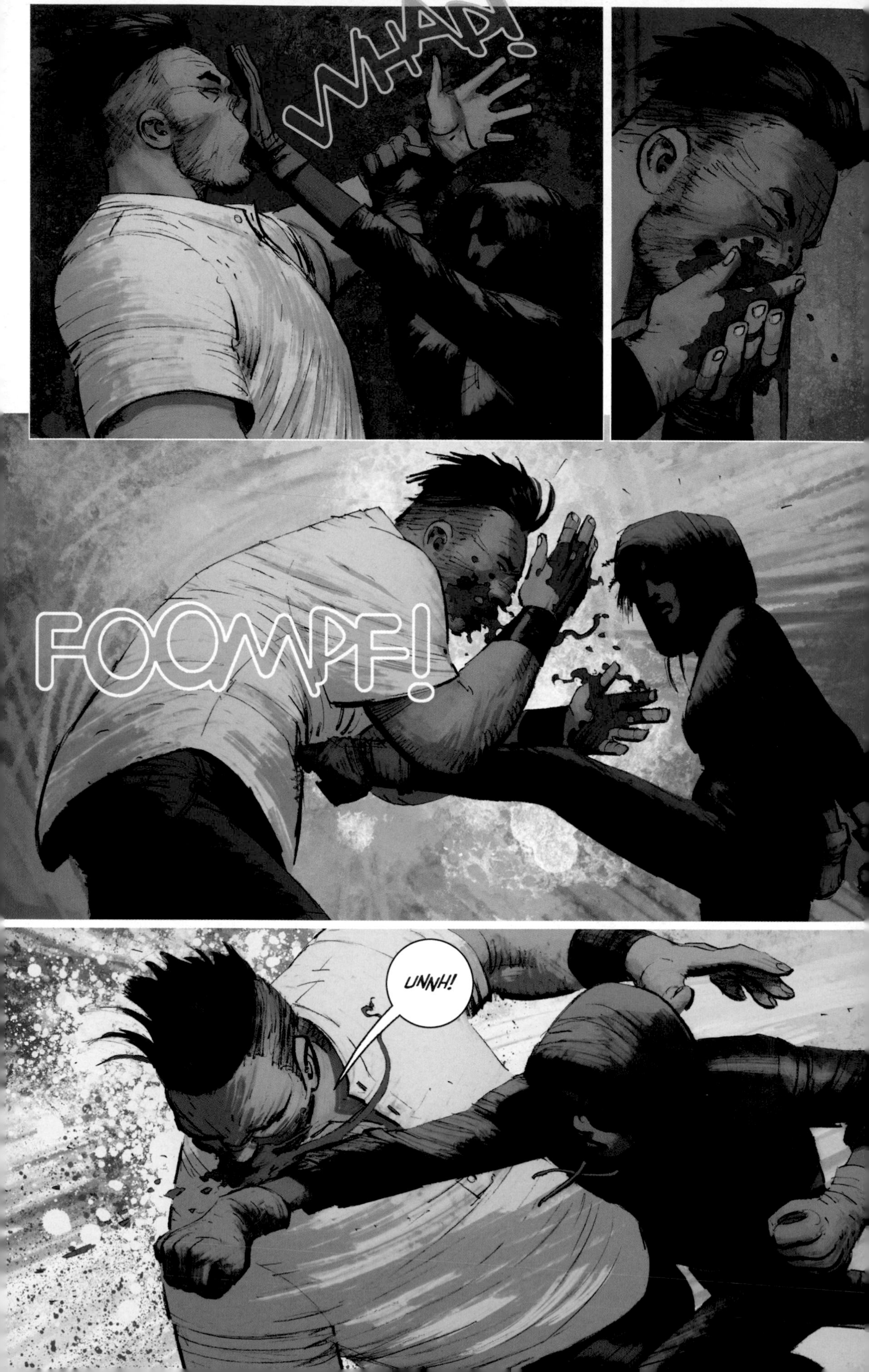
WHAP!
FOOMPF!
UNNH!

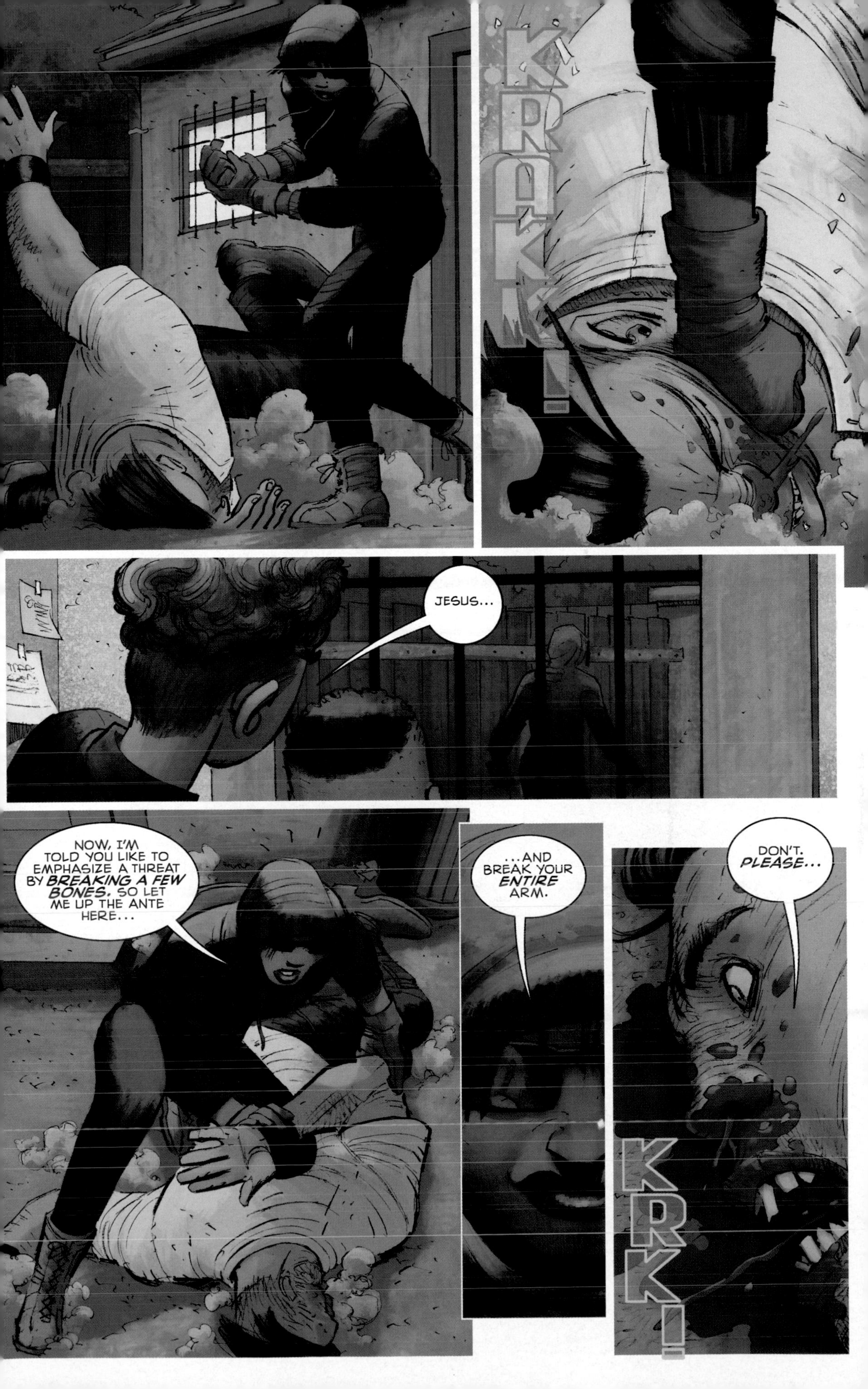
KRAK!
JESUS...
NOW, I'M TOLD YOU LIKE TO EMPHASIZE A THREAT BY BREAKING A FEW BONES. SO LET ME UP THE ANTE HERE...
...AND BREAK YOUR ENTIRE ARM.
DON'T. PLEASE...
KRK!

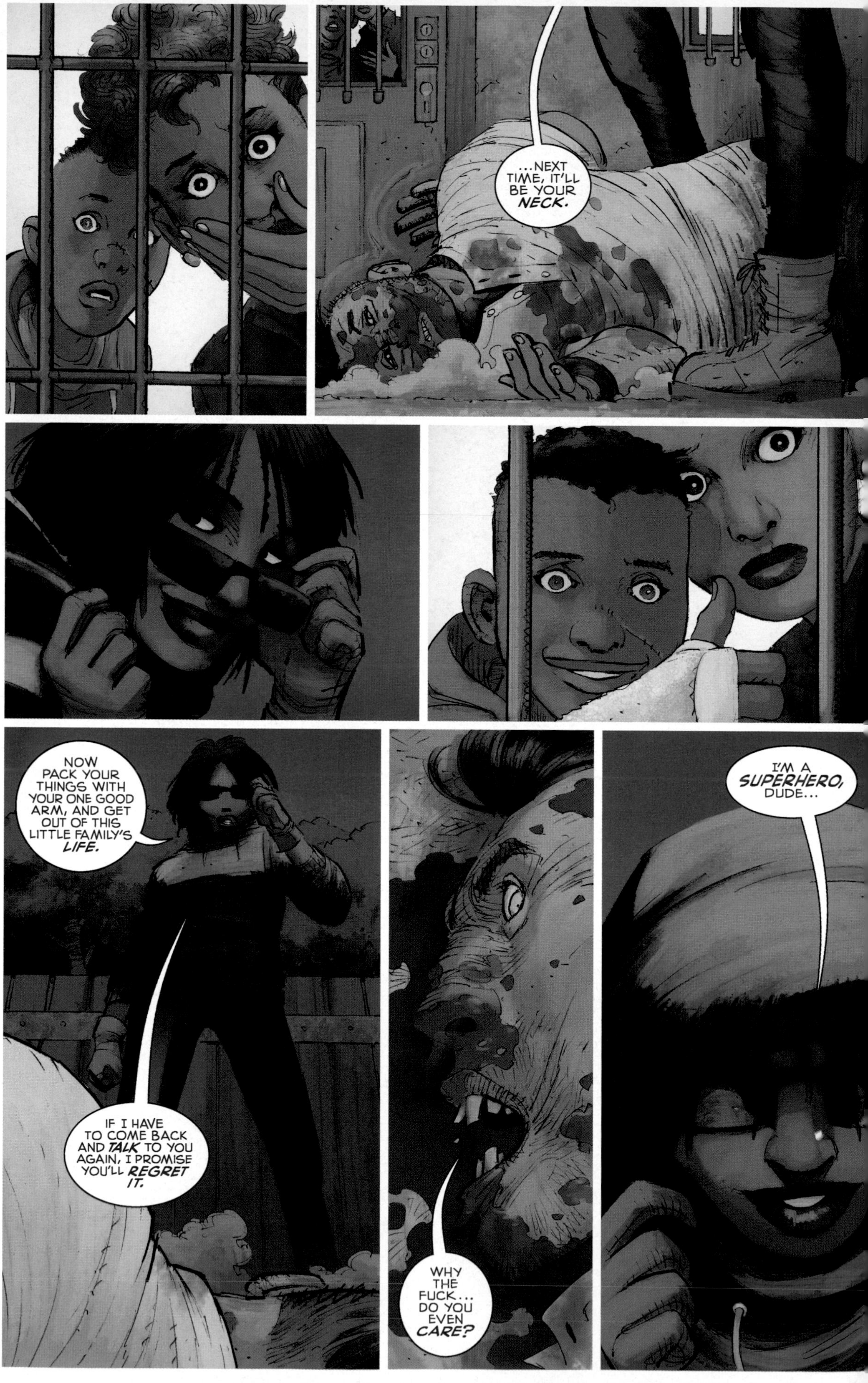
...NEXT TIME, IT'LL BE YOUR *NECK.*
NOW PACK YOUR THINGS WITH YOUR ONE GOOD ARM, AND GET OUT OF THIS LITTLE FAMILY'S *LIFE.*
IF I HAVE TO COME BACK AND *TALK* TO YOU AGAIN, I PROMISE YOU'LL *REGRET IT.*
WHY THE FUCK... DO YOU EVEN *CARE?*
I'M A *SUPERHERO,* DUDE...

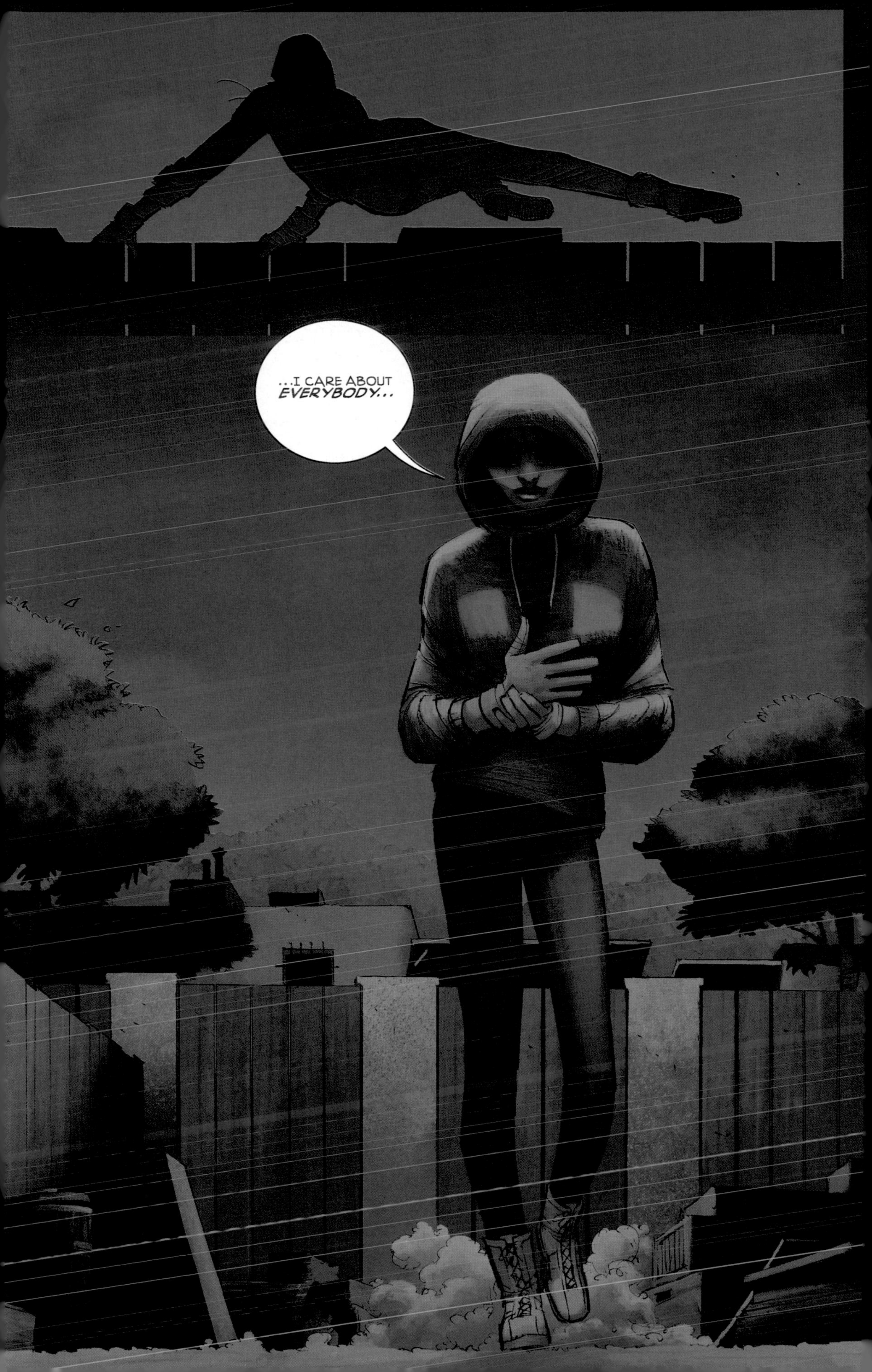
...I CARE ABOUT *EVERYBODY*...

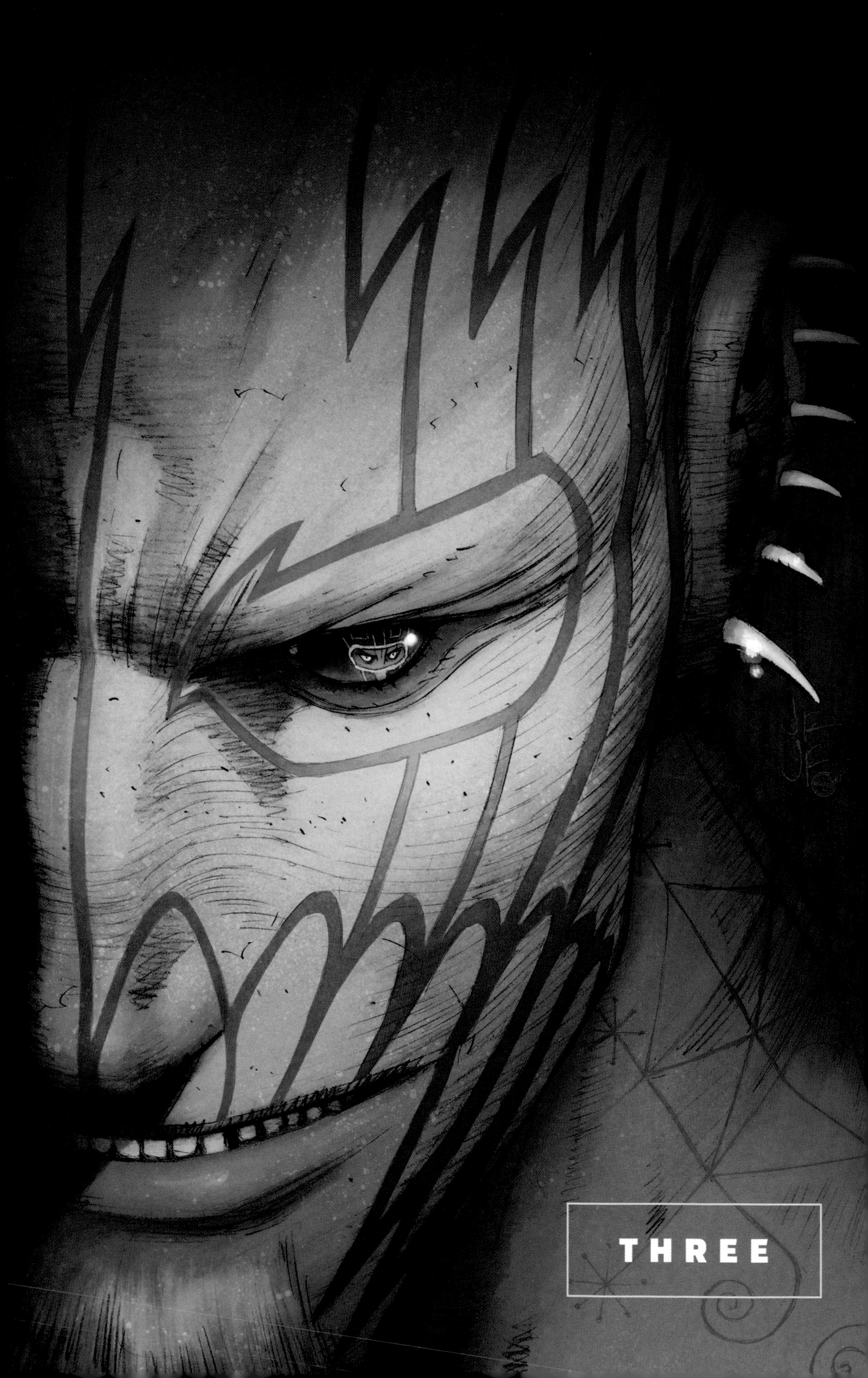
THREE

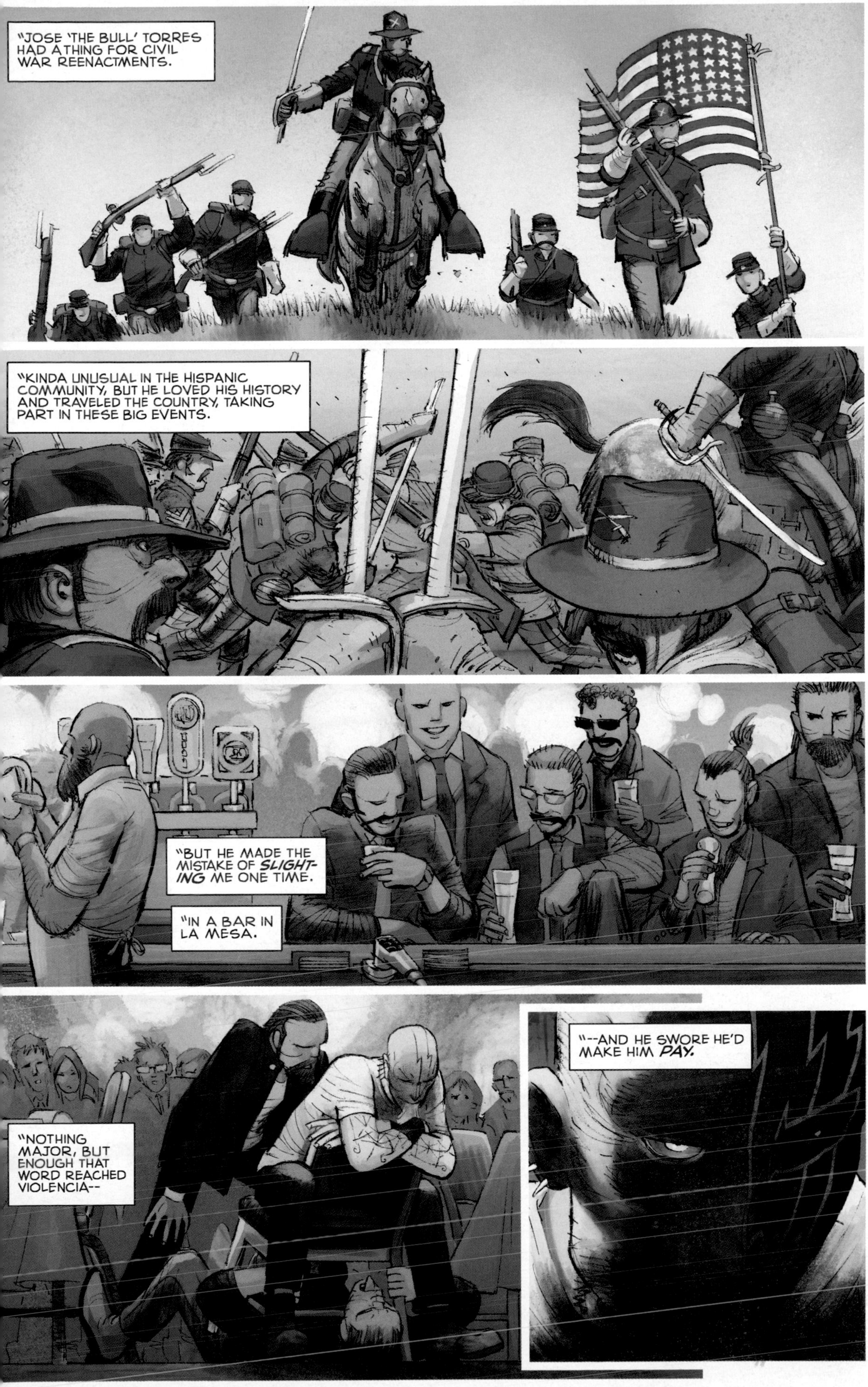
"JOSE 'THE BULL' TORRES HAD A THING FOR CIVIL WAR REENACTMENTS.
"KINDA UNUSUAL IN THE HISPANIC COMMUNITY, BUT HE LOVED HIS HISTORY AND TRAVELED THE COUNTRY, TAKING PART IN THESE BIG EVENTS.
"BUT HE MADE THE MISTAKE OF *SLIGHTING* ME ONE TIME.
"IN A BAR IN LA MESA.
"NOTHING MAJOR, BUT ENOUGH THAT WORD REACHED VIOLENCIA--
"--AND HE SWORE HE'D MAKE HIM *PAY.*

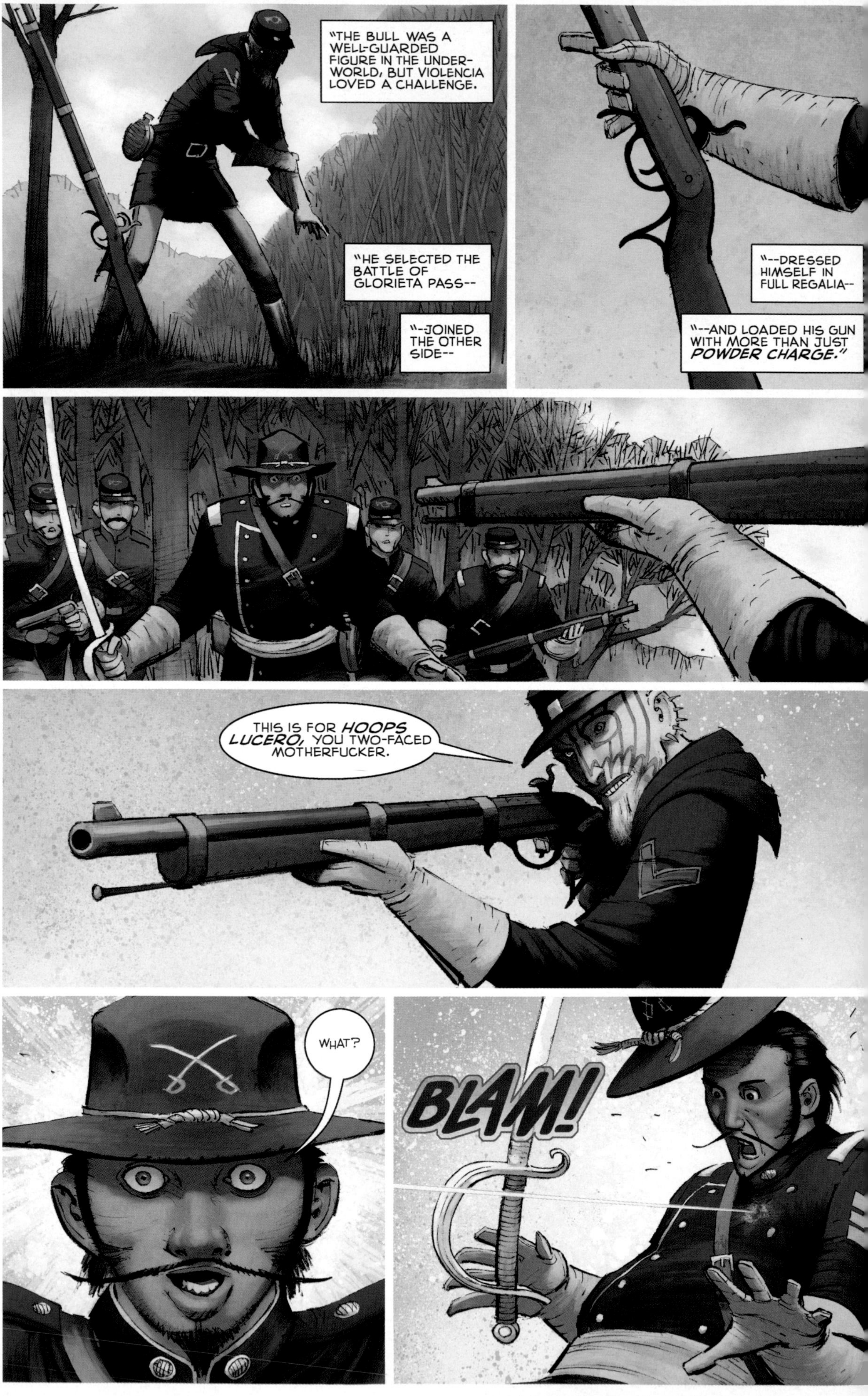
"THE BULL WAS A WELL-GUARDED FIGURE IN THE UNDER-WORLD, BUT VIOLENCIA LOVED A CHALLENGE.
"HE SELECTED THE BATTLE OF GLORIETA PASS--
"-JOINED THE OTHER SIDE--
"--DRESSED HIMSELF IN FULL REGALIA--
"--AND LOADED HIS GUN WITH MORE THAN JUST *POWDER CHARGE.*"
THIS IS FOR *HOOPS LUCERO,* YOU TWO-FACED MOTHERFUCKER.
WHAT?
BLAM!

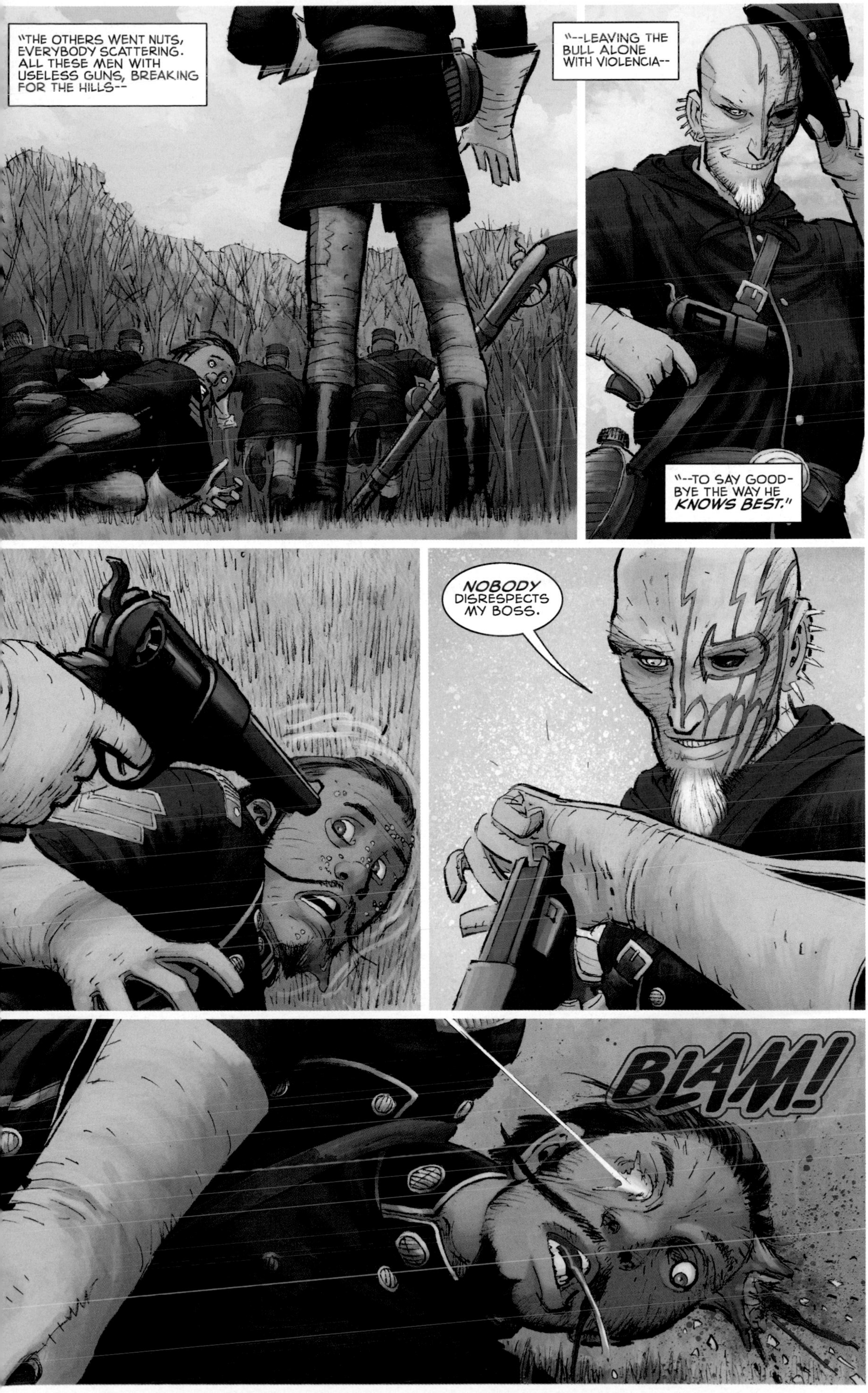
"THE OTHERS WENT NUTS, EVERYBODY SCATTERING. ALL THESE MEN WITH USELESS GUNS, BREAKING FOR THE HILLS--
"--LEAVING THE BULL ALONE WITH VIOLENCIA--
"--TO SAY GOOD-BYE THE WAY HE *KNOWS BEST.*"
NOBODY DISRESPECTS MY BOSS.
BLAM!

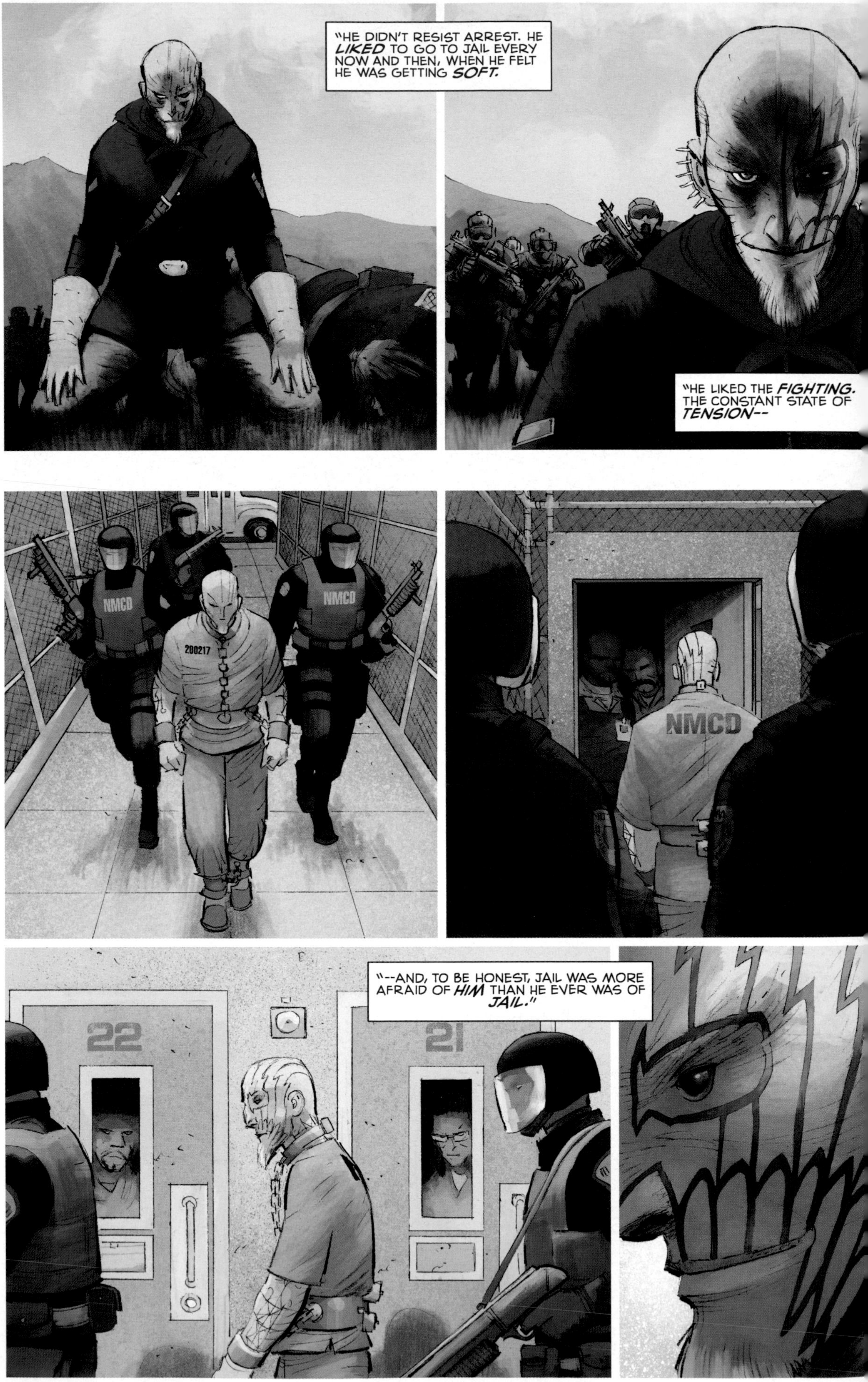
"HE DIDN'T RESIST ARREST. HE *LIKED* TO GO TO JAIL EVERY NOW AND THEN, WHEN HE FELT HE WAS GETTING *SOFT.*
"HE LIKED THE *FIGHTING.* THE CONSTANT STATE OF *TENSION*--
NMCD
NMCD
200217
NMCD
22
21
"--AND, TO BE HONEST, JAIL WAS MORE AFRAID OF *HIM* THAN HE EVER WAS OF *JAIL.*"

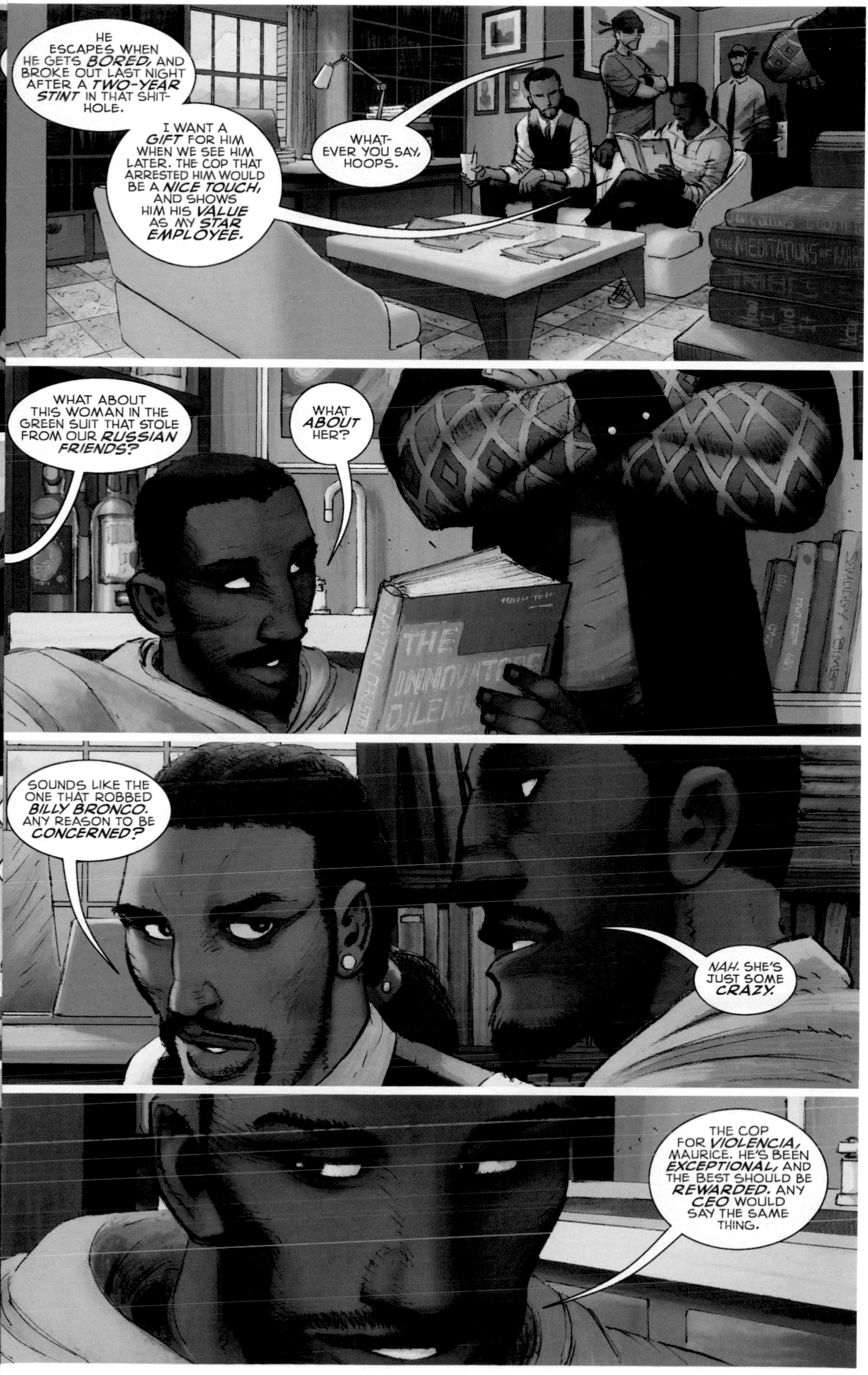
HE ESCAPES WHEN HE GETS BORED, AND BROKE OUT LAST NIGHT AFTER A TWO-YEAR STINT IN THAT SHIT-HOLE.
I WANT A GIFT FOR HIM WHEN WE SEE HIM LATER. THE COP THAT ARRESTED HIM WOULD BE A NICE TOUCH, AND SHOWS HIM HIS VALUE AS MY STAR EMPLOYEE.
WHAT-EVER YOU SAY, HOOPS.
THE MEDITATIONS OF MARC
WHAT ABOUT THIS WOMAN IN THE GREEN SUIT THAT STOLE FROM OUR RUSSIAN FRIENDS?
WHAT ABOUT HER?
THE INNOVATOR'S DILEMMA
SOUNDS LIKE THE ONE THAT ROBBED BILLY BRONCO. ANY REASON TO BE CONCERNED?
NAH. SHE'S JUST SOME CRAZY.
THE COP FOR VIOLENCIA, MAURICE. HE'S BEEN EXCEPTIONAL, AND THE BEST SHOULD BE REWARDED. ANY CEO WOULD SAY THE SAME THING.

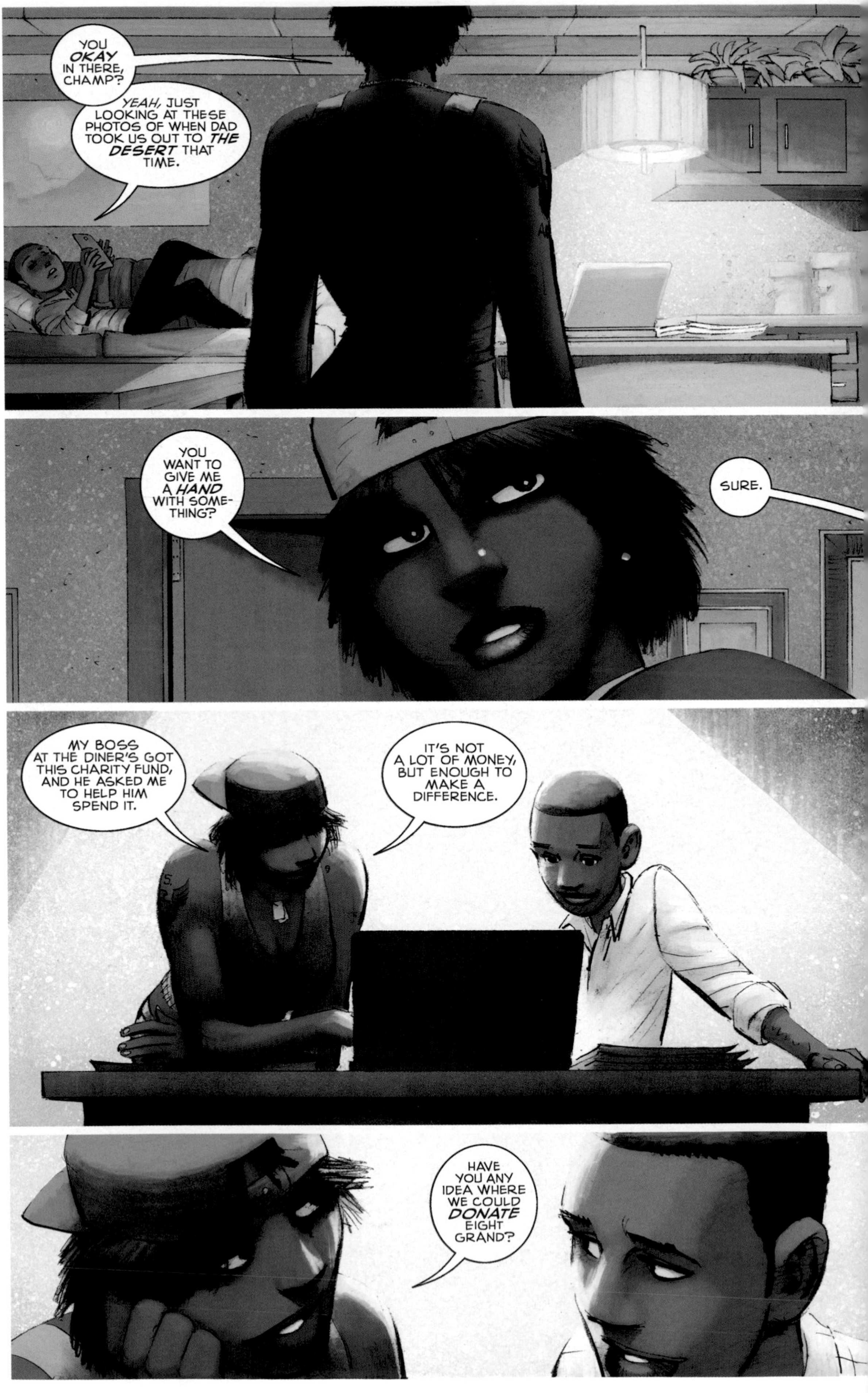
YOU *OKAY* IN THERE, CHAMP?
YEAH, JUST LOOKING AT THESE PHOTOS OF WHEN DAD TOOK US OUT TO *THE DESERT* THAT TIME.
YOU WANT TO GIVE ME A *HAND* WITH SOME-THING?
SURE.
MY BOSS AT THE DINER'S GOT THIS CHARITY FUND, AND HE ASKED ME TO HELP HIM SPEND IT.
IT'S NOT A LOT OF MONEY, BUT ENOUGH TO MAKE A DIFFERENCE.
HAVE YOU ANY IDEA WHERE WE COULD *DONATE* EIGHT GRAND?

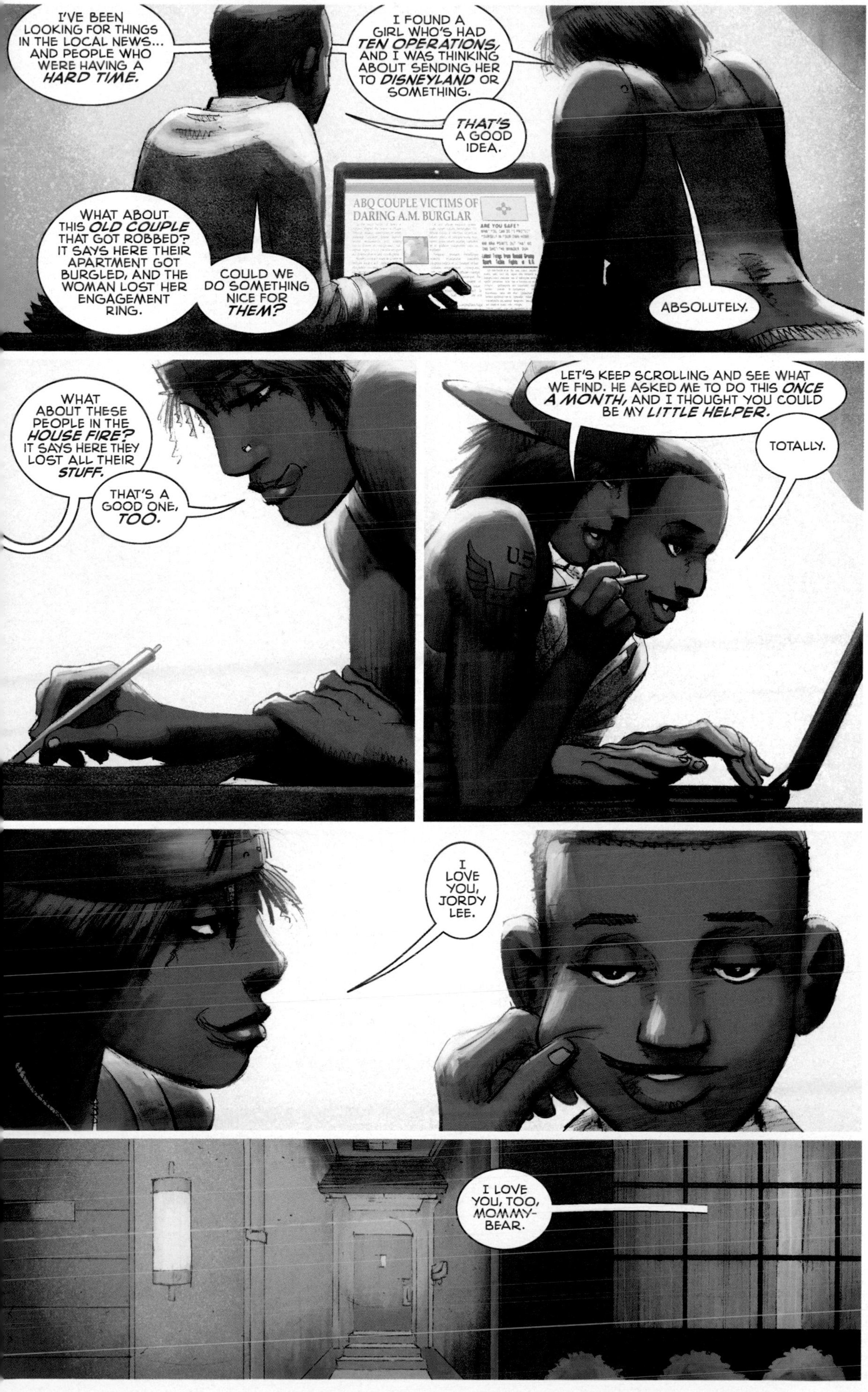
I'VE BEEN LOOKING FOR THINGS IN THE LOCAL NEWS... AND PEOPLE WHO WERE HAVING A *HARD TIME.*
I FOUND A GIRL WHO'S HAD *TEN OPERATIONS,* AND I WAS THINKING ABOUT SENDING HER TO *DISNEYLAND* OR SOMETHING.
THAT'S A GOOD IDEA.
ABQ COUPLE VICTIMS OF DARING A.M. BURGLAR
ARE YOU SAFE?
WHAT ABOUT THIS *OLD COUPLE* THAT GOT ROBBED? IT SAYS HERE THEIR APARTMENT GOT BURGLED, AND THE WOMAN LOST HER ENGAGEMENT RING.
COULD WE DO SOMETHING NICE FOR *THEM?*
ABSOLUTELY.
WHAT ABOUT THESE PEOPLE IN THE *HOUSE FIRE?* IT SAYS HERE THEY LOST ALL THEIR *STUFF.*
THAT'S A GOOD ONE, *TOO.*
LET'S KEEP SCROLLING AND SEE WHAT WE FIND. HE ASKED ME TO DO THIS *ONCE A MONTH,* AND I THOUGHT YOU COULD BE MY *LITTLE HELPER.*
TOTALLY.
I LOVE YOU, JORDY LEE.
I LOVE YOU, TOO, MOMMY-BEAR.

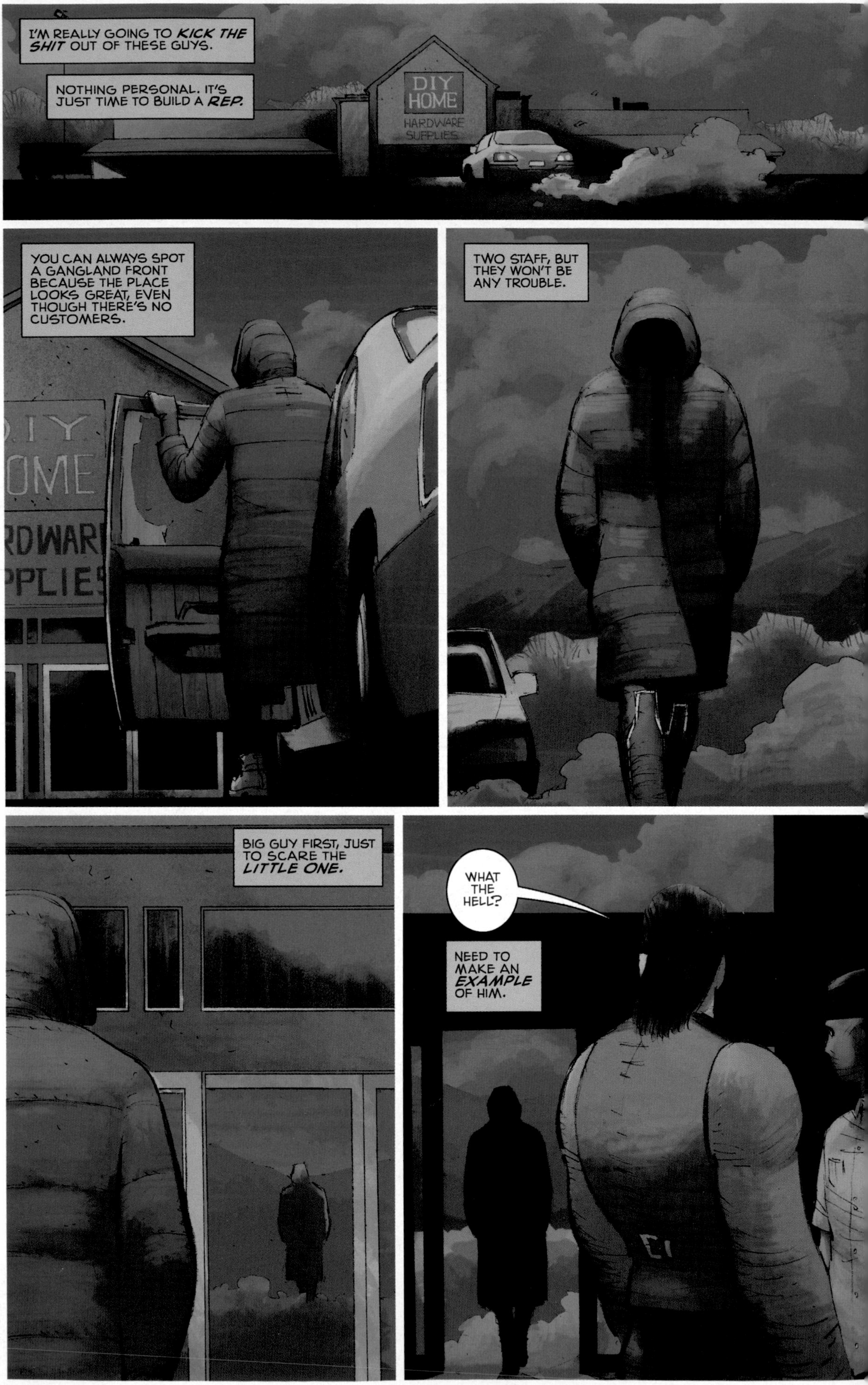
I'M REALLY GOING TO KICK THE SHIT OUT OF THESE GUYS.
NOTHING PERSONAL. IT'S JUST TIME TO BUILD A REP.
DIY HOME HARDWARE SUPPLIES
YOU CAN ALWAYS SPOT A GANGLAND FRONT BECAUSE THE PLACE LOOKS GREAT, EVEN THOUGH THERE'S NO CUSTOMERS.
TWO STAFF, BUT THEY WON'T BE ANY TROUBLE.
BIG GUY FIRST, JUST TO SCARE THE LITTLE ONE.
WHAT THE HELL?
NEED TO MAKE AN EXAMPLE OF HIM.

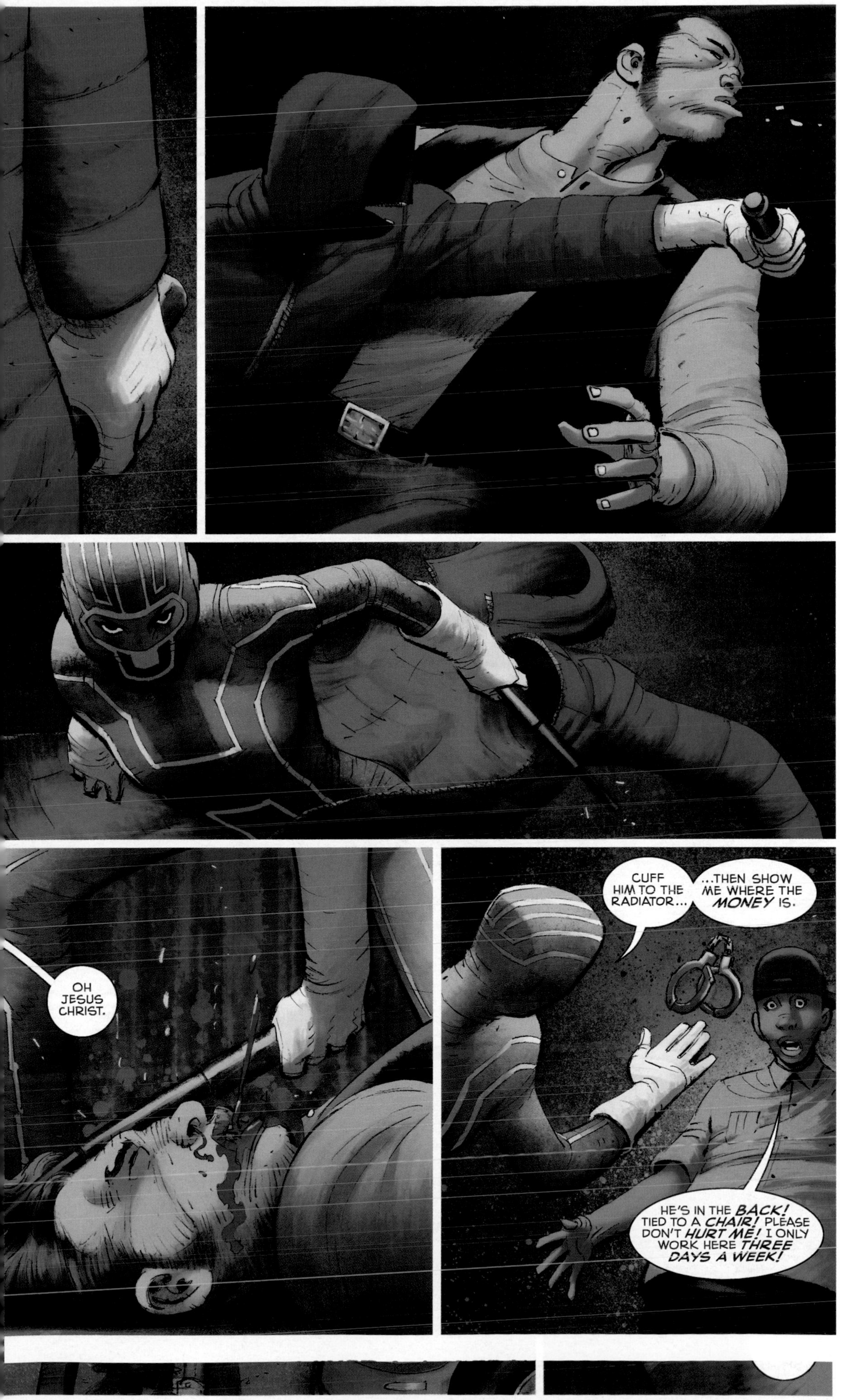
OH JESUS CHRIST.
CUFF HIM TO THE RADIATOR...
...THEN SHOW ME WHERE THE MONEY IS.
HE'S IN THE BACK! TIED TO A CHAIR! PLEASE DON'T HURT ME! I ONLY WORK HERE THREE DAYS A WEEK!

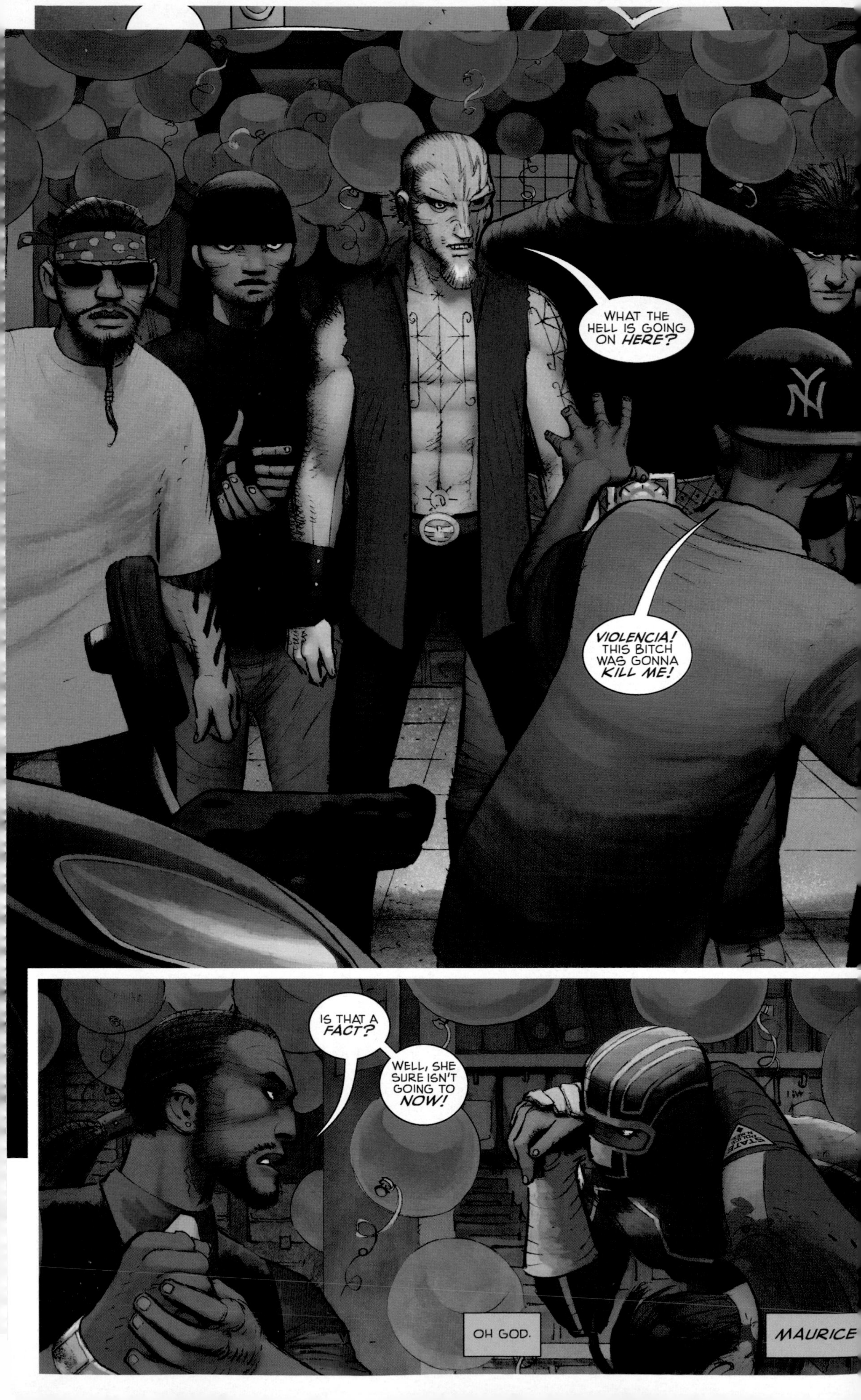

WHAT THE HELL IS GOING ON *HERE?*
VIOLENCIA! THIS BITCH WAS GONNA *KILL ME!*
IS THAT A *FACT?*
WELL, SHE SURE ISN'T GOING TO *NOW!*
OH GOD.
MAURICE

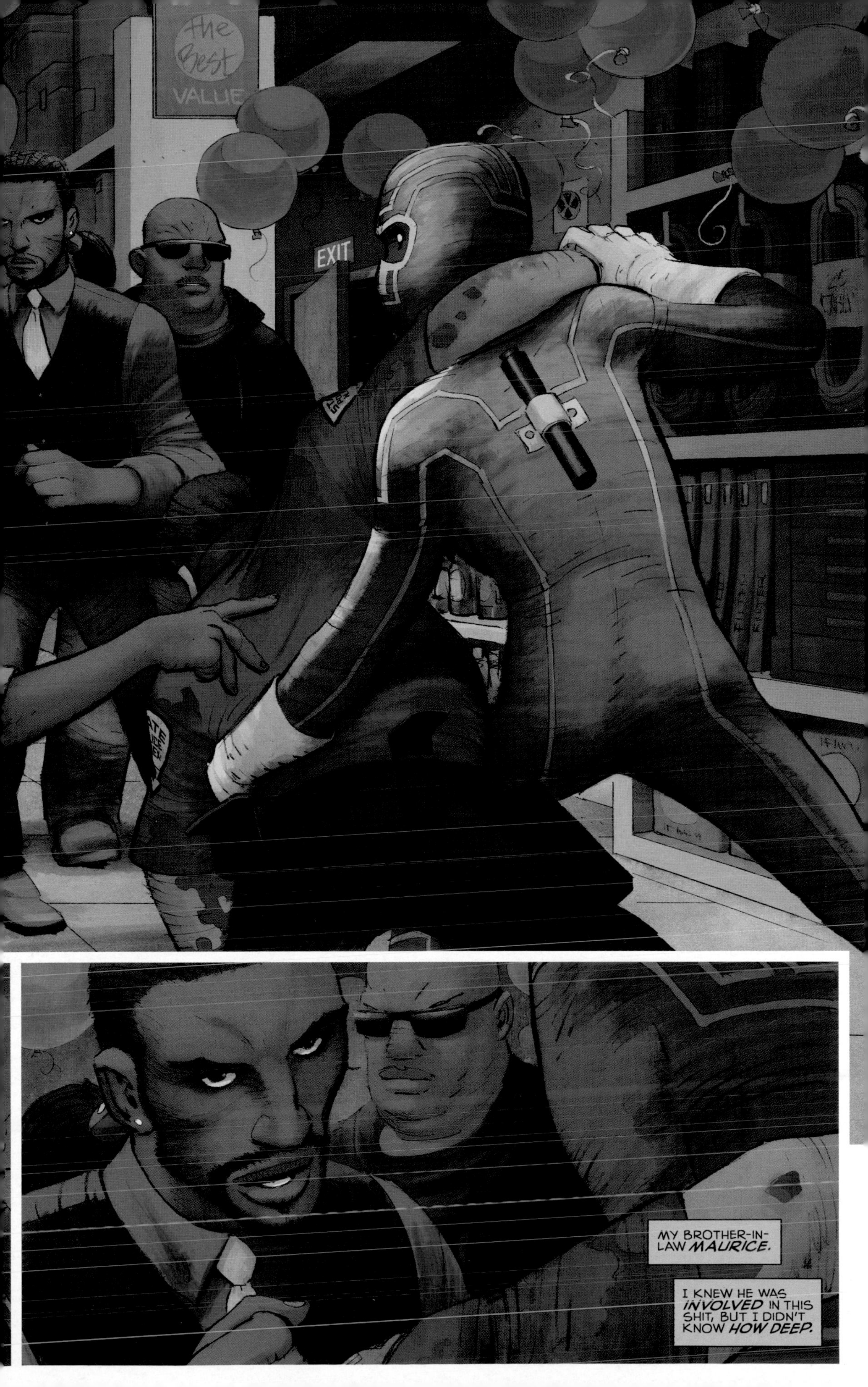
the Best VALUE
EXIT
MY BROTHER-IN-LAW *MAURICE.*
I KNEW HE WAS *INVOLVED* IN THIS SHIT, BUT I DIDN'T KNOW *HOW DEEP.*

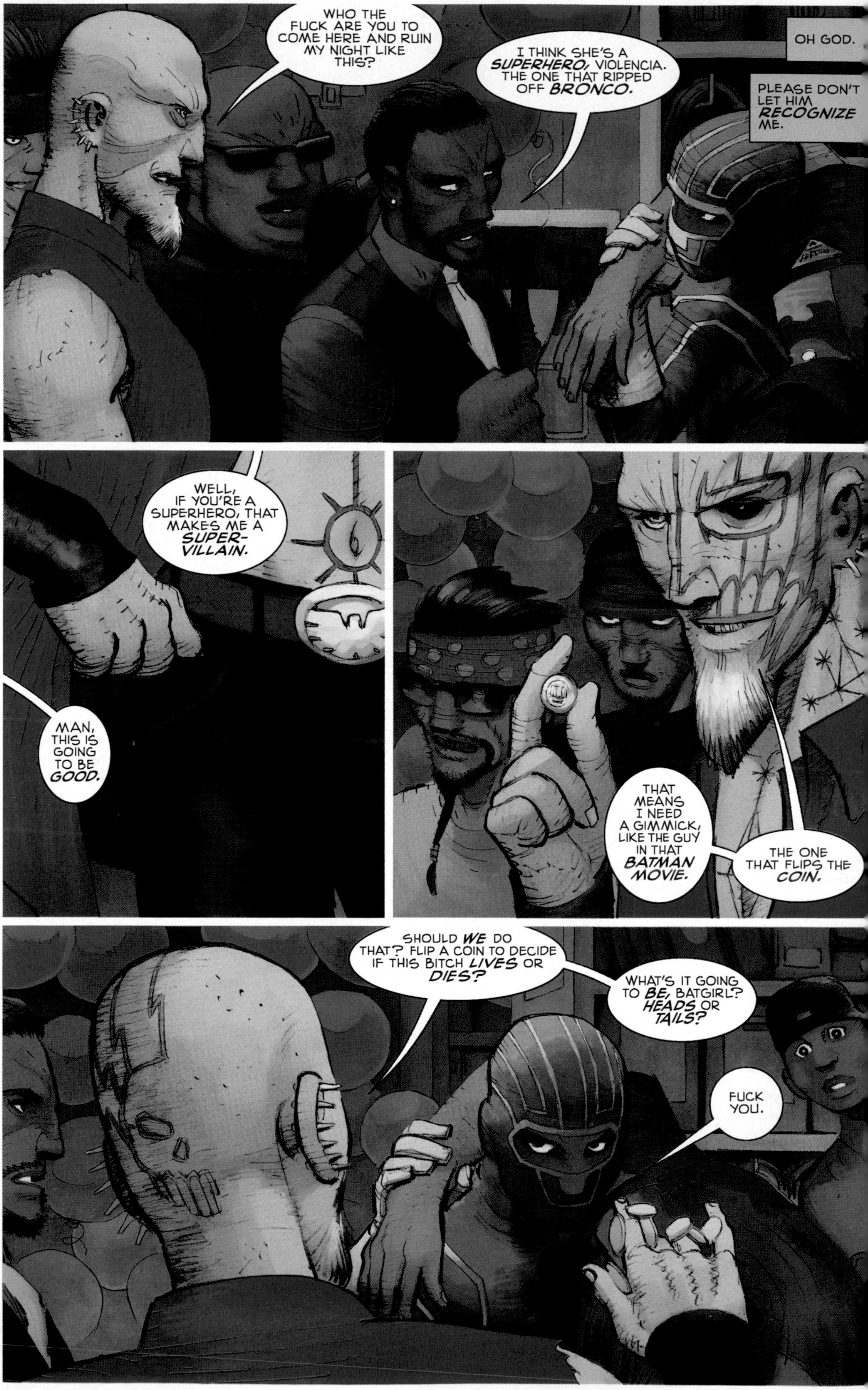
WHO THE FUCK ARE YOU TO COME HERE AND RUIN MY NIGHT LIKE THIS?
I THINK SHE'S A SUPERHERO, VIOLENCIA. THE ONE THAT RIPPED OFF BRONCO.
OH GOD.
PLEASE DON'T LET HIM RECOGNIZE ME.
WELL, IF YOU'RE A SUPERHERO, THAT MAKES ME A SUPER-VILLAIN.
MAN, THIS IS GOING TO BE GOOD.
THAT MEANS I NEED A GIMMICK, LIKE THE GUY IN THAT BATMAN MOVIE.
THE ONE THAT FLIPS THE COIN.
SHOULD WE DO THAT? FLIP A COIN TO DECIDE IF THIS BITCH LIVES OR DIES?
WHAT'S IT GOING TO BE, BATGIRL? HEADS OR TAILS?
FUCK YOU.

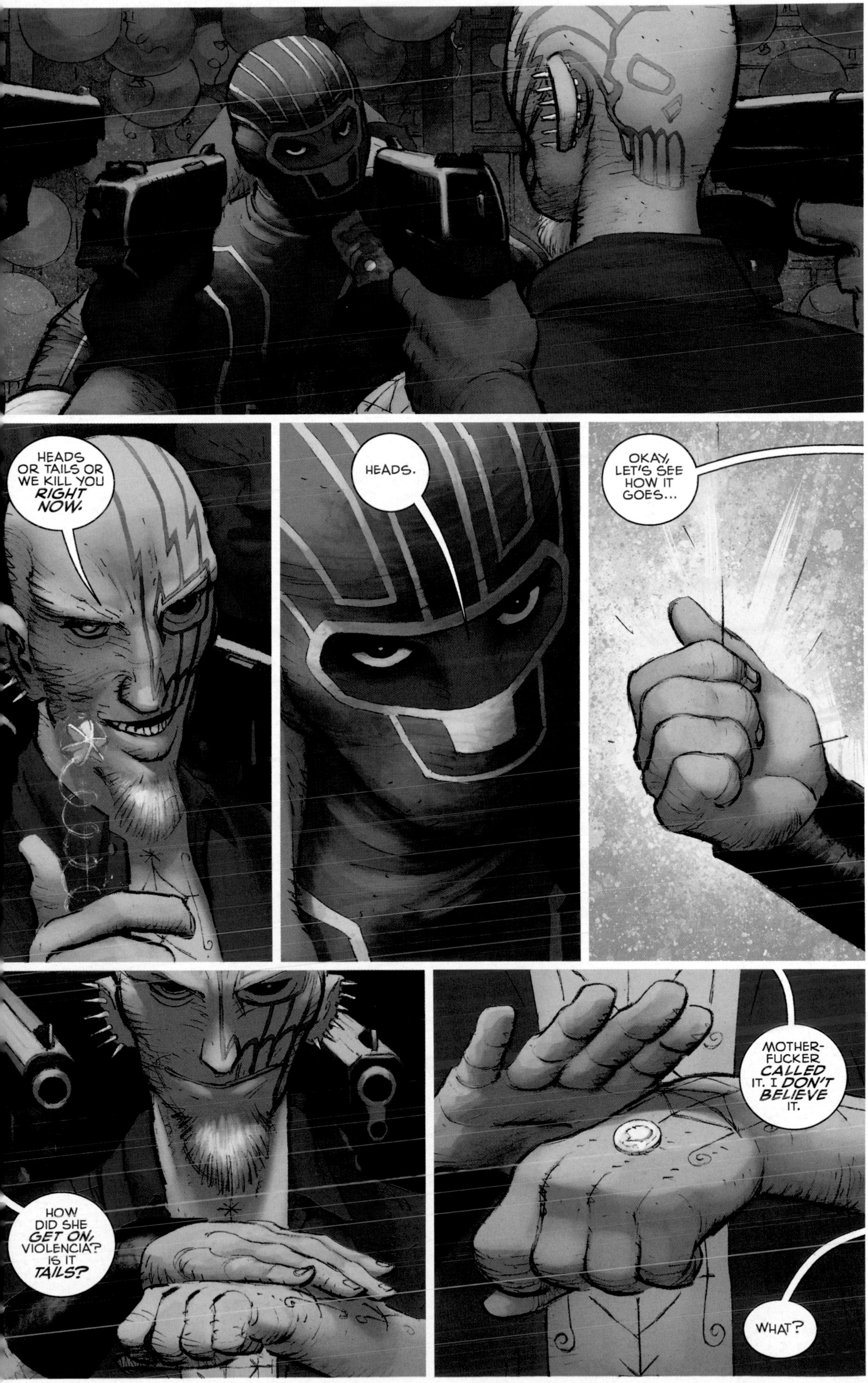
HEADS OR TAILS OR WE KILL YOU *RIGHT NOW.*
HEADS.
OKAY, LET'S SEE HOW IT GOES...
HOW DID SHE *GET ON,* VIOLENCIA? IS IT *TAILS?*
MOTHER-FUCKER *CALLED* IT. I *DON'T BELIEVE* IT.
WHAT?

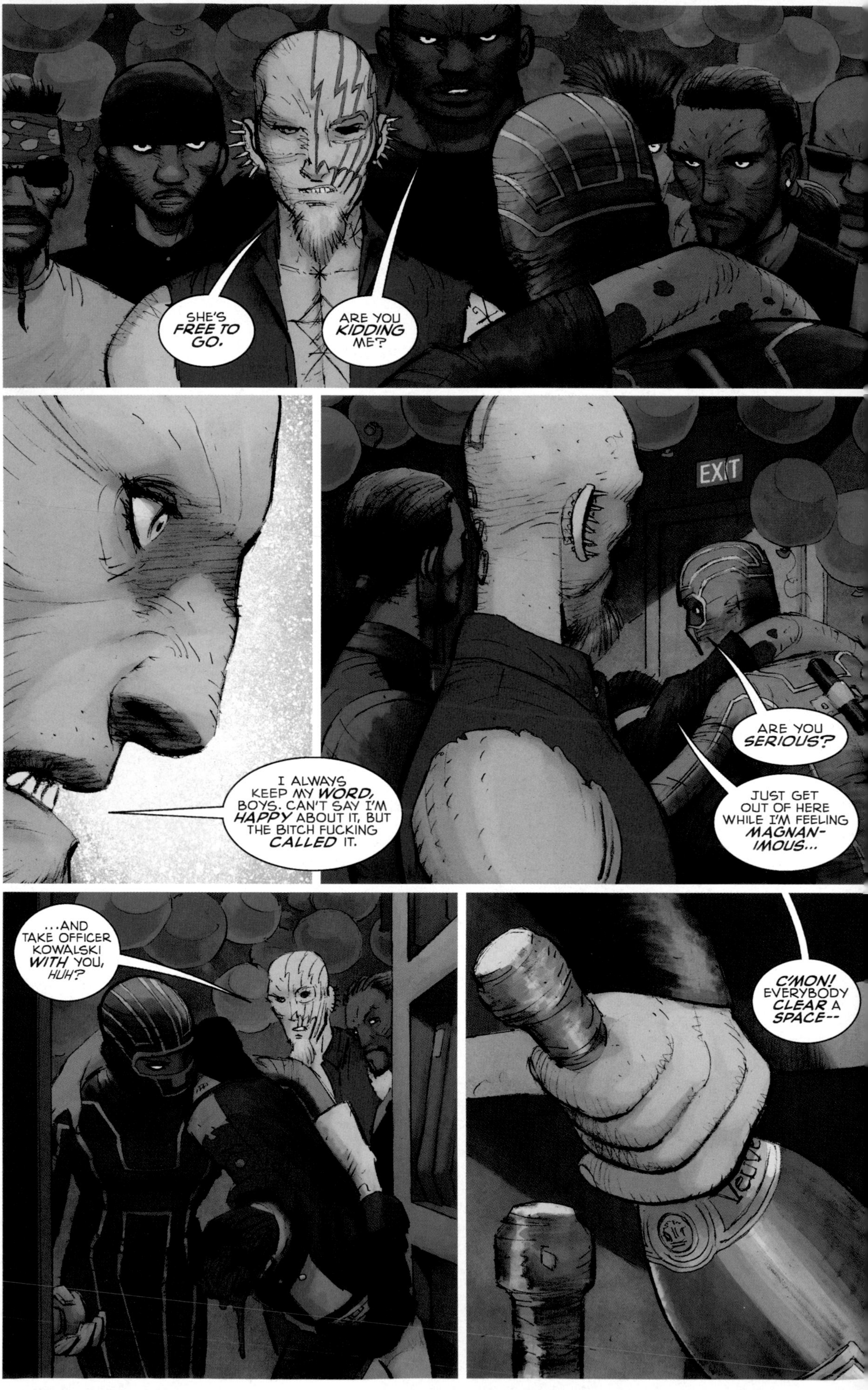
SHE'S FREE TO GO.
ARE YOU KIDDING ME?
I ALWAYS KEEP MY WORD, BOYS. CAN'T SAY I'M HAPPY ABOUT IT, BUT THE BITCH FUCKING CALLED IT.
EXIT
ARE YOU SERIOUS?
JUST GET OUT OF HERE WHILE I'M FEELING MAGNAN-IMOUS...
...AND TAKE OFFICER KOWALSKI WITH YOU, HUH?
C'MON! EVERYBODY CLEAR A SPACE--

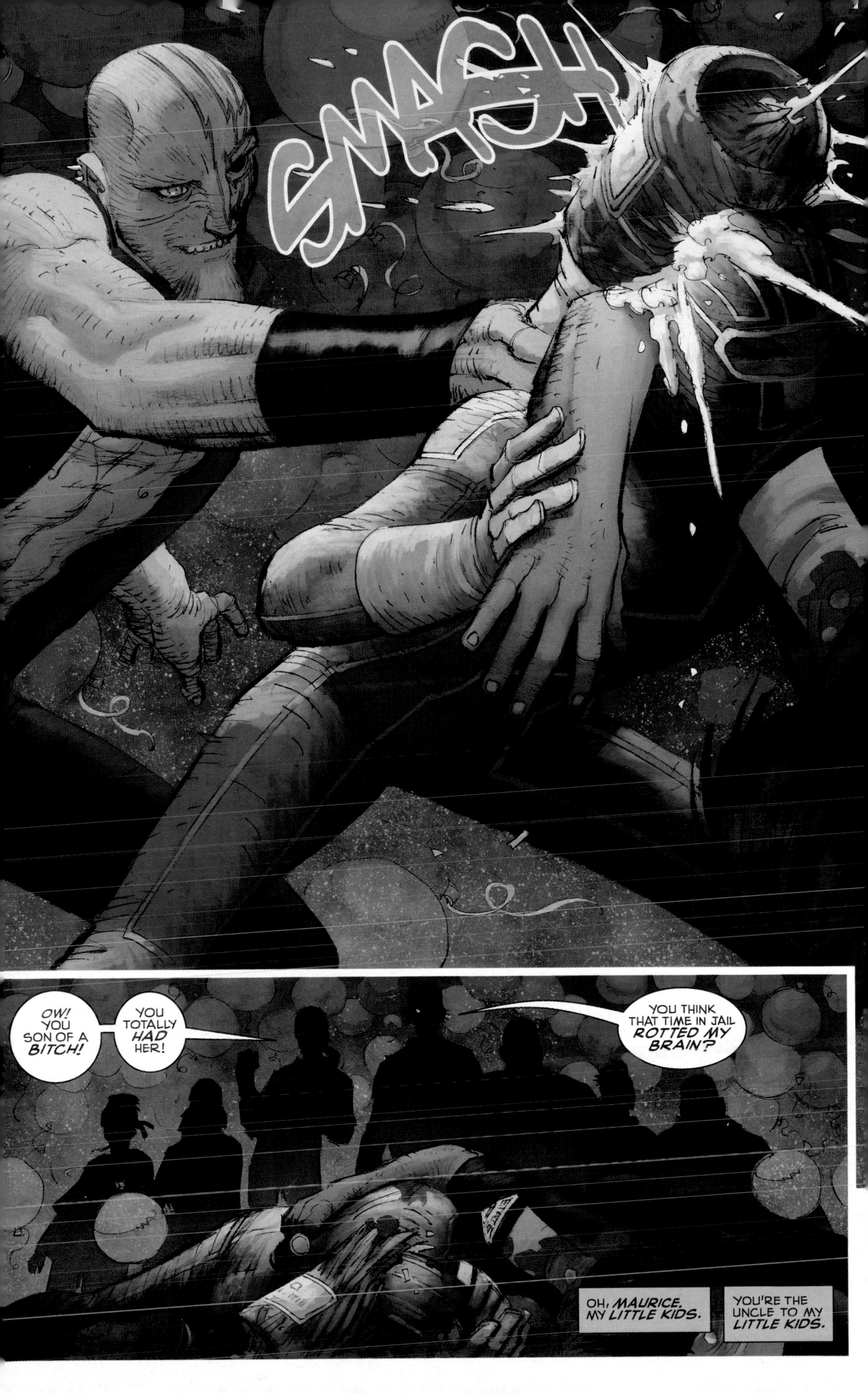
SMASH
OW! YOU SON OF A BITCH!
YOU TOTALLY HAD HER!
YOU THINK THAT TIME IN JAIL ROTTED MY BRAIN?
OH, MAURICE. MY LITTLE KIDS.
YOU'RE THE UNCLE TO MY LITTLE KIDS.

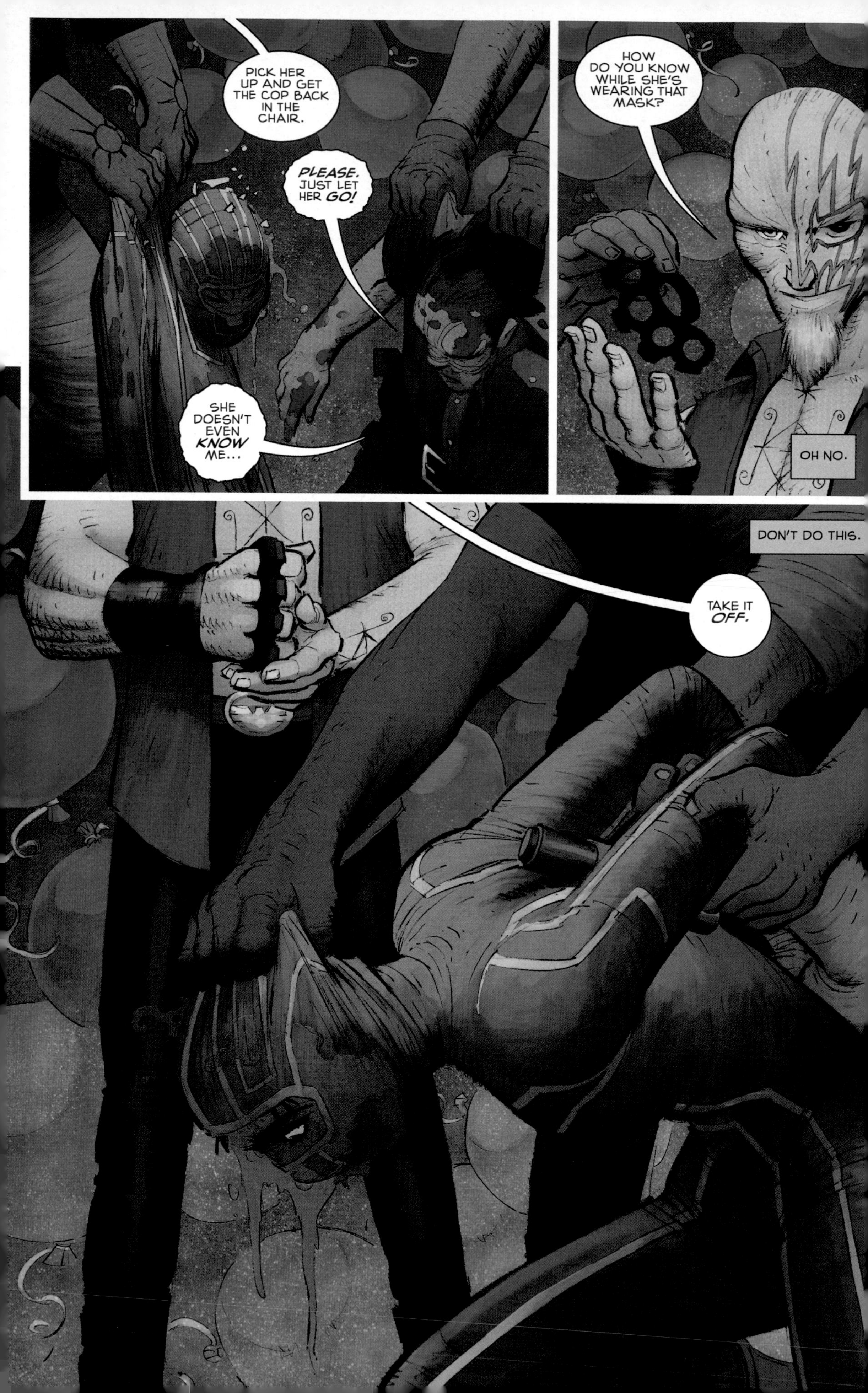
PICK HER UP AND GET THE COP BACK IN THE CHAIR.
PLEASE. JUST LET HER GO!
SHE DOESN'T EVEN KNOW ME...
HOW DO YOU KNOW WHILE SHE'S WEARING THAT MASK?
OH NO.
DON'T DO THIS.
TAKE IT OFF.

FOUR

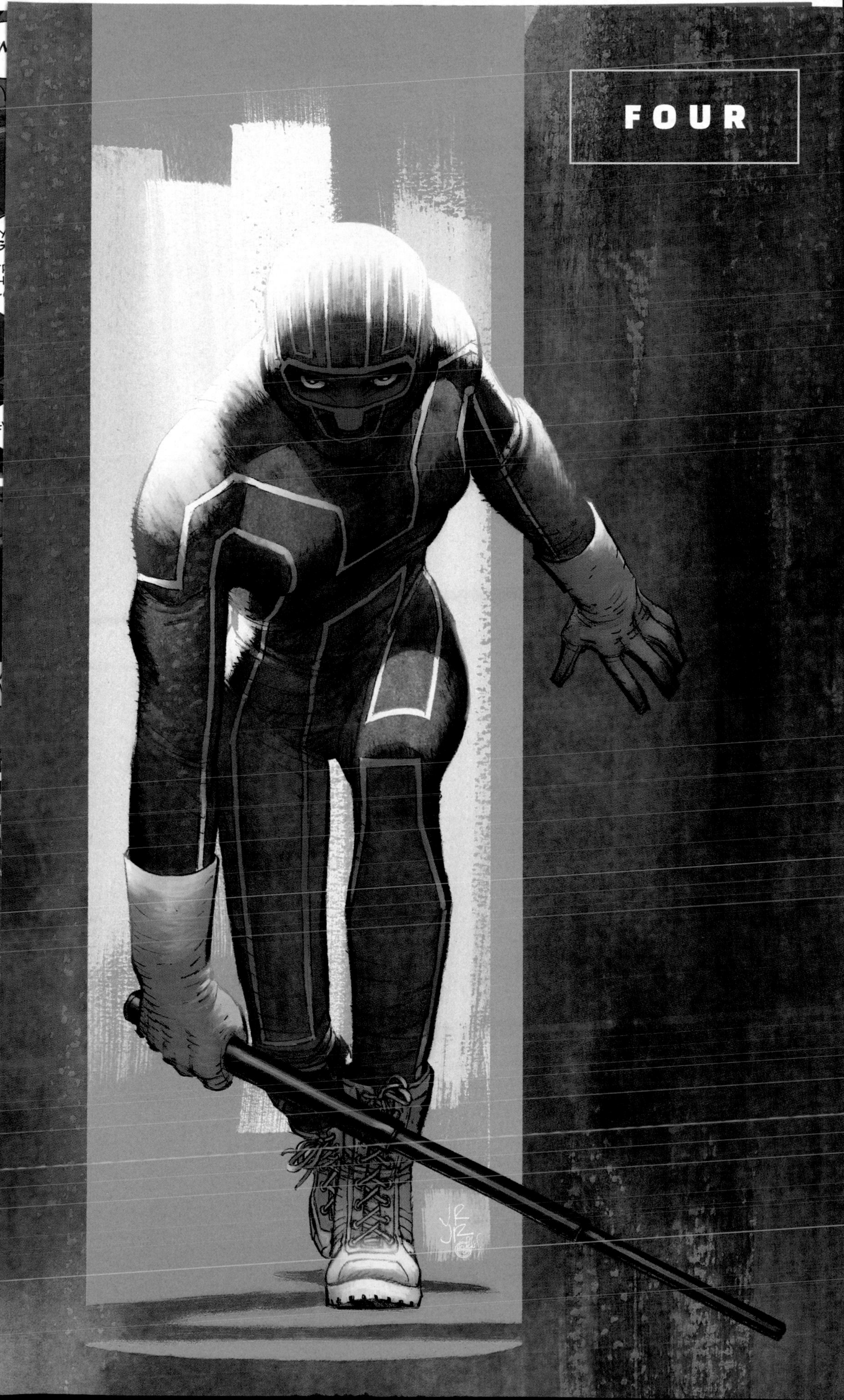

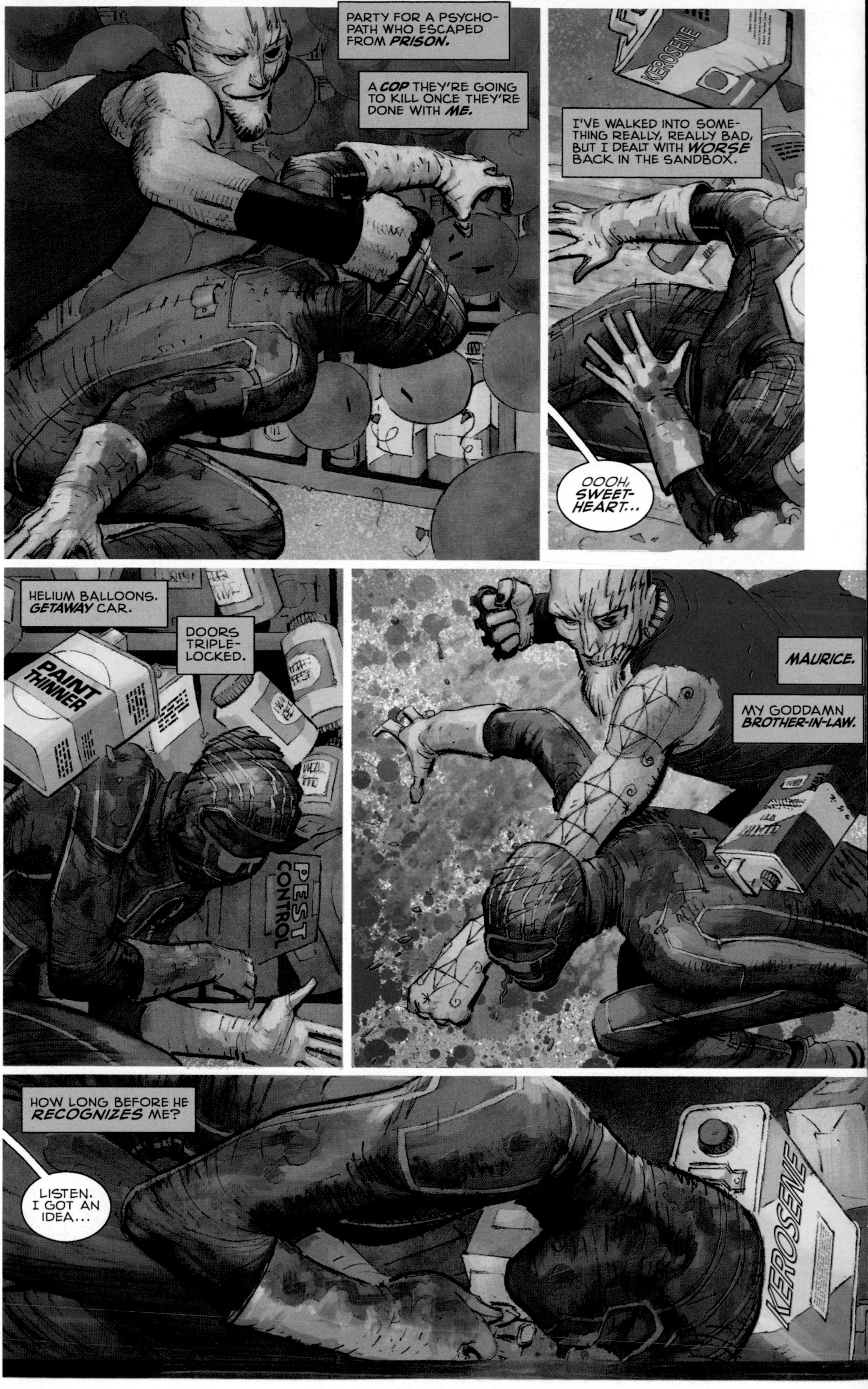
PARTY FOR A PSYCHOPATH WHO ESCAPED FROM PRISON.
A COP THEY'RE GOING TO KILL ONCE THEY'RE DONE WITH ME.
KEROSENE
I'VE WALKED INTO SOMETHING REALLY, REALLY BAD, BUT I DEALT WITH WORSE BACK IN THE SANDBOX.
OOOH, SWEETHEART...
HELIUM BALLOONS. GETAWAY CAR.
DOORS TRIPLE-LOCKED.
PAINT THINNER
PEST CONTROL
MAURICE.
MY GODDAMN BROTHER-IN-LAW.
HOW LONG BEFORE HE RECOGNIZES ME?
LISTEN. I GOT AN IDEA...
KEROSENE

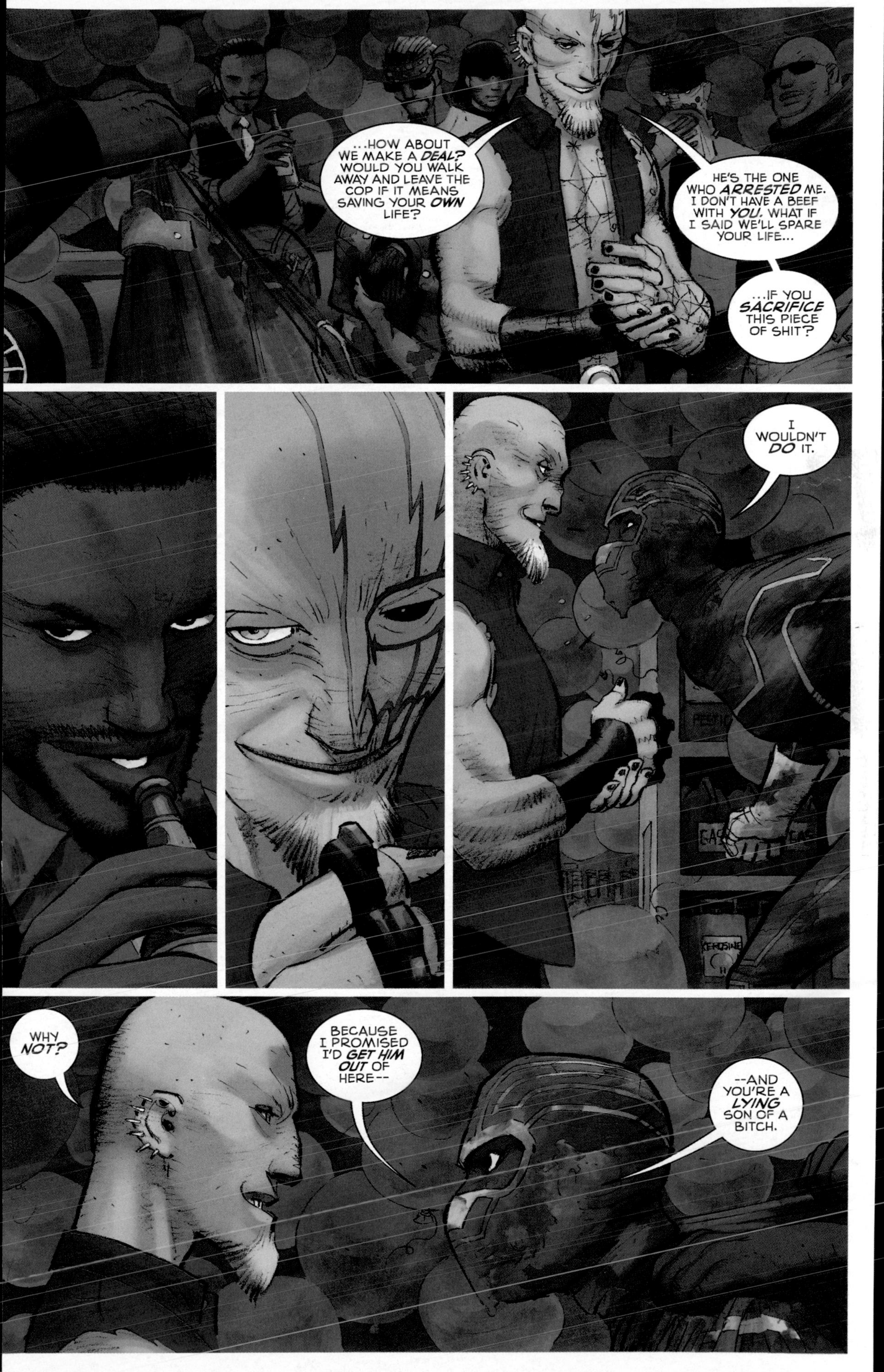
...HOW ABOUT WE MAKE A DEAL? WOULD YOU WALK AWAY AND LEAVE THE COP IF IT MEANS SAVING YOUR OWN LIFE?
HE'S THE ONE WHO ARRESTED ME. I DON'T HAVE A BEEF WITH YOU. WHAT IF I SAID WE'LL SPARE YOUR LIFE...
...IF YOU SACRIFICE THIS PIECE OF SHIT?
I WOULDN'T DO IT.
WHY NOT?
BECAUSE I PROMISED I'D GET HIM OUT OF HERE--
--AND YOU'RE A LYING SON OF A BITCH.

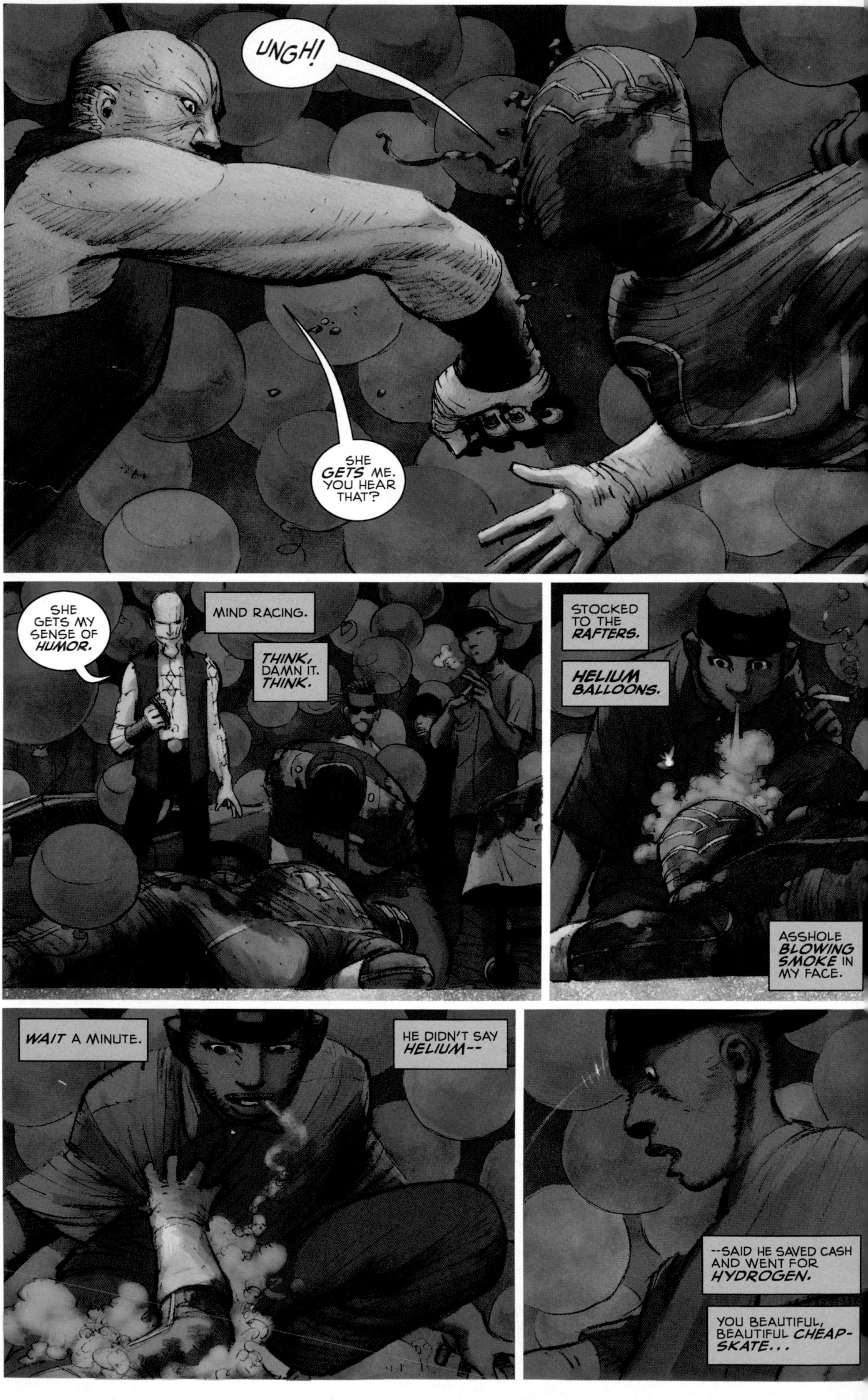
UNGH!
SHE *GETS* ME. YOU HEAR THAT?
SHE GETS MY SENSE OF *HUMOR.*
MIND RACING.
THINK, DAMN IT. *THINK.*
STOCKED TO THE *RAFTERS.*
HELIUM BALLOONS.
ASSHOLE *BLOWING SMOKE* IN MY FACE.
WAIT A MINUTE.
HE DIDN'T SAY *HELIUM*--
--SAID HE SAVED CASH AND WENT FOR *HYDROGEN.*
YOU BEAUTIFUL, BEAUTIFUL *CHEAP-SKATE...*

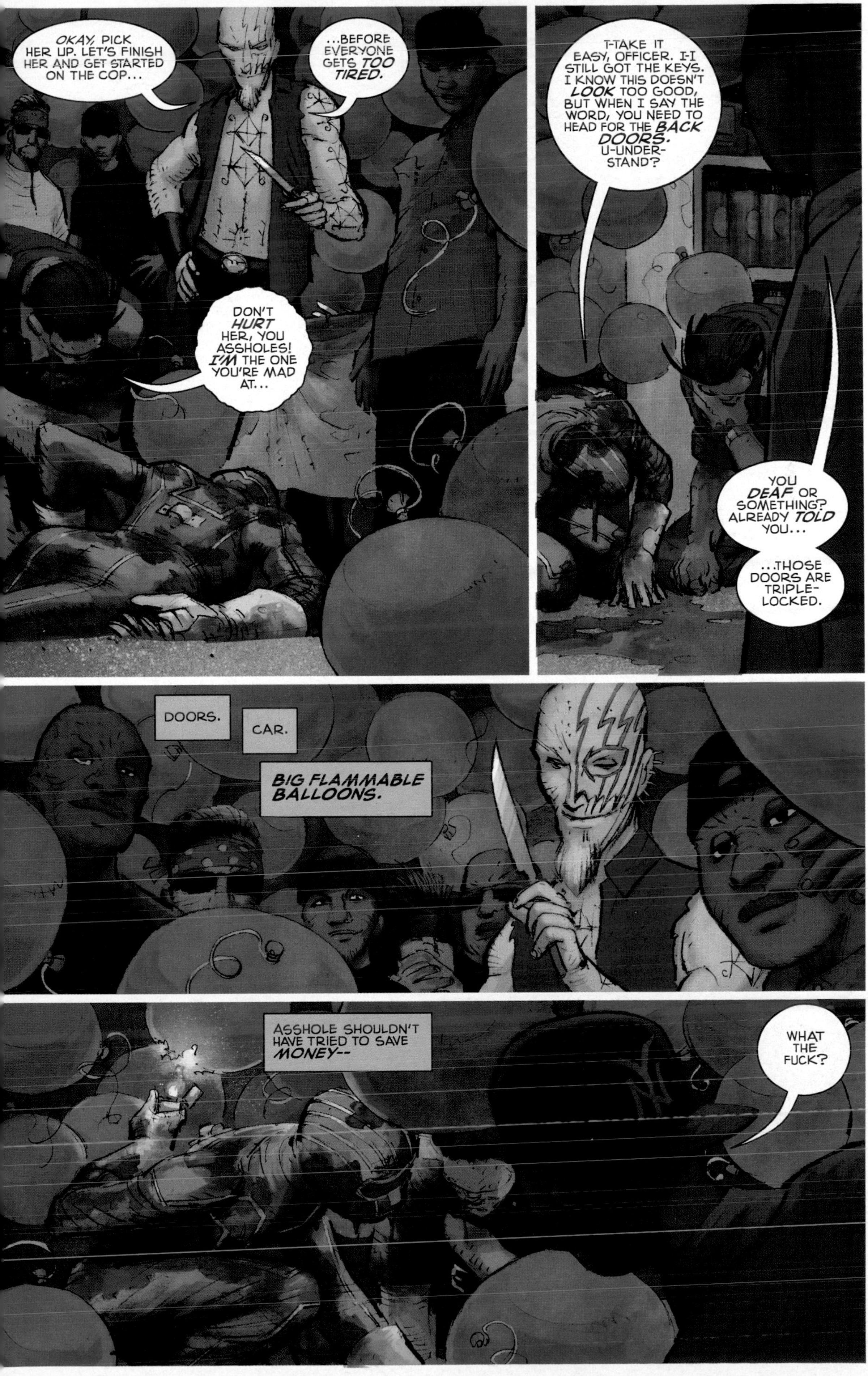
OKAY, PICK HER UP. LET'S FINISH HER AND GET STARTED ON THE COP...
...BEFORE EVERYONE GETS TOO TIRED.
DON'T HURT HER, YOU ASSHOLES! I'M THE ONE YOU'RE MAD AT...
T-TAKE IT EASY, OFFICER. I-I STILL GOT THE KEYS. I KNOW THIS DOESN'T LOOK TOO GOOD, BUT WHEN I SAY THE WORD, YOU NEED TO HEAD FOR THE BACK DOORS. U-UNDER-STAND?
YOU DEAF OR SOMETHING? ALREADY TOLD YOU...
...THOSE DOORS ARE TRIPLE-LOCKED.
DOORS.
CAR.
BIG FLAMMABLE BALLOONS.
ASSHOLE SHOULDN'T HAVE TRIED TO SAVE MONEY--
WHAT THE FUCK?

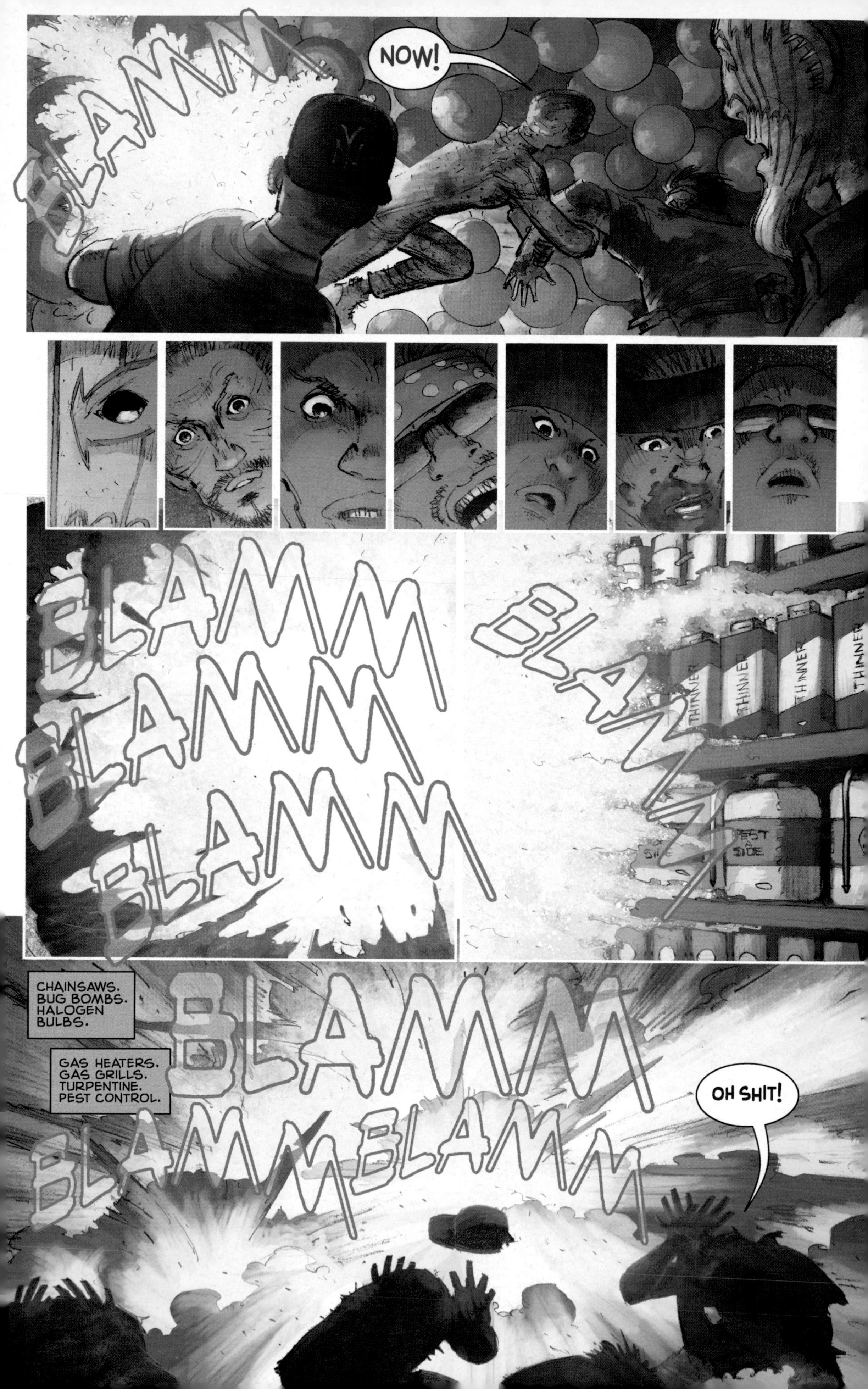
BLAMM
NOW!
BLAMM
BLAMM
BLAMM
BLAMM
THINNER
THINNER
THINNER
THINNER
CHAINSAWS. BUG BOMBS. HALOGEN BULBS.
GAS HEATERS. GAS GRILLS. TURPENTINE. PEST CONTROL.
BLAMM
BLAMM
BLAMM
OH SHIT!

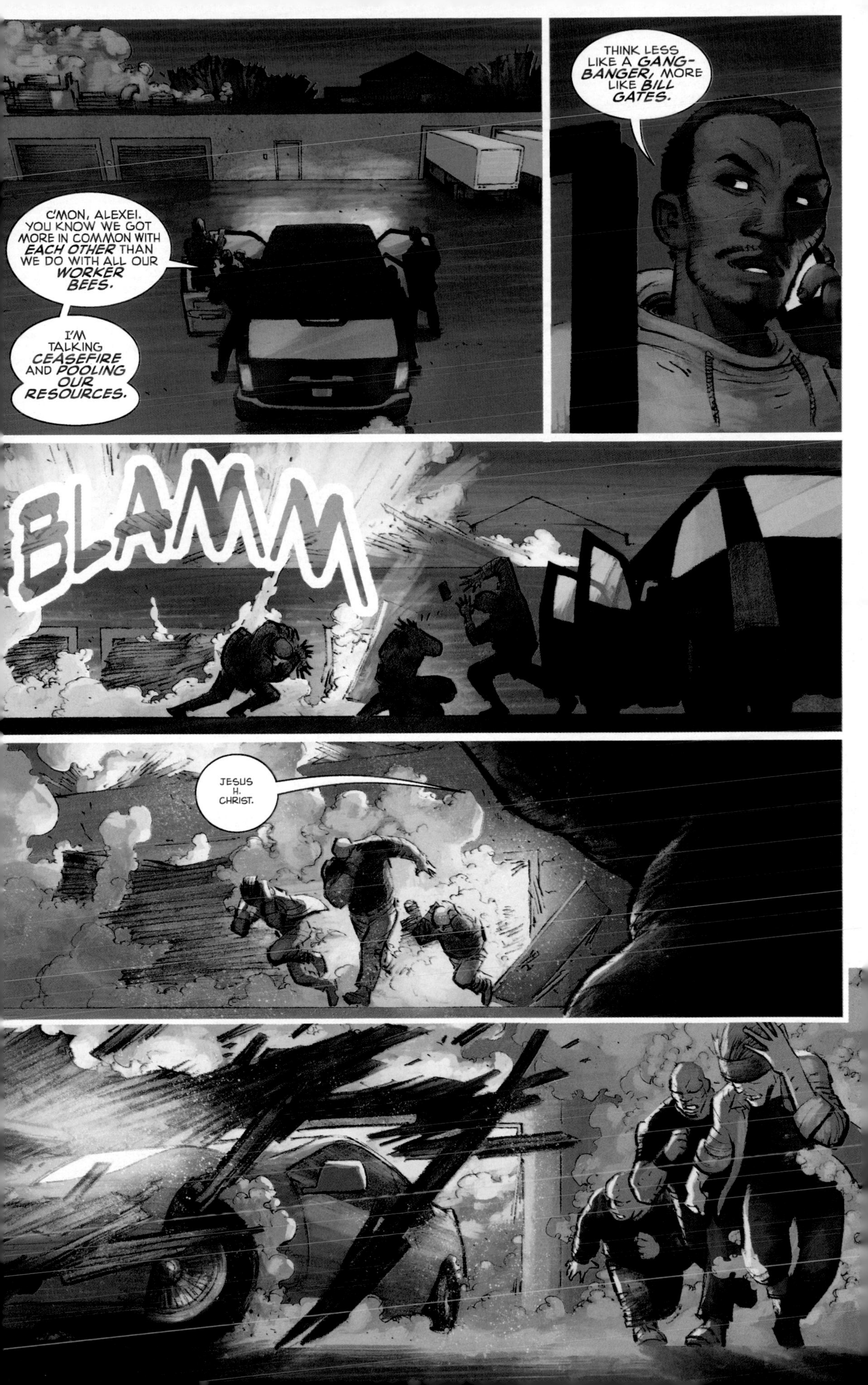
C'MON, ALEXEI. YOU KNOW WE GOT MORE IN COMMON WITH EACH OTHER THAN WE DO WITH ALL OUR WORKER BEES.
I'M TALKING CEASEFIRE AND POOLING OUR RESOURCES.
THINK LESS LIKE A GANG-BANGER, MORE LIKE BILL GATES.
BLAMM
JESUS H. CHRIST.

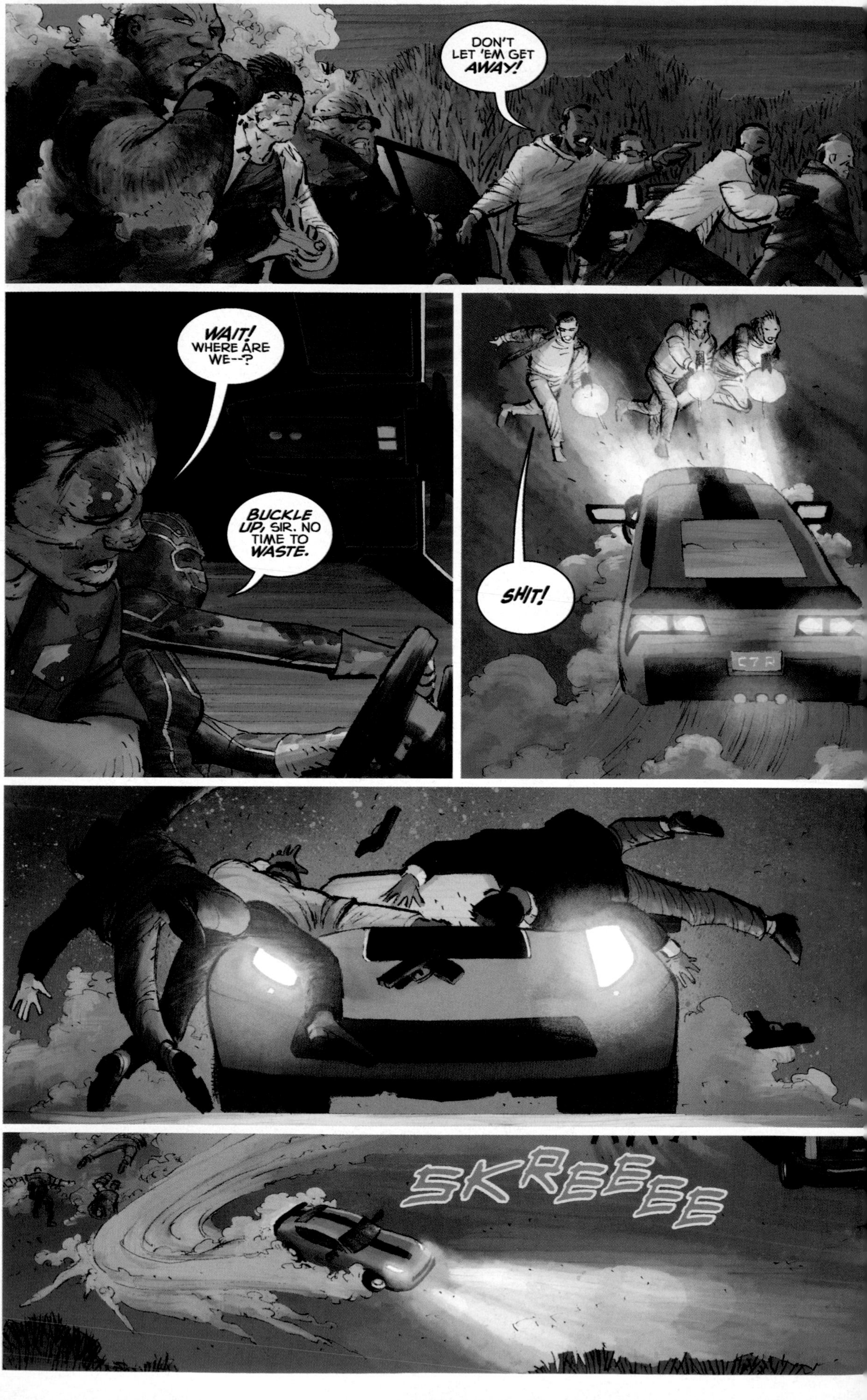
DON'T LET 'EM GET AWAY!
WAIT! WHERE ARE WE--?
BUCKLE UP, SIR. NO TIME TO WASTE.
SHIT!
SKREEEEE

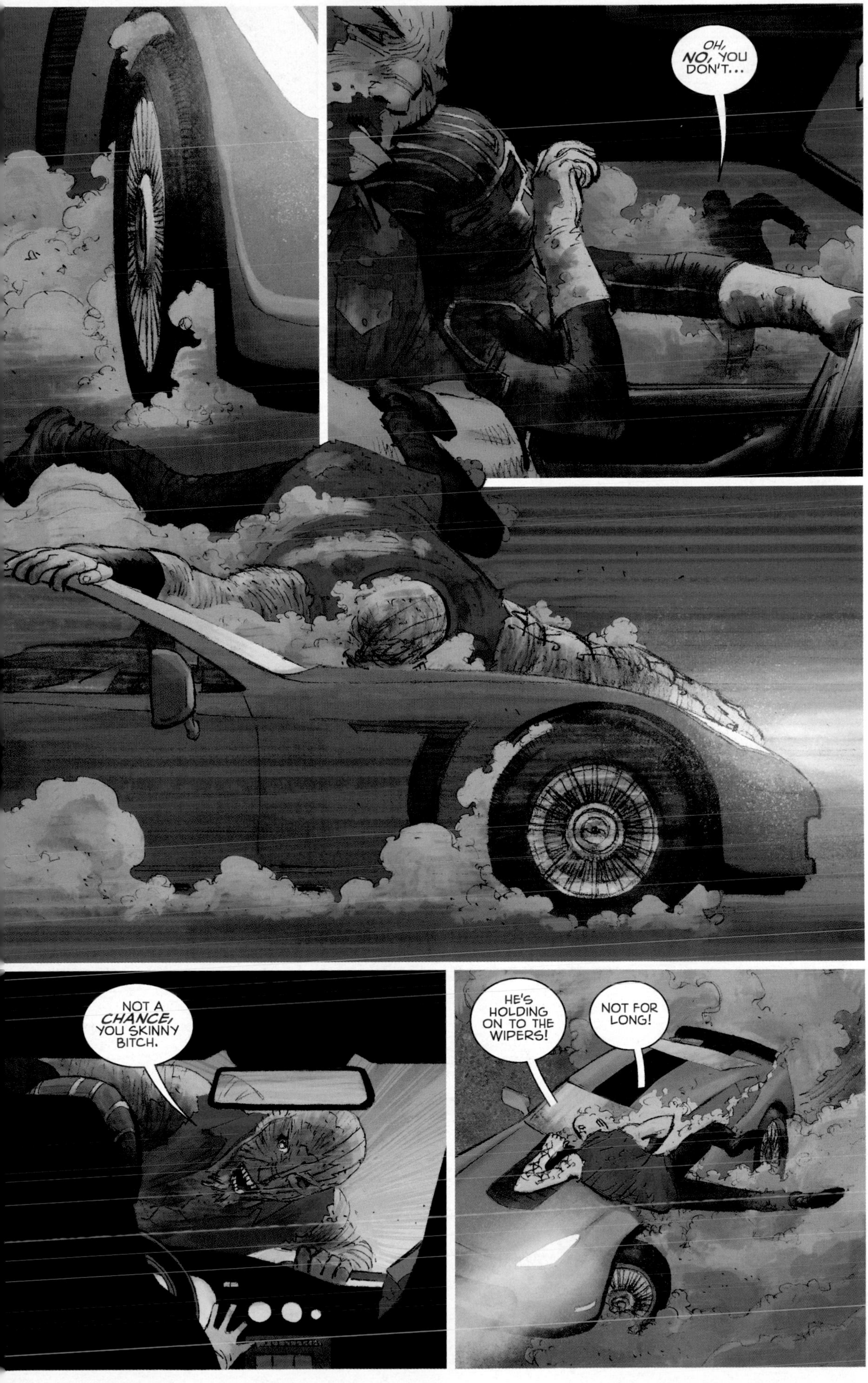
OH, NO, YOU DON'T...
NOT A CHANCE, YOU SKINNY BITCH.
HE'S HOLDING ON TO THE WIPERS!
NOT FOR LONG!

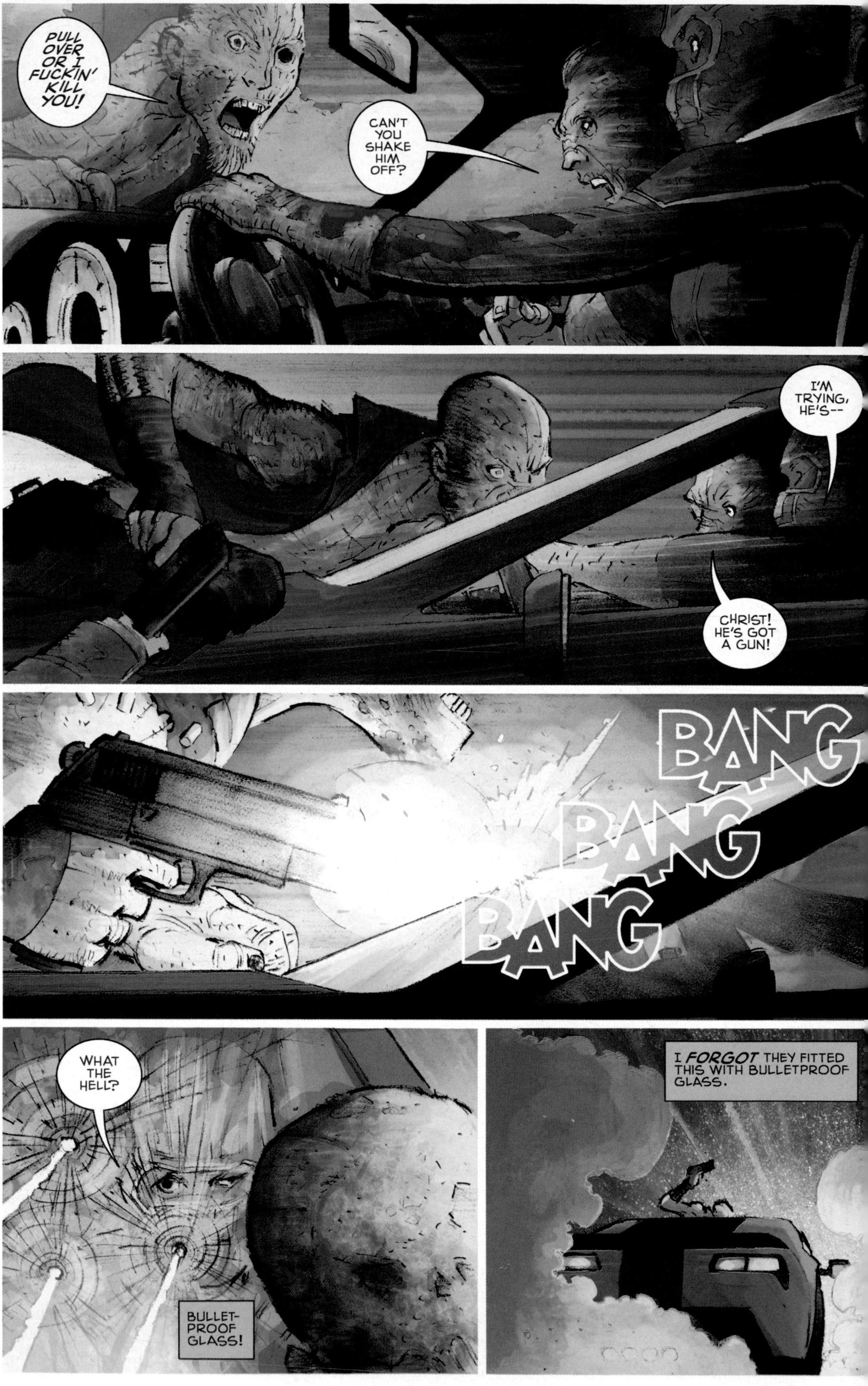
PULL OVER OR I FUCKIN' KILL YOU!
CAN'T YOU SHAKE HIM OFF?
I'M TRYING, HE'S--
CHRIST! HE'S GOT A GUN!
BANG
BANG
BANG
WHAT THE HELL?
BULLET-PROOF GLASS!
I *FORGOT* THEY FITTED THIS WITH BULLETPROOF GLASS.

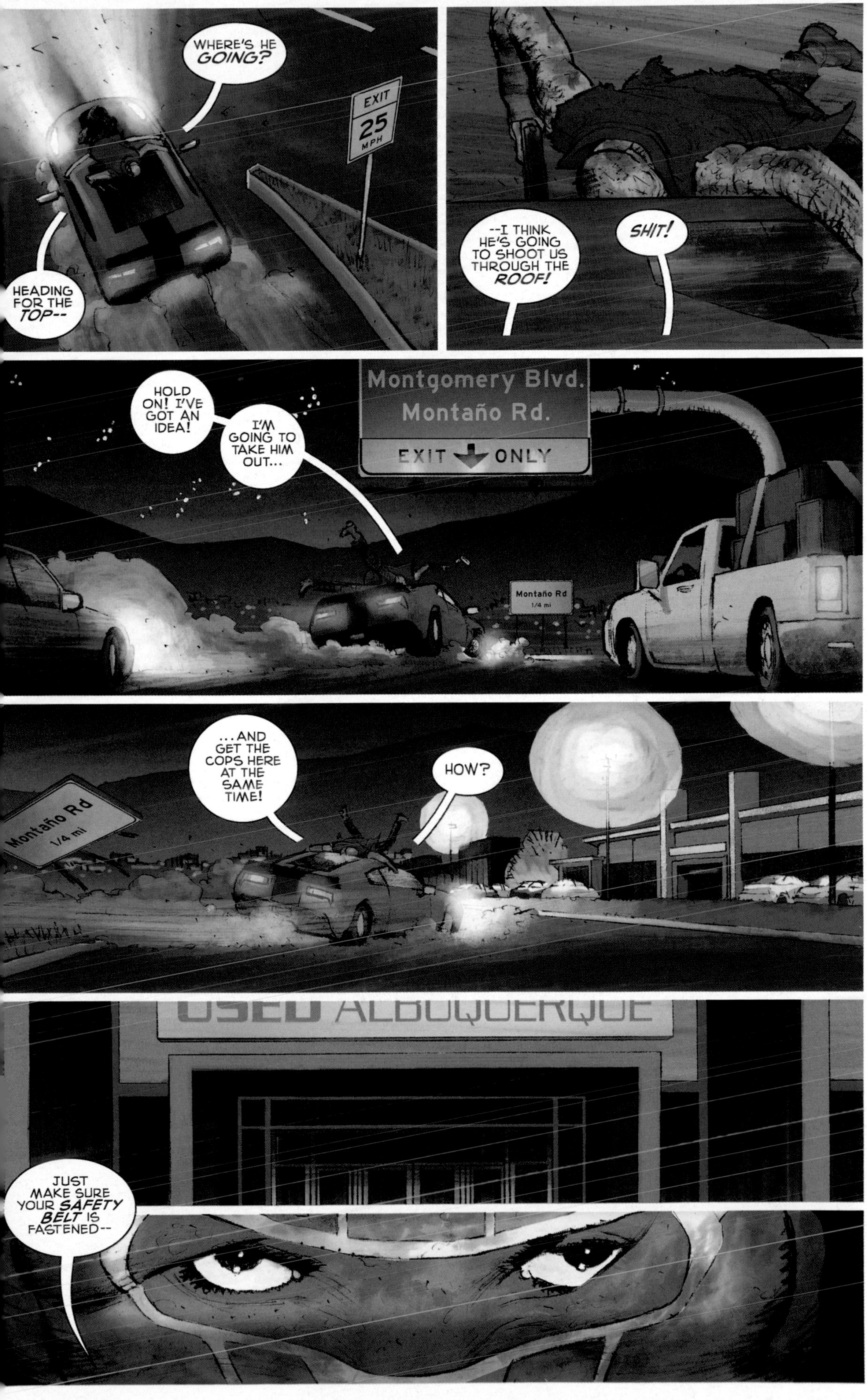
WHERE'S HE GOING?
EXIT 25 MPH
HEADING FOR THE TOP--
--I THINK HE'S GOING TO SHOOT US THROUGH THE ROOF!
SHIT!
Montgomery Blvd. Montaño Rd. EXIT ONLY
HOLD ON! I'VE GOT AN IDEA!
I'M GOING TO TAKE HIM OUT...
Montaño Rd 1/4 mi
...AND GET THE COPS HERE AT THE SAME TIME!
HOW?
Montaño Rd 1/4 mi
USED ALBUQUERQUE
JUST MAKE SURE YOUR SAFETY BELT IS FASTENED--

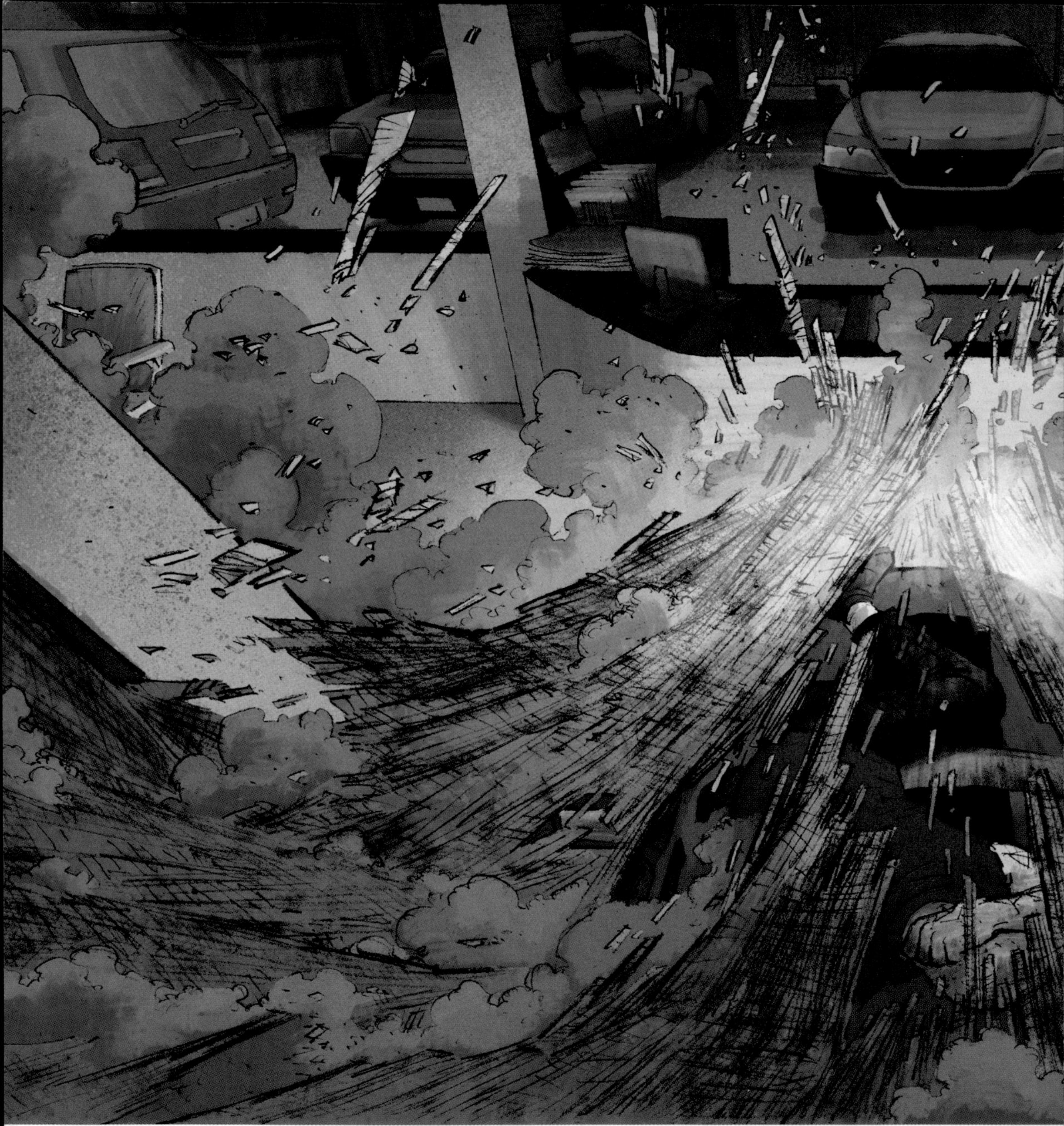

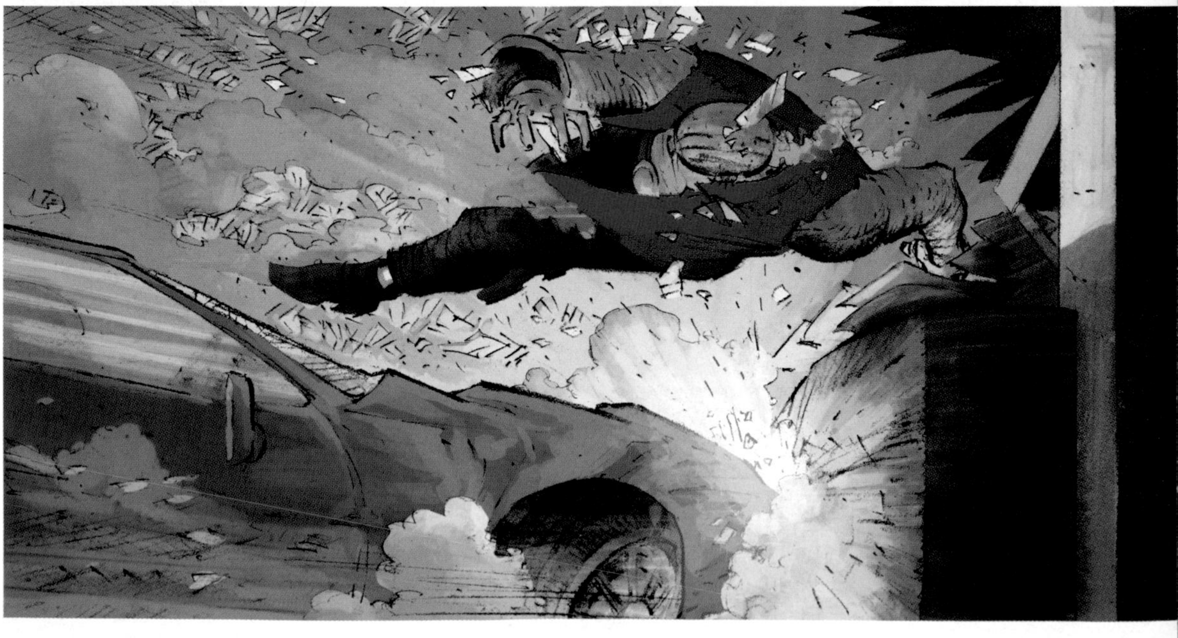

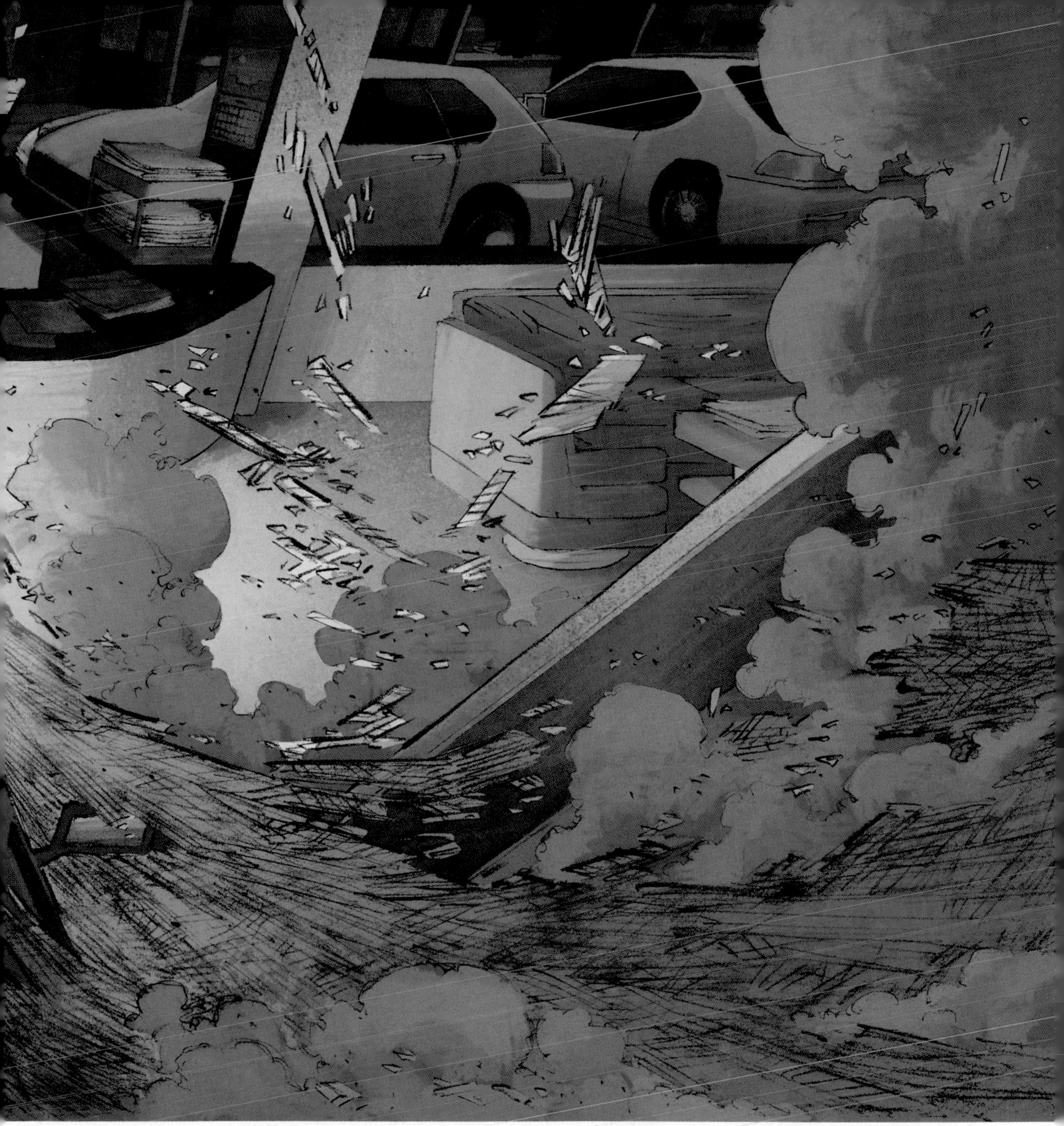
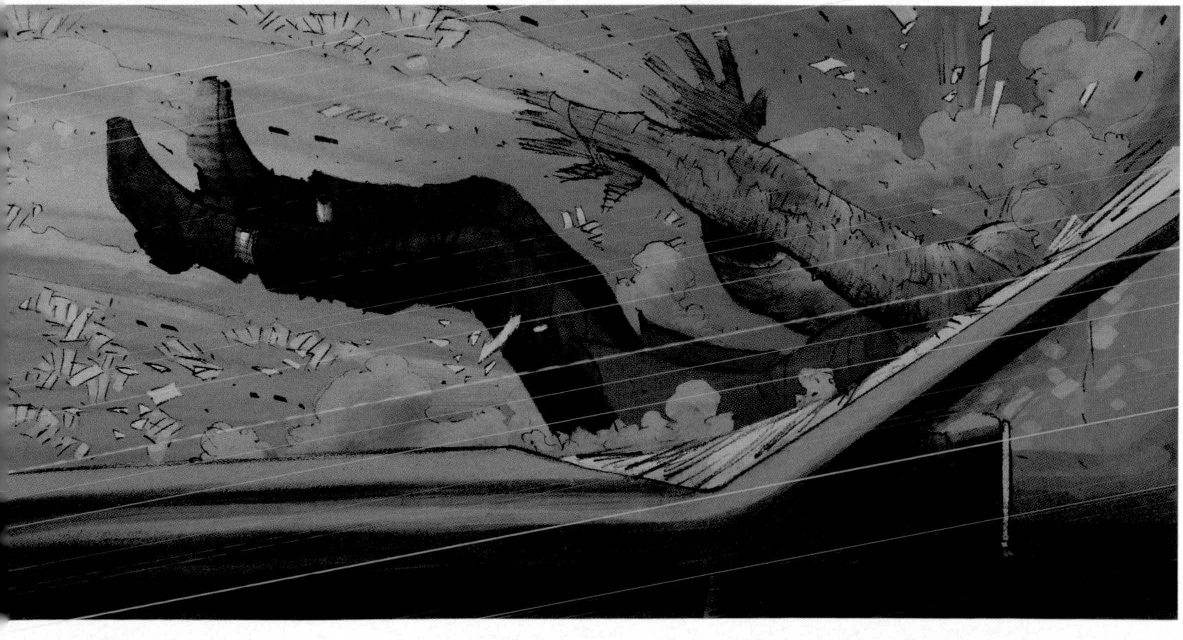

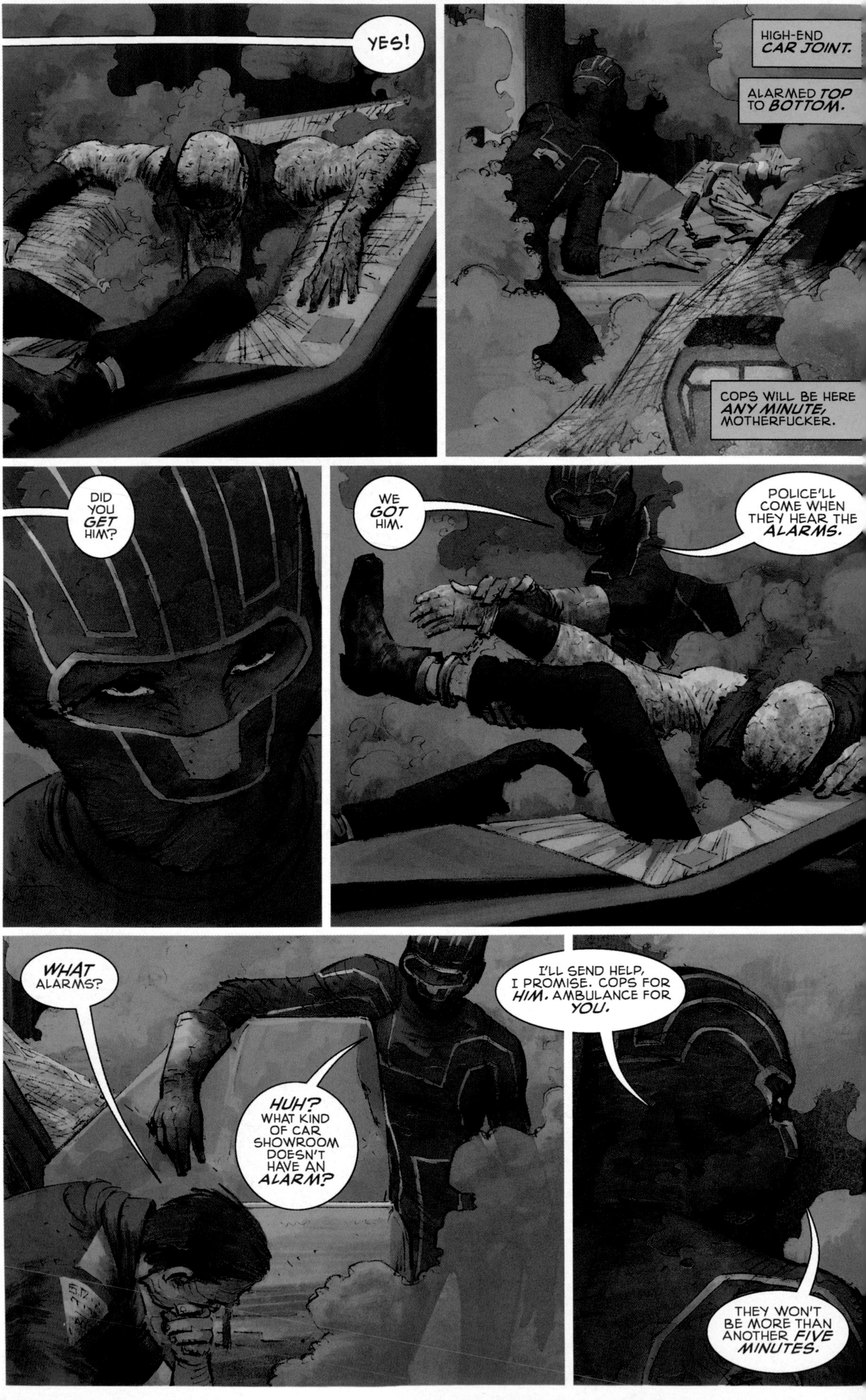
YES!
HIGH-END CAR JOINT.
ALARMED TOP TO BOTTOM.
COPS WILL BE HERE ANY MINUTE, MOTHERFUCKER.
DID YOU GET HIM?
WE GOT HIM.
POLICE'LL COME WHEN THEY HEAR THE ALARMS.
WHAT ALARMS?
HUH? WHAT KIND OF CAR SHOWROOM DOESN'T HAVE AN ALARM?
I'LL SEND HELP, I PROMISE. COPS FOR HIM. AMBULANCE FOR YOU.
THEY WON'T BE MORE THAN ANOTHER FIVE MINUTES.

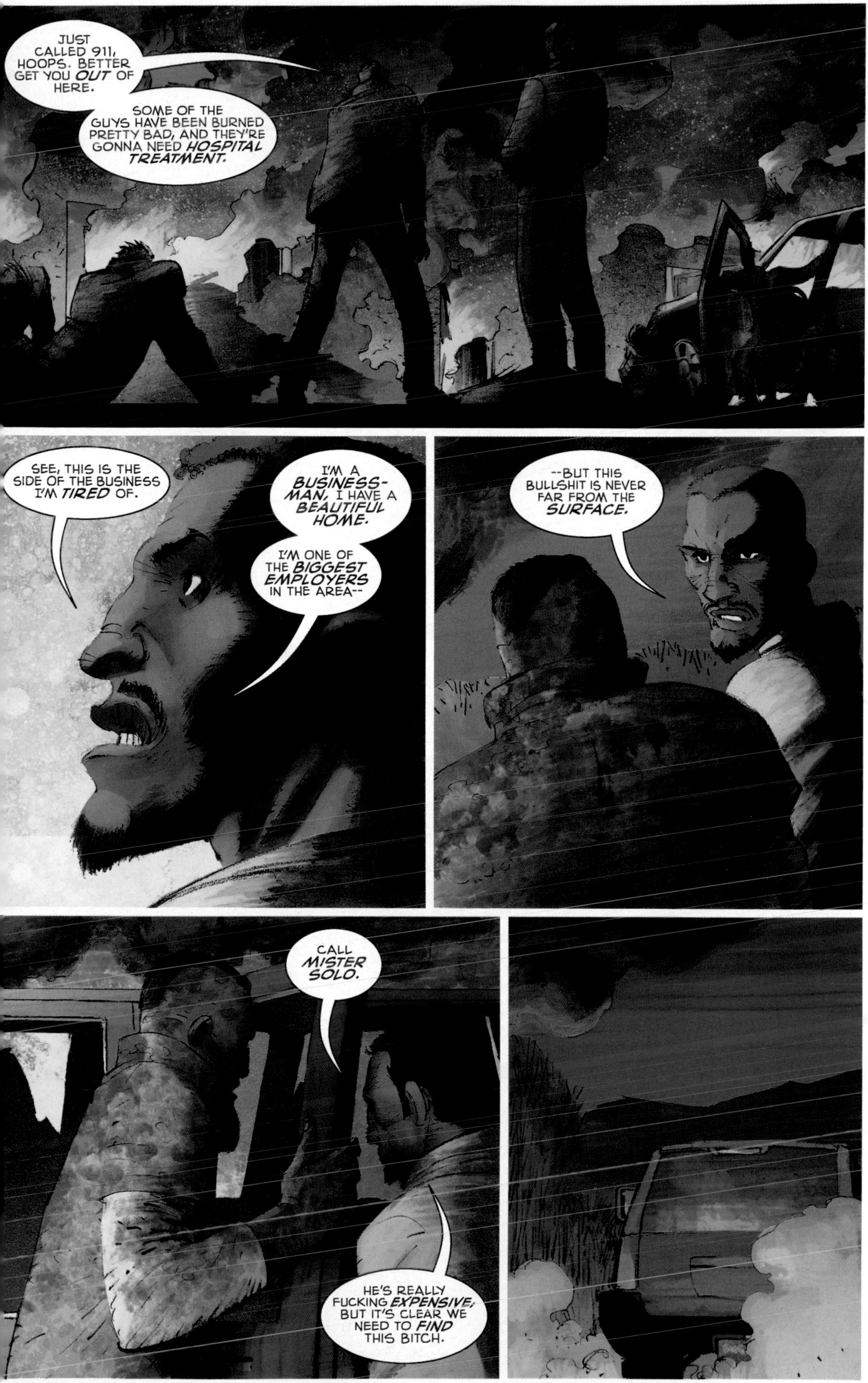
JUST CALLED 911, HOOPS. BETTER GET YOU OUT OF HERE.
SOME OF THE GUYS HAVE BEEN BURNED PRETTY BAD, AND THEY'RE GONNA NEED HOSPITAL TREATMENT.
SEE, THIS IS THE SIDE OF THE BUSINESS I'M TIRED OF.
I'M A BUSINESS-MAN, I HAVE A BEAUTIFUL HOME.
I'M ONE OF THE BIGGEST EMPLOYERS IN THE AREA--
--BUT THIS BULLSHIT IS NEVER FAR FROM THE SURFACE.
CALL MISTER SOLO.
HE'S REALLY FUCKING EXPENSIVE, BUT IT'S CLEAR WE NEED TO FIND THIS BITCH.

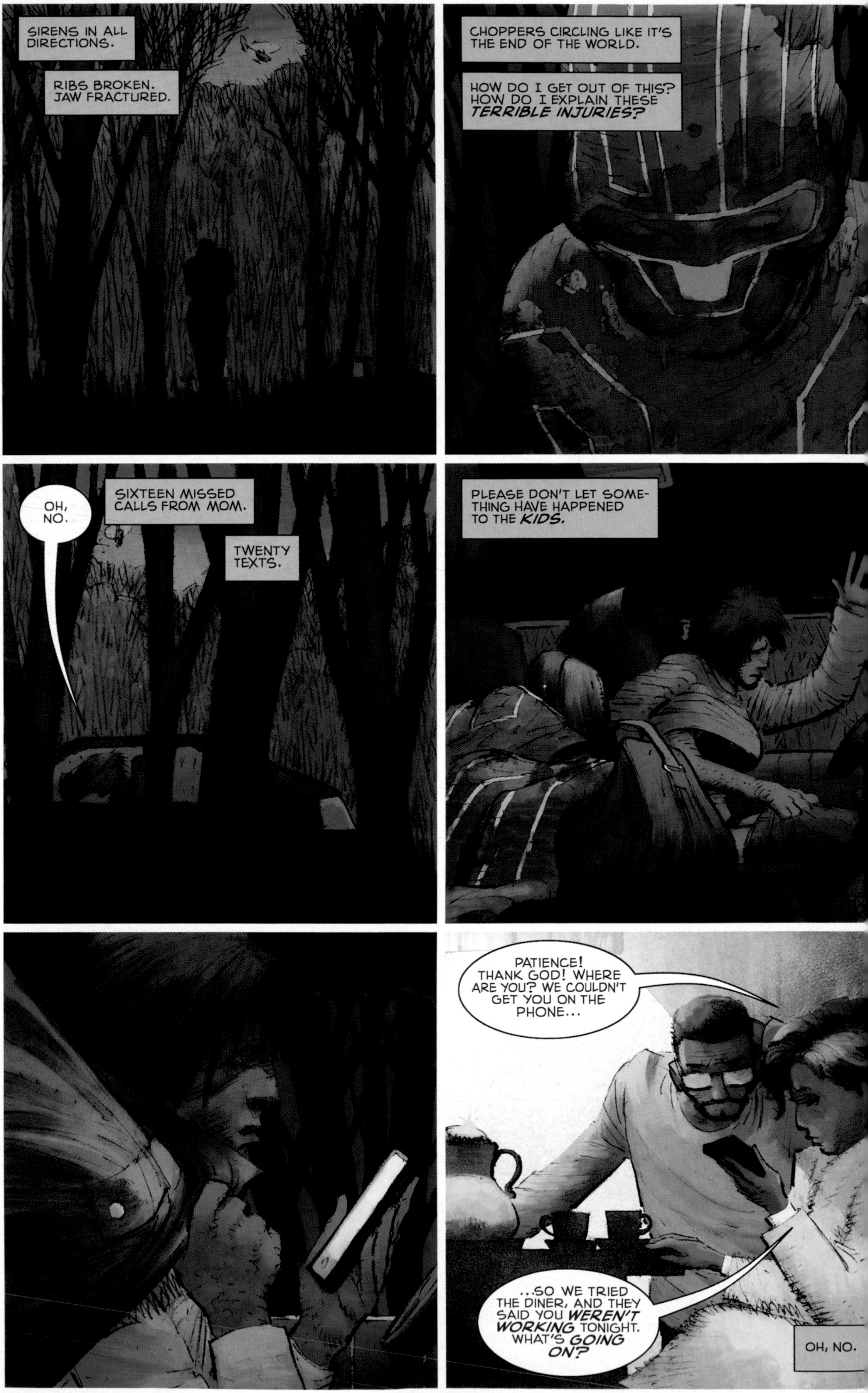
SIRENS IN ALL DIRECTIONS.
RIBS BROKEN. JAW FRACTURED.
CHOPPERS CIRCLING LIKE IT'S THE END OF THE WORLD.
HOW DO I GET OUT OF THIS? HOW DO I EXPLAIN THESE *TERRIBLE INJURIES?*
SIXTEEN MISSED CALLS FROM MOM.
OH, NO.
TWENTY TEXTS.
PLEASE DON'T LET SOME-THING HAVE HAPPENED TO THE *KIDS.*
PATIENCE! THANK GOD! WHERE ARE YOU? WE COULDN'T GET YOU ON THE PHONE...
...SO WE TRIED THE DINER, AND THEY SAID YOU *WEREN'T WORKING* TONIGHT. WHAT'S *GOING ON?*
OH, NO.

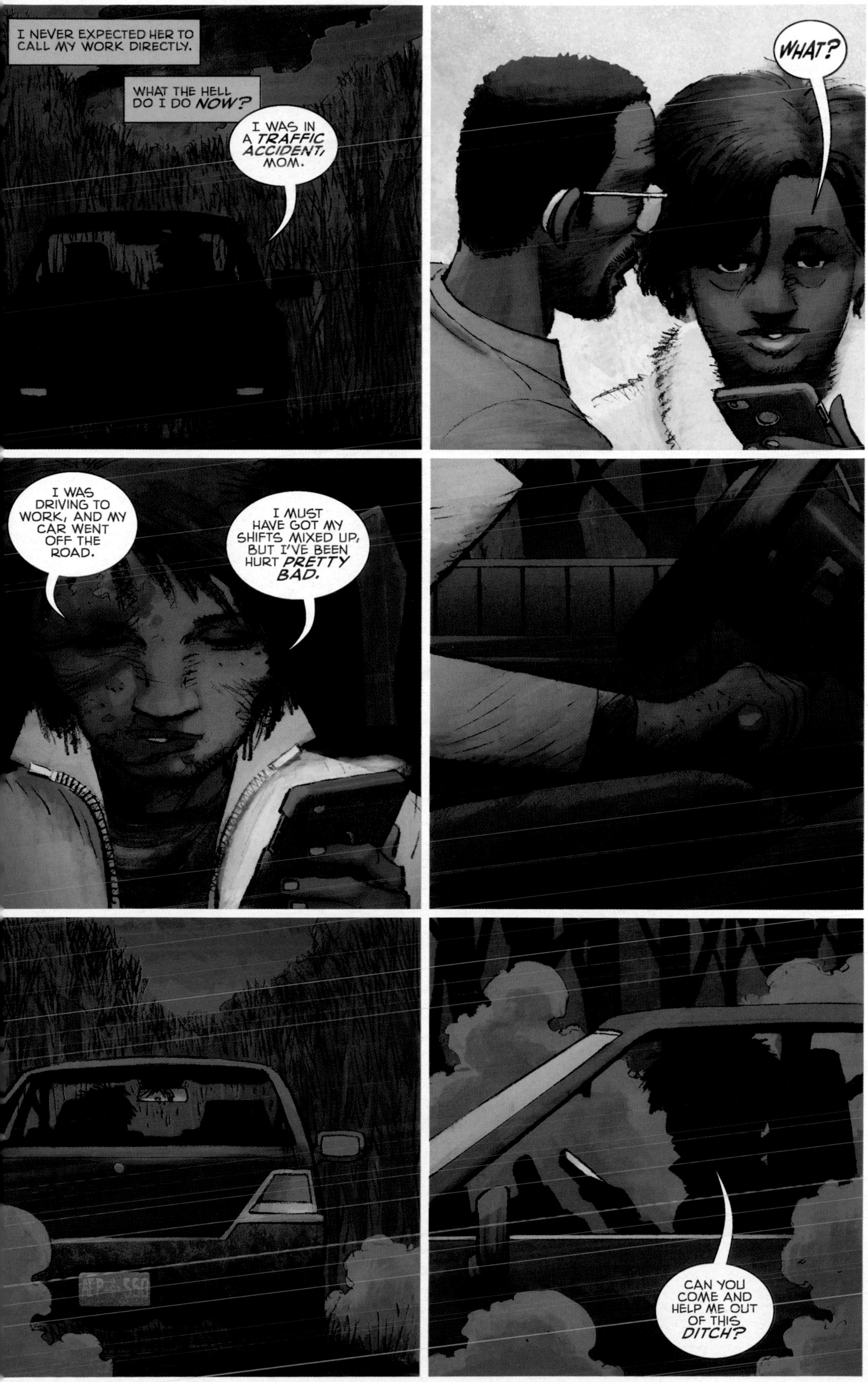
I NEVER EXPECTED HER TO CALL MY WORK DIRECTLY.
WHAT THE HELL DO I DO NOW?
I WAS IN A TRAFFIC ACCIDENT, MOM.
WHAT?
I WAS DRIVING TO WORK, AND MY CAR WENT OFF THE ROAD.
I MUST HAVE GOT MY SHIFTS MIXED UP, BUT I'VE BEEN HURT PRETTY BAD.
CAN YOU COME AND HELP ME OUT OF THIS DITCH?

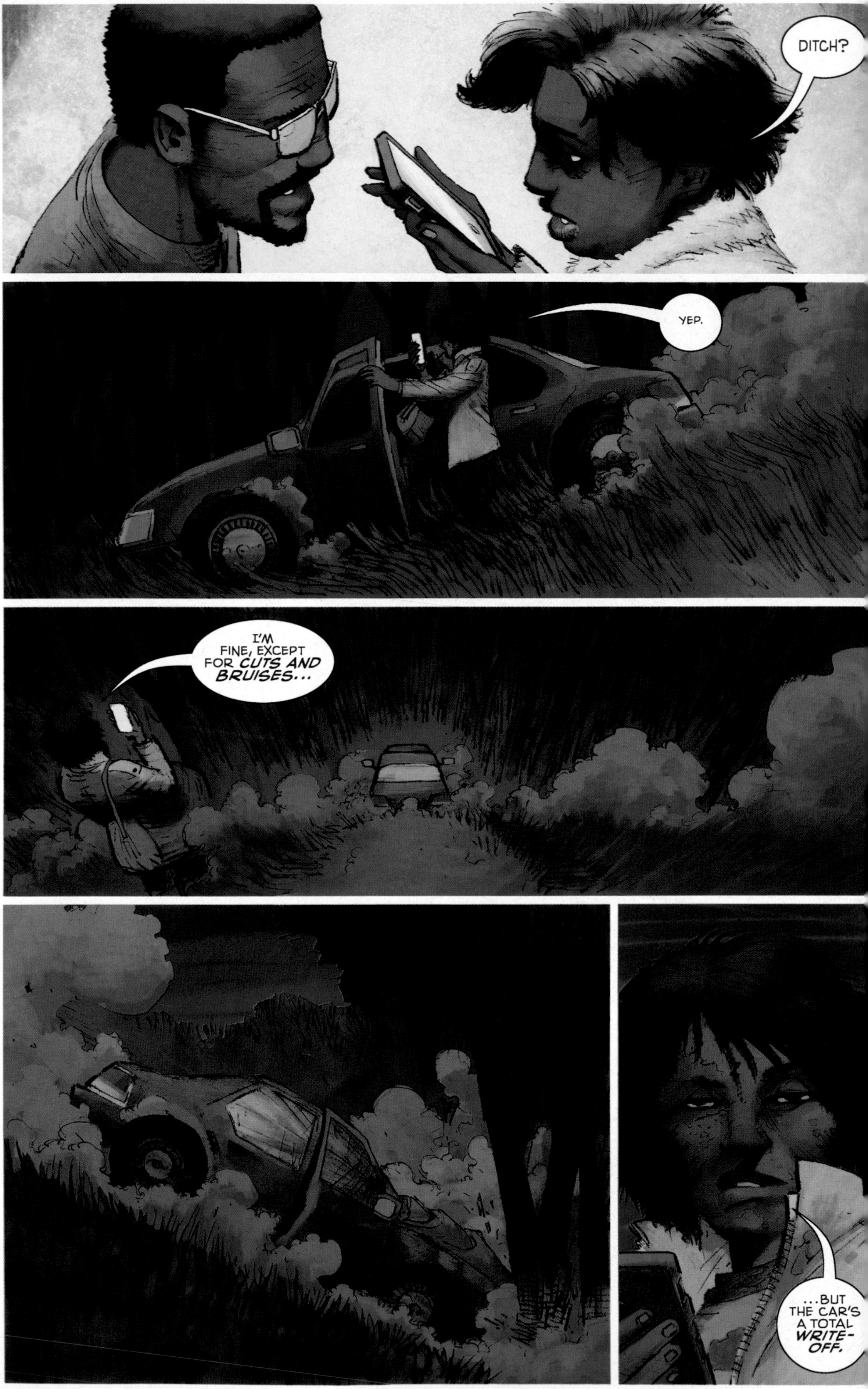
DITCH?
YEP.
I'M FINE, EXCEPT FOR CUTS AND BRUISES...
...BUT THE CAR'S A TOTAL WRITE-OFF.

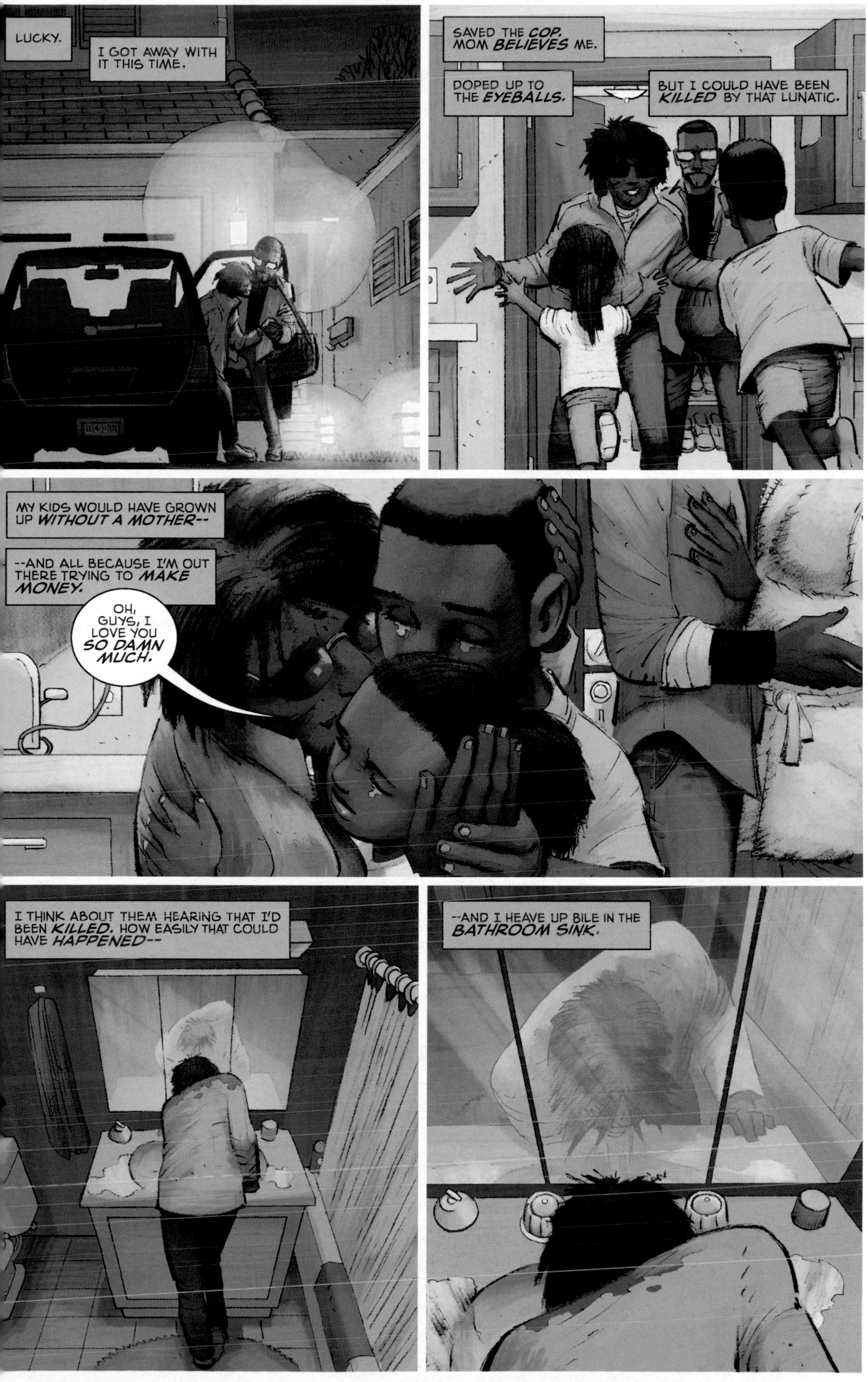
LUCKY.
I GOT AWAY WITH IT THIS TIME.
SAVED THE COP. MOM BELIEVES ME.
DOPED UP TO THE EYEBALLS.
BUT I COULD HAVE BEEN KILLED BY THAT LUNATIC.
MY KIDS WOULD HAVE GROWN UP WITHOUT A MOTHER--
--AND ALL BECAUSE I'M OUT THERE TRYING TO MAKE MONEY.
OH, GUYS, I LOVE YOU SO DAMN MUCH.
I THINK ABOUT THEM HEARING THAT I'D BEEN KILLED. HOW EASILY THAT COULD HAVE HAPPENED--
--AND I HEAVE UP BILE IN THE BATHROOM SINK.

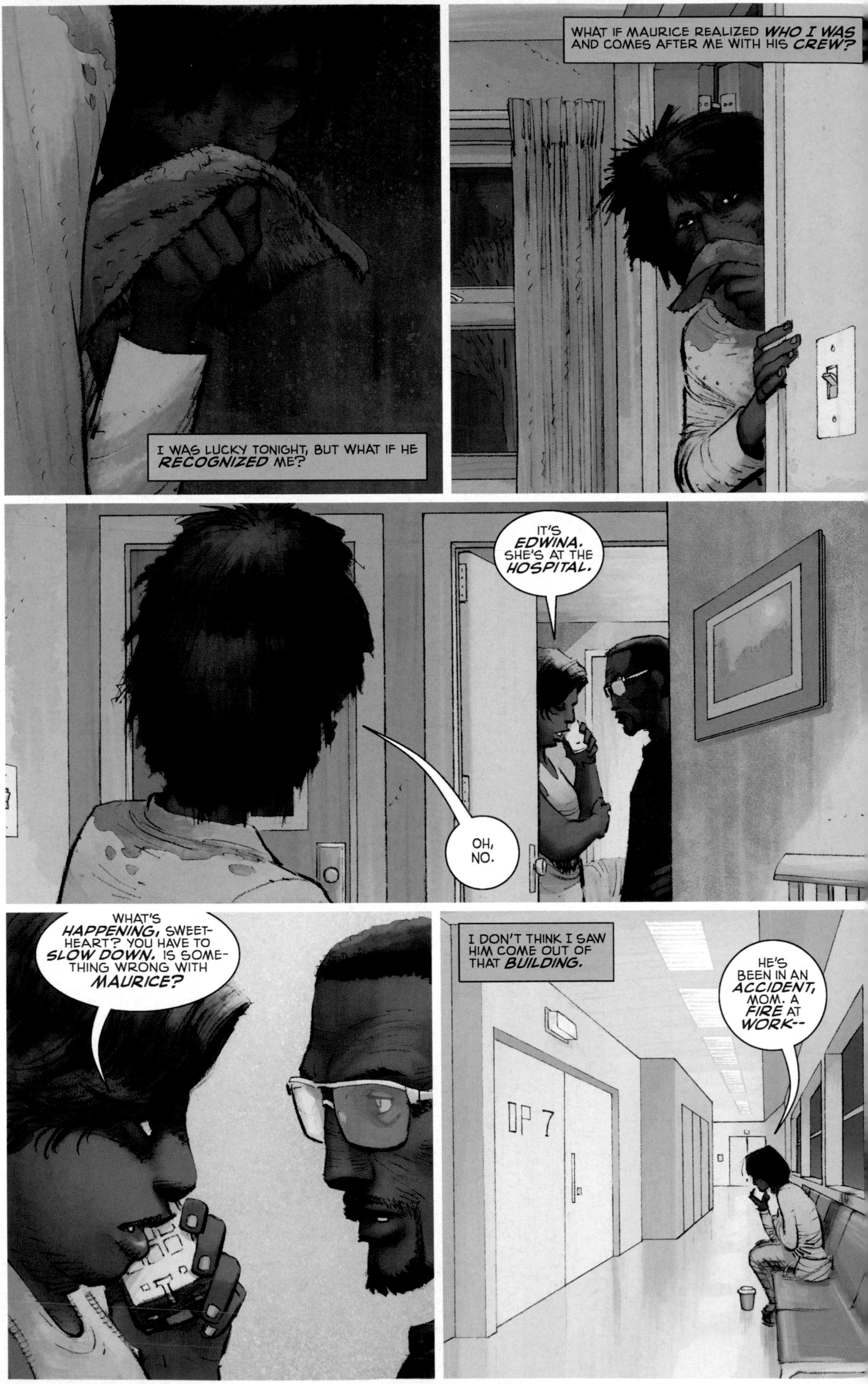
I WAS LUCKY TONIGHT, BUT WHAT IF HE RECOGNIZED ME?
WHAT IF MAURICE REALIZED WHO I WAS AND COMES AFTER ME WITH HIS CREW?
IT'S EDWINA. SHE'S AT THE HOSPITAL.
OH, NO.
WHAT'S HAPPENING, SWEET-HEART? YOU HAVE TO SLOW DOWN. IS SOME-THING WRONG WITH MAURICE?
I DON'T THINK I SAW HIM COME OUT OF THAT BUILDING.
HE'S BEEN IN AN ACCIDENT, MOM. A FIRE AT WORK--
OP 7

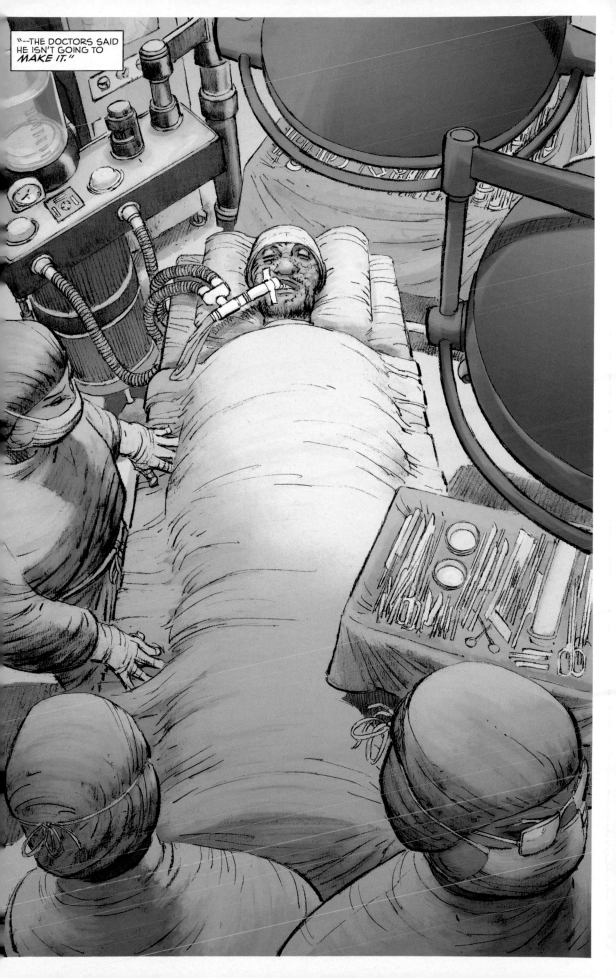

"--THE DOCTORS SAID HE ISN'T GOING TO *MAKE IT*."

FIVE

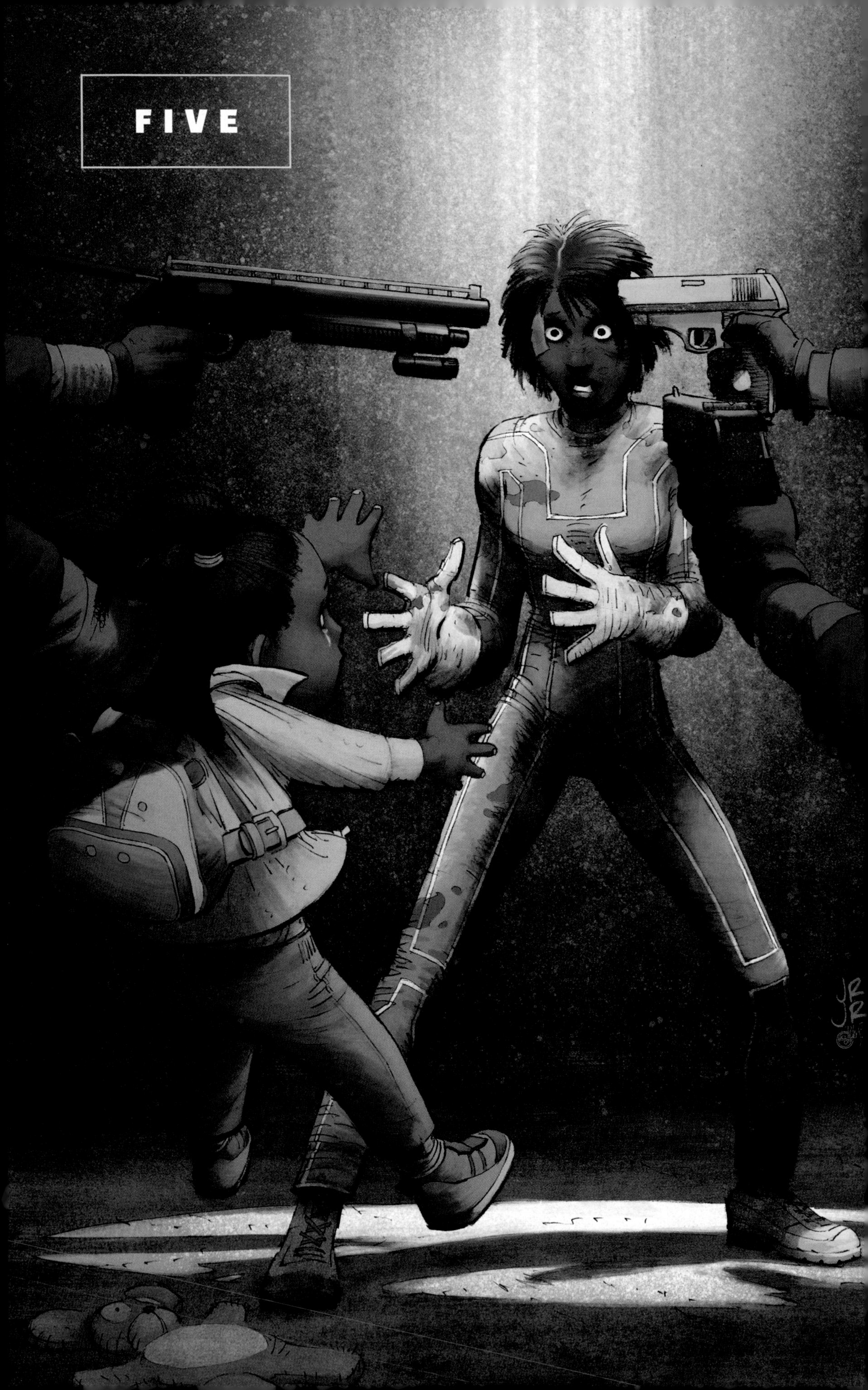

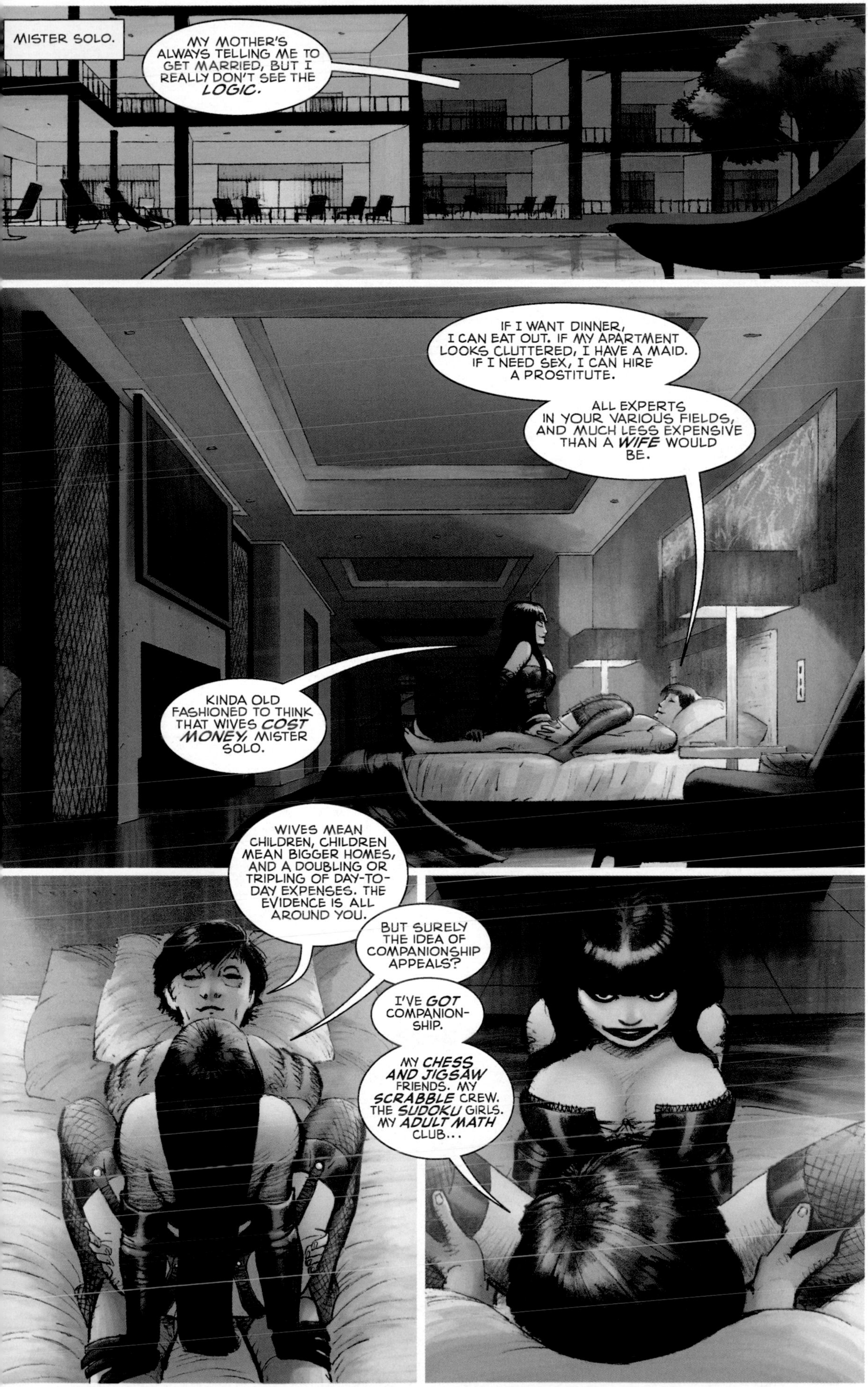
MISTER SOLO.
MY MOTHER'S ALWAYS TELLING ME TO GET MARRIED, BUT I REALLY DON'T SEE THE LOGIC.
IF I WANT DINNER, I CAN EAT OUT. IF MY APARTMENT LOOKS CLUTTERED, I HAVE A MAID. IF I NEED SEX, I CAN HIRE A PROSTITUTE.
ALL EXPERTS IN YOUR VARIOUS FIELDS, AND MUCH LESS EXPENSIVE THAN A WIFE WOULD BE.
KINDA OLD FASHIONED TO THINK THAT WIVES COST MONEY, MISTER SOLO.
WIVES MEAN CHILDREN, CHILDREN MEAN BIGGER HOMES, AND A DOUBLING OR TRIPLING OF DAY-TO-DAY EXPENSES. THE EVIDENCE IS ALL AROUND YOU.
BUT SURELY THE IDEA OF COMPANIONSHIP APPEALS?
I'VE GOT COMPANIONSHIP.
MY CHESS AND JIGSAW FRIENDS. MY SCRABBLE CREW. THE SUDOKU GIRLS. MY ADULT MATH CLUB...

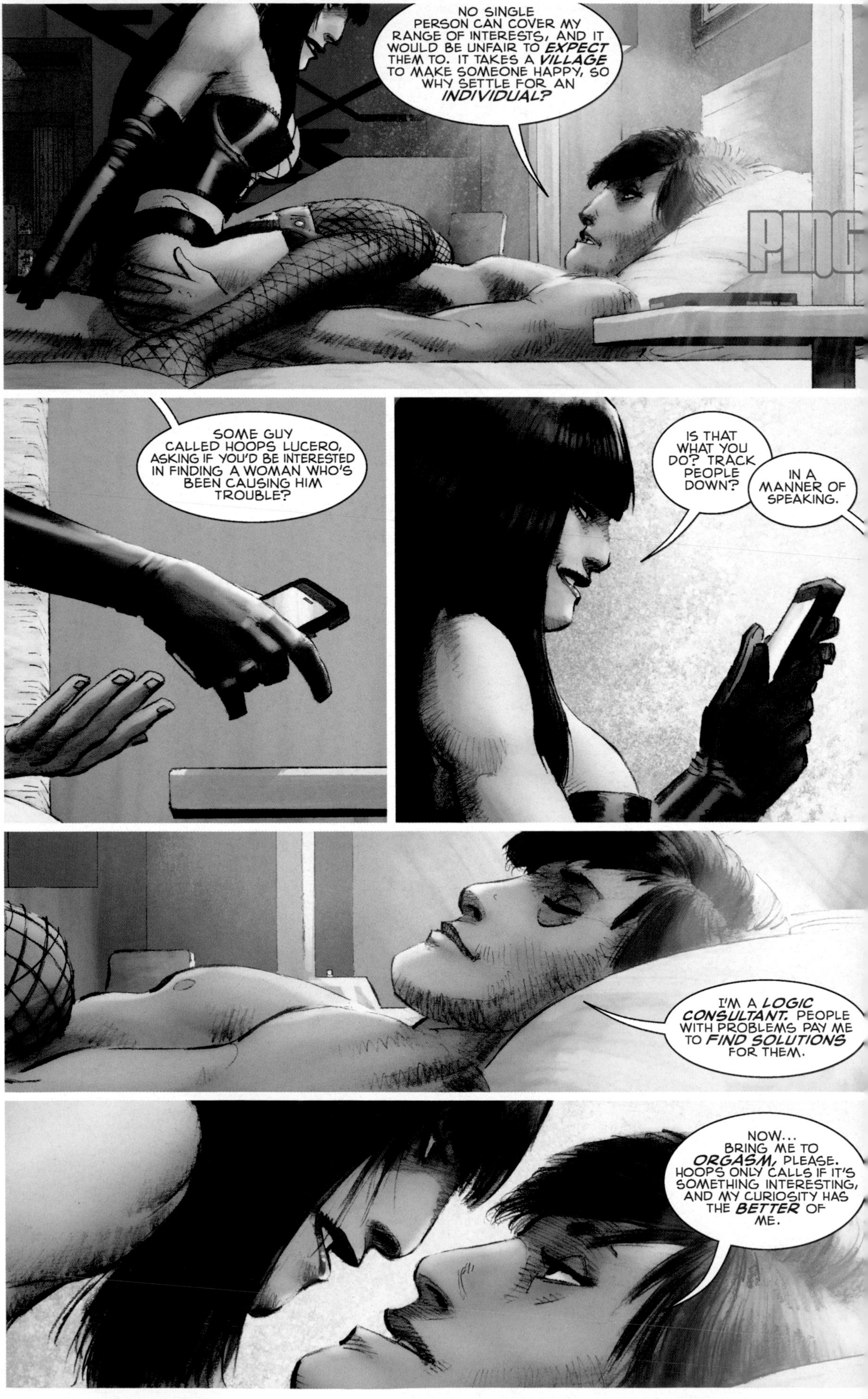
NO SINGLE PERSON CAN COVER MY RANGE OF INTERESTS, AND IT WOULD BE UNFAIR TO EXPECT THEM TO. IT TAKES A VILLAGE TO MAKE SOMEONE HAPPY, SO WHY SETTLE FOR AN INDIVIDUAL?
SOME GUY CALLED HOOPS LUCERO, ASKING IF YOU'D BE INTERESTED IN FINDING A WOMAN WHO'S BEEN CAUSING HIM TROUBLE?
IS THAT WHAT YOU DO? TRACK PEOPLE DOWN?
IN A MANNER OF SPEAKING.
I'M A LOGIC CONSULTANT. PEOPLE WITH PROBLEMS PAY ME TO FIND SOLUTIONS FOR THEM.
NOW... BRING ME TO ORGASM, PLEASE. HOOPS ONLY CALLS IF IT'S SOMETHING INTERESTING, AND MY CURIOSITY HAS THE BETTER OF ME.

MY NAME IS PATIENCE LEE, AND I'M A STAFF SERGEANT IN THE *160TH SOAR* HOLED UP IN AFGHANISTAN.

TEN SECONDS AGO, OUR *MRAP* HIT A DAISY-CHAINED *IED*, BLOWING A HOLE IN THE DOOR'S PNEUMATICS AND TRAPPING US ALL INSIDE.

I NEED TO GET MY BOYS OUT OF HERE, OR WE'RE GOING TO BE SITTING DUCKS.

UP THROUGH THE *TURRET!* IT'S OUR *ONLY* EXIT!

HAJIS'LL *TORCH* US IF THEY TRAP US IN THERE.

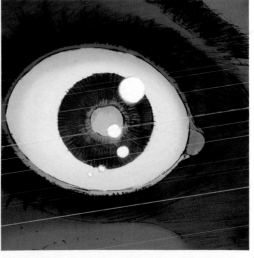

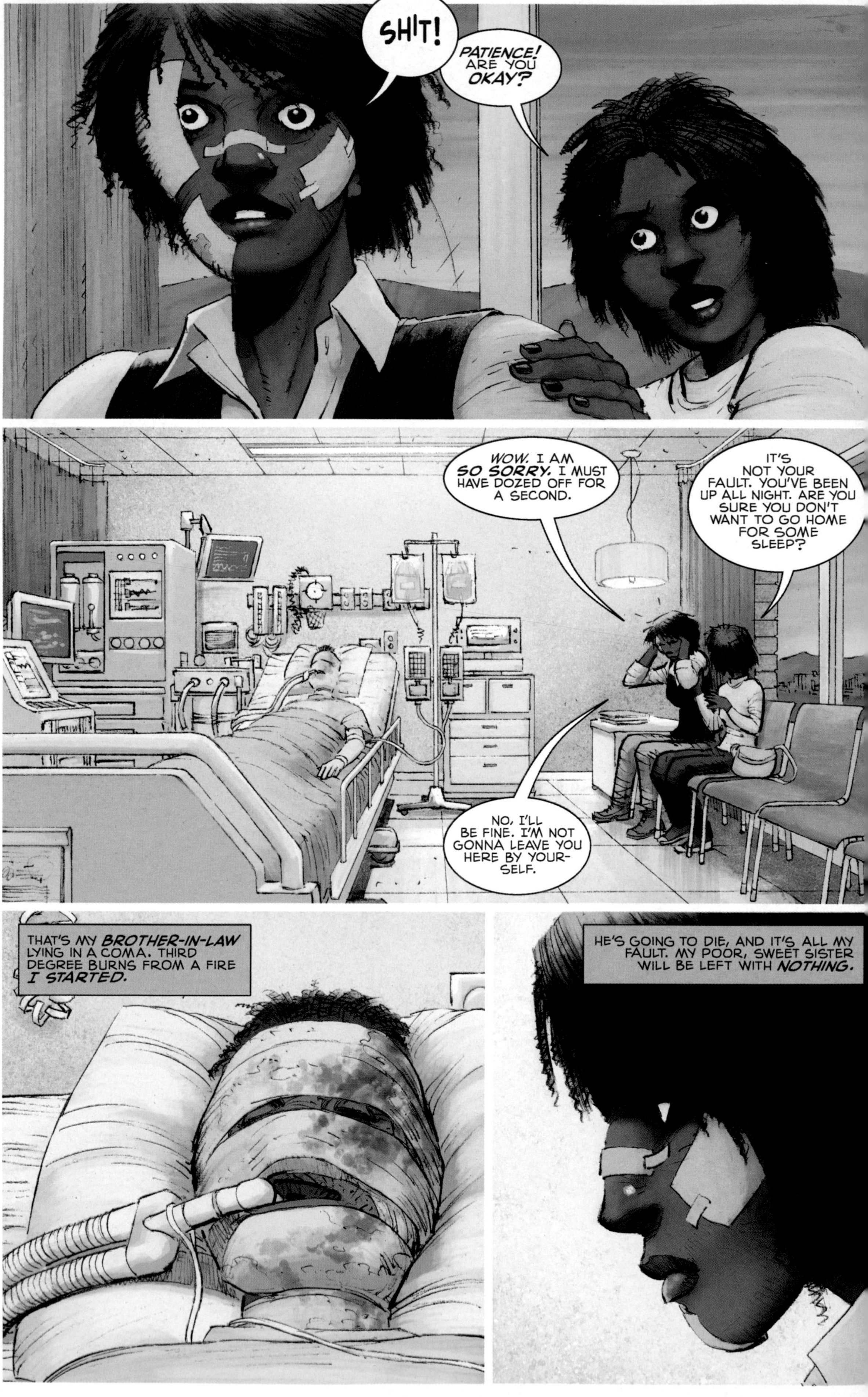
SHIT!
PATIENCE! ARE YOU OKAY?
WOW. I AM SO SORRY. I MUST HAVE DOZED OFF FOR A SECOND.
IT'S NOT YOUR FAULT. YOU'VE BEEN UP ALL NIGHT. ARE YOU SURE YOU DON'T WANT TO GO HOME FOR SOME SLEEP?
NO, I'LL BE FINE. I'M NOT GONNA LEAVE YOU HERE BY YOUR-SELF.
THAT'S MY BROTHER-IN-LAW LYING IN A COMA. THIRD DEGREE BURNS FROM A FIRE I STARTED.
HE'S GOING TO DIE, AND IT'S ALL MY FAULT. MY POOR, SWEET SISTER WILL BE LEFT WITH NOTHING.

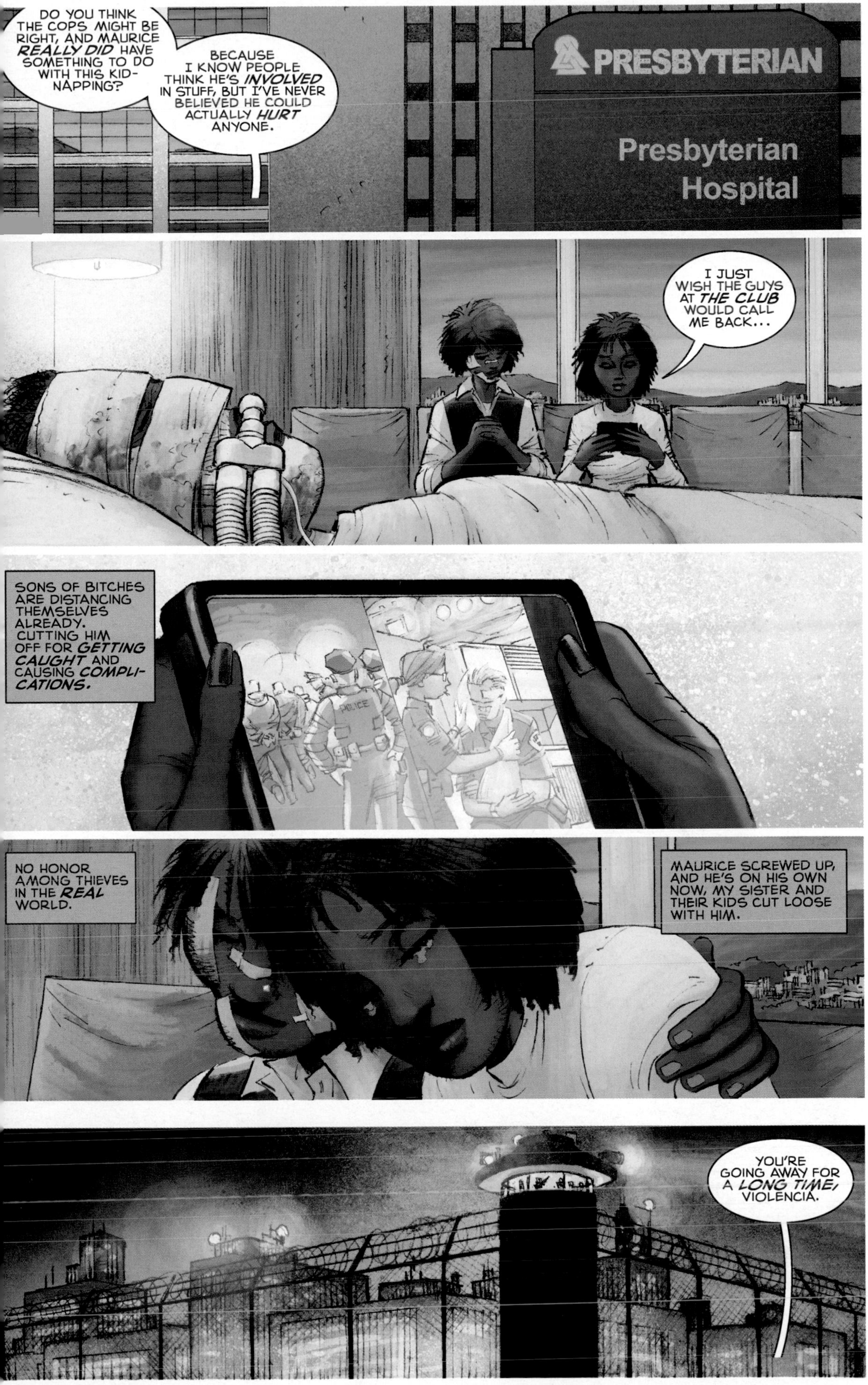
DO YOU THINK THE COPS MIGHT BE RIGHT, AND MAURICE REALLY DID HAVE SOMETHING TO DO WITH THIS KID-NAPPING?
BECAUSE I KNOW PEOPLE THINK HE'S INVOLVED IN STUFF, BUT I'VE NEVER BELIEVED HE COULD ACTUALLY HURT ANYONE.
PRESBYTERIAN
Presbyterian Hospital
I JUST WISH THE GUYS AT THE CLUB WOULD CALL ME BACK...
SONS OF BITCHES ARE DISTANCING THEMSELVES ALREADY. CUTTING HIM OFF FOR GETTING CAUGHT AND CAUSING COMPLI-CATIONS.
POLICE
NO HONOR AMONG THIEVES IN THE REAL WORLD.
MAURICE SCREWED UP, AND HE'S ON HIS OWN NOW, MY SISTER AND THEIR KIDS CUT LOOSE WITH HIM.
YOU'RE GOING AWAY FOR A LONG TIME, VIOLENCIA.

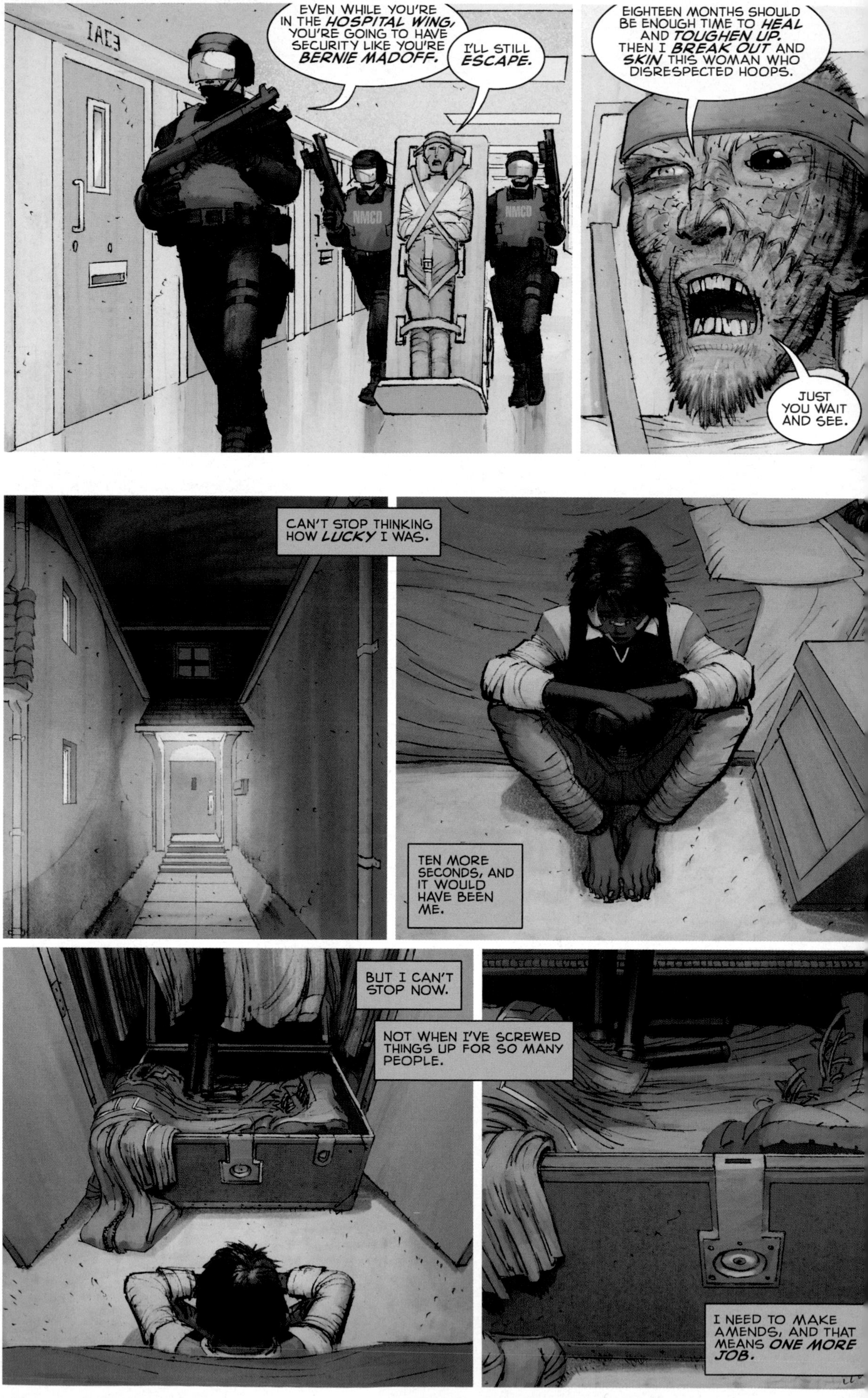
EVEN WHILE YOU'RE IN THE HOSPITAL WING, YOU'RE GOING TO HAVE SECURITY LIKE YOU'RE BERNIE MADOFF.
I'LL STILL ESCAPE.
EIGHTEEN MONTHS SHOULD BE ENOUGH TIME TO HEAL AND TOUGHEN UP. THEN I BREAK OUT AND SKIN THIS WOMAN WHO DISRESPECTED HOOPS.
JUST YOU WAIT AND SEE.
CAN'T STOP THINKING HOW LUCKY I WAS.
TEN MORE SECONDS, AND IT WOULD HAVE BEEN ME.
BUT I CAN'T STOP NOW.
NOT WHEN I'VE SCREWED THINGS UP FOR SO MANY PEOPLE.
I NEED TO MAKE AMENDS, AND THAT MEANS ONE MORE JOB.

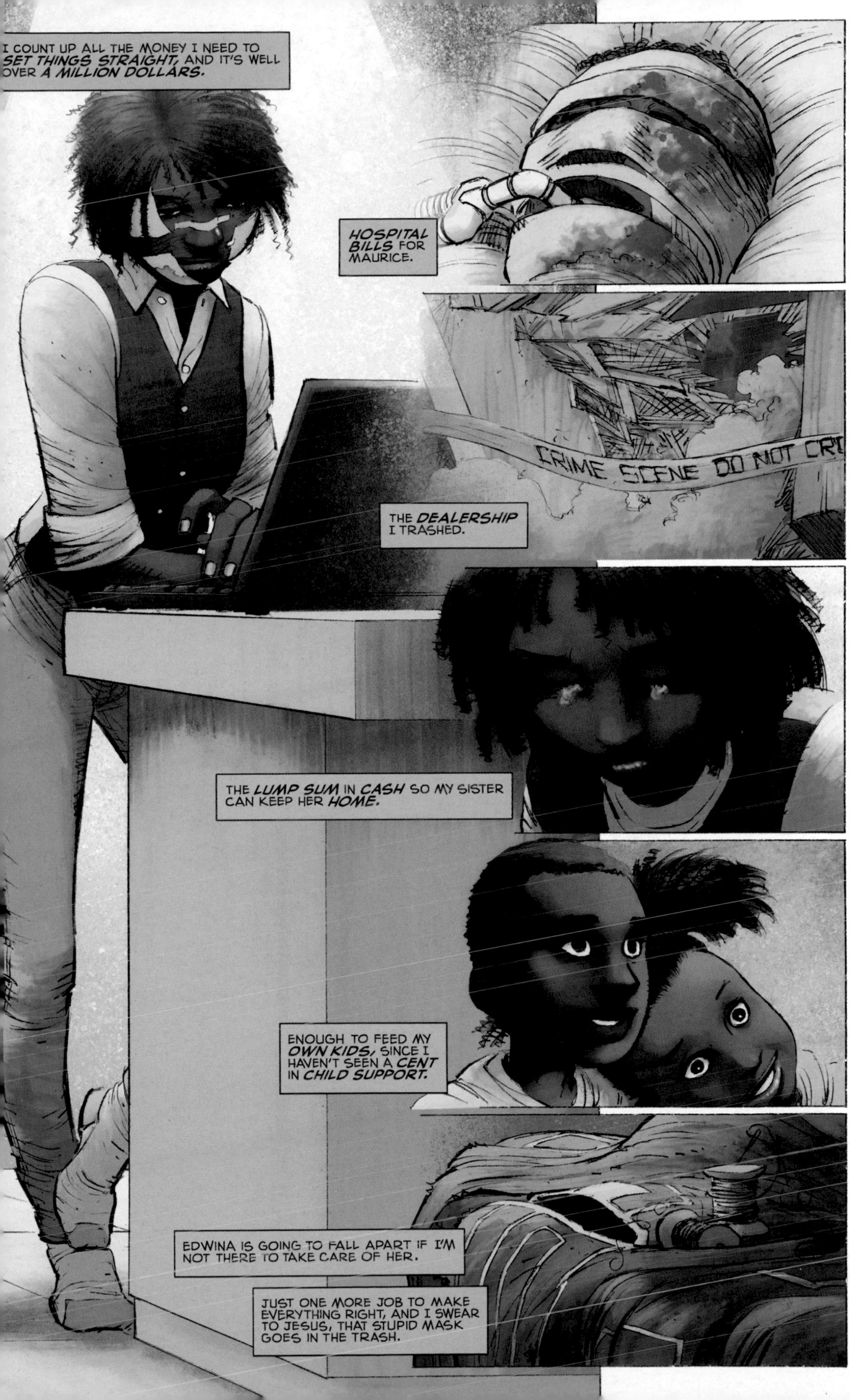
I COUNT UP ALL THE MONEY I NEED TO SET THINGS STRAIGHT, AND IT'S WELL OVER A MILLION DOLLARS.
HOSPITAL BILLS FOR MAURICE.
CRIME SCENE DO NOT CR
THE DEALERSHIP I TRASHED.
THE LUMP SUM IN CASH SO MY SISTER CAN KEEP HER HOME.
ENOUGH TO FEED MY OWN KIDS, SINCE I HAVEN'T SEEN A CENT IN CHILD SUPPORT.
EDWINA IS GOING TO FALL APART IF I'M NOT THERE TO TAKE CARE OF HER.
JUST ONE MORE JOB TO MAKE EVERYTHING RIGHT, AND I SWEAR TO JESUS, THAT STUPID MASK GOES IN THE TRASH.

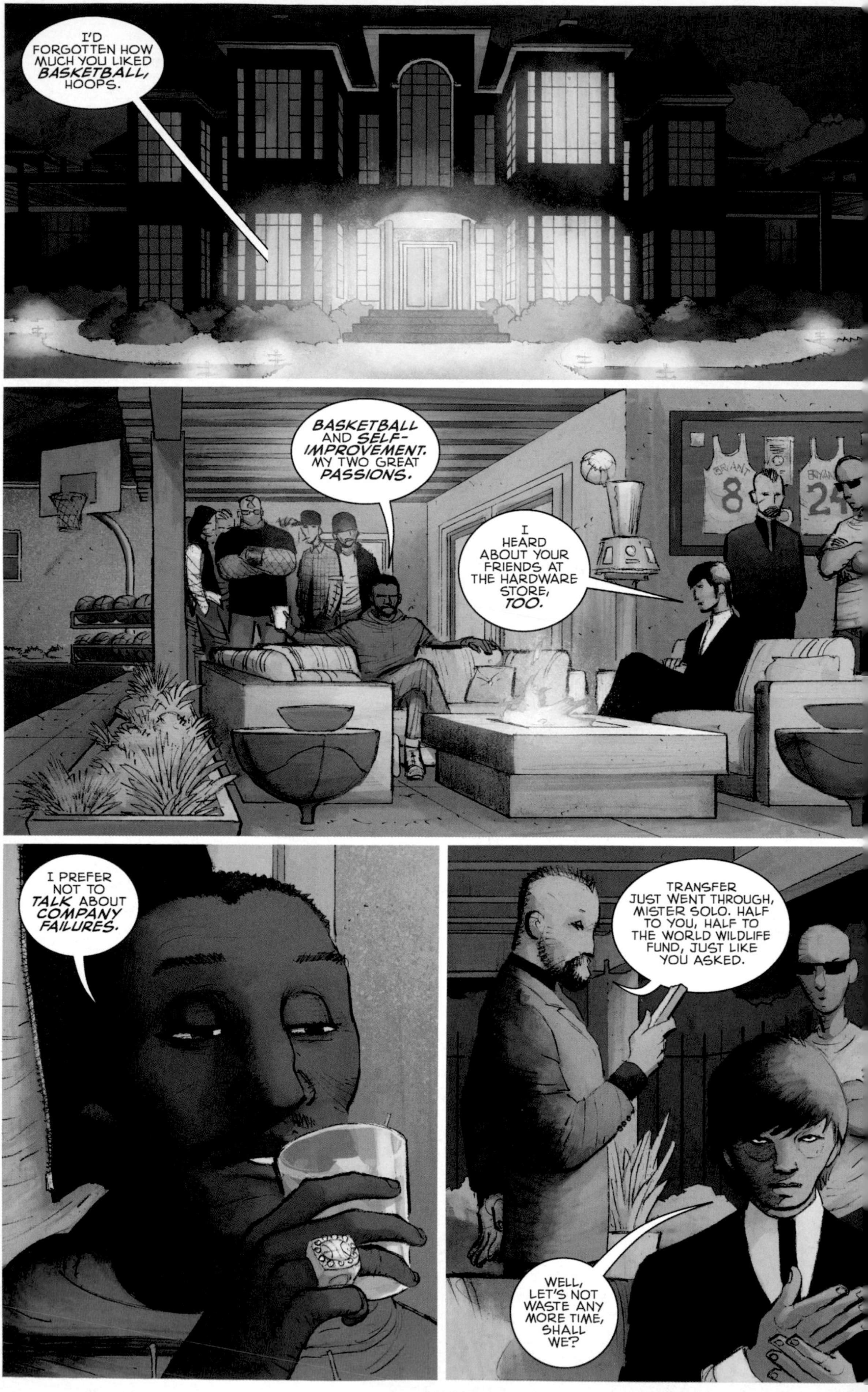
I'D FORGOTTEN HOW MUCH YOU LIKED BASKETBALL, HOOPS.
BASKETBALL AND SELF-IMPROVEMENT. MY TWO GREAT PASSIONS.
I HEARD ABOUT YOUR FRIENDS AT THE HARDWARE STORE, TOO.
BRYANT 8
BRYANT 24
I PREFER NOT TO TALK ABOUT COMPANY FAILURES.
TRANSFER JUST WENT THROUGH, MISTER SOLO. HALF TO YOU, HALF TO THE WORLD WILDLIFE FUND, JUST LIKE YOU ASKED.
WELL, LET'S NOT WASTE ANY MORE TIME, SHALL WE?

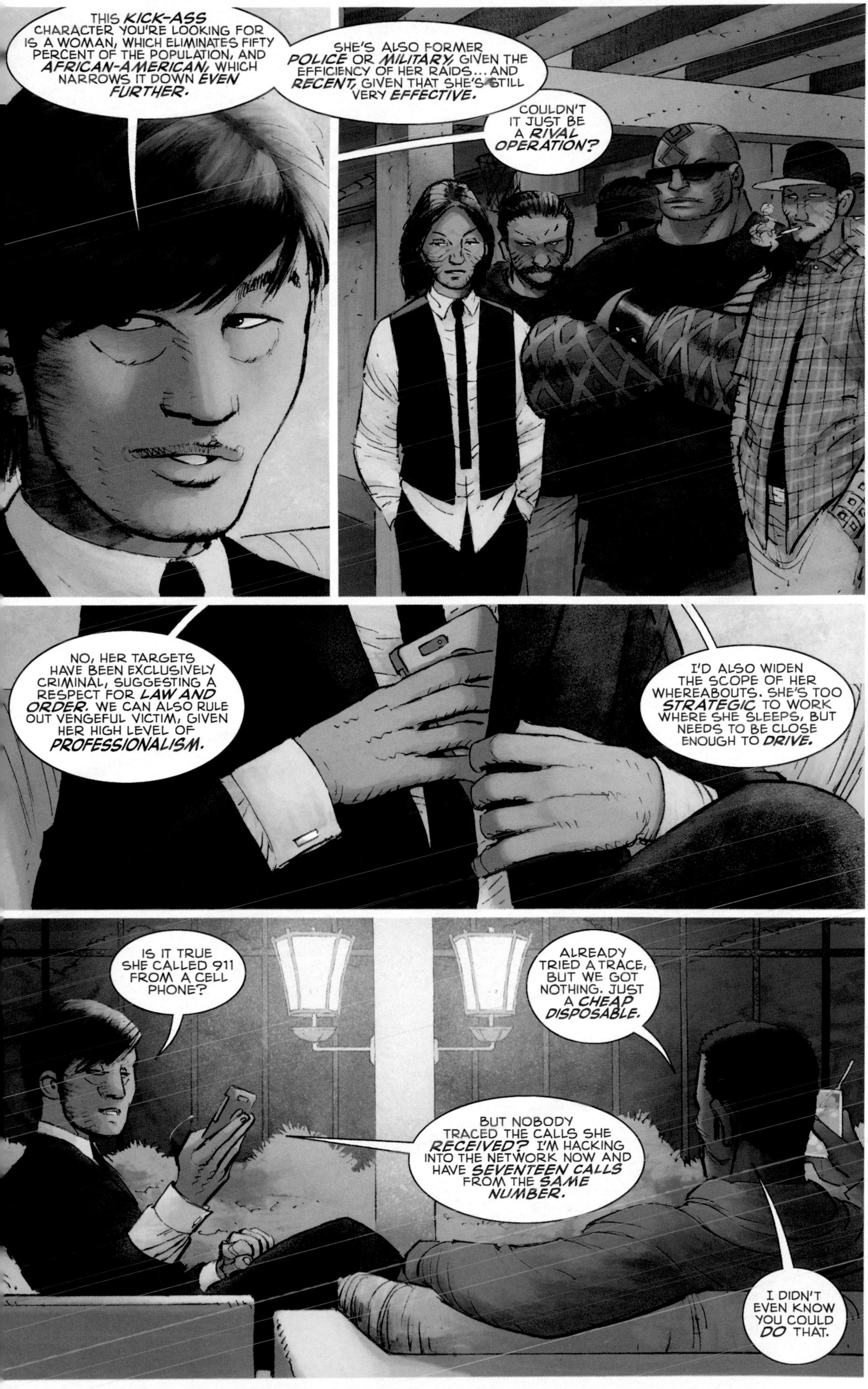
THIS KICK-ASS CHARACTER YOU'RE LOOKING FOR IS A WOMAN, WHICH ELIMINATES FIFTY PERCENT OF THE POPULATION, AND AFRICAN-AMERICAN, WHICH NARROWS IT DOWN EVEN FURTHER.
SHE'S ALSO FORMER POLICE OR MILITARY, GIVEN THE EFFICIENCY OF HER RAIDS... AND RECENT, GIVEN THAT SHE'S STILL VERY EFFECTIVE.
COULDN'T IT JUST BE A RIVAL OPERATION?
NO, HER TARGETS HAVE BEEN EXCLUSIVELY CRIMINAL, SUGGESTING A RESPECT FOR LAW AND ORDER. WE CAN ALSO RULE OUT VENGEFUL VICTIM, GIVEN HER HIGH LEVEL OF PROFESSIONALISM.
I'D ALSO WIDEN THE SCOPE OF HER WHEREABOUTS. SHE'S TOO STRATEGIC TO WORK WHERE SHE SLEEPS, BUT NEEDS TO BE CLOSE ENOUGH TO DRIVE.
IS IT TRUE SHE CALLED 911 FROM A CELL PHONE?
ALREADY TRIED A TRACE, BUT WE GOT NOTHING. JUST A CHEAP DISPOSABLE.
BUT NOBODY TRACED THE CALLS SHE RECEIVED? I'M HACKING INTO THE NETWORK NOW AND HAVE SEVENTEEN CALLS FROM THE SAME NUMBER.
I DIDN'T EVEN KNOW YOU COULD DO THAT.

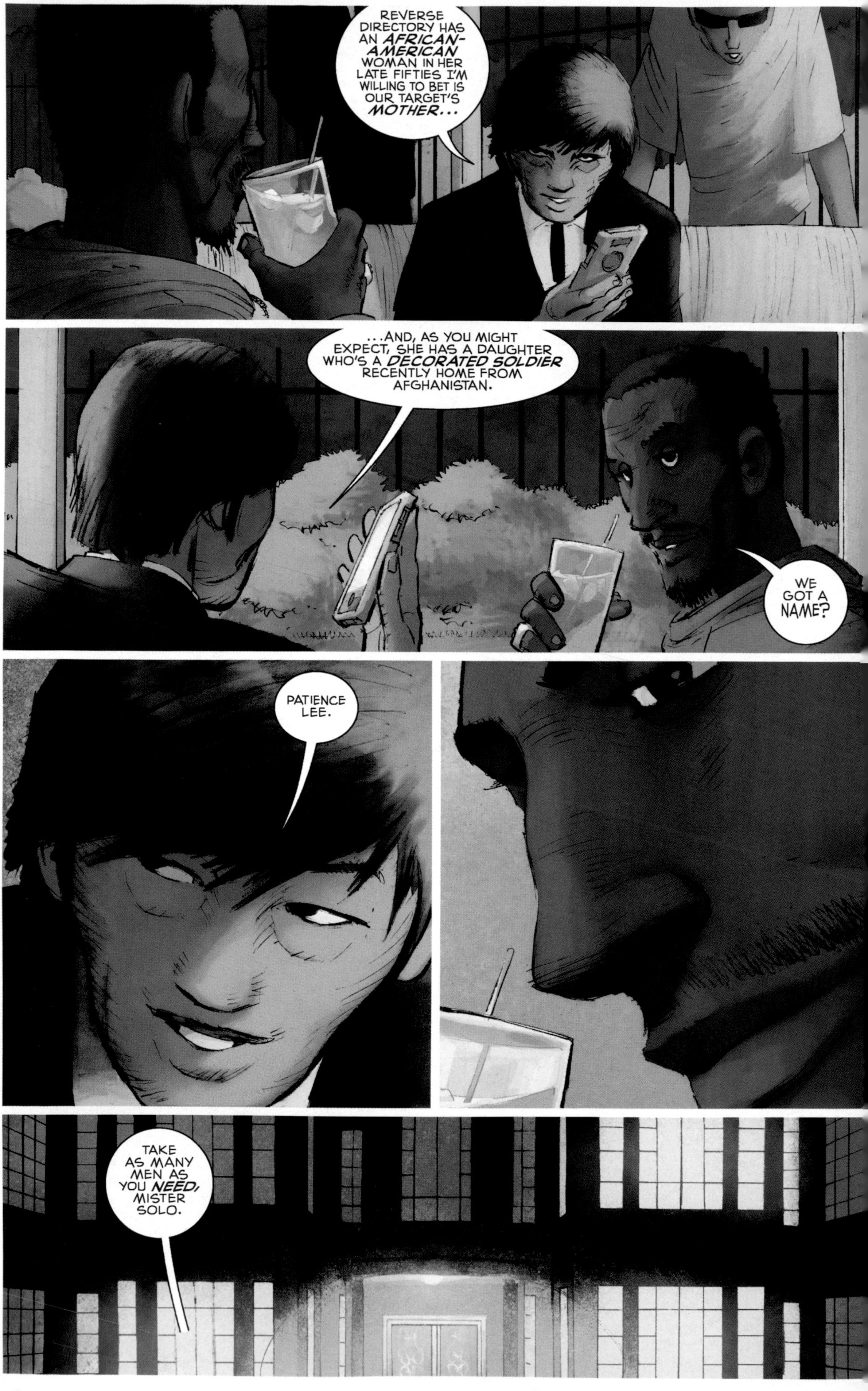
REVERSE DIRECTORY HAS AN AFRICAN-AMERICAN WOMAN IN HER LATE FIFTIES I'M WILLING TO BET IS OUR TARGET'S MOTHER...
...AND, AS YOU MIGHT EXPECT, SHE HAS A DAUGHTER WHO'S A DECORATED SOLDIER RECENTLY HOME FROM AFGHANISTAN.
WE GOT A NAME?
PATIENCE LEE.
TAKE AS MANY MEN AS YOU NEED, MISTER SOLO.

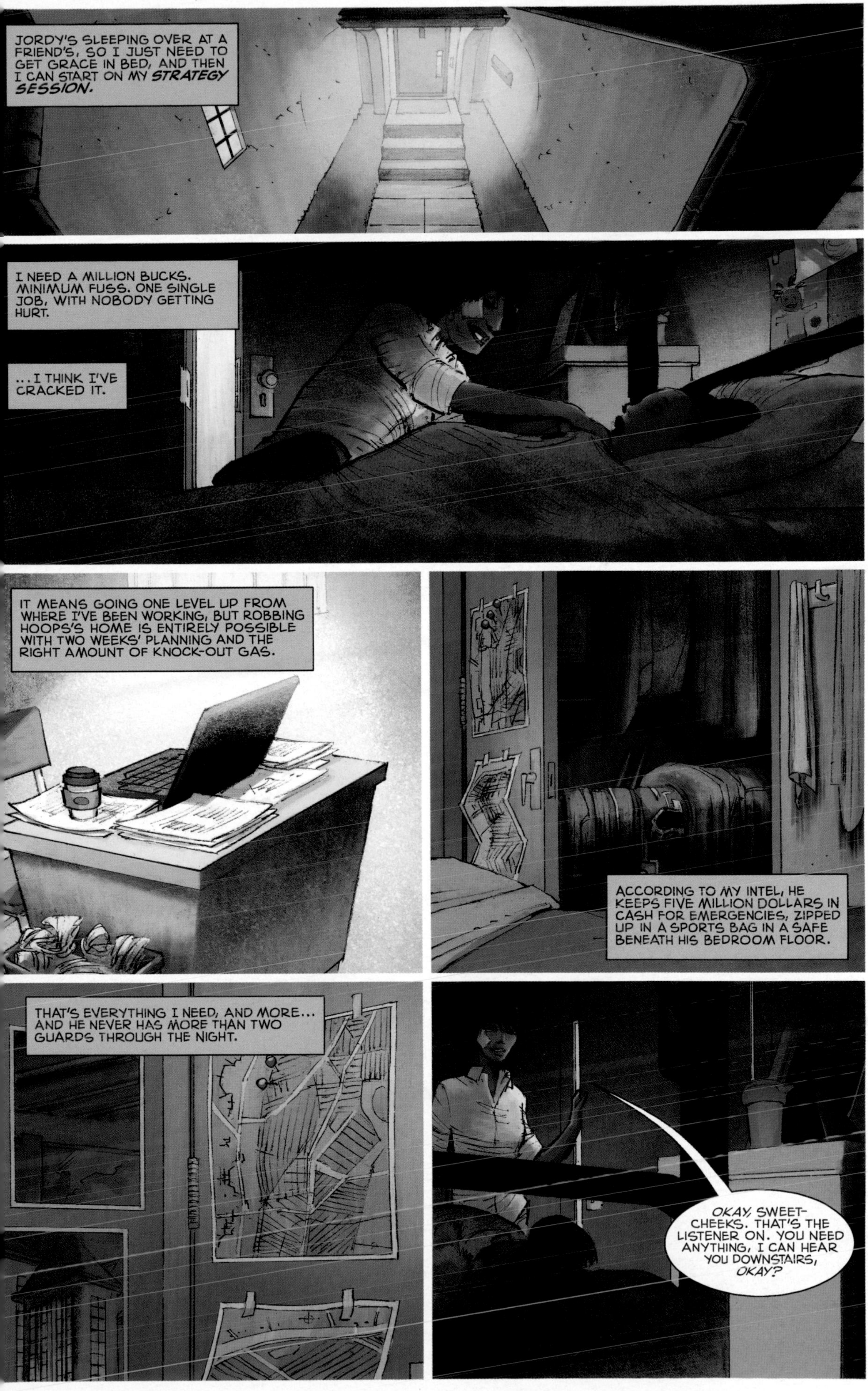
JORDY'S SLEEPING OVER AT A FRIEND'S, SO I JUST NEED TO GET GRACE IN BED, AND THEN I CAN START ON MY *STRATEGY SESSION.*
I NEED A MILLION BUCKS. MINIMUM FUSS. ONE SINGLE JOB, WITH NOBODY GETTING HURT.
...I THINK I'VE CRACKED IT.
IT MEANS GOING ONE LEVEL UP FROM WHERE I'VE BEEN WORKING, BUT ROBBING HOOPS'S HOME IS ENTIRELY POSSIBLE WITH TWO WEEKS' PLANNING AND THE RIGHT AMOUNT OF KNOCK-OUT GAS.
ACCORDING TO MY INTEL, HE KEEPS FIVE MILLION DOLLARS IN CASH FOR EMERGENCIES, ZIPPED UP IN A SPORTS BAG IN A SAFE BENEATH HIS BEDROOM FLOOR.
THAT'S EVERYTHING I NEED, AND MORE... AND HE NEVER HAS MORE THAN TWO GUARDS THROUGH THE NIGHT.
OKAY, SWEET-CHEEKS. THAT'S THE LISTENER ON. YOU NEED ANYTHING, I CAN HEAR YOU DOWNSTAIRS, *OKAY?*

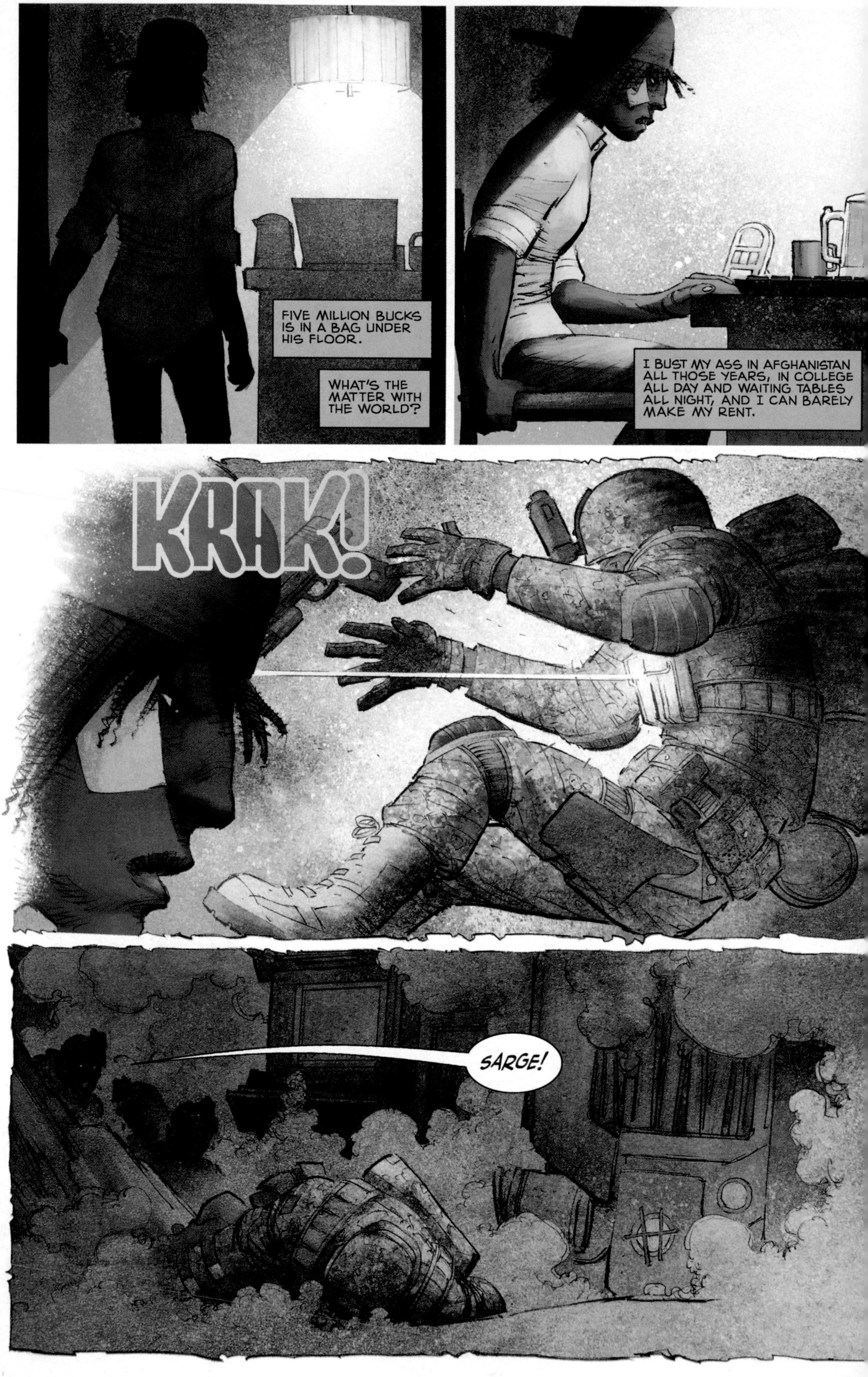
FIVE MILLION BUCKS IS IN A BAG UNDER HIS FLOOR.
WHAT'S THE MATTER WITH THE WORLD?
I BUST MY ASS IN AFGHANISTAN ALL THOSE YEARS, IN COLLEGE ALL DAY AND WAITING TABLES ALL NIGHT, AND I CAN BARELY MAKE MY RENT.
KRAK!
SARGE!

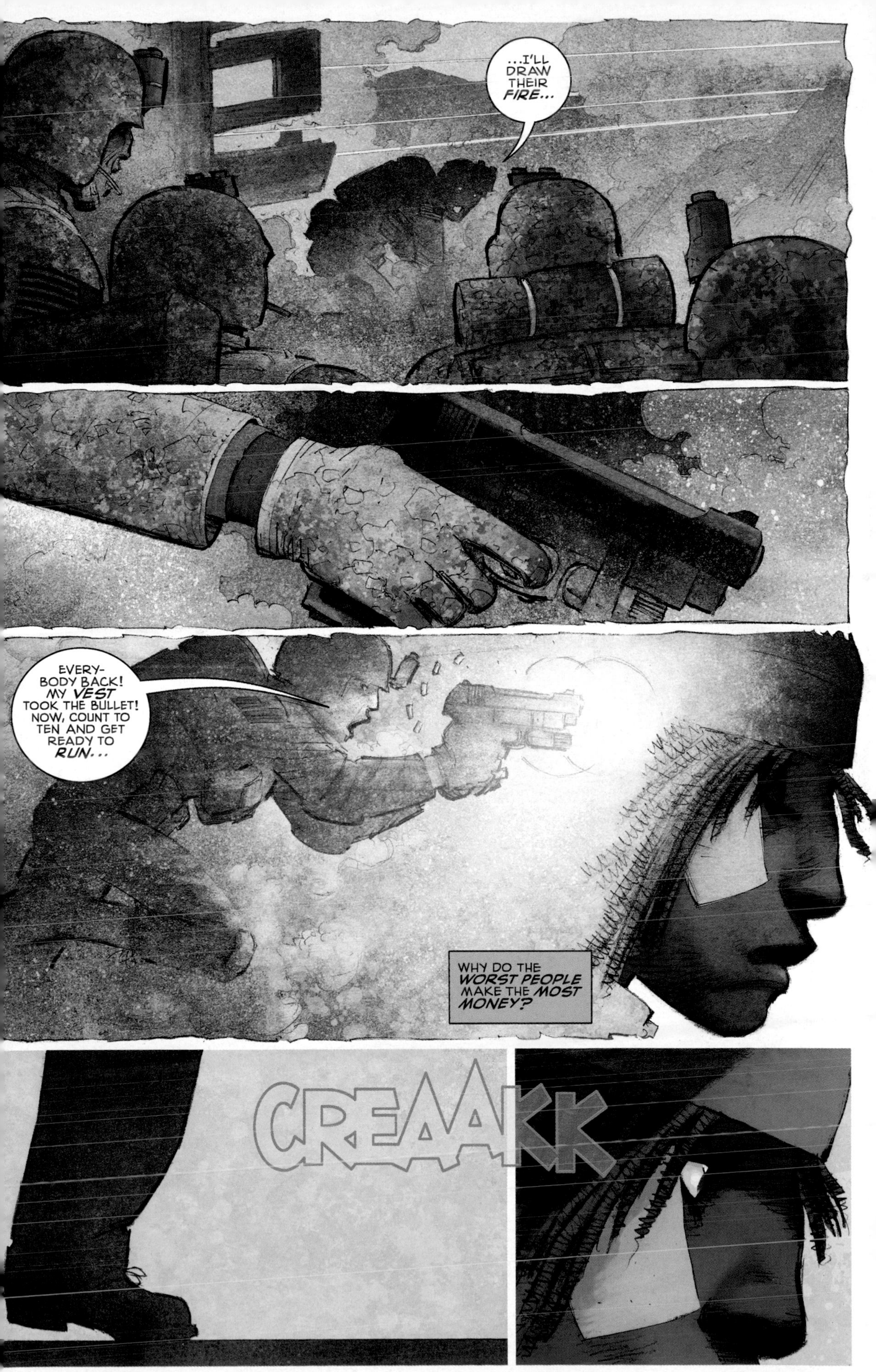
...I'LL DRAW THEIR FIRE...
EVERY-BODY BACK! MY VEST TOOK THE BULLET! NOW, COUNT TO TEN AND GET READY TO RUN...
WHY DO THE WORST PEOPLE MAKE THE MOST MONEY?
CREAAKK

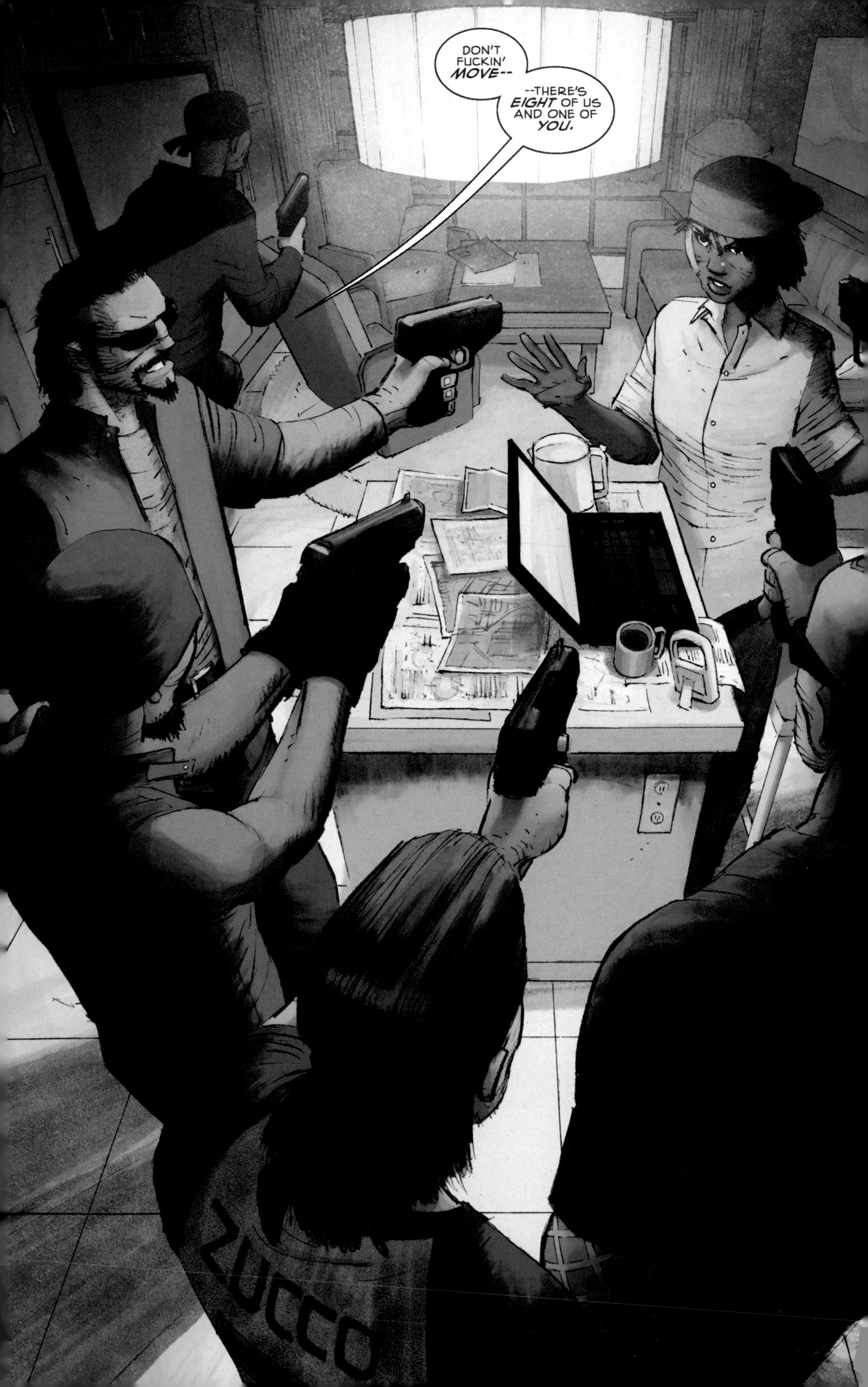
DON'T FUCKIN' MOVE--
--THERE'S EIGHT OF US AND ONE OF YOU.
ZUCCO

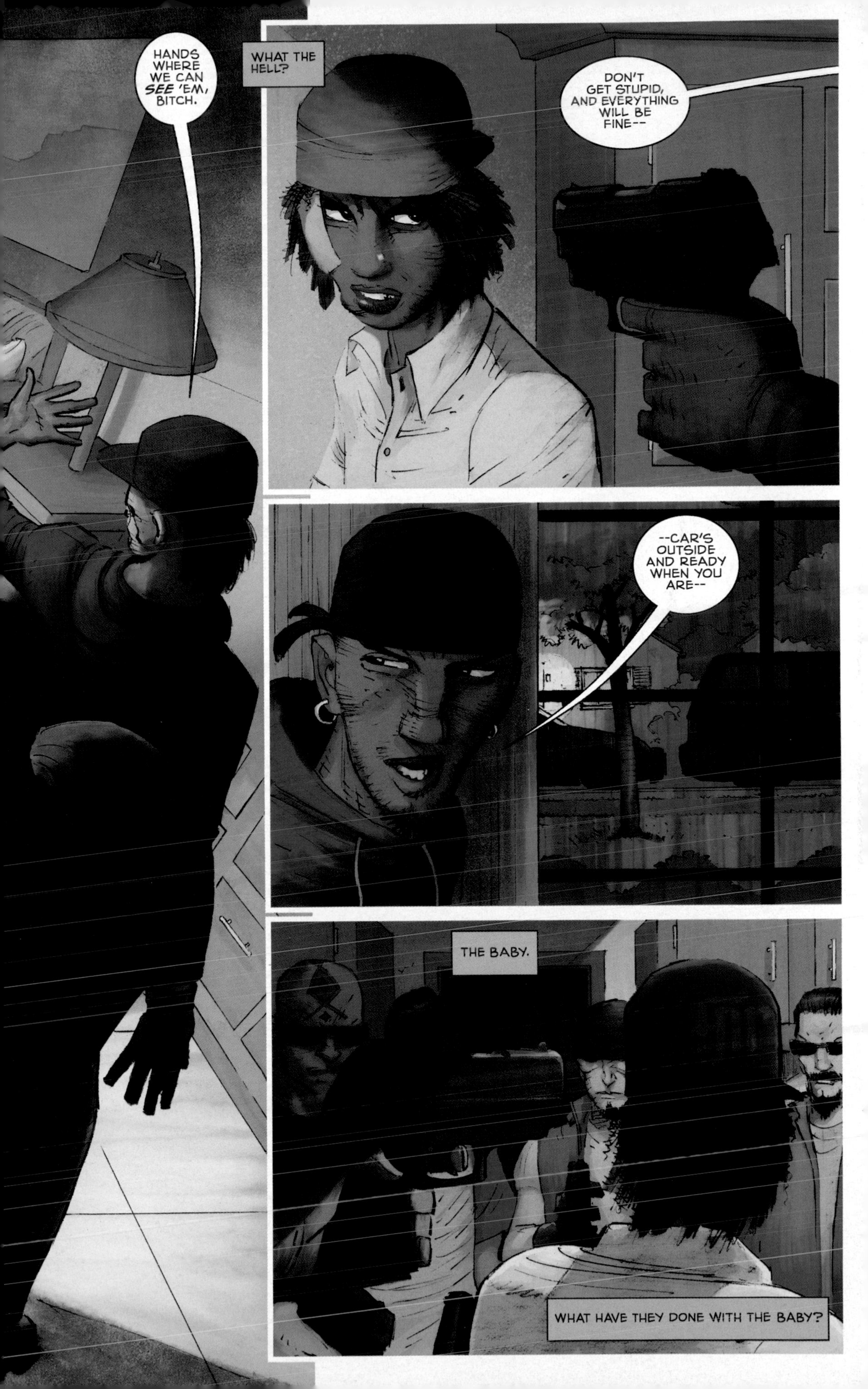
HANDS WHERE WE CAN SEE 'EM, BITCH.
WHAT THE HELL?
DON'T GET STUPID, AND EVERYTHING WILL BE FINE--
--CAR'S OUTSIDE AND READY WHEN YOU ARE--
THE BABY.
WHAT HAVE THEY DONE WITH THE BABY?

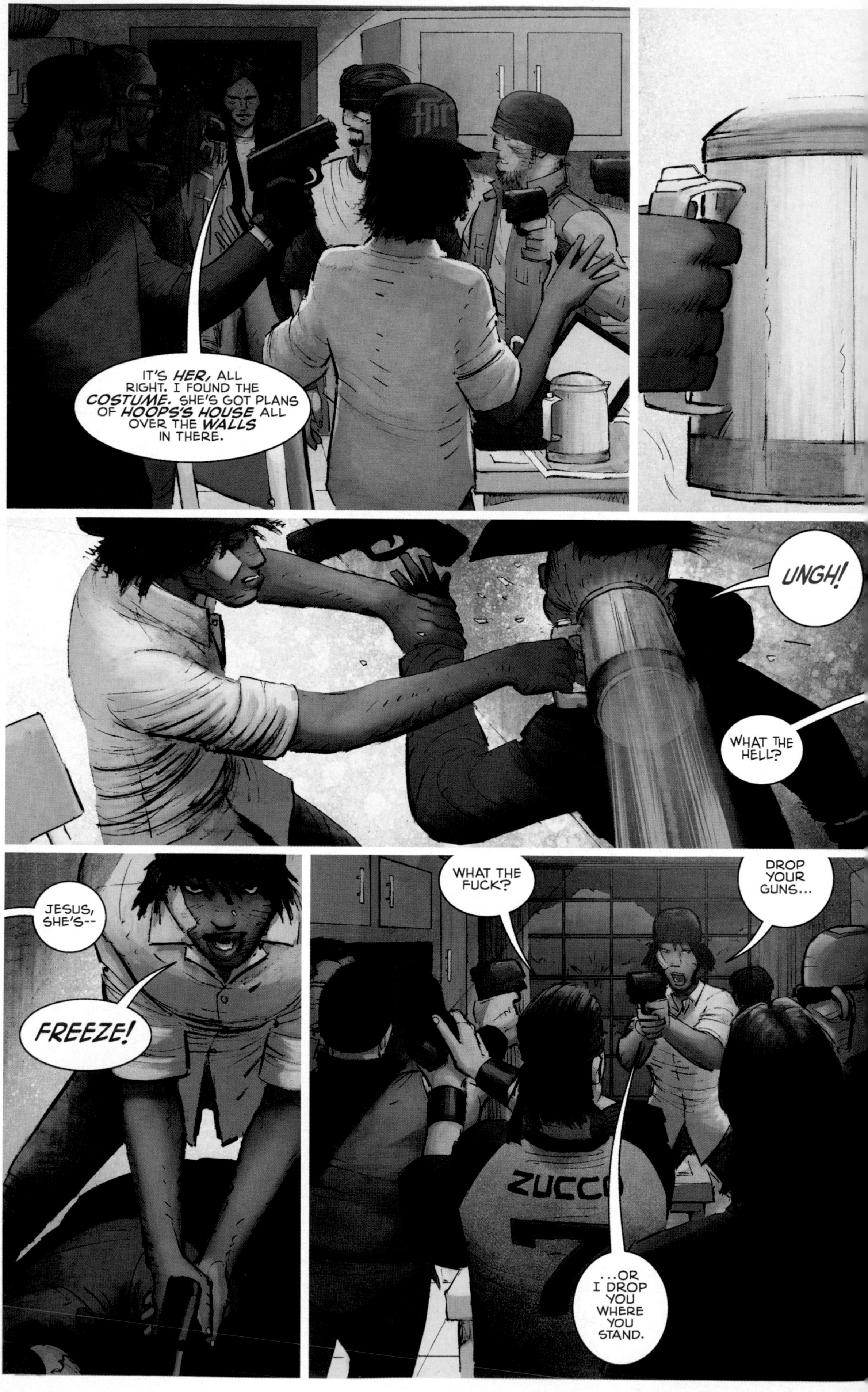
IT'S HER, ALL RIGHT. I FOUND THE COSTUME. SHE'S GOT PLANS OF HOOPS'S HOUSE ALL OVER THE WALLS IN THERE.
UNGH!
WHAT THE HELL?
JESUS, SHE'S--
FREEZE!
WHAT THE FUCK?
DROP YOUR GUNS...
...OR I DROP YOU WHERE YOU STAND.
ZUCCO

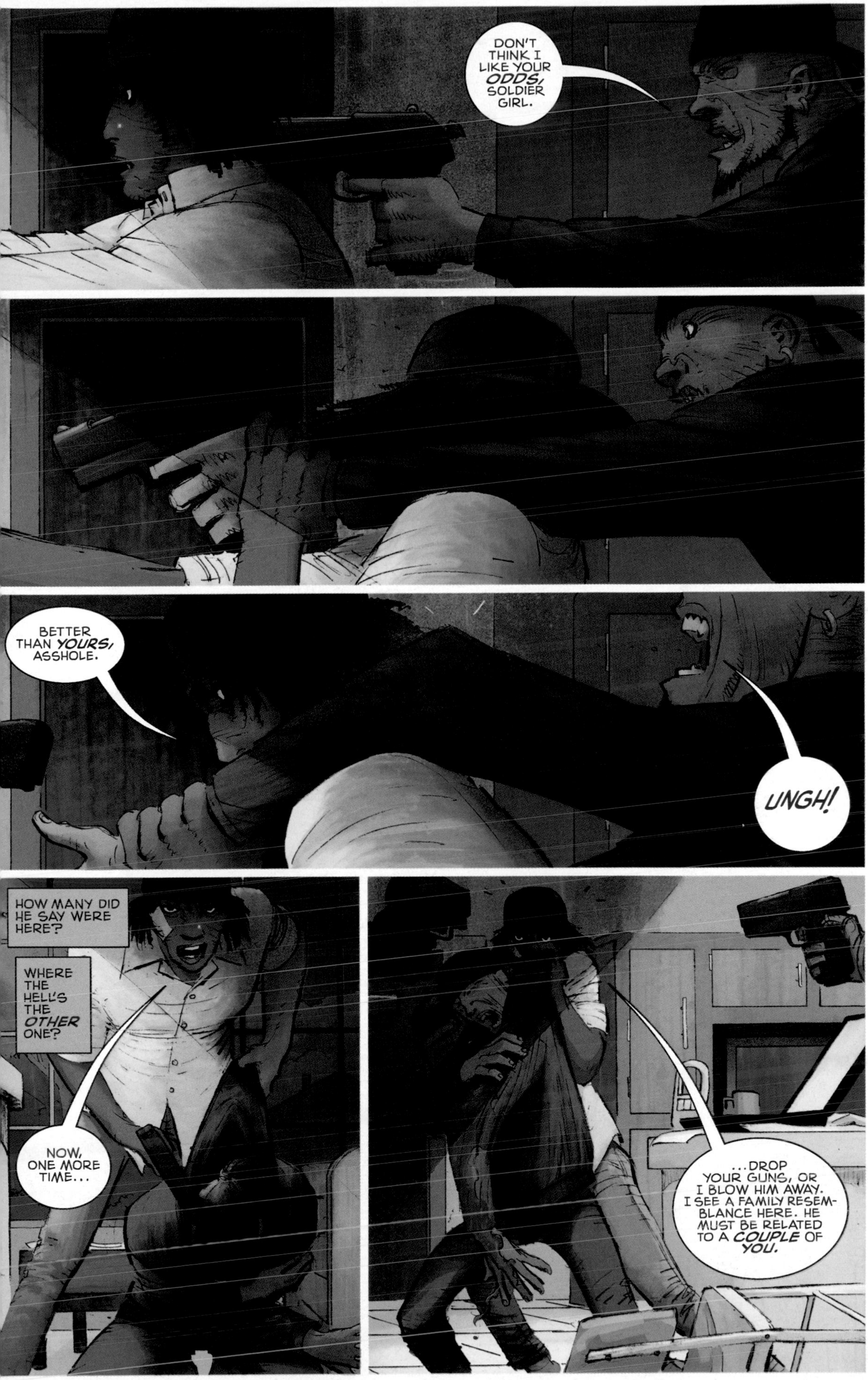
DON'T THINK I LIKE YOUR *ODDS*, SOLDIER GIRL.
BETTER THAN *YOURS*, ASSHOLE.
UNGH!
HOW MANY DID HE SAY WERE HERE?
WHERE THE HELL'S THE *OTHER* ONE?
NOW, ONE MORE TIME...
...DROP YOUR GUNS, OR I BLOW HIM AWAY. I SEE A FAMILY RESEMBLANCE HERE. HE MUST BE RELATED TO A *COUPLE* OF *YOU*.

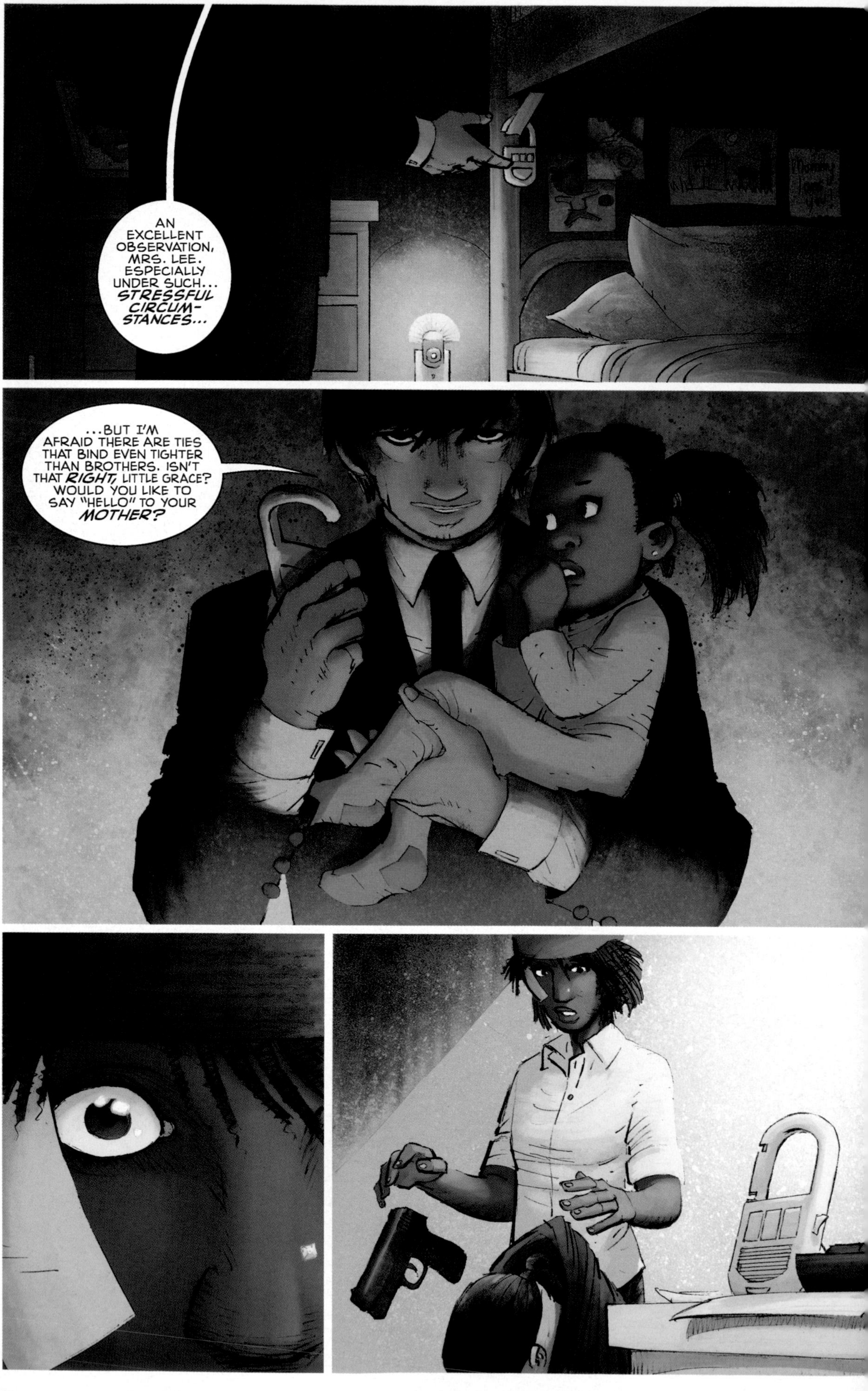
AN EXCELLENT OBSERVATION, MRS. LEE. ESPECIALLY UNDER SUCH... STRESSFUL CIRCUM-STANCES...
...BUT I'M AFRAID THERE ARE TIES THAT BIND EVEN TIGHTER THAN BROTHERS. ISN'T THAT RIGHT, LITTLE GRACE? WOULD YOU LIKE TO SAY "HELLO" TO YOUR MOTHER?

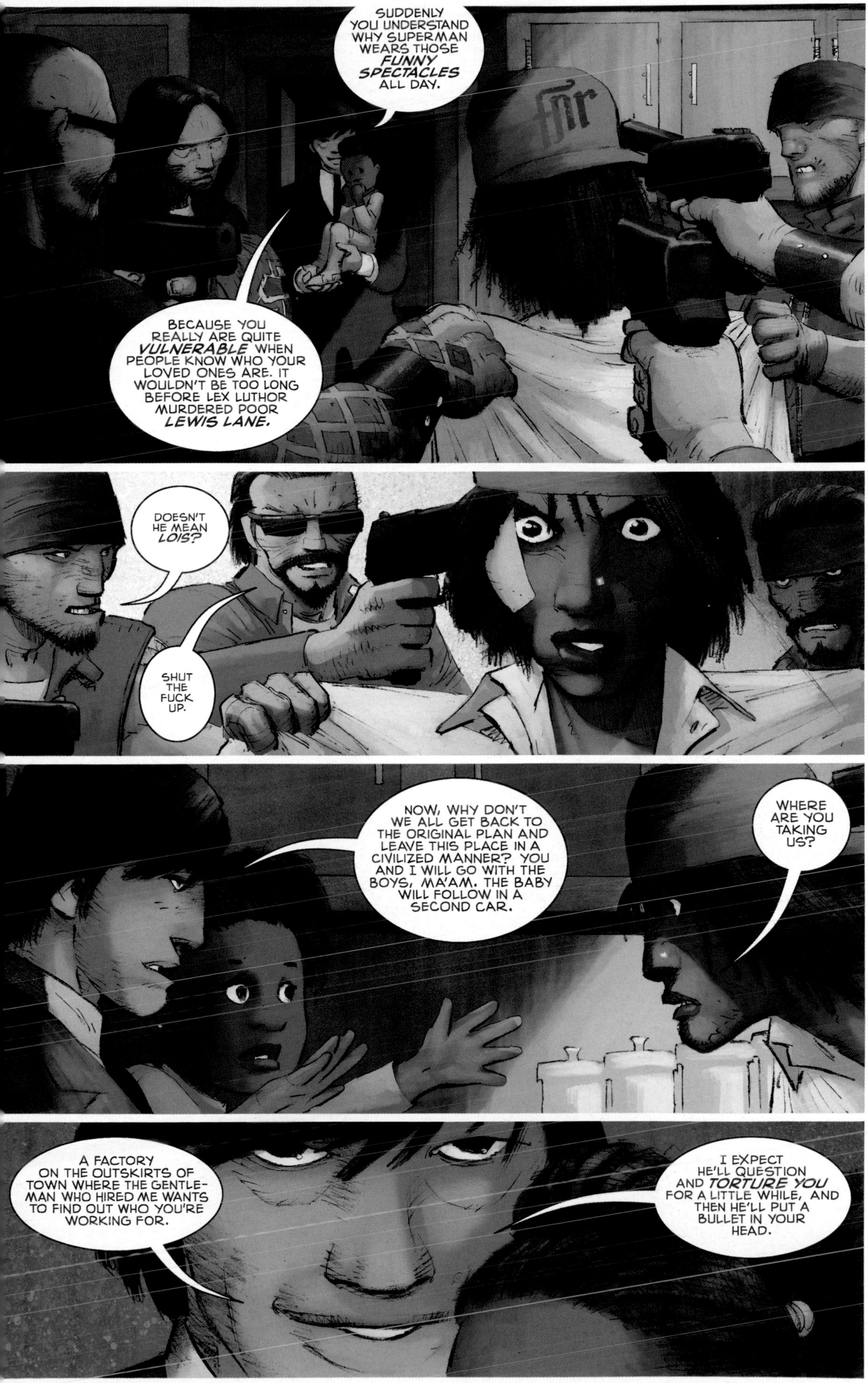
SUDDENLY YOU UNDERSTAND WHY SUPERMAN WEARS THOSE *FUNNY SPECTACLES* ALL DAY.
BECAUSE YOU REALLY ARE QUITE *VULNERABLE* WHEN PEOPLE KNOW WHO YOUR LOVED ONES ARE. IT WOULDN'T BE TOO LONG BEFORE LEX LUTHOR MURDERED POOR *LEWIS LANE.*
DOESN'T HE MEAN *LOIS?*
SHUT THE FUCK UP.
NOW, WHY DON'T WE ALL GET BACK TO THE ORIGINAL PLAN AND LEAVE THIS PLACE IN A CIVILIZED MANNER? YOU AND I WILL GO WITH THE BOYS, MA'AM. THE BABY WILL FOLLOW IN A SECOND CAR.
WHERE ARE YOU TAKING US?
A FACTORY ON THE OUTSKIRTS OF TOWN WHERE THE GENTLEMAN WHO HIRED ME WANTS TO FIND OUT WHO YOU'RE WORKING FOR.
I EXPECT HE'LL QUESTION AND *TORTURE YOU* FOR A LITTLE WHILE, AND THEN HE'LL PUT A BULLET IN YOUR HEAD.

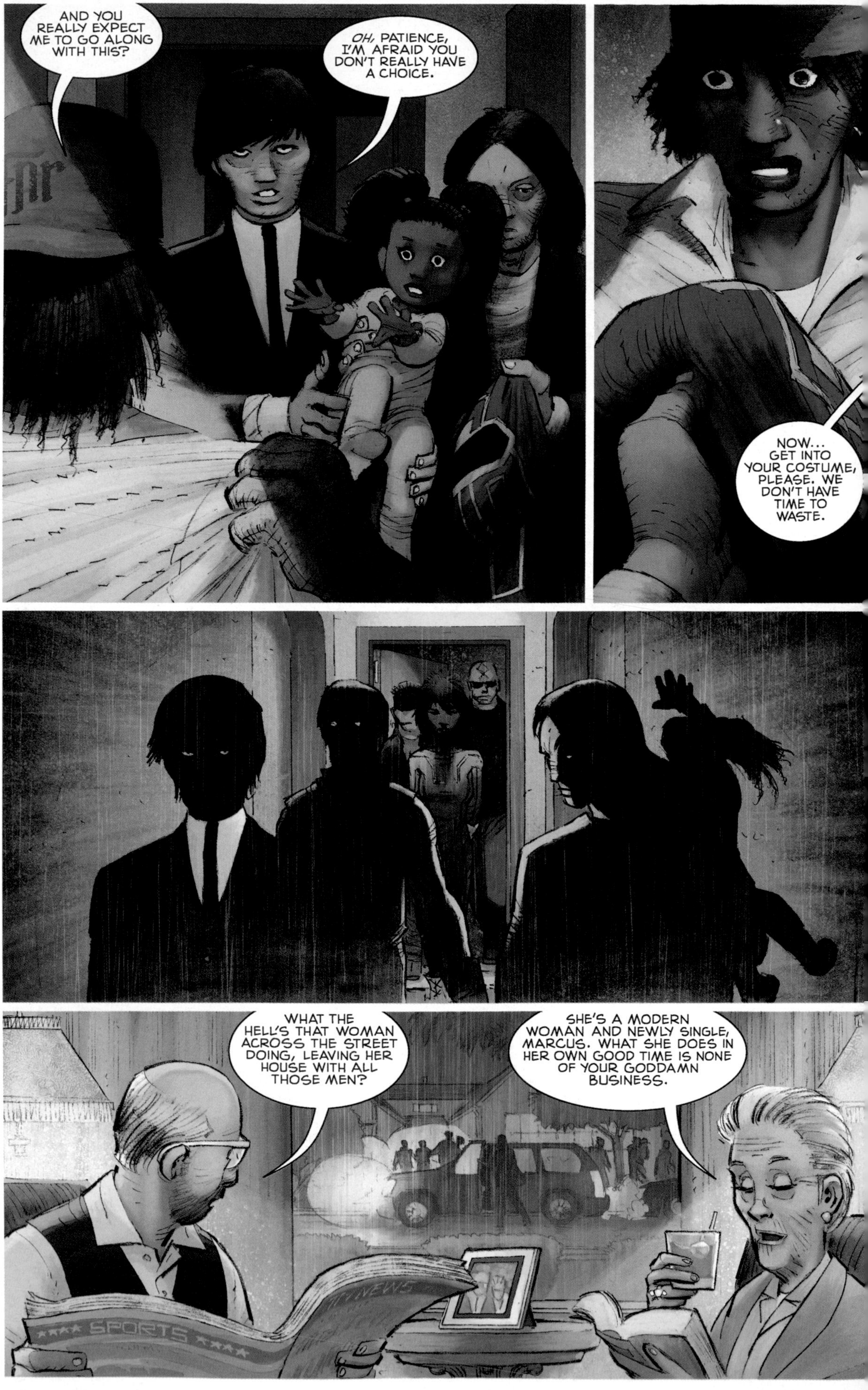
AND YOU REALLY EXPECT ME TO GO ALONG WITH THIS?
OH, PATIENCE, I'M AFRAID YOU DON'T REALLY HAVE A CHOICE.
NOW... GET INTO YOUR COSTUME, PLEASE. WE DON'T HAVE TIME TO WASTE.
WHAT THE HELL'S THAT WOMAN ACROSS THE STREET DOING, LEAVING HER HOUSE WITH ALL THOSE MEN?
SHE'S A MODERN WOMAN AND NEWLY SINGLE, MARCUS. WHAT SHE DOES IN HER OWN GOOD TIME IS NONE OF YOUR GODDAMN BUSINESS.
SPORTS

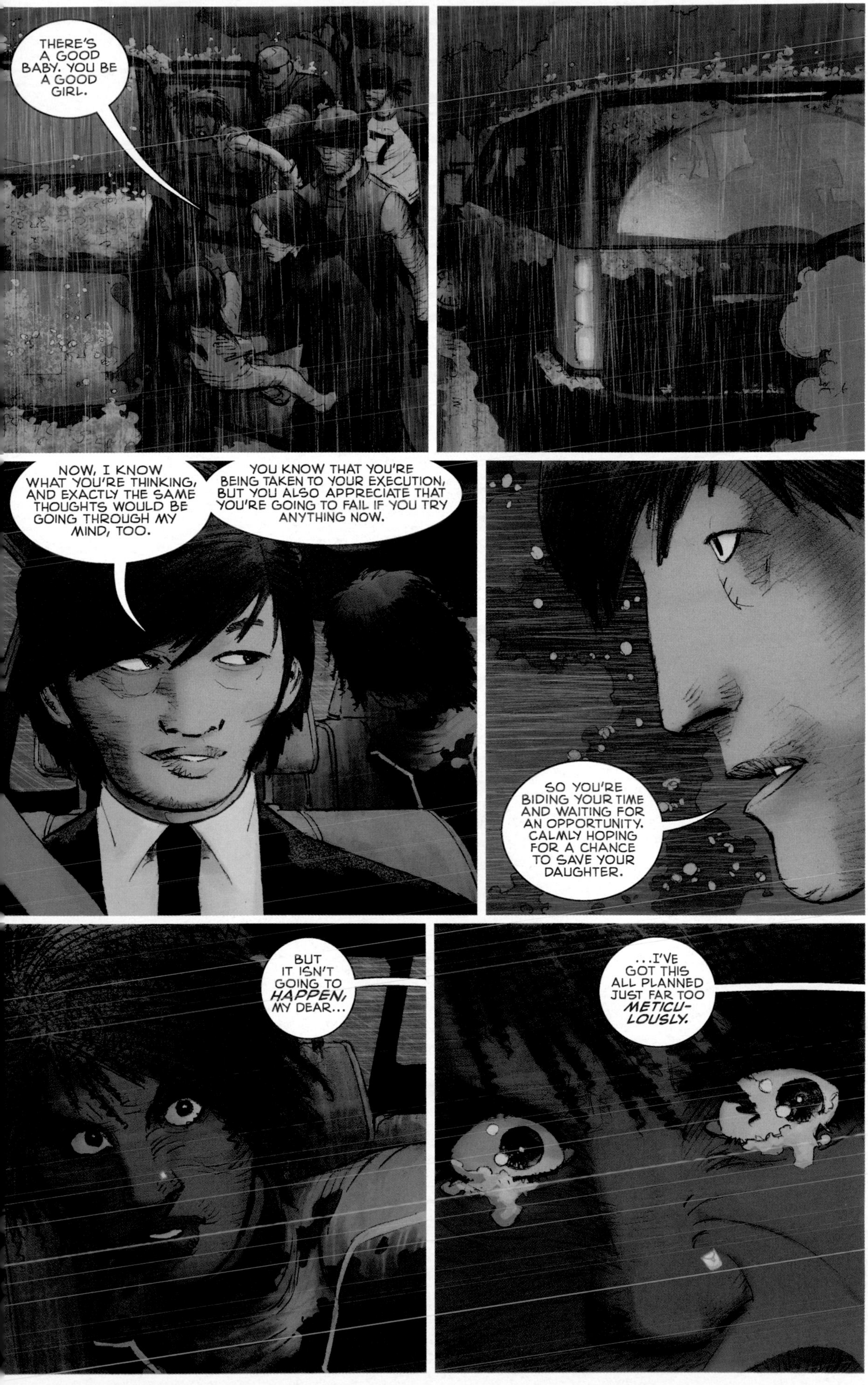
THERE'S A GOOD BABY. YOU BE A GOOD GIRL.
NOW, I KNOW WHAT YOU'RE THINKING, AND EXACTLY THE SAME THOUGHTS WOULD BE GOING THROUGH MY MIND, TOO.
YOU KNOW THAT YOU'RE BEING TAKEN TO YOUR EXECUTION, BUT YOU ALSO APPRECIATE THAT YOU'RE GOING TO FAIL IF YOU TRY ANYTHING NOW.
SO YOU'RE BIDING YOUR TIME AND WAITING FOR AN OPPORTUNITY. CALMLY HOPING FOR A CHANCE TO SAVE YOUR DAUGHTER.
BUT IT ISN'T GOING TO *HAPPEN,* MY DEAR...
...I'VE GOT THIS ALL PLANNED JUST FAR TOO *METICU-LOUSLY.*

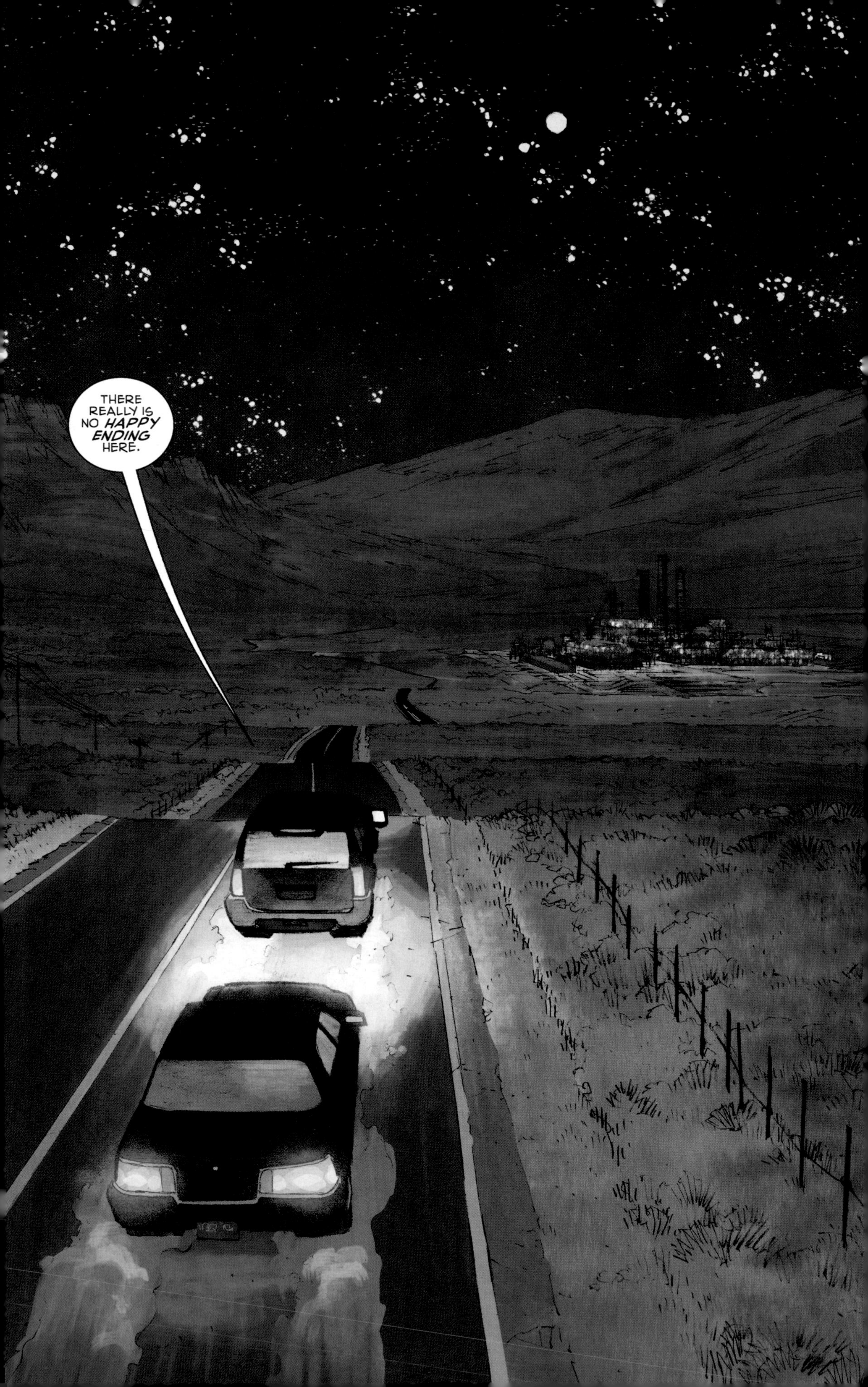
THERE REALLY IS NO *HAPPY ENDING* HERE.

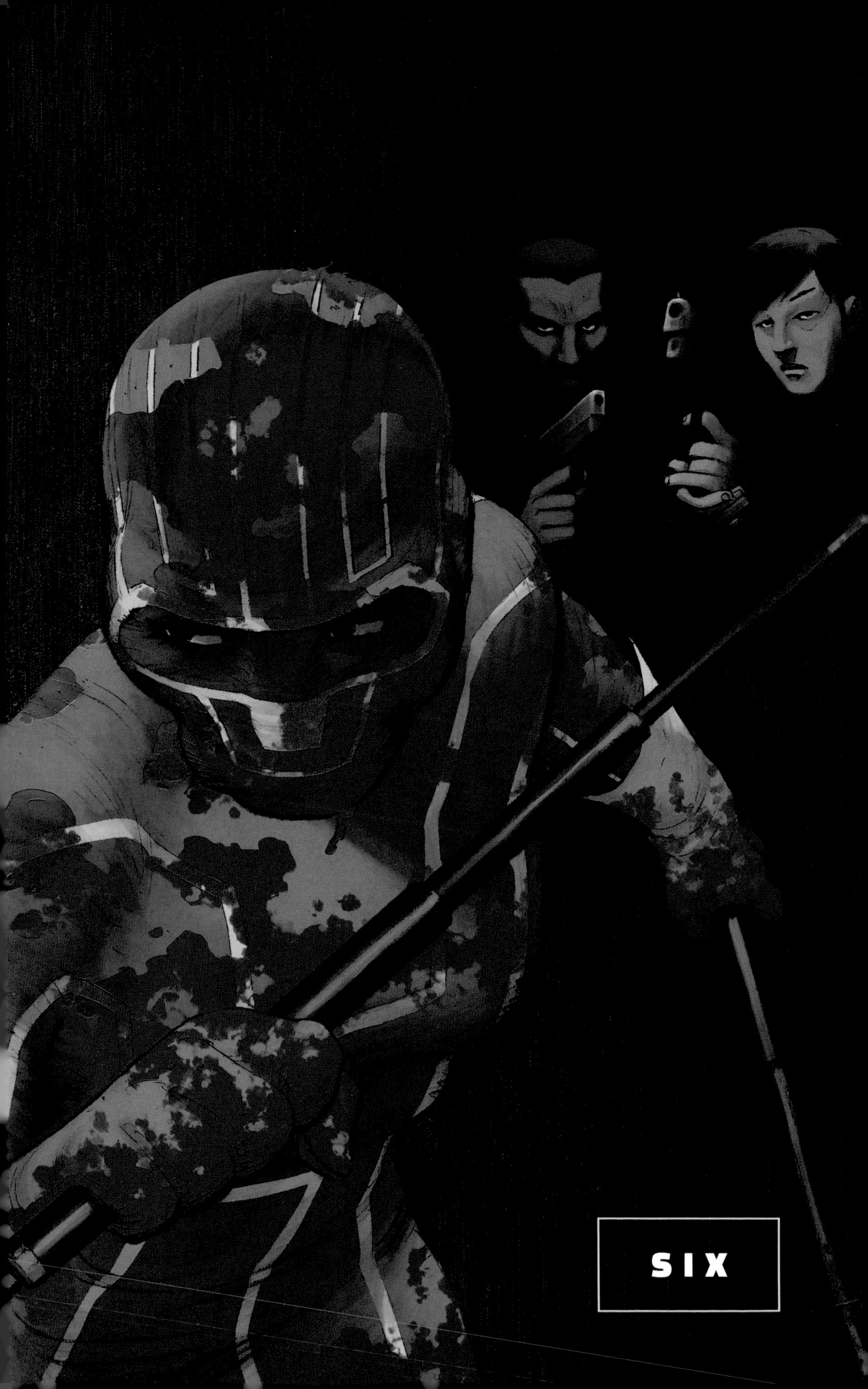
SIX

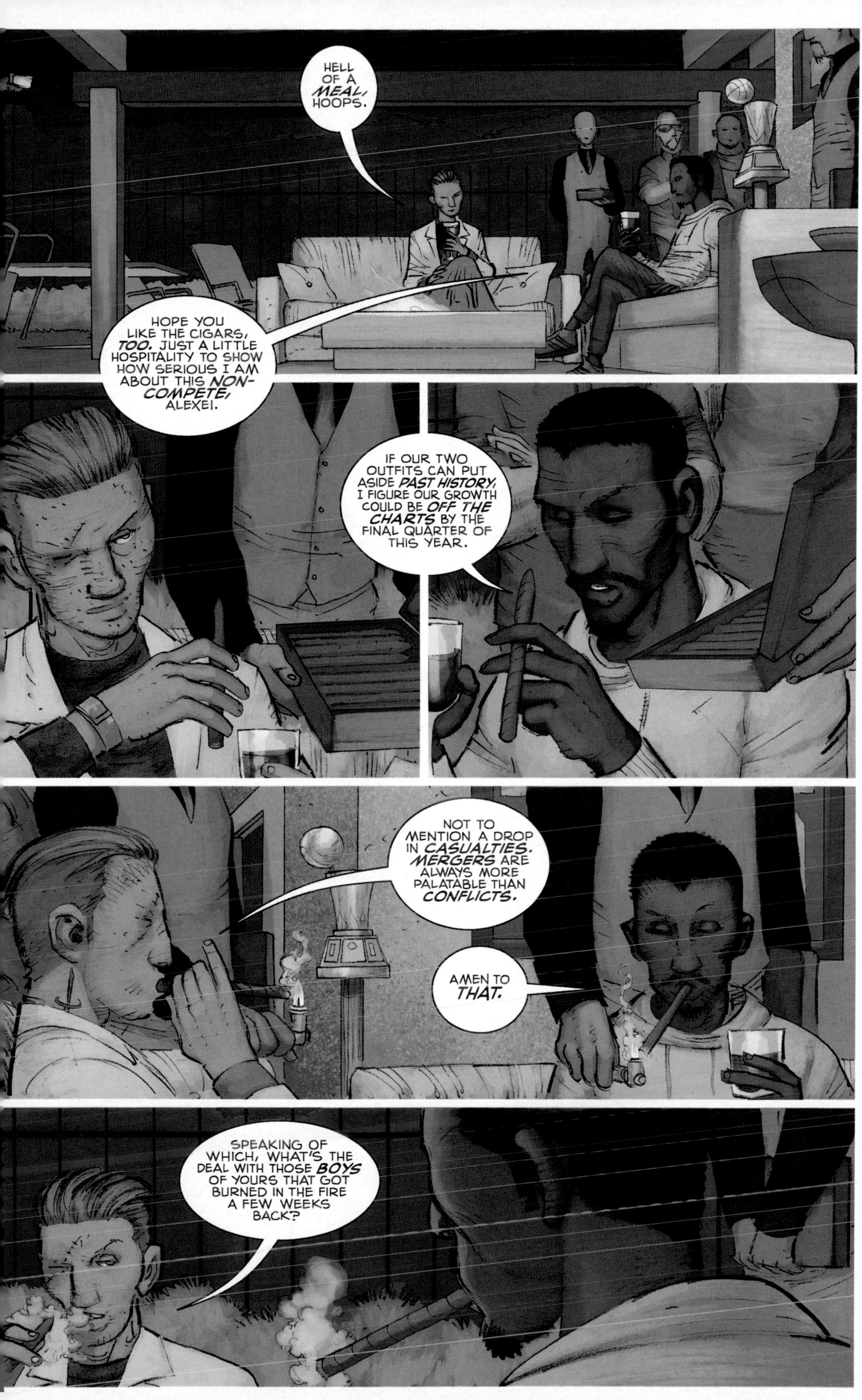
HELL OF A MEAL, HOOPS.
HOPE YOU LIKE THE CIGARS, TOO. JUST A LITTLE HOSPITALITY TO SHOW HOW SERIOUS I AM ABOUT THIS NON-COMPETE, ALEXEI.
IF OUR TWO OUTFITS CAN PUT ASIDE PAST HISTORY, I FIGURE OUR GROWTH COULD BE OFF THE CHARTS BY THE FINAL QUARTER OF THIS YEAR.
NOT TO MENTION A DROP IN CASUALTIES. MERGERS ARE ALWAYS MORE PALATABLE THAN CONFLICTS.
AMEN TO THAT.
SPEAKING OF WHICH, WHAT'S THE DEAL WITH THOSE BOYS OF YOURS THAT GOT BURNED IN THE FIRE A FEW WEEKS BACK?

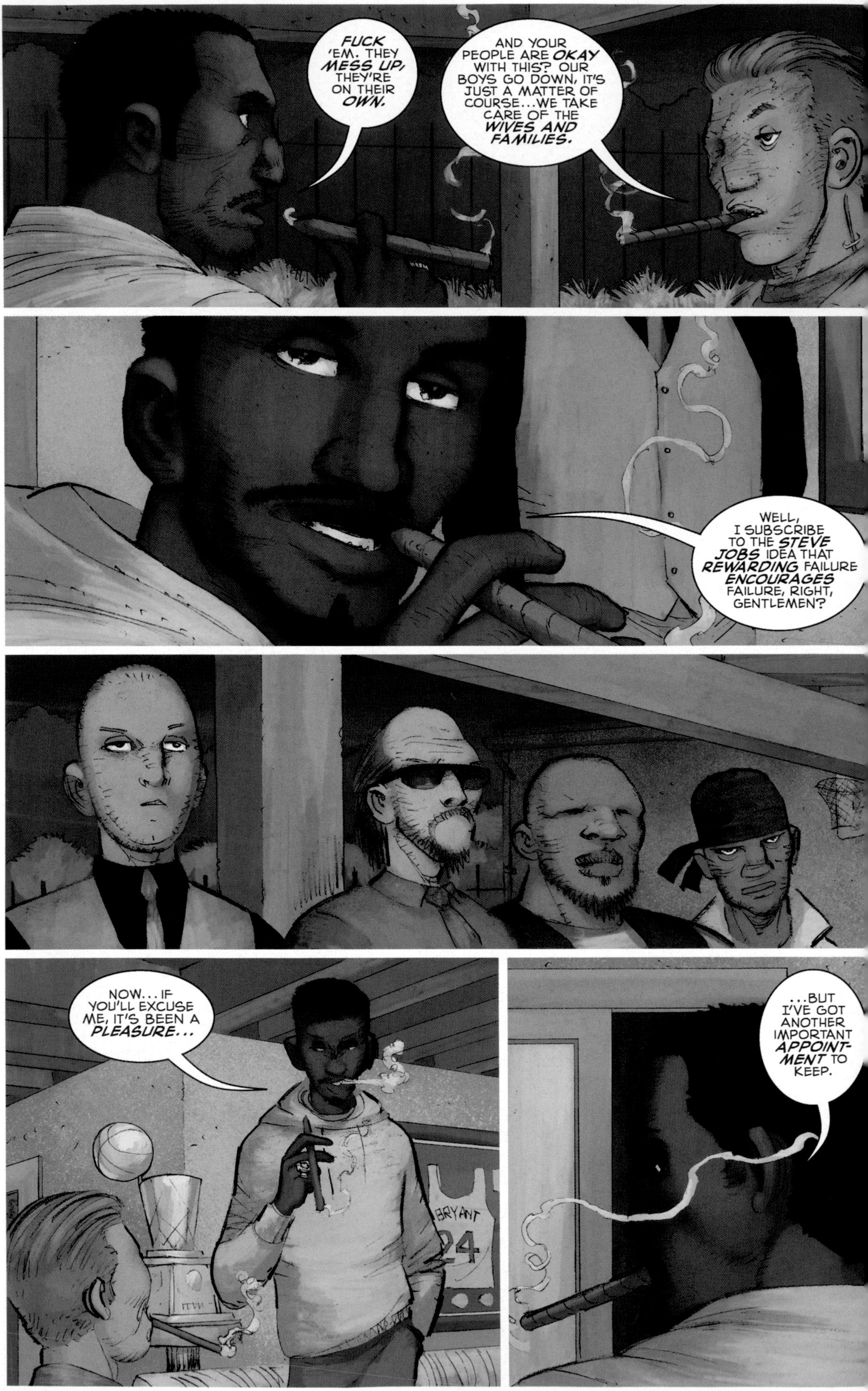
FUCK 'EM. THEY MESS UP, THEY'RE ON THEIR OWN.
AND YOUR PEOPLE ARE OKAY WITH THIS? OUR BOYS GO DOWN, IT'S JUST A MATTER OF COURSE...WE TAKE CARE OF THE WIVES AND FAMILIES.
WELL, I SUBSCRIBE TO THE STEVE JOBS IDEA THAT REWARDING FAILURE ENCOURAGES FAILURE, RIGHT, GENTLEMEN?
NOW... IF YOU'LL EXCUSE ME, IT'S BEEN A PLEASURE...
BRYANT
24
...BUT I'VE GOT ANOTHER IMPORTANT APPOINTMENT TO KEEP.

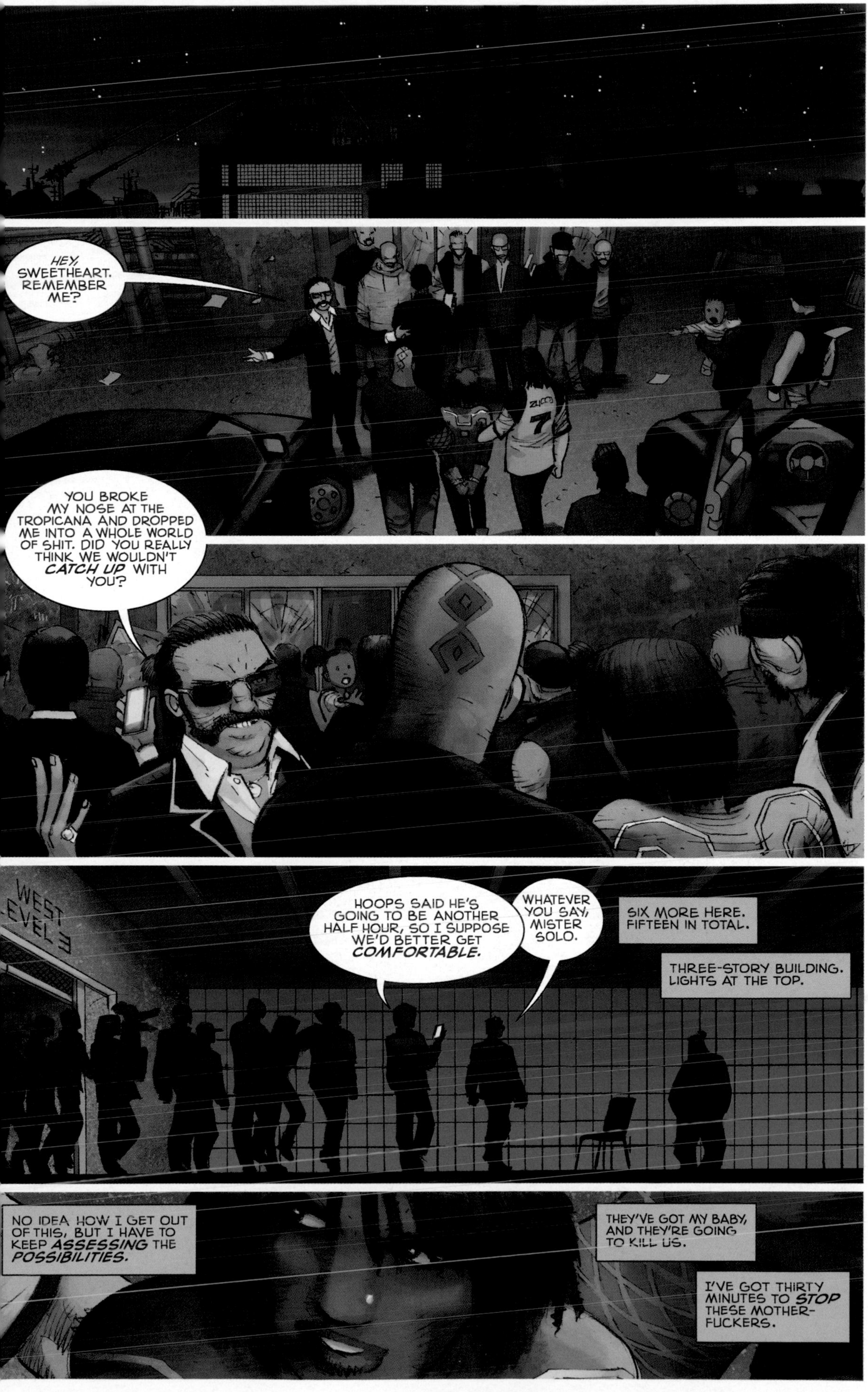
HEY, SWEETHEART. REMEMBER ME?
YOU BROKE MY NOSE AT THE TROPICANA AND DROPPED ME INTO A WHOLE WORLD OF SHIT. DID YOU REALLY THINK WE WOULDN'T CATCH UP WITH YOU?
WEST LEVEL 3
HOOPS SAID HE'S GOING TO BE ANOTHER HALF HOUR, SO I SUPPOSE WE'D BETTER GET COMFORTABLE.
WHATEVER YOU SAY, MISTER SOLO.
SIX MORE HERE. FIFTEEN IN TOTAL.
THREE-STORY BUILDING. LIGHTS AT THE TOP.
NO IDEA HOW I GET OUT OF THIS, BUT I HAVE TO KEEP ASSESSING THE POSSIBILITIES.
THEY'VE GOT MY BABY, AND THEY'RE GOING TO KILL US.
I'VE GOT THIRTY MINUTES TO STOP THESE MOTHER-FUCKERS.

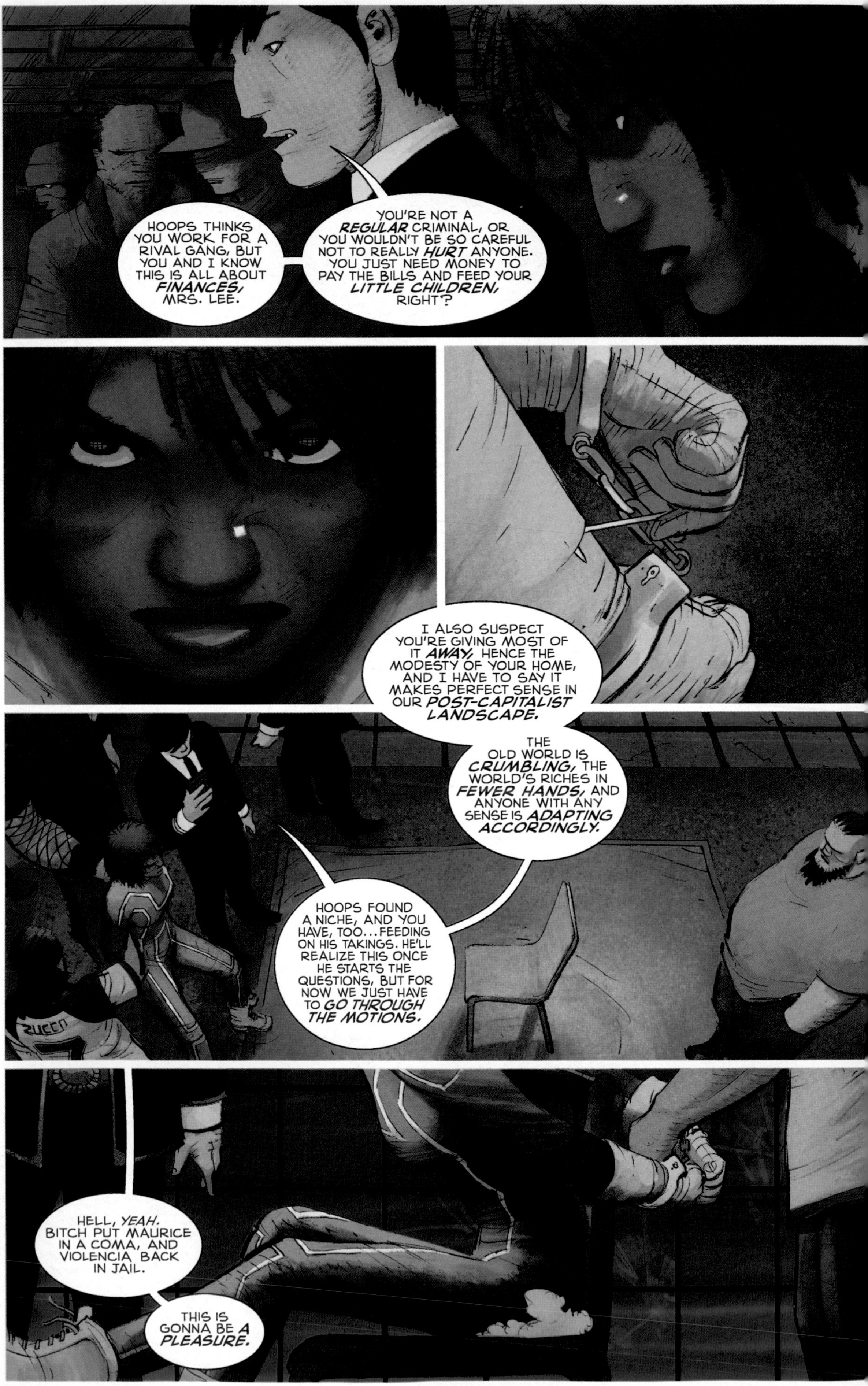
HOOPS THINKS YOU WORK FOR A RIVAL GANG, BUT YOU AND I KNOW THIS IS ALL ABOUT FINANCES, MRS. LEE.
YOU'RE NOT A REGULAR CRIMINAL, OR YOU WOULDN'T BE SO CAREFUL NOT TO REALLY HURT ANYONE. YOU JUST NEED MONEY TO PAY THE BILLS AND FEED YOUR LITTLE CHILDREN, RIGHT?
I ALSO SUSPECT YOU'RE GIVING MOST OF IT AWAY, HENCE THE MODESTY OF YOUR HOME, AND I HAVE TO SAY IT MAKES PERFECT SENSE IN OUR POST-CAPITALIST LANDSCAPE.
THE OLD WORLD IS CRUMBLING, THE WORLD'S RICHES IN FEWER HANDS, AND ANYONE WITH ANY SENSE IS ADAPTING ACCORDINGLY.
HOOPS FOUND A NICHE, AND YOU HAVE, TOO...FEEDING ON HIS TAKINGS. HE'LL REALIZE THIS ONCE HE STARTS THE QUESTIONS, BUT FOR NOW WE JUST HAVE TO GO THROUGH THE MOTIONS.
HELL, YEAH. BITCH PUT MAURICE IN A COMA, AND VIOLENCIA BACK IN JAIL.
THIS IS GONNA BE A PLEASURE.

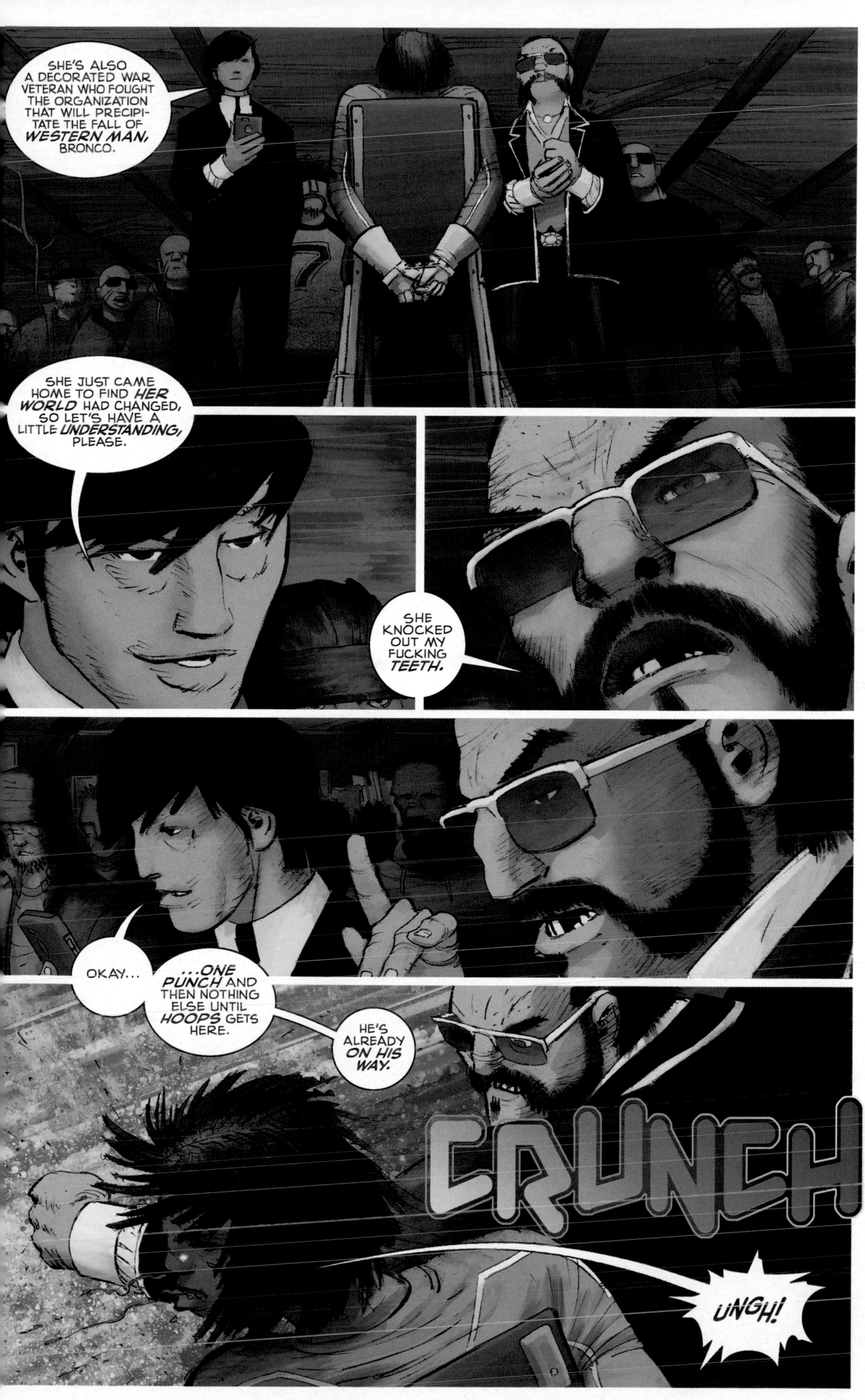
SHE'S ALSO A DECORATED WAR VETERAN WHO FOUGHT THE ORGANIZATION THAT WILL PRECIPITATE THE FALL OF WESTERN MAN, BRONCO.
SHE JUST CAME HOME TO FIND HER WORLD HAD CHANGED, SO LET'S HAVE A LITTLE UNDERSTANDING, PLEASE.
SHE KNOCKED OUT MY FUCKING TEETH.
OKAY...
...ONE PUNCH AND THEN NOTHING ELSE UNTIL HOOPS GETS HERE.
HE'S ALREADY ON HIS WAY.
CRUNCH
UNGH!

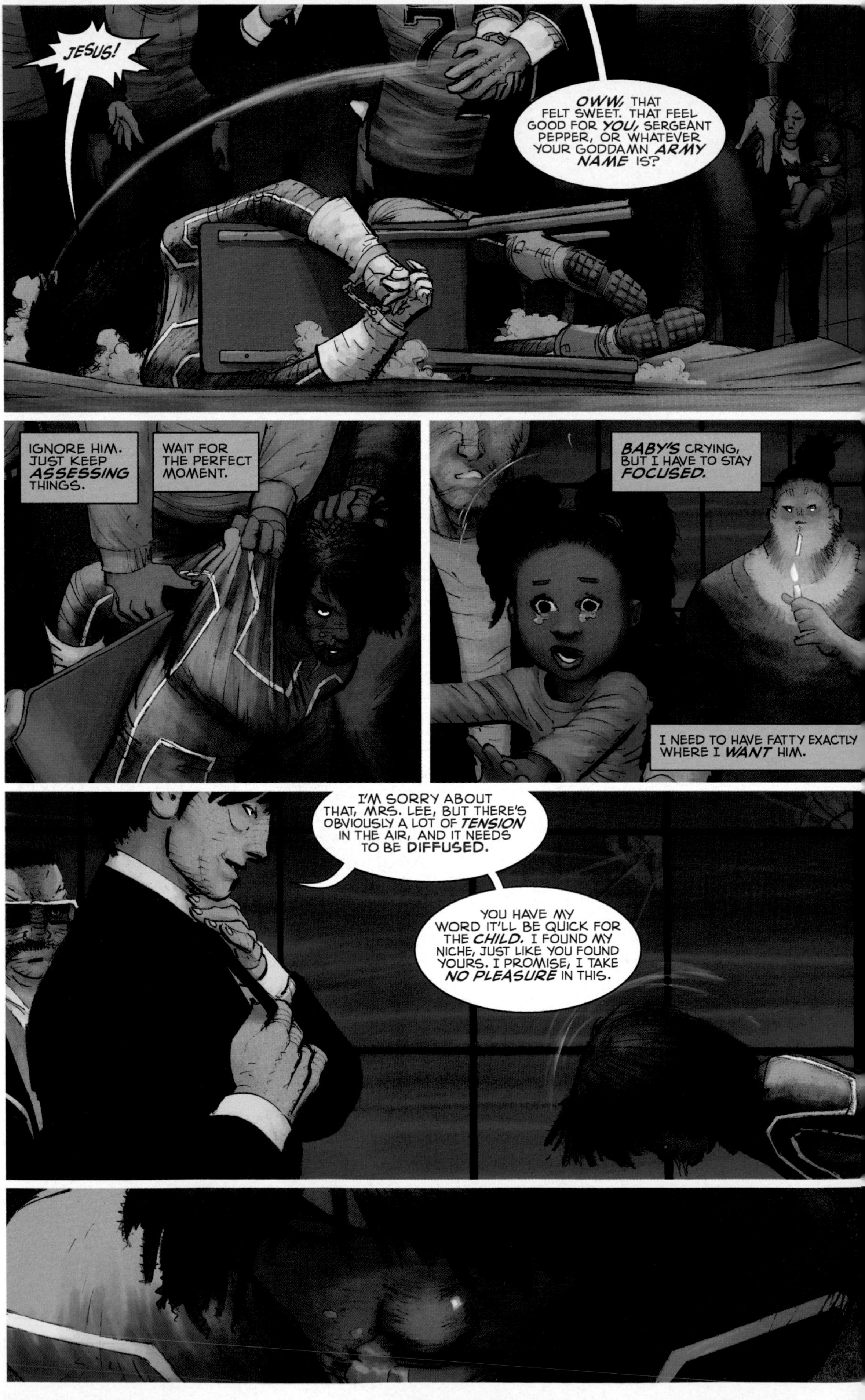
JESUS!
OWW, THAT FELT SWEET. THAT FEEL GOOD FOR YOU, SERGEANT PEPPER, OR WHATEVER YOUR GODDAMN ARMY NAME IS?
IGNORE HIM. JUST KEEP ASSESSING THINGS.
WAIT FOR THE PERFECT MOMENT.
BABY'S CRYING, BUT I HAVE TO STAY FOCUSED.
I NEED TO HAVE FATTY EXACTLY WHERE I WANT HIM.
I'M SORRY ABOUT THAT, MRS. LEE, BUT THERE'S OBVIOUSLY A LOT OF TENSION IN THE AIR, AND IT NEEDS TO BE DIFFUSED.
YOU HAVE MY WORD IT'LL BE QUICK FOR THE CHILD. I FOUND MY NICHE, JUST LIKE YOU FOUND YOURS. I PROMISE, I TAKE NO PLEASURE IN THIS.

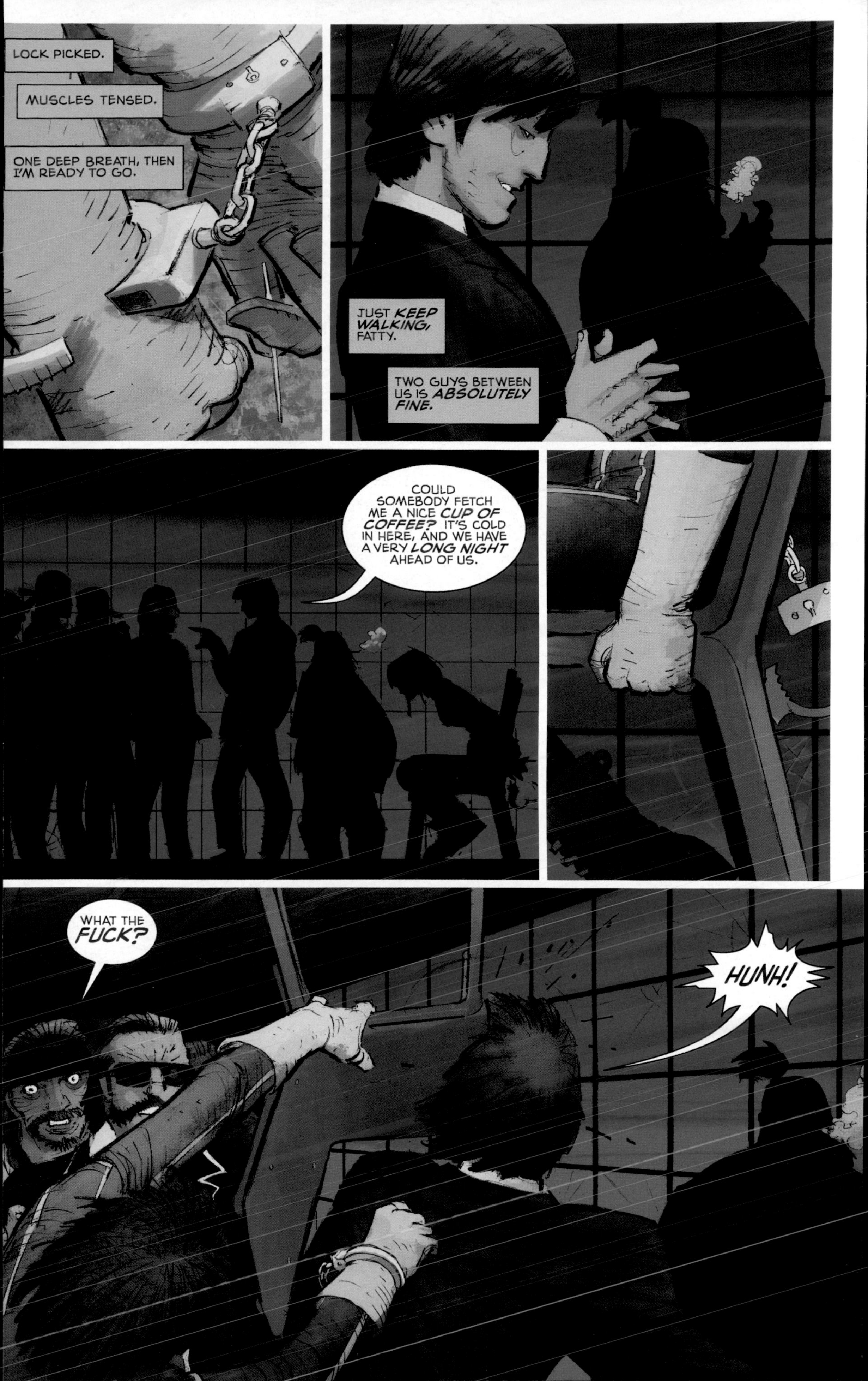
LOCK PICKED.
MUSCLES TENSED.
ONE DEEP BREATH, THEN I'M READY TO GO.
JUST KEEP WALKING, FATTY.
TWO GUYS BETWEEN US IS ABSOLUTELY FINE.
COULD SOMEBODY FETCH ME A NICE CUP OF COFFEE? IT'S COLD IN HERE, AND WE HAVE A VERY LONG NIGHT AHEAD OF US.
WHAT THE FUCK?
HUNH!

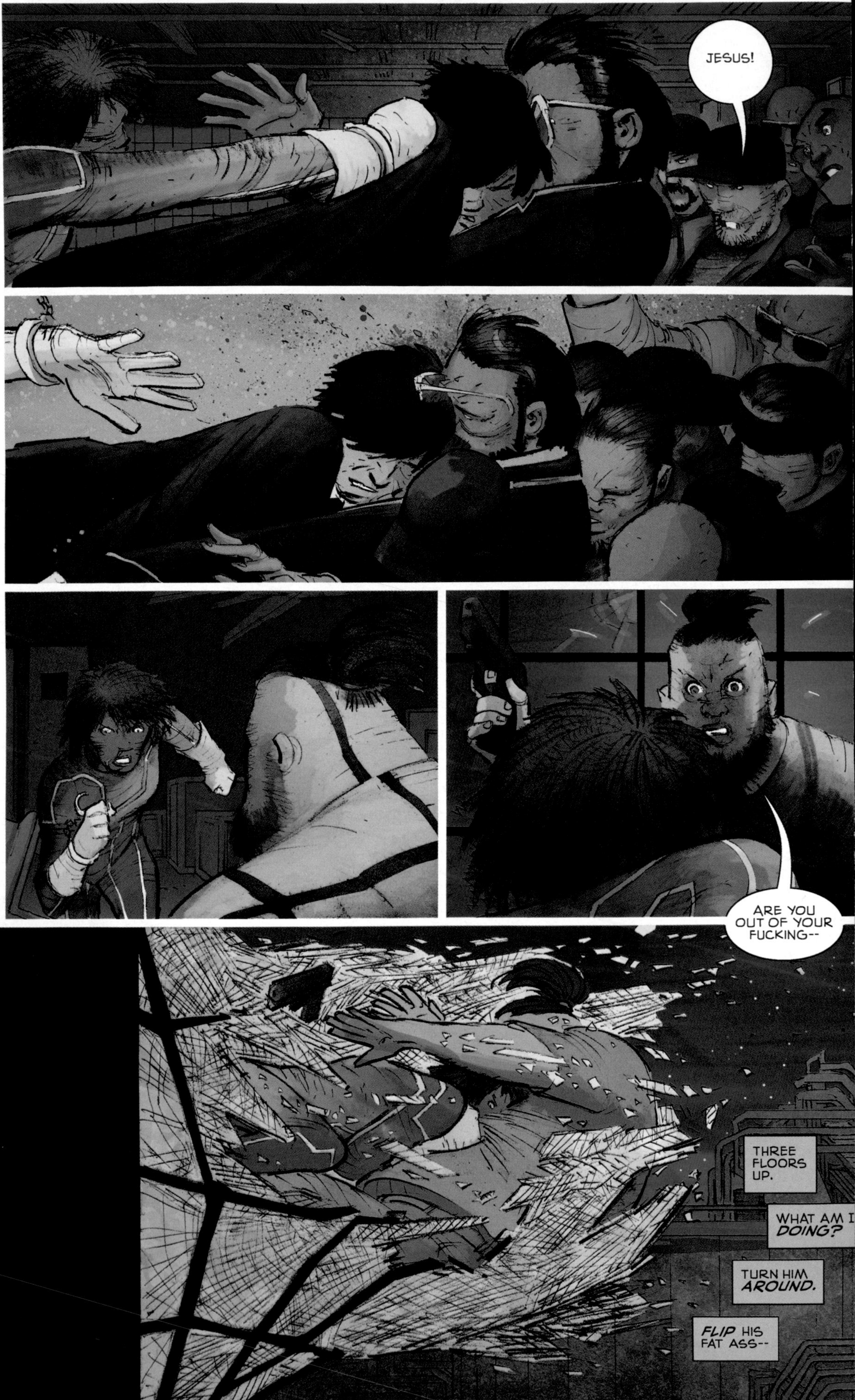
JESUS!
ARE YOU OUT OF YOUR FUCKING--
THREE FLOORS UP.
WHAT AM I *DOING?*
TURN HIM *AROUND.*
FLIP HIS FAT ASS--

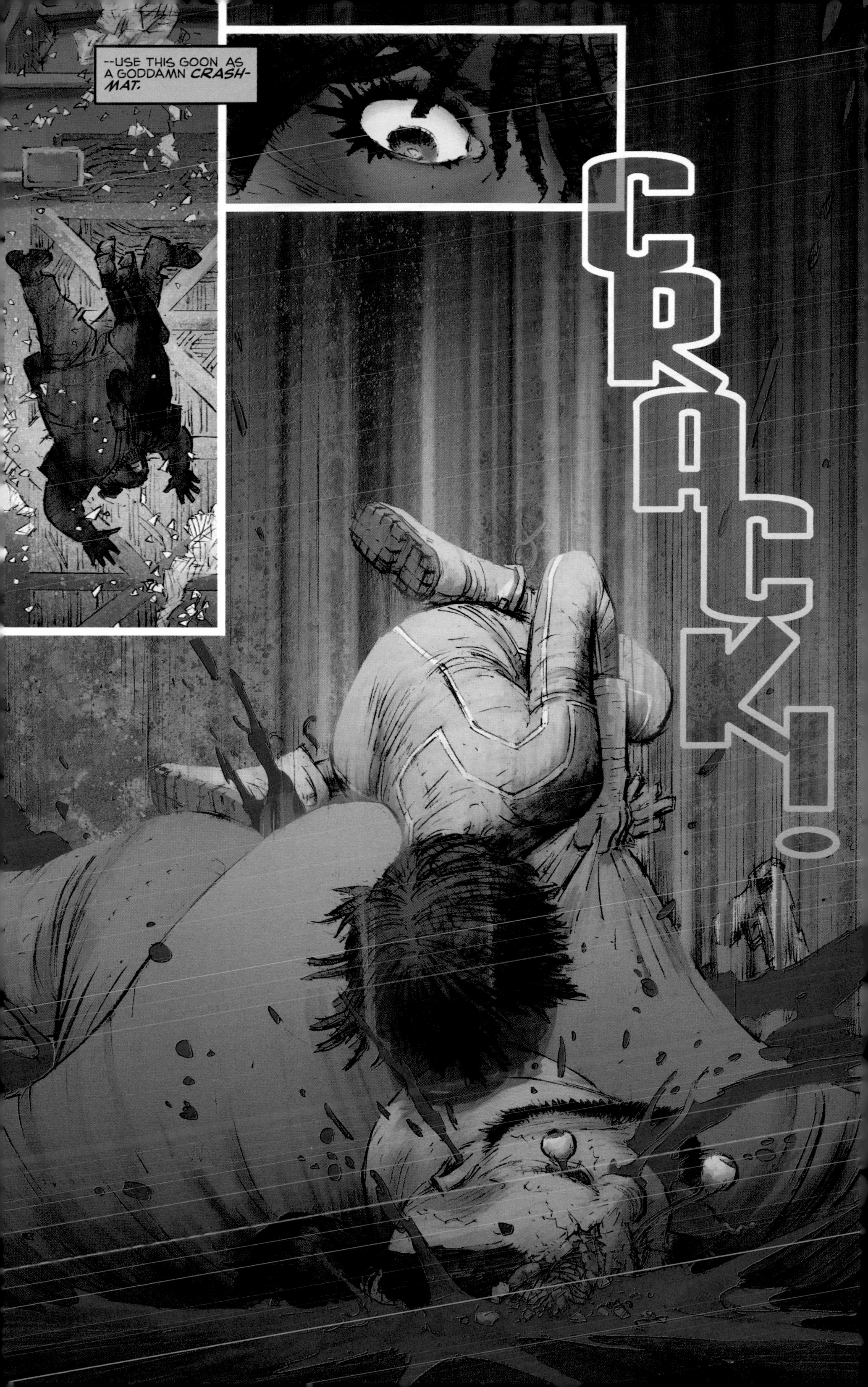
--USE THIS GOON AS A GODDAMN CRASH-MAT.
CRACK!

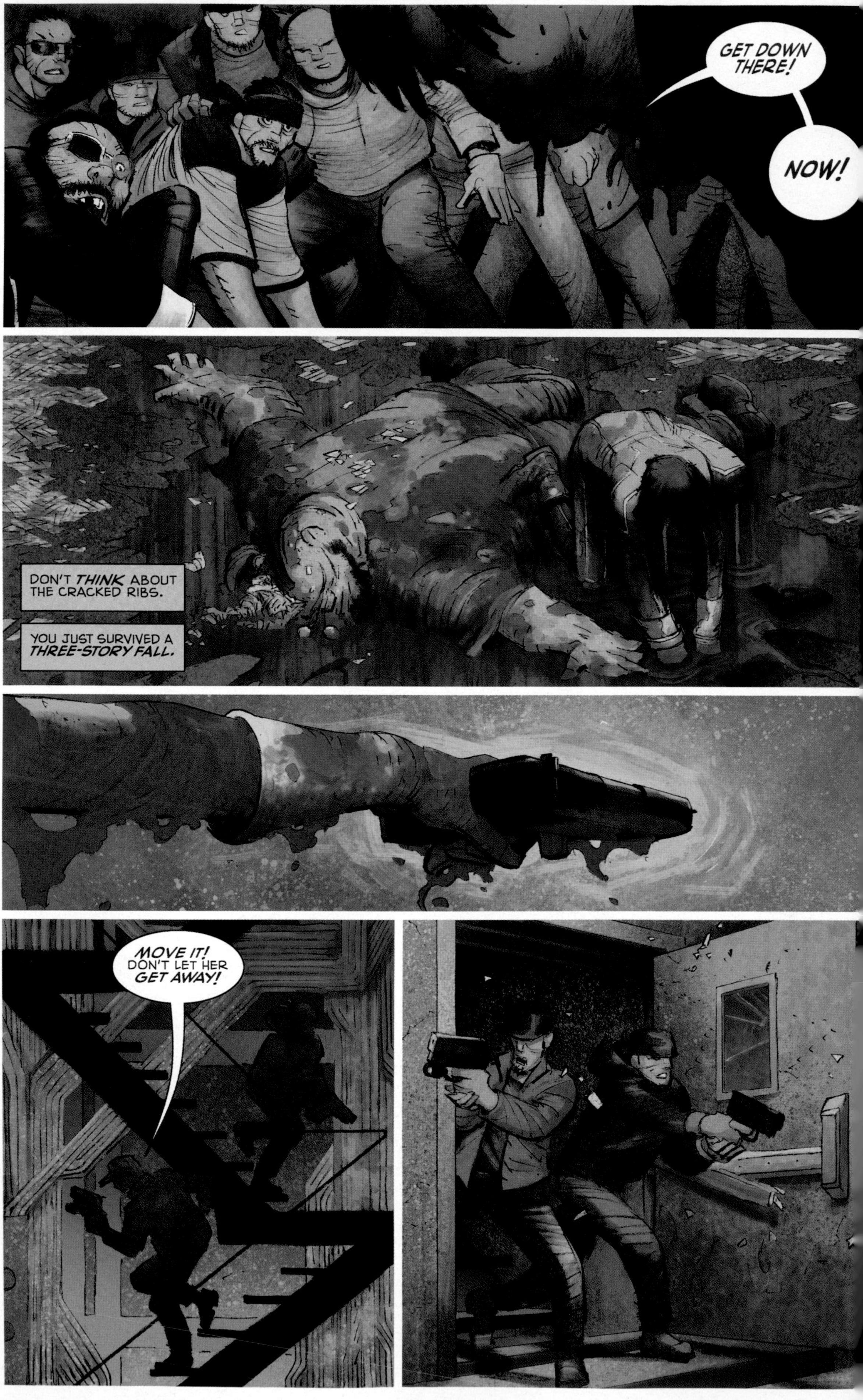
GET DOWN THERE!
NOW!
DON'T THINK ABOUT THE CRACKED RIBS.
YOU JUST SURVIVED A THREE-STORY FALL.
MOVE IT! DON'T LET HER GET AWAY!

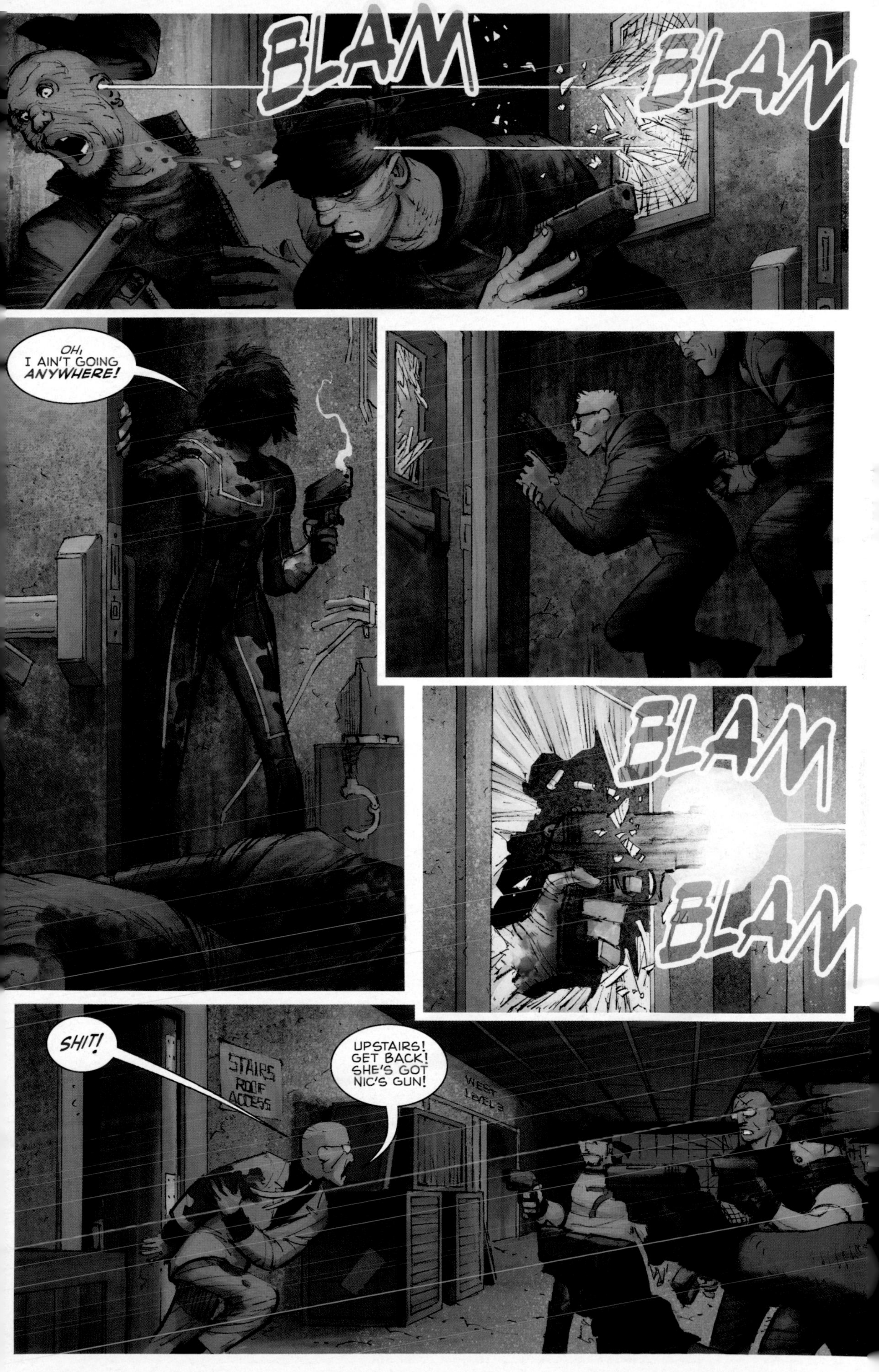
BLAM
BLAM
OH, I AIN'T GOING ANYWHERE!
BLAM
BLAM
SHIT!
UPSTAIRS! GET BACK! SHE'S GOT NIC'S GUN!
STAIRS ROOF ACCESS
WEST LEVEL 3

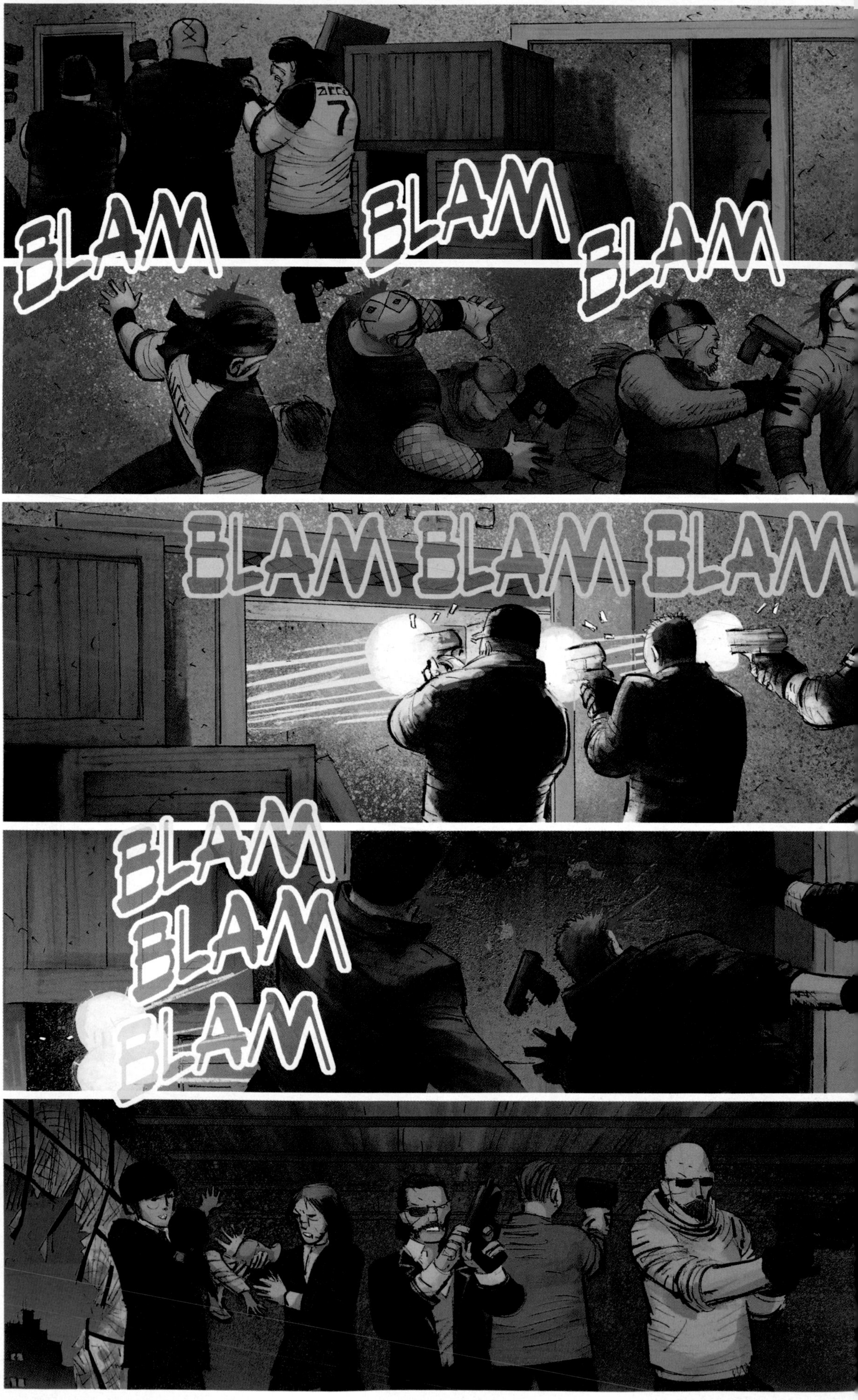
BLAM
BLAM
BLAM
BLAM BLAM BLAM
BLAM
BLAM
BLAM

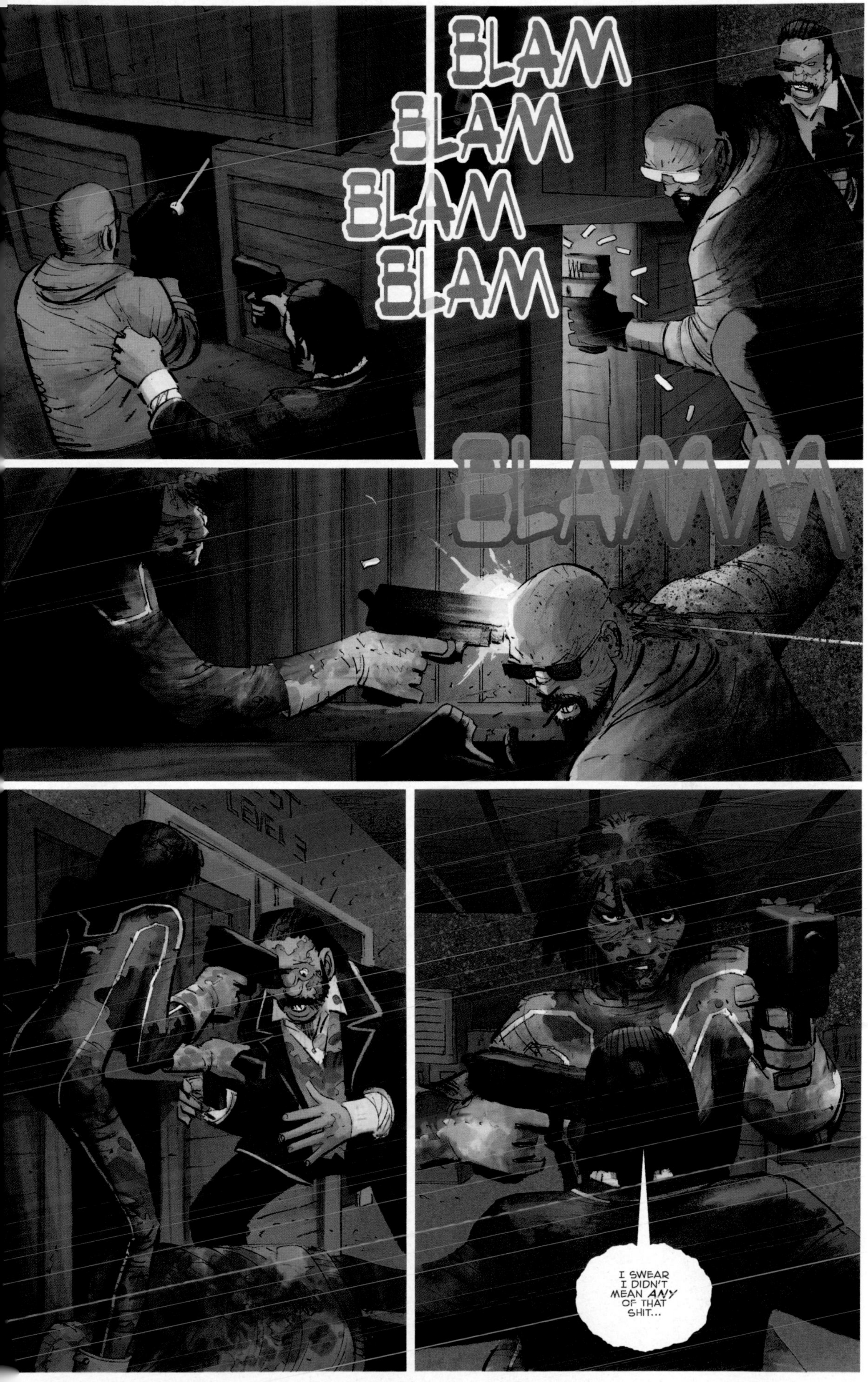
BLAM
BLAM
BLAM
BLAM
BLAMM
I SWEAR I DIDN'T MEAN *ANY* OF THAT SHIT...

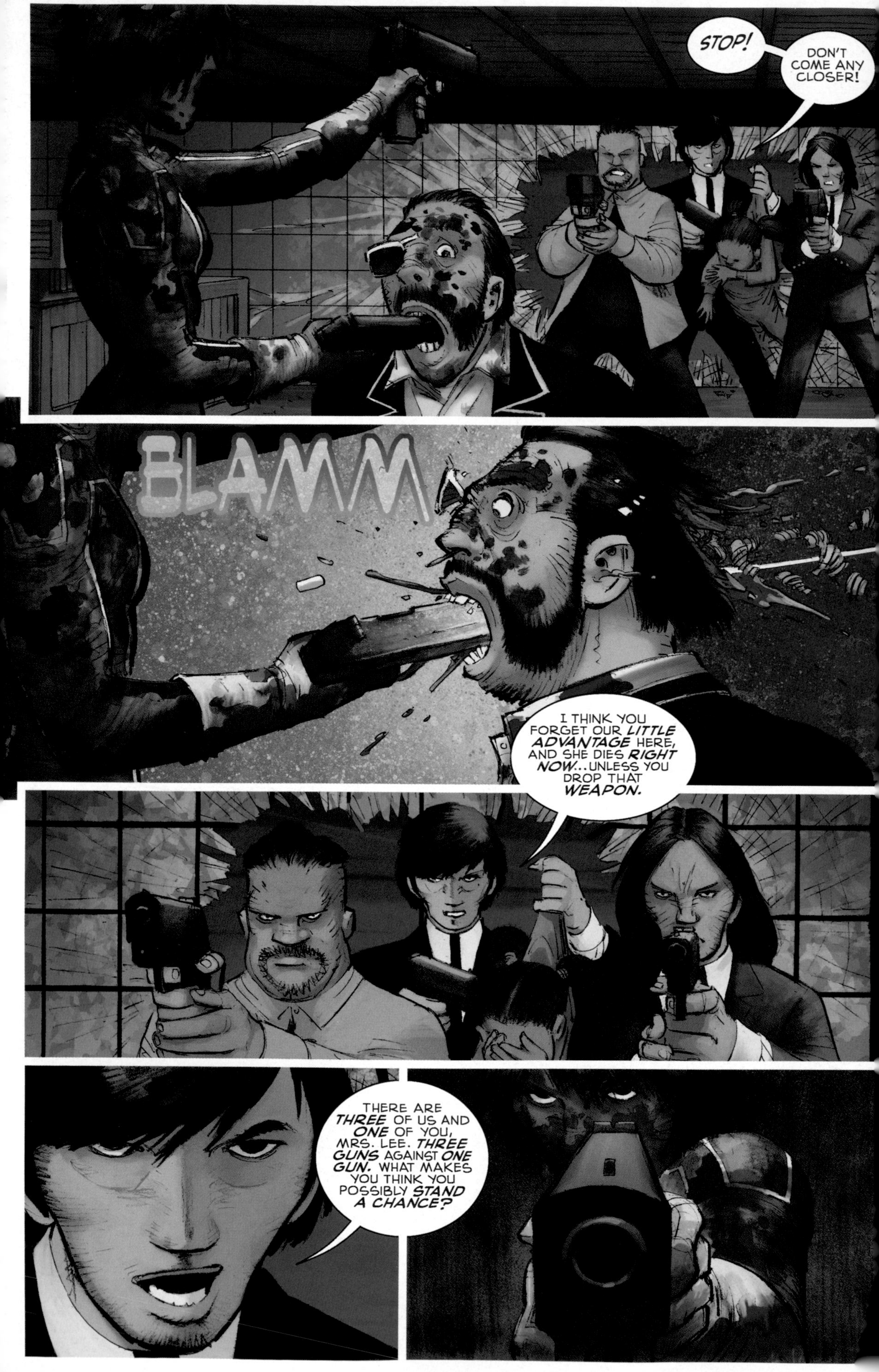
STOP!
DON'T COME ANY CLOSER!
BLAMM
I THINK YOU FORGET OUR LITTLE ADVANTAGE HERE, AND SHE DIES RIGHT NOW...UNLESS YOU DROP THAT WEAPON.
THERE ARE THREE OF US AND ONE OF YOU, MRS. LEE. THREE GUNS AGAINST ONE GUN. WHAT MAKES YOU THINK YOU POSSIBLY STAND A CHANCE?

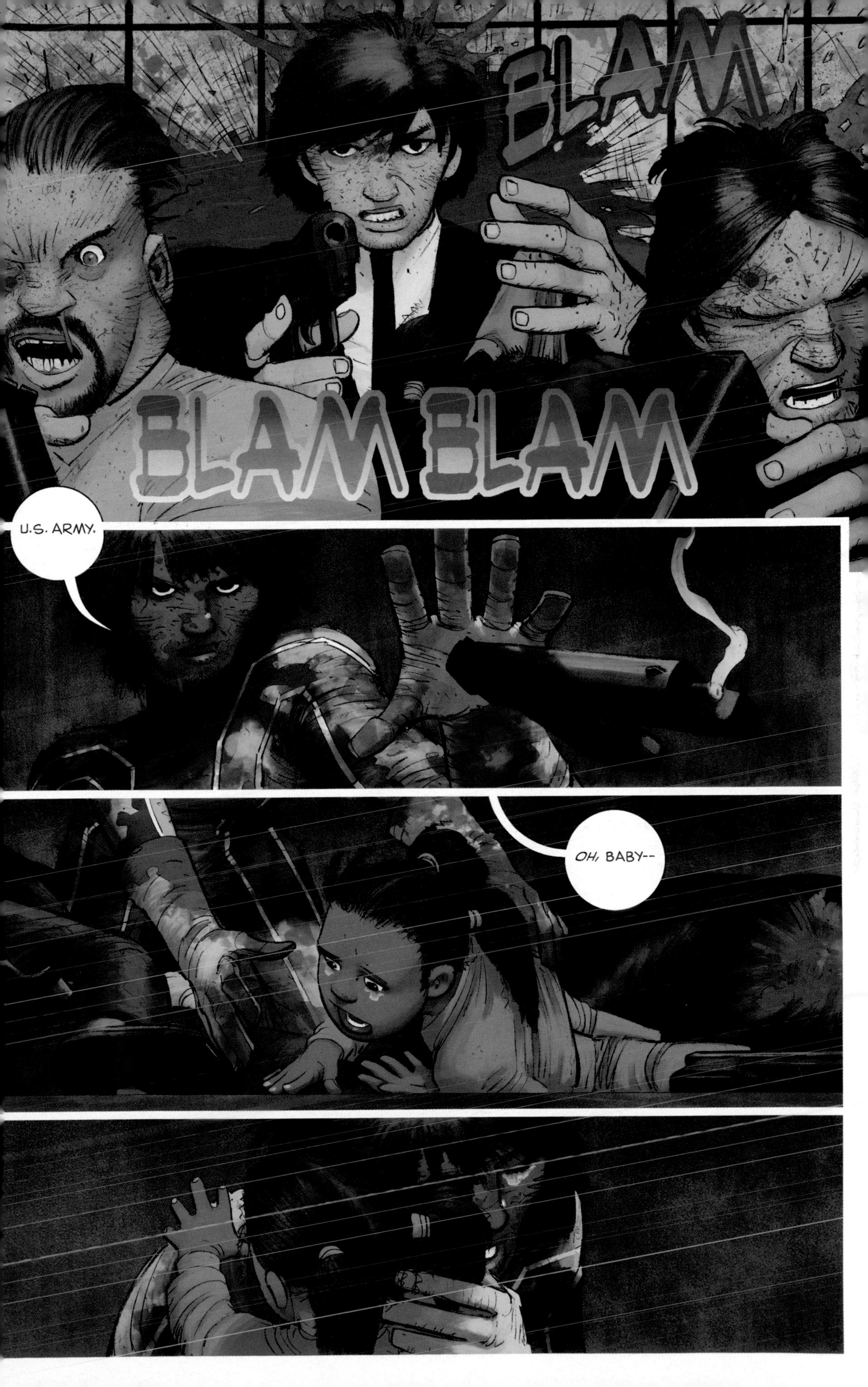
BLAM
BLAM BLAM
U.S. ARMY.
OH, BABY--

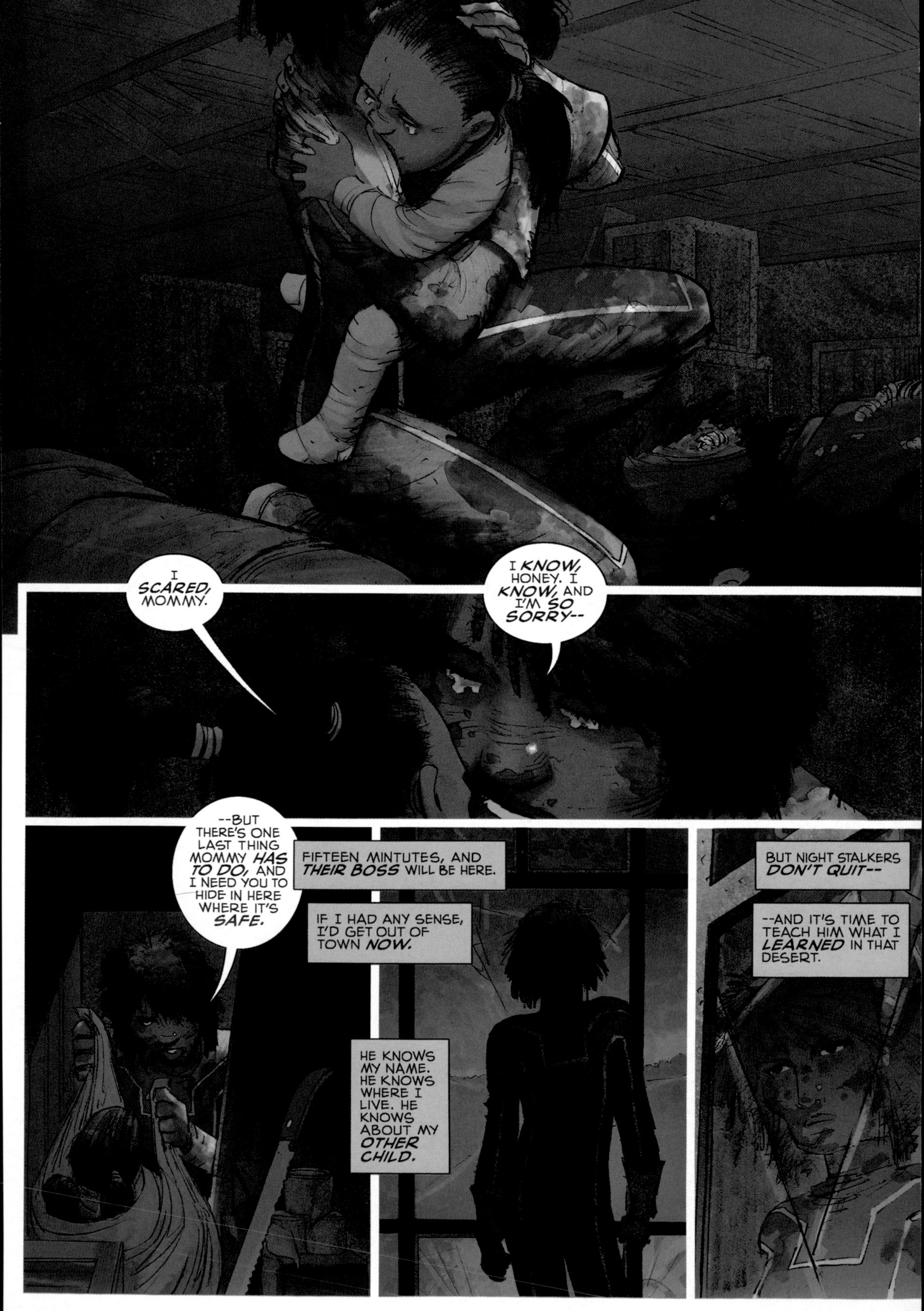
I SCARED, MOMMY.
I KNOW, HONEY. I KNOW, AND I'M SO SORRY--
--BUT THERE'S ONE LAST THING MOMMY HAS TO DO, AND I NEED YOU TO HIDE IN HERE WHERE IT'S SAFE.
FIFTEEN MINTUTES, AND THEIR BOSS WILL BE HERE.
IF I HAD ANY SENSE, I'D GET OUT OF TOWN NOW.
HE KNOWS MY NAME. HE KNOWS WHERE I LIVE. HE KNOWS ABOUT MY OTHER CHILD.
BUT NIGHT STALKERS DON'T QUIT--
--AND IT'S TIME TO TEACH HIM WHAT I LEARNED IN THAT DESERT.

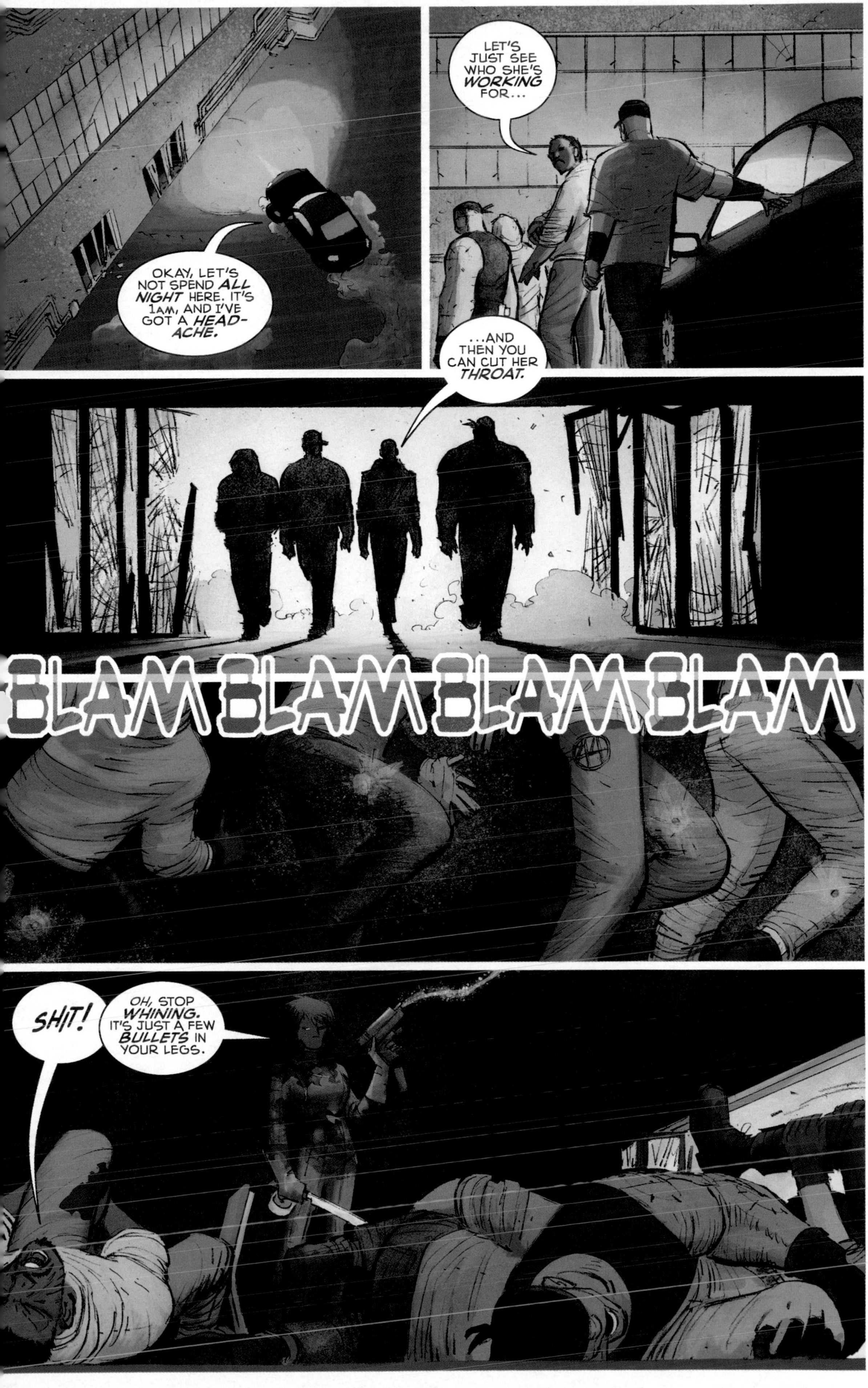
OKAY, LET'S NOT SPEND ALL NIGHT HERE. IT'S 1AM, AND I'VE GOT A HEAD-ACHE.
LET'S JUST SEE WHO SHE'S WORKING FOR...
...AND THEN YOU CAN CUT HER THROAT.
BLAM BLAM BLAM BLAM
SHIT!
OH, STOP WHINING. IT'S JUST A FEW BULLETS IN YOUR LEGS.

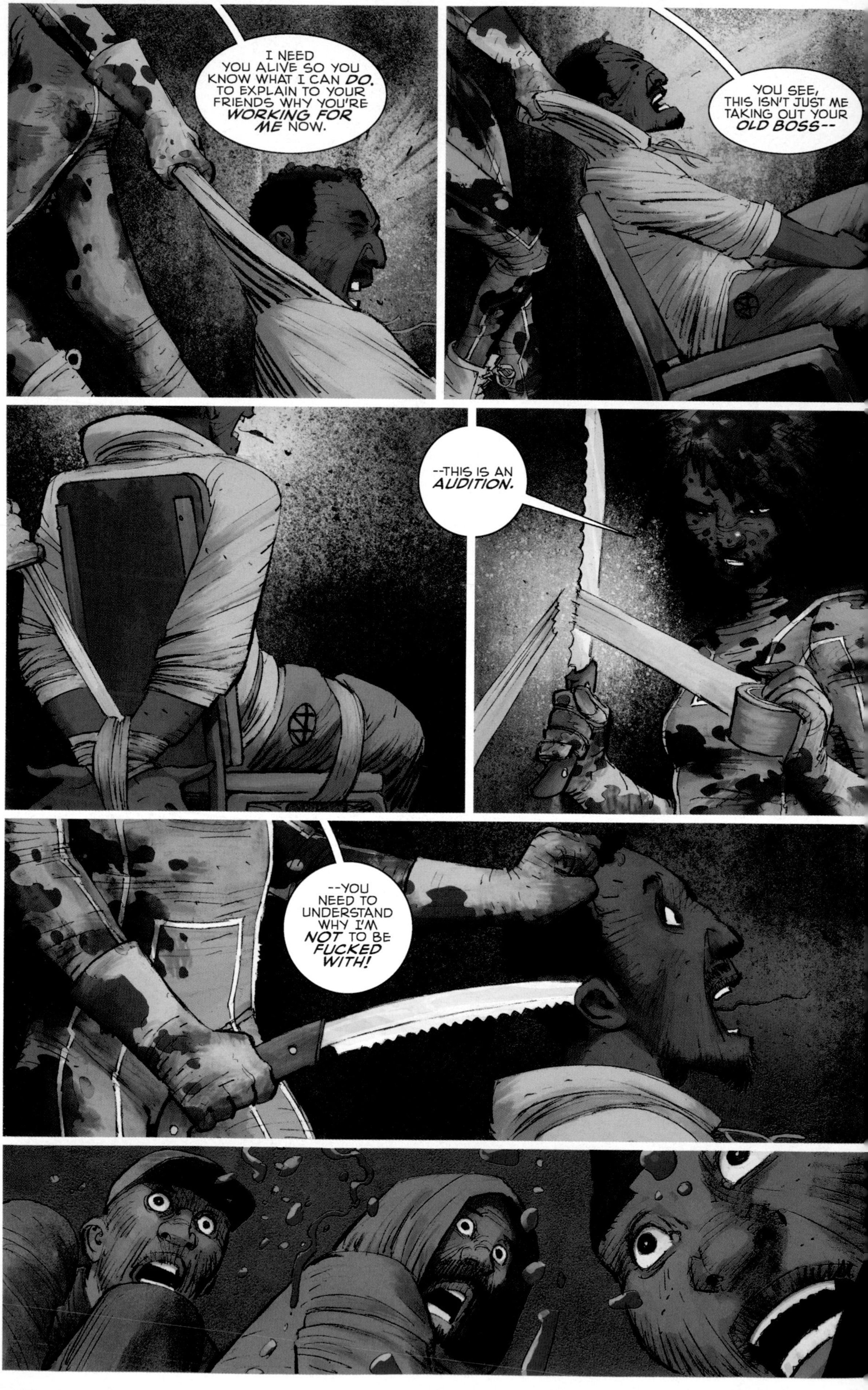
I NEED YOU ALIVE SO YOU KNOW WHAT I CAN *DO.* TO EXPLAIN TO YOUR FRIENDS WHY YOU'RE *WORKING FOR ME* NOW.
YOU SEE, THIS ISN'T JUST ME TAKING OUT YOUR *OLD BOSS--*
--THIS IS AN *AUDITION.*
--YOU NEED TO UNDERSTAND WHY I'M *NOT* TO BE *FUCKED WITH!*

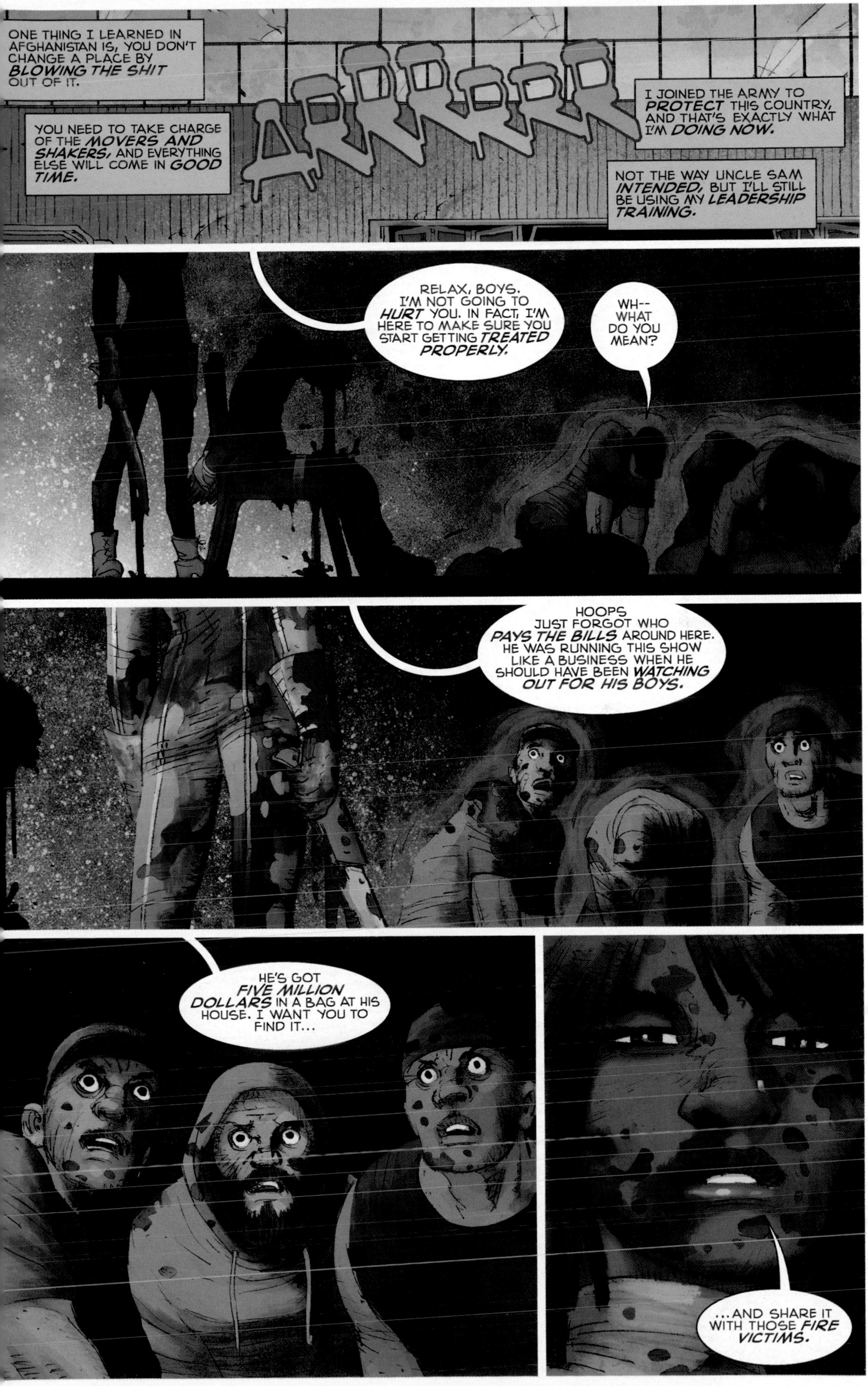
ONE THING I LEARNED IN AFGHANISTAN IS, YOU DON'T CHANGE A PLACE BY BLOWING THE SHIT OUT OF IT.
YOU NEED TO TAKE CHARGE OF THE MOVERS AND SHAKERS, AND EVERYTHING ELSE WILL COME IN GOOD TIME.
ARRRRRR
I JOINED THE ARMY TO PROTECT THIS COUNTRY, AND THAT'S EXACTLY WHAT I'M DOING NOW.
NOT THE WAY UNCLE SAM INTENDED, BUT I'LL STILL BE USING MY LEADERSHIP TRAINING.
RELAX, BOYS. I'M NOT GOING TO HURT YOU. IN FACT, I'M HERE TO MAKE SURE YOU START GETTING TREATED PROPERLY.
WH-- WHAT DO YOU MEAN?
HOOPS JUST FORGOT WHO PAYS THE BILLS AROUND HERE. HE WAS RUNNING THIS SHOW LIKE A BUSINESS WHEN HE SHOULD HAVE BEEN WATCHING OUT FOR HIS BOYS.
HE'S GOT FIVE MILLION DOLLARS IN A BAG AT HIS HOUSE. I WANT YOU TO FIND IT...
...AND SHARE IT WITH THOSE FIRE VICTIMS.

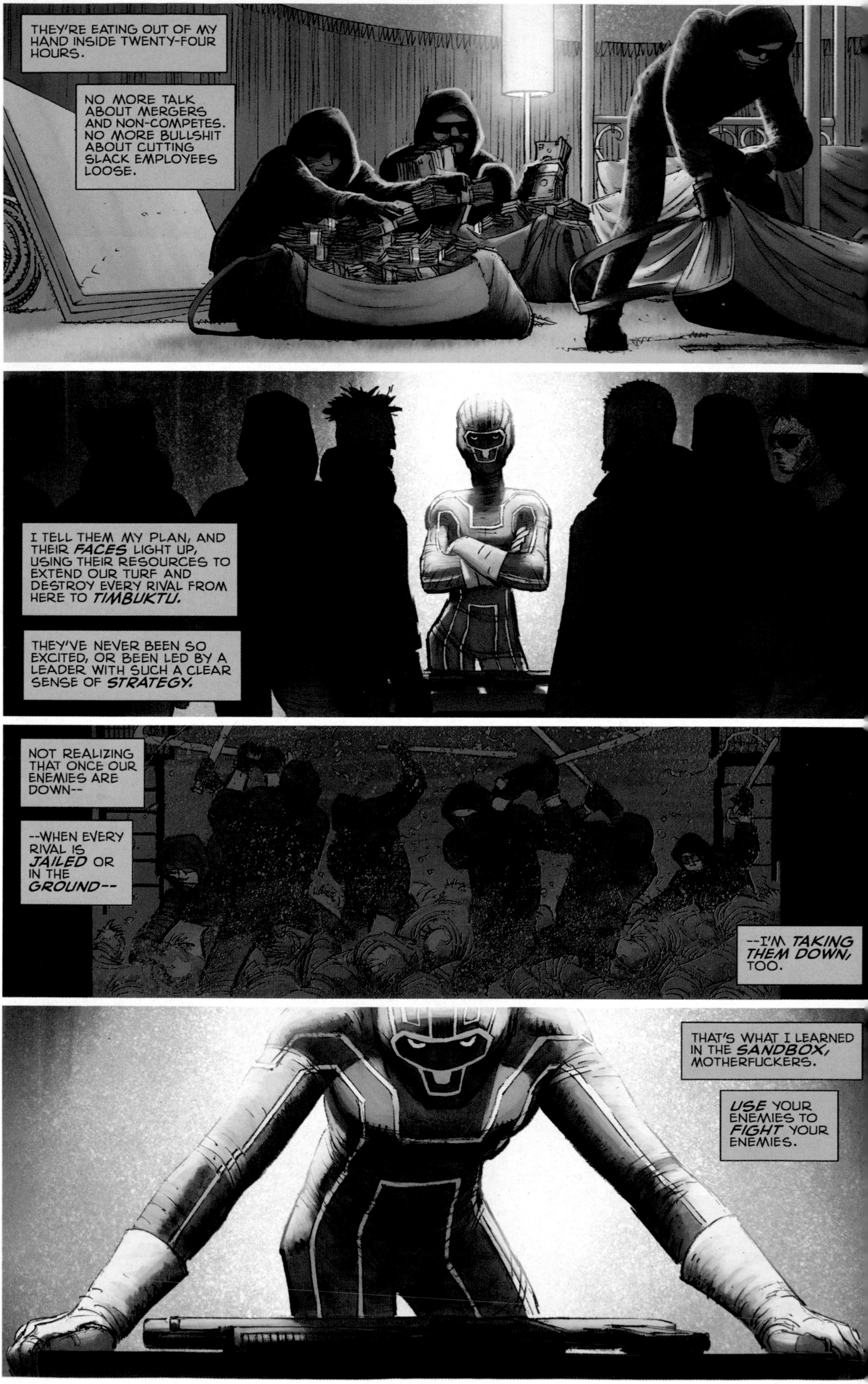
THEY'RE EATING OUT OF MY HAND INSIDE TWENTY-FOUR HOURS.
NO MORE TALK ABOUT MERGERS AND NON-COMPETES. NO MORE BULLSHIT ABOUT CUTTING SLACK EMPLOYEES LOOSE.
I TELL THEM MY PLAN, AND THEIR *FACES* LIGHT UP, USING THEIR RESOURCES TO EXTEND OUR TURF AND DESTROY EVERY RIVAL FROM HERE TO *TIMBUKTU.*
THEY'VE NEVER BEEN SO EXCITED, OR BEEN LED BY A LEADER WITH SUCH A CLEAR SENSE OF *STRATEGY.*
NOT REALIZING THAT ONCE OUR ENEMIES ARE DOWN--
--WHEN EVERY RIVAL IS *JAILED* OR IN THE *GROUND--*
--I'M *TAKING THEM DOWN,* TOO.
THAT'S WHAT I LEARNED IN THE *SANDBOX,* MOTHERFUCKERS.
USE YOUR ENEMIES TO *FIGHT* YOUR ENEMIES.

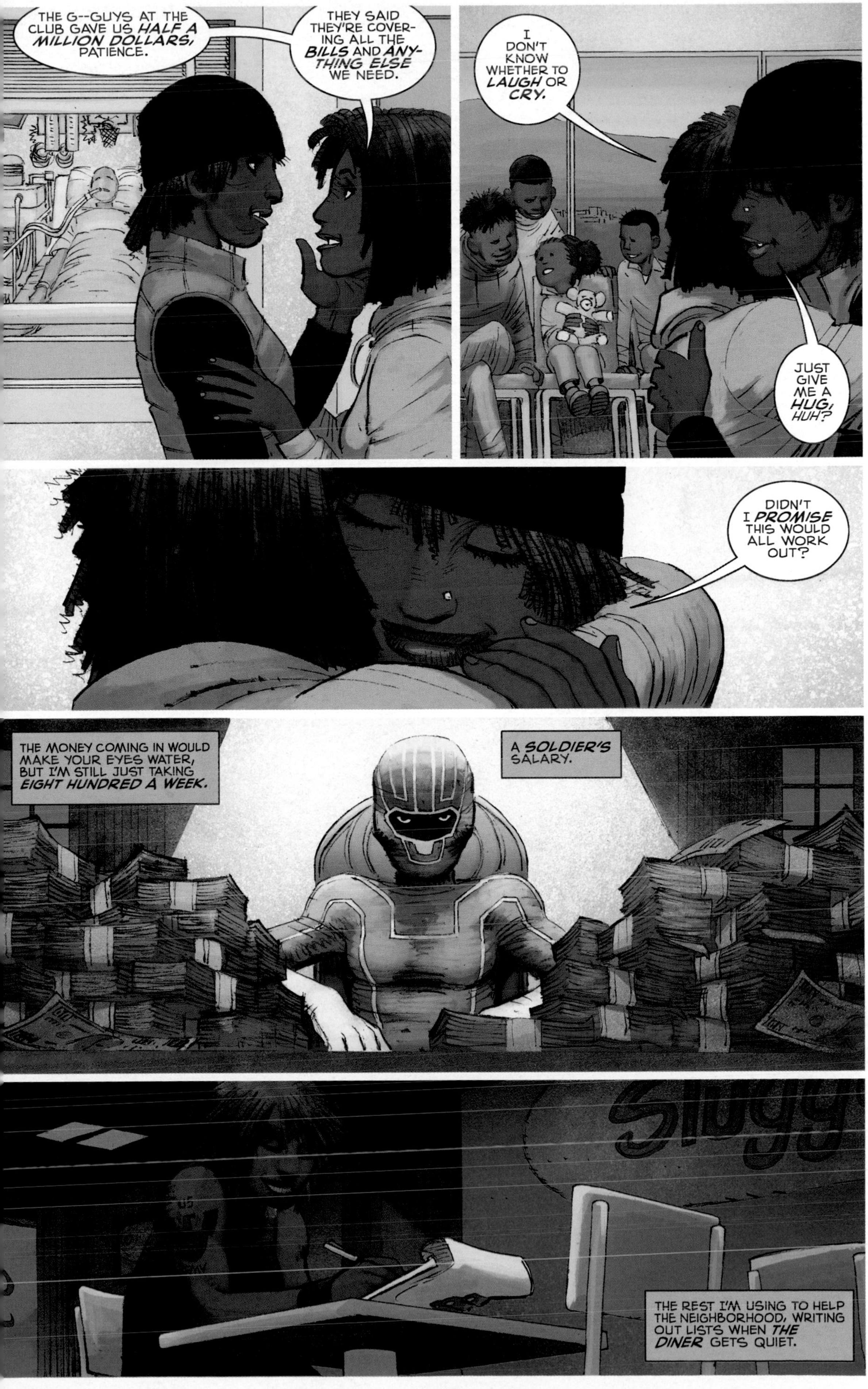

THE G--GUYS AT THE CLUB GAVE US HALF A MILLION DOLLARS, PATIENCE.
THEY SAID THEY'RE COVERING ALL THE BILLS AND ANYTHING ELSE WE NEED.
I DON'T KNOW WHETHER TO LAUGH OR CRY.
JUST GIVE ME A HUG, HUH?
DIDN'T I PROMISE THIS WOULD ALL WORK OUT?
THE MONEY COMING IN WOULD MAKE YOUR EYES WATER, BUT I'M STILL JUST TAKING EIGHT HUNDRED A WEEK.
A SOLDIER'S SALARY.
THE REST I'M USING TO HELP THE NEIGHBORHOOD, WRITING OUT LISTS WHEN THE DINER GETS QUIET.

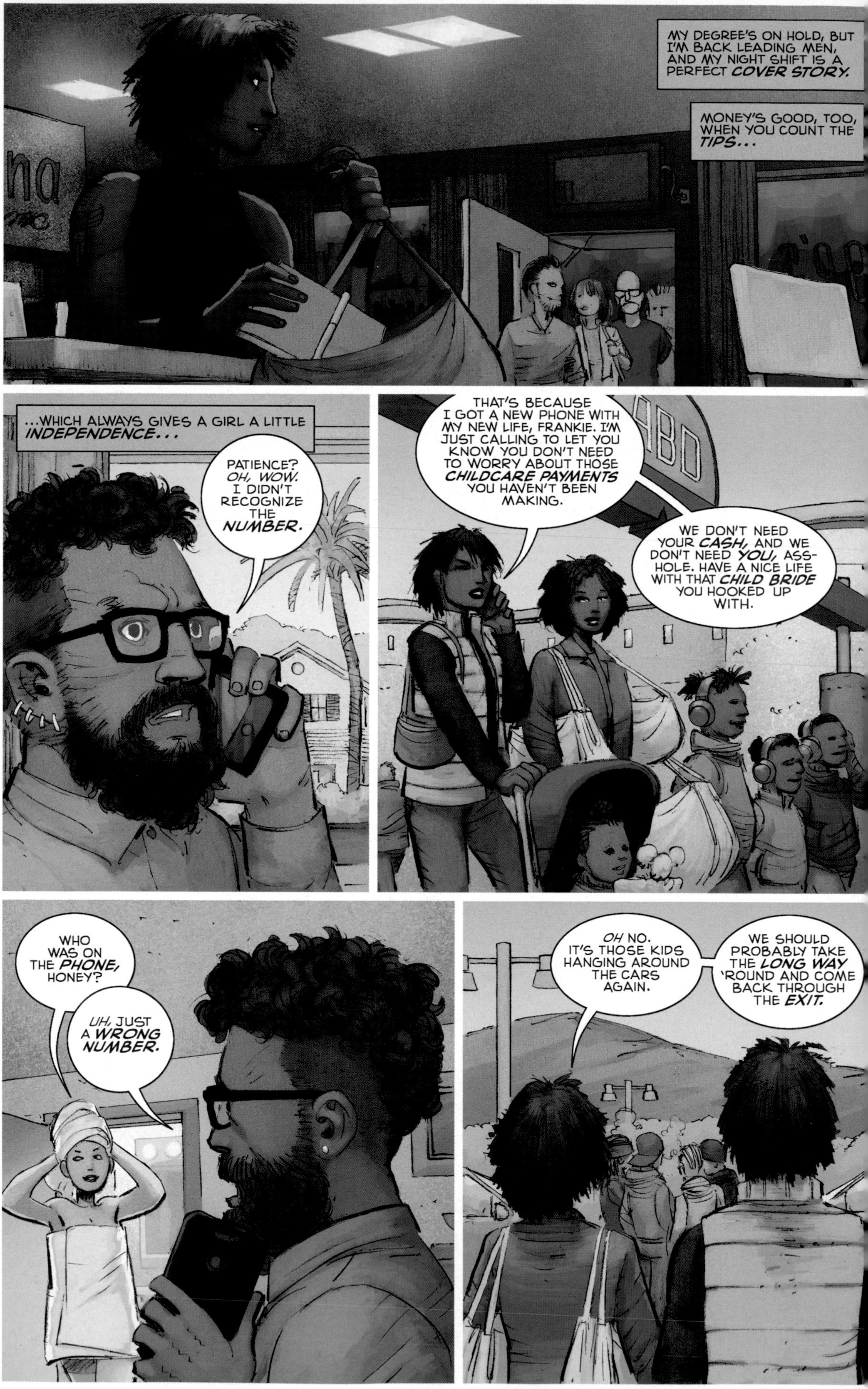
MY DEGREE'S ON HOLD, BUT I'M BACK LEADING MEN, AND MY NIGHT SHIFT IS A PERFECT COVER STORY.
MONEY'S GOOD, TOO, WHEN YOU COUNT THE TIPS...
...WHICH ALWAYS GIVES A GIRL A LITTLE INDEPENDENCE...
PATIENCE? OH, WOW. I DIDN'T RECOGNIZE THE NUMBER.
THAT'S BECAUSE I GOT A NEW PHONE WITH MY NEW LIFE, FRANKIE. I'M JUST CALLING TO LET YOU KNOW YOU DON'T NEED TO WORRY ABOUT THOSE CHILDCARE PAYMENTS YOU HAVEN'T BEEN MAKING.
WE DON'T NEED YOUR CASH, AND WE DON'T NEED YOU, ASS-HOLE. HAVE A NICE LIFE WITH THAT CHILD BRIDE YOU HOOKED UP WITH.
WHO WAS ON THE PHONE, HONEY?
UH, JUST A WRONG NUMBER.
OH NO. IT'S THOSE KIDS HANGING AROUND THE CARS AGAIN.
WE SHOULD PROBABLY TAKE THE LONG WAY 'ROUND AND COME BACK THROUGH THE EXIT.

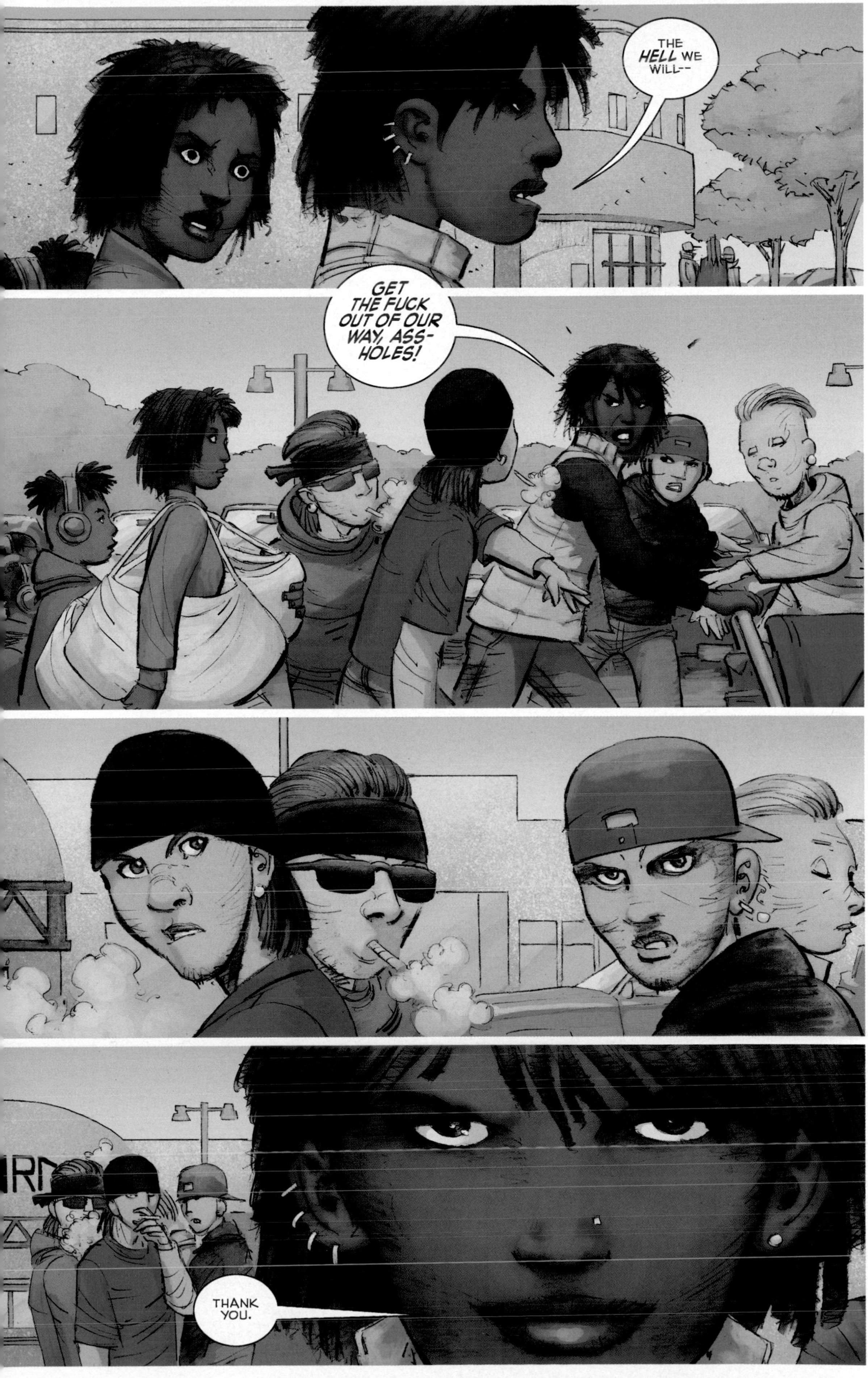
THE HELL WE WILL--
GET THE FUCK OUT OF OUR WAY, ASS-HOLES!
THANK YOU.

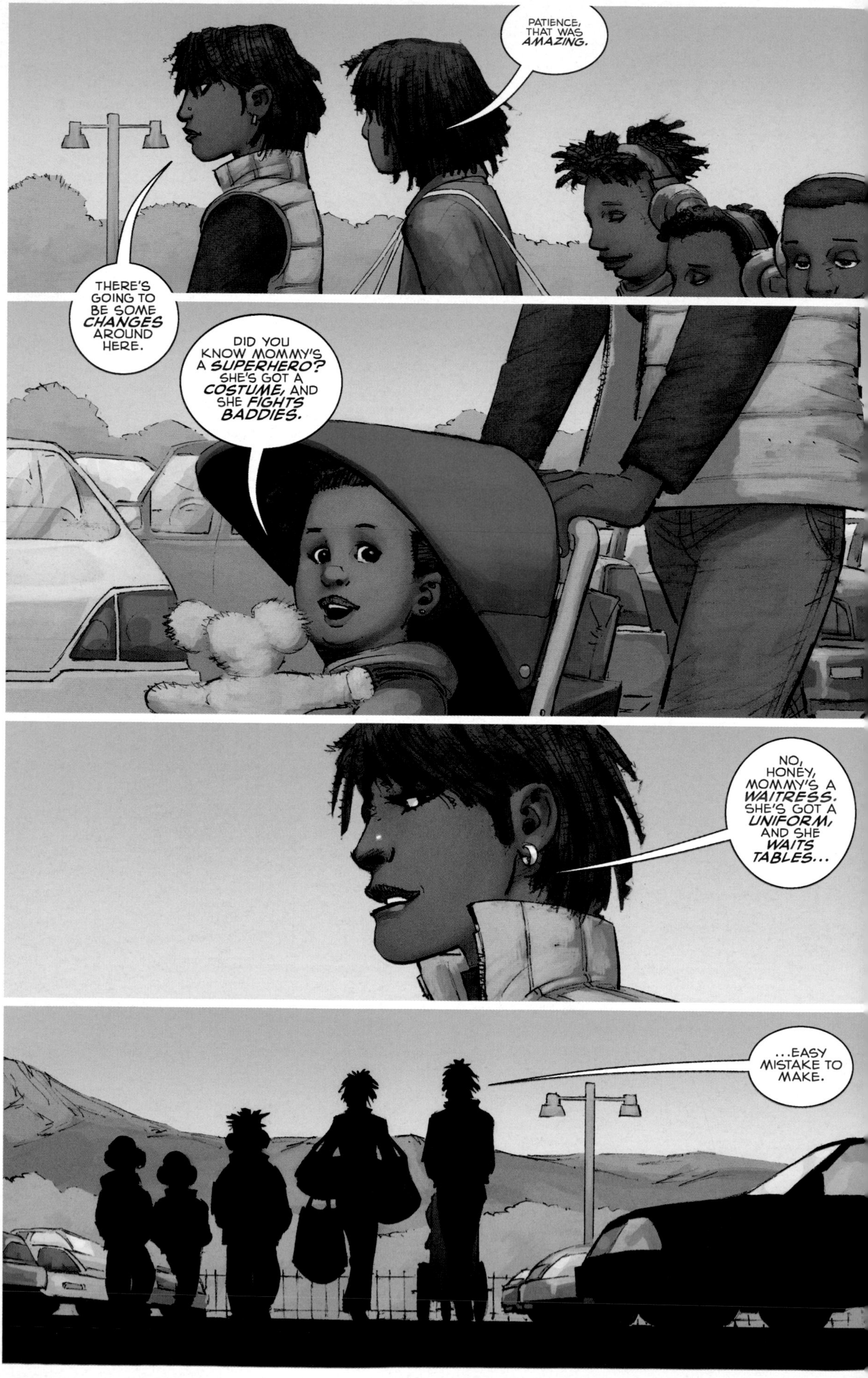
PATIENCE, THAT WAS AMAZING.
THERE'S GOING TO BE SOME CHANGES AROUND HERE.
DID YOU KNOW MOMMY'S A SUPERHERO? SHE'S GOT A COSTUME, AND SHE FIGHTS BADDIES.
NO, HONEY, MOMMY'S A WAITRESS. SHE'S GOT A UNIFORM, AND SHE WAITS TABLES...
...EASY MISTAKE TO MAKE.

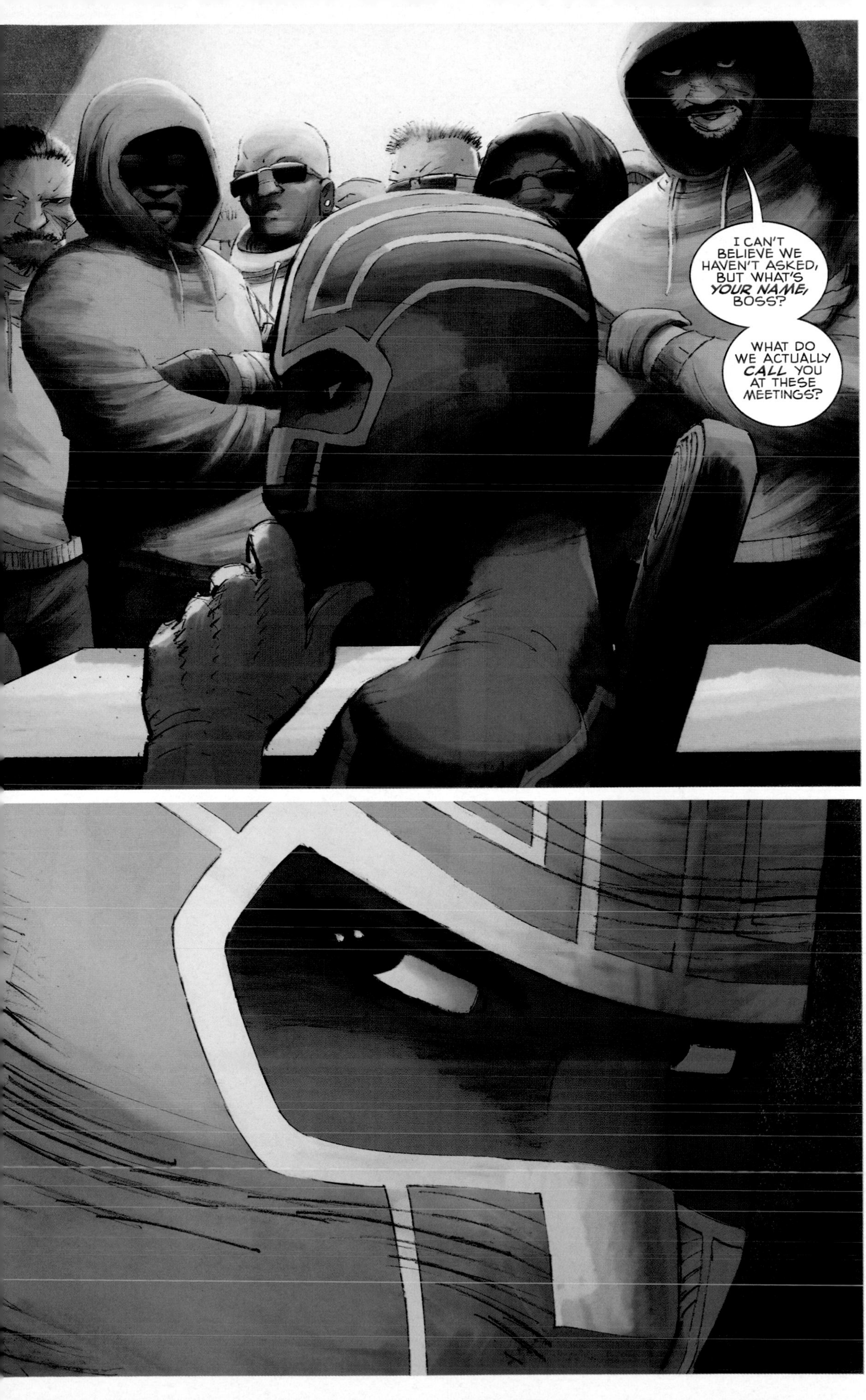
I CAN'T BELIEVE WE HAVEN'T ASKED, BUT WHAT'S YOUR NAME, BOSS?
WHAT DO WE ACTUALLY CALL YOU AT THESE MEETINGS?

KICK

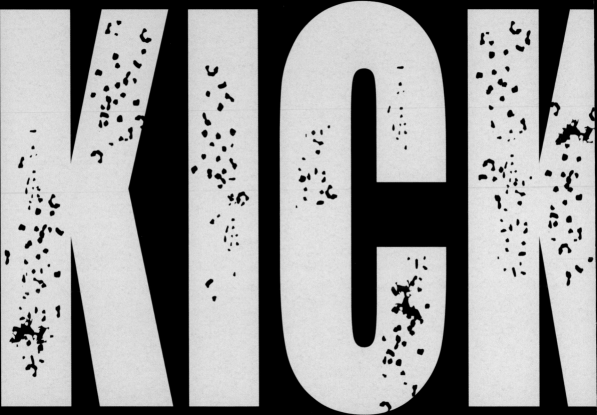

-ASS

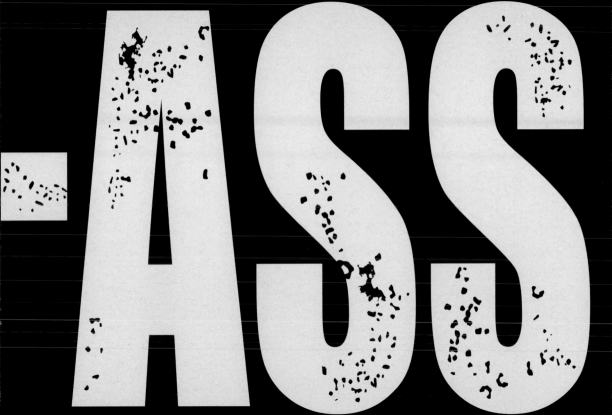

TO BE CONTINUED IN...

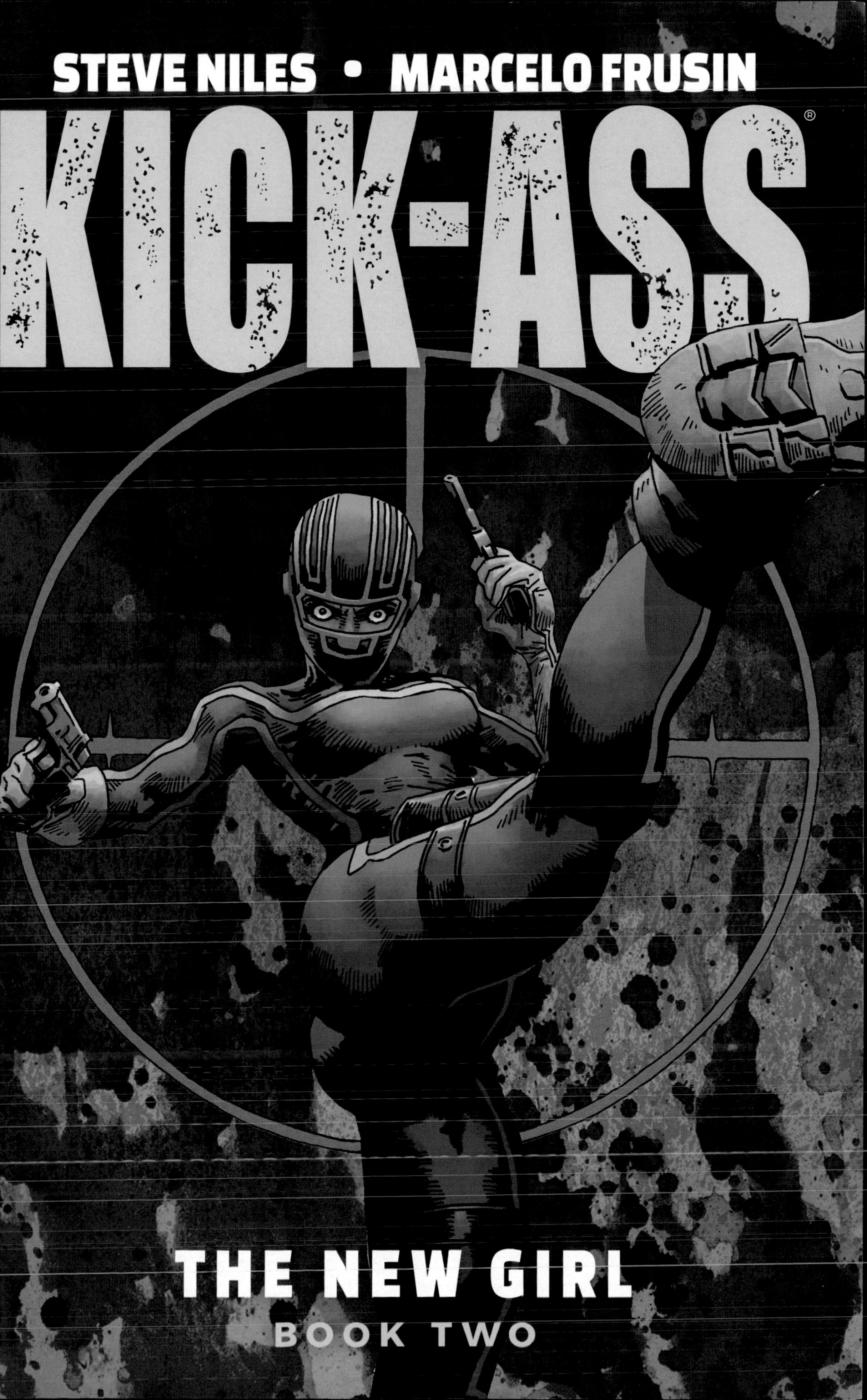
STEVE NILES • MARCELO FRUSIN
KICK-ASS®
THE NEW GIRL
BOOK TWO

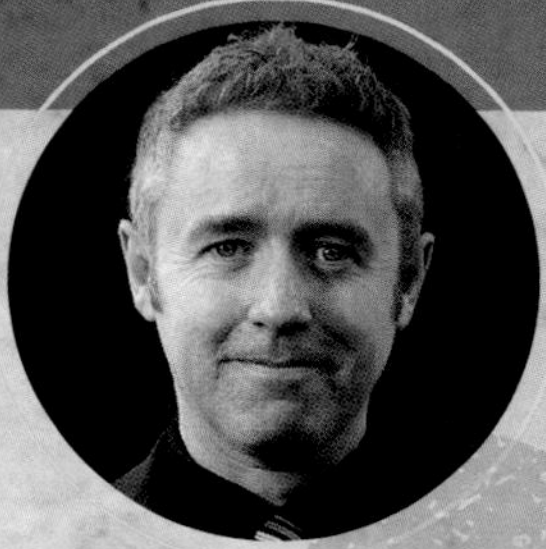

MARK MILLAR

is the *New York Times* bestselling author of **KICK-ASS**, **WANTED**, and **KINGSMAN: THE SECRET SERVICE**, all of which have been adapted into Hollywood franchises.

His DC Comics work includes the seminal **SUPERMAN: RED SON**. At Marvel Comics he created **THE ULTIMATES**, selected by *Time* magazine as the comic book of the decade, and described by screenwriter Zak Penn as his major inspiration for **THE AVENGERS** movie. Millar also created **WOLVERINE: OLD MAN LOGAN** and **CIVIL WAR**, Marvel's two biggest-selling graphic novels ever. **CIVIL WAR** was the basis of the **CAPTAIN AMERICA: CIVIL WAR** movie, and **OLD MAN LOGAN** was the inspiration for Fox's **LOGAN** movie in 2017.

Mark has been an executive producer on all his movies, and for four years worked as a creative consultant to Fox Studios on their Marvel slate of movies. In 2017, Netflix bought Millarworld in the company's first ever acquisition, and employed Mark as President to continue creating comics, TV shows, and movies. His much-anticipated autobiography, **BE YOUR OWN SURGEON**, will be published next year.

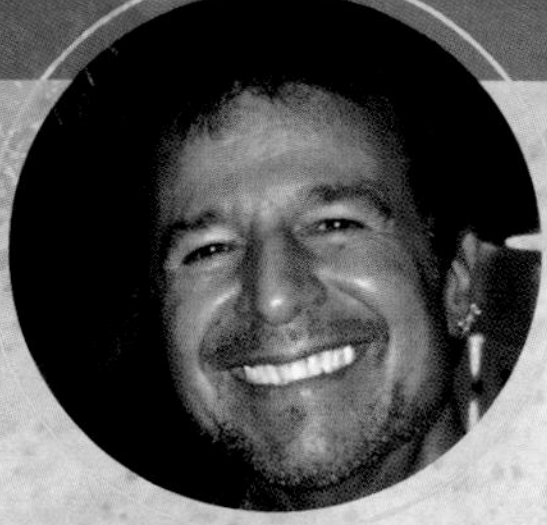

JOHN ROMITA JR.

is a modern-day comics legend. He has followed in his father's footsteps and helped keep the Romita name on the list of top-shelf talent.

Timeless runs on **IRON MAN**, **UNCANNY X-MEN**, **AMAZING SPIDER-MAN** and **DAREDEVIL** helped establish him as his own man artistically, and his art on **WOLVERINE** is arguably the most explosive comic art of its decade — trumped perhaps only by his work on the massive blockbuster **WORLD WAR HULK**. He and Mark Millar created the bestselling, original **KICK-ASS** and **HIT-GIRL** stories, which went on to be the basis of two Hollywood blockbusters.

John has also paired with renowned writer Neil Gaiman for **THE ETERNALS**, worked on DC Comics' flagship title **SUPERMAN** with Geoff Johns, and in 2016 joined forces with Scott Snyder on the **ALL-STAR BATMAN** series as part of the DC Rebirth launch.

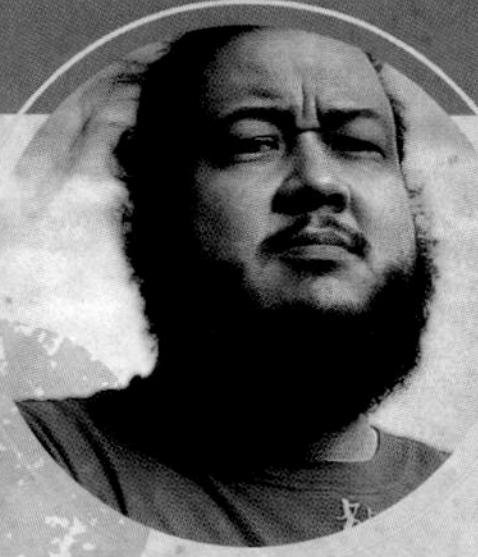

PETER STEIGERWALD

Born and raised in Honolulu, Hawai'i, now living in Los Angeles, Peter Steigerwald has had a long career in comics. During that career, he has done nearly every job possible. He is best known as a colorist and for his artistic collaborations with Michael Turner.

In 2003, he and Frank Mastromauro helped Michael found Aspen Comics. Since Turner's death in 2008, Peter has continued as co-owner of Aspen Comics with Frank, keeping Michael's legacy alive and creating new projects and characters.

Peter has also had a coloring hand in many high-profile events and covers for Marvel, **LADY MECHANIKA** and DC comics where he first collaborated with John Romita Jr. on **THE DARK KNIGHT RETURNS: THE LAST CRUSADE**. That collaboration was so successful and fun for John and Peter that they did it again here, in this book you hold in your hands.

If you're looking for Peter he can be most easily found at Aspen's offices, working through the night on any number of things, including his creator-owned book that he writes, illustrates, and letters: **THE ZOOHUNTERS**.

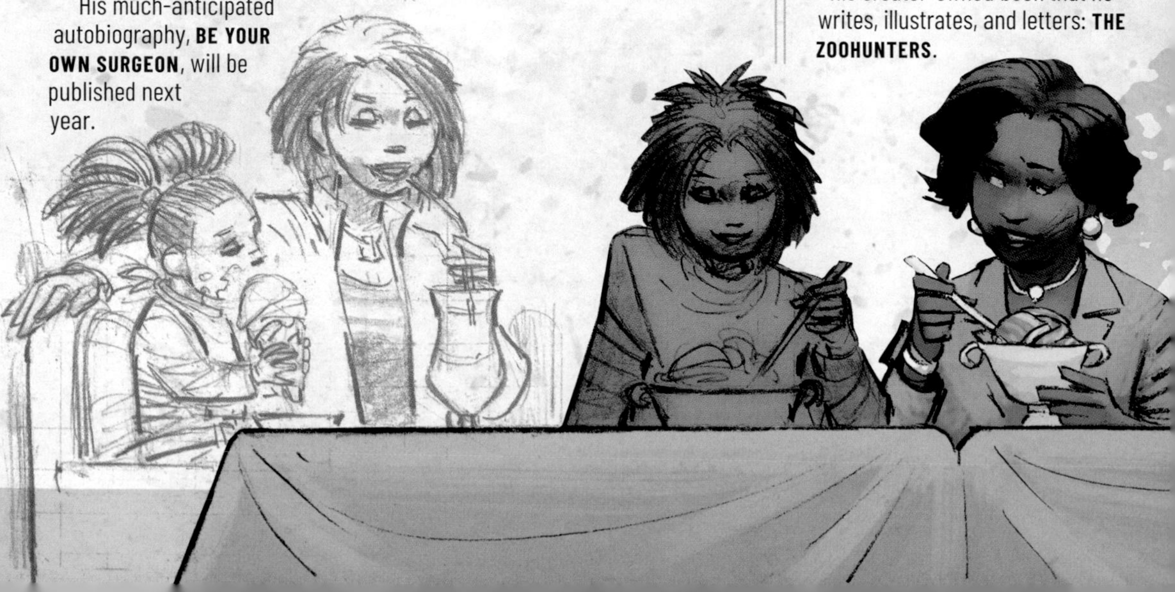

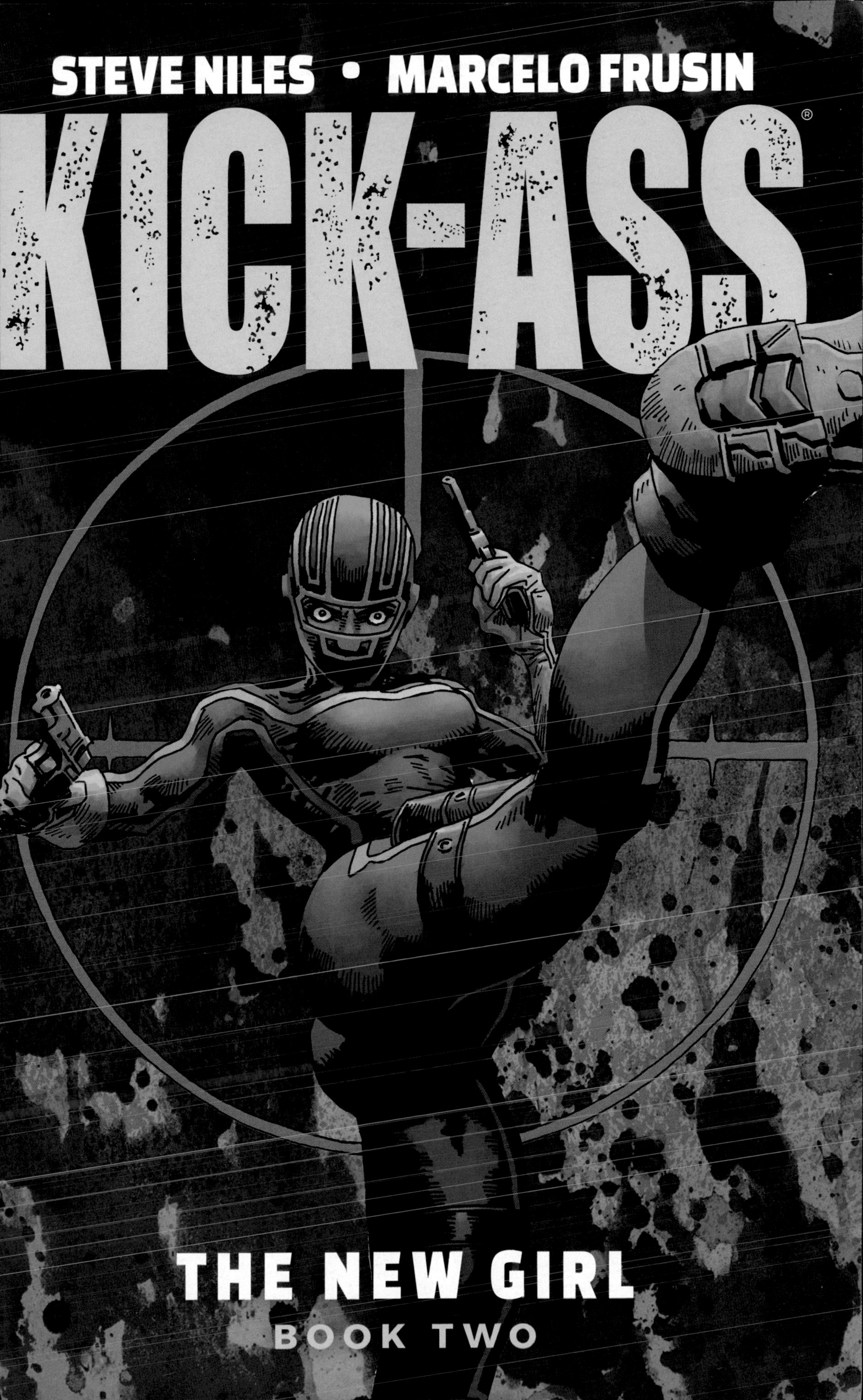
STEVE NILES • MARCELO FRUSIN
KICK-ASS®
THE NEW GIRL
BOOK TWO

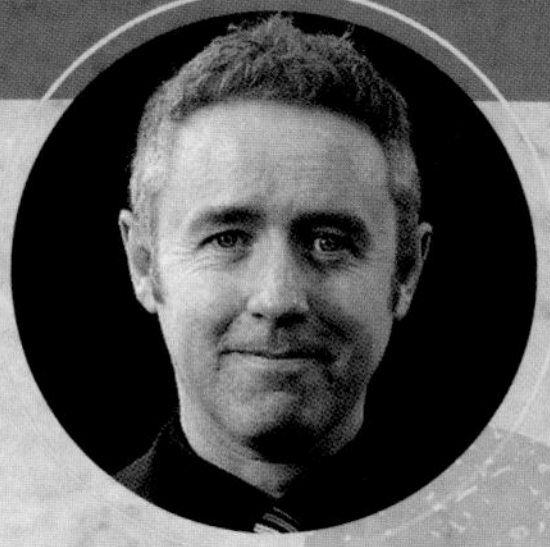

MARK MILLAR

is the *New York Times* bestselling author of **KICK-ASS**, **WANTED**, and **KINGSMAN: THE SECRET SERVICE**, all of which have been adapted into Hollywood franchises.

His DC Comics work includes the seminal **SUPERMAN: RED SON**. At Marvel Comics he created **THE ULTIMATES**, selected by *Time* magazine as the comic book of the decade, and described by screenwriter Zak Penn as his major inspiration for **THE AVENGERS** movie. Millar also created **WOLVERINE: OLD MAN LOGAN** and **CIVIL WAR**, Marvel's two biggest-selling graphic novels ever. **CIVIL WAR** was the basis of the **CAPTAIN AMERICA: CIVIL WAR** movie, and **OLD MAN LOGAN** was the inspiration for Fox's **LOGAN** movie in 2017.

Mark has been an executive producer on all his movies, and for four years worked as a creative consultant to Fox Studios on their Marvel slate of movies. In 2017, Netflix bought Millarworld in the company's first ever acquisition, and employed Mark as President to continue creating comics, TV shows, and movies. His much-anticipated autobiography, **BE YOUR OWN SURGEON**, will be published next year.

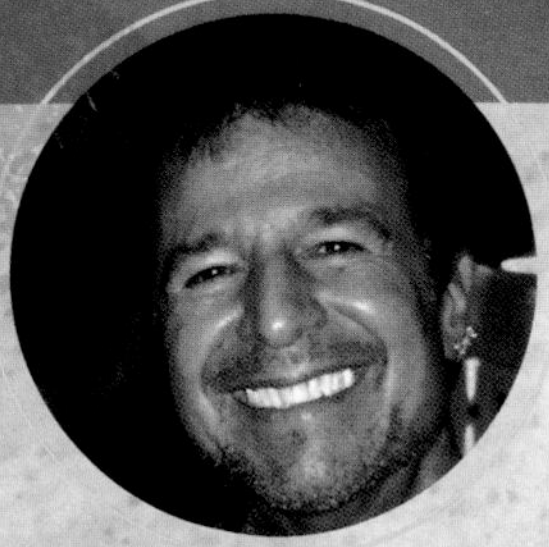

JOHN ROMITA JR.

is a modern-day comics legend. He has followed in his father's footsteps and helped keep the Romita name on the list of top-shelf talent.

Timeless runs on **IRON MAN**, **UNCANNY X-MEN**, **AMAZING SPIDER-MAN** and **DAREDEVIL** helped establish him as his own man artistically, and his art on **WOLVERINE** is arguably the most explosive comic art of its decade — trumped perhaps only by his work on the massive blockbuster **WORLD WAR HULK**. He and Mark Millar created the bestselling, original **KICK-ASS** and **HIT-GIRL** stories, which went on to be the basis of two Hollywood blockbusters.

John has also paired with renowned writer Neil Gaiman for **THE ETERNALS**, worked on DC Comics' flagship title **SUPERMAN** with Geoff Johns, and in 2016 joined forces with Scott Snyder on the **ALL-STAR BATMAN** series as part of the DC Rebirth launch.

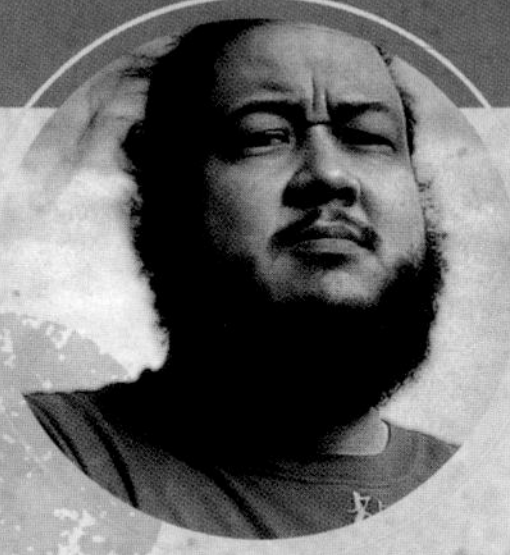

PETER STEIGERWALD

Born and raised in Honolulu, Hawai'i, now living in Los Angeles, Peter Steigerwald has had a long career in comics. During that career, he has done nearly every job possible. He is best known as a colorist and for his artistic collaborations with Michael Turner.

In 2003, he and Frank Mastromauro helped Michael found Aspen Comics. Since Turner's death in 2008, Peter has continued as co-owner of Aspen Comics with Frank, keeping Michael's legacy alive and creating new projects and characters.

Peter has also had a coloring hand in many high-profile events and covers for Marvel, **LADY MECHANIKA** and DC comics where he first collaborated with John Romita Jr. on **THE DARK KNIGHT RETURNS: THE LAST CRUSADE**. That collaboration was so successful and fun for John and Peter that they did it again here, in this book you hold in your hands.

If you're looking for Peter he can be most easily found at Aspen's offices, working through the night on any number of things, including his creator-owned book that he writes, illustrates, and letters: **THE ZOOHUNTERS**.

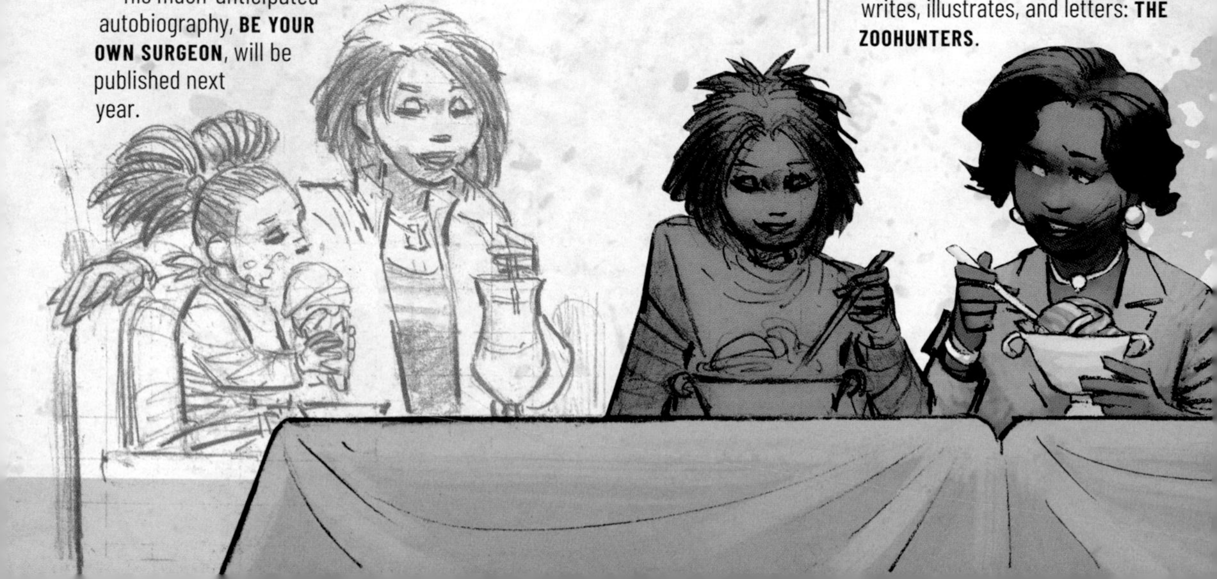

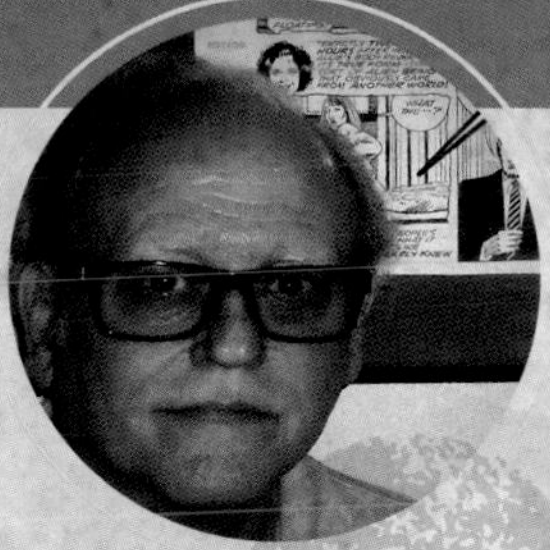

JOHN WORKMAN

managed to turn a love for the comics form into a career. During the past five decades, he has held the positions of editor, writer, art director, penciler, inker, colorist, letterer, production director, and book designer for various companies.

He created (with some help from Bhob Stewart and Bob Smith) the offbeat stories in **WILD THINGS** (with much of that material having first appeared in *Star*Reach* and *Heavy Metal*) and both wrote and drew the comics series **SINDY**, **FALLEN ANGELS** and **ROMA**.

In 1991, he reflected on model Bettie Page in **BETTY BEING BAD** (Eros) and later produced the hardbounds **HEAVY METAL: 25 YEARS OF CLASSIC COVERS AND INNOCENT IMAGES: THE SEXY FANTASY FEMALES OF VIPER AND KISS**, as well as **THE ADVENTURES OF ROMA**, a reformatted graphic novel version of his earlier series.

He continues to write, draw, and do a whole lot of lettering for a number of comics companies on an international level.

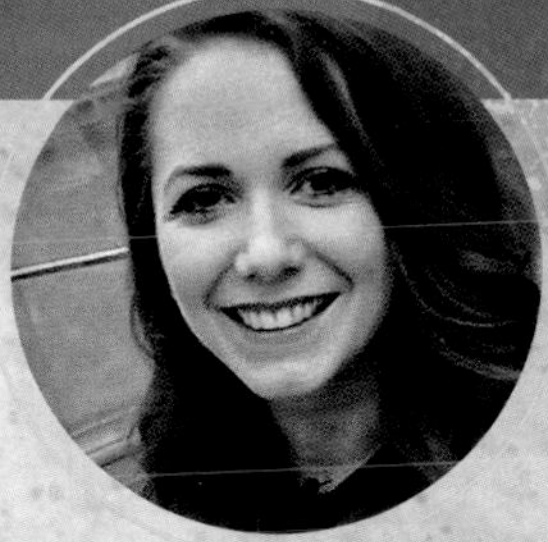

RACHAEL FULTON

is series editor of Mark Millar and John Romita Jr's monthly ongoing **KICK-ASS** series, as well as the monthly ongoing **HIT-GIRL** series, working with talent such as Eduardo Risso, Rafael Albuquerque and Goran Parlov. She is editor of Netflix's Millarworld division, where she is currently producing **THE MAGIC ORDER** with Mark Millar and Olivier Coipel. Her past credits as series editor include **EMPRESS**, **JUPITER'S LEGACY 2**, **REBORN**, and **KINGSMAN: THE RED DIAMOND**. She is collections editor for the most recent editions of **KINGSMAN: THE SECRET SERVICE** and all volumes of **KICK-ASS: THE DAVE LIZEWSKI YEARS**.

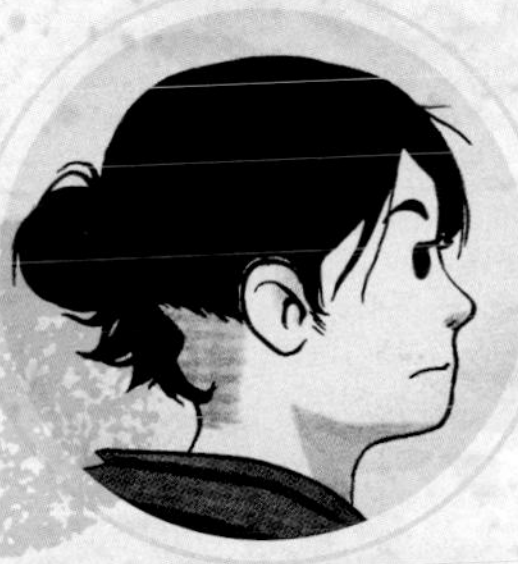

MEGAN SHIRK

is an illustrator based in Southern California, who goes by the name "ZombieTeddie" pretty much everywhere online.

She loves to create her own comics and stories, and regularly participates in artist alleys at various conventions with her husband. **KICK-ASS: THE NEW GIRL** is her first published work, and hopefully won't be the last!

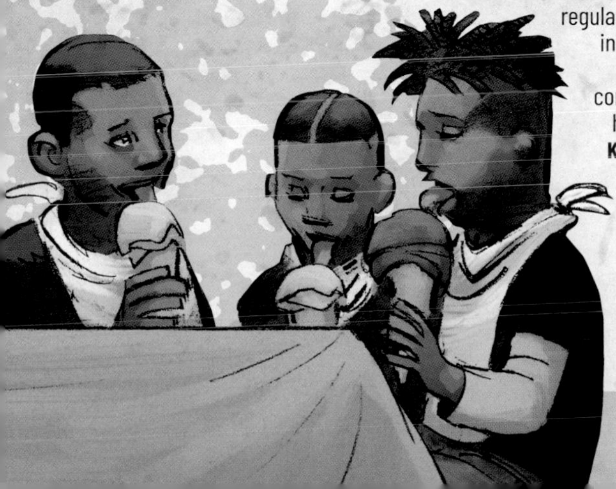

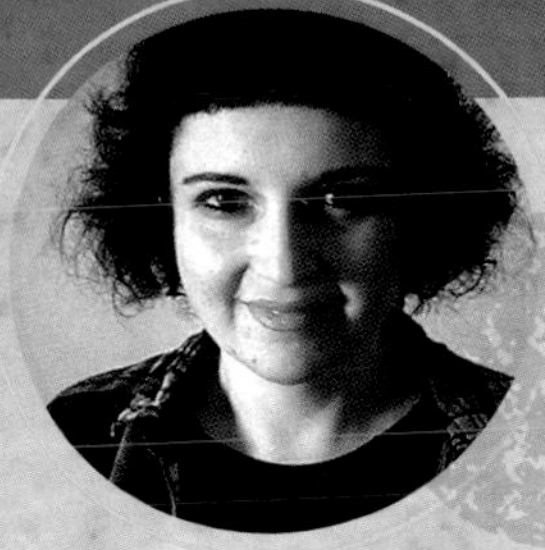

MELINA MIKULIC

hasn't yet won an Eisner Award for Best Publication Design, for one simple reason: she's designed more than a thousand gorgeous comic books (including Fibra's editions of Moebius and Tezuka, and Marjane Satrapi's **PERSEPOLIS**) but all on the wrong continent. That is about to change.

She is a Master of Arts, and graduated from the Faculty of Design in Zagreb, Croatia, where she was born. As a graphic designer, she is primarily engaged in design for print, with a growing interest in illustration and interactive media. She now lives in Rijeka, where despite enjoying the Mediterranean climate, she rarely sees the sun, as she spends her time wandering through shadowy landscapes of fonts and letters.

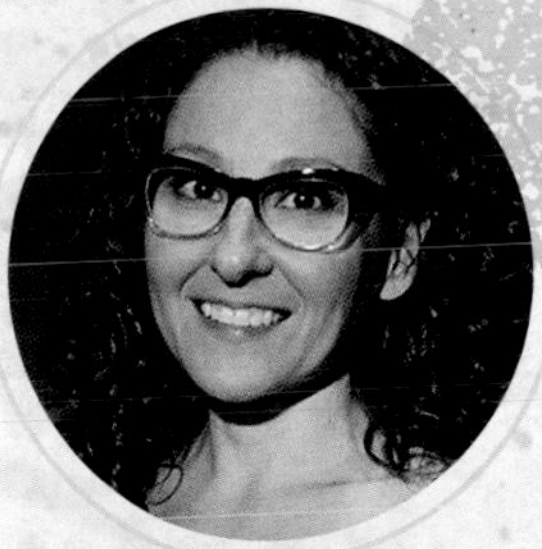

BETH SOTELO

In 2001 Beth Sotelo began working in the comic book industry as a colorist for Top Cow Productions, and has since worked for Aspen Comics, DC, and Marvel. Her recent coloring credits include DC Comic's **SUICIDE SQUAD: MOST WANTED**, Joe Benitez's **LADY MECHANIKA** and coloring/illustration work for 20th Century Fox.

Beth is also working on a second book to follow her OGN titled **GRUMP** which was successfully funded through Kickstarter. Beth can be found at www.BethSotelo.com and on Twitter and Instagram @Midimew.

OLIVIER COIPEL
VARIANT COVER **ISSUE #1**

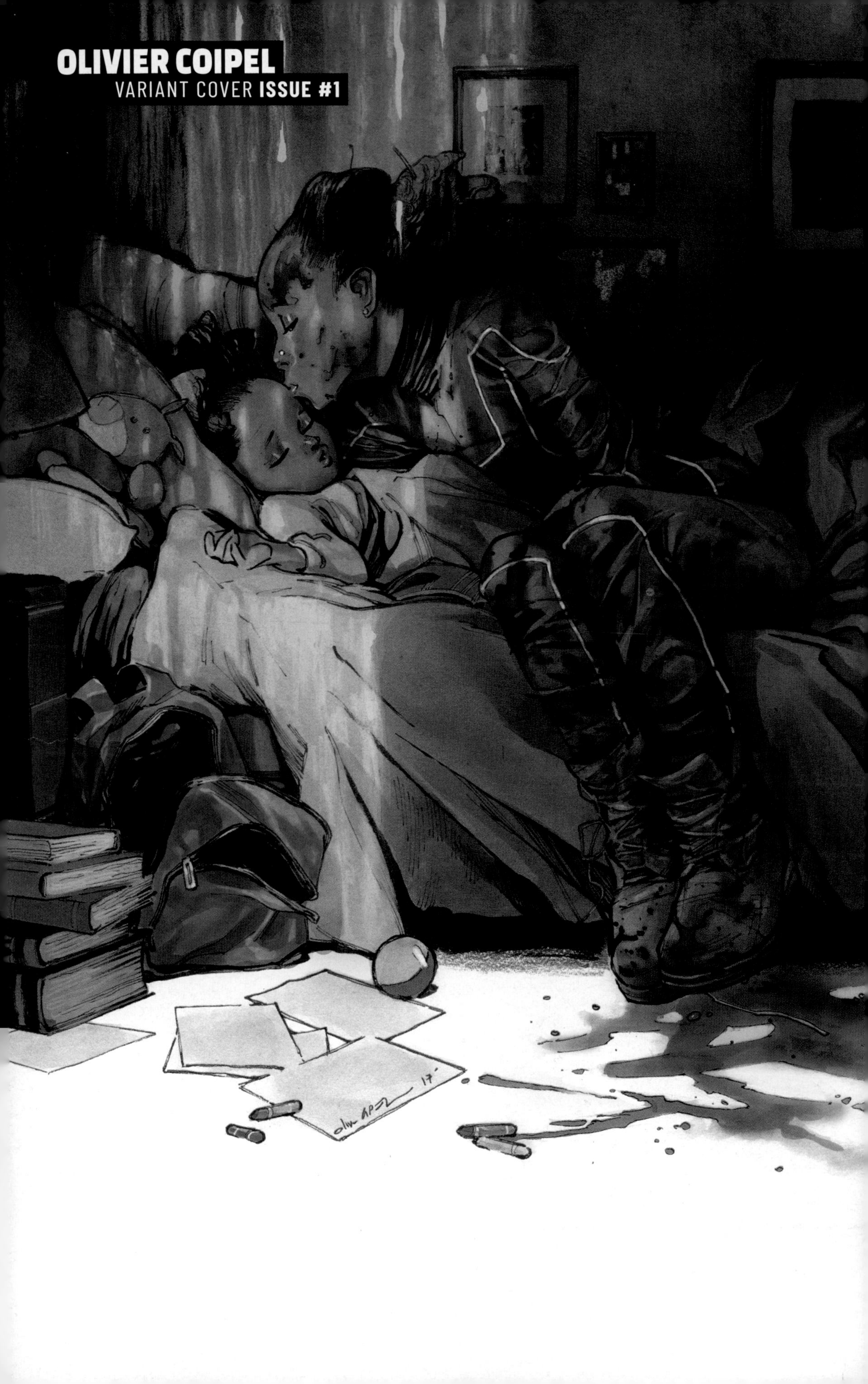

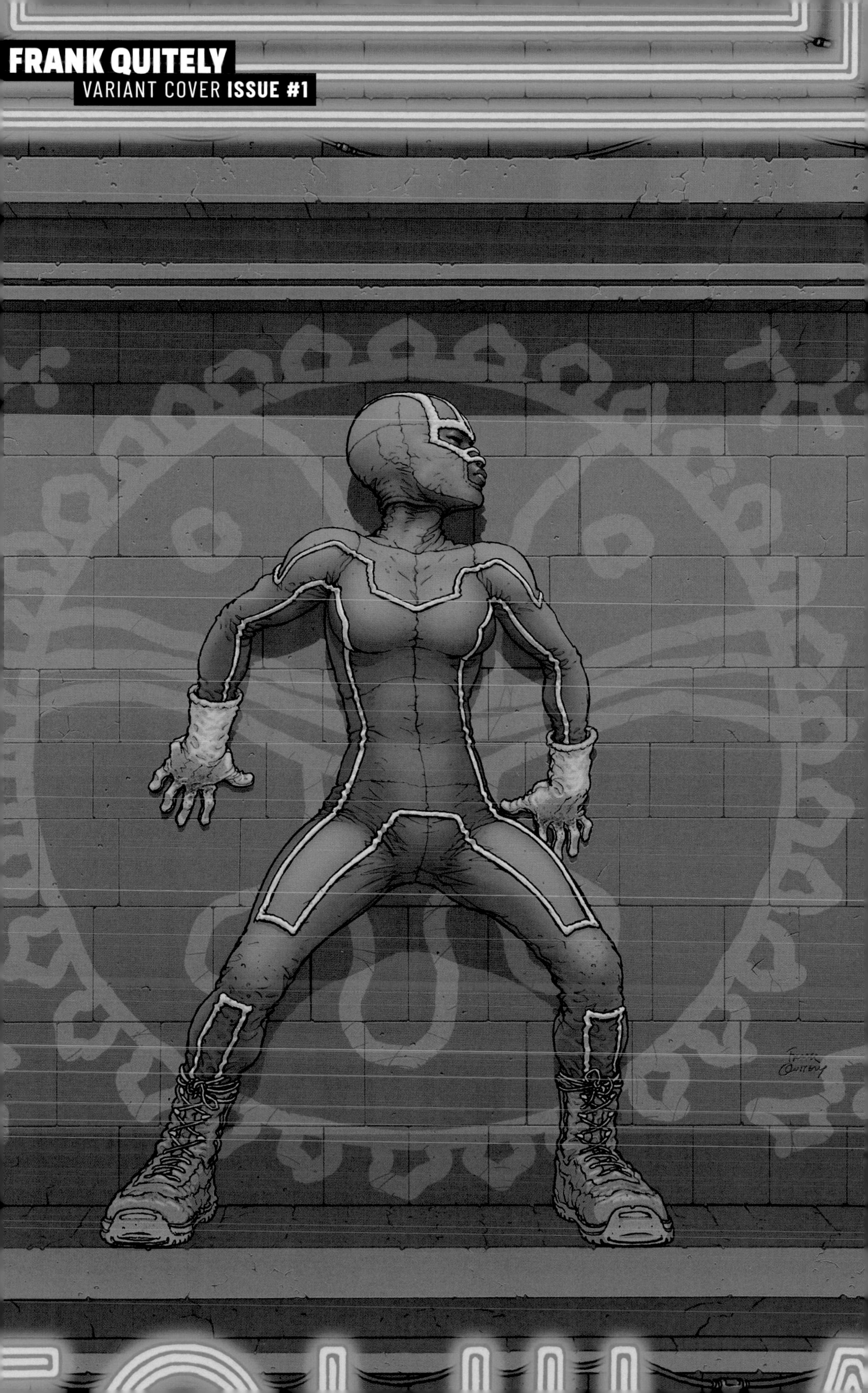
FRANK QUITELY
VARIANT COVER ISSUE #1

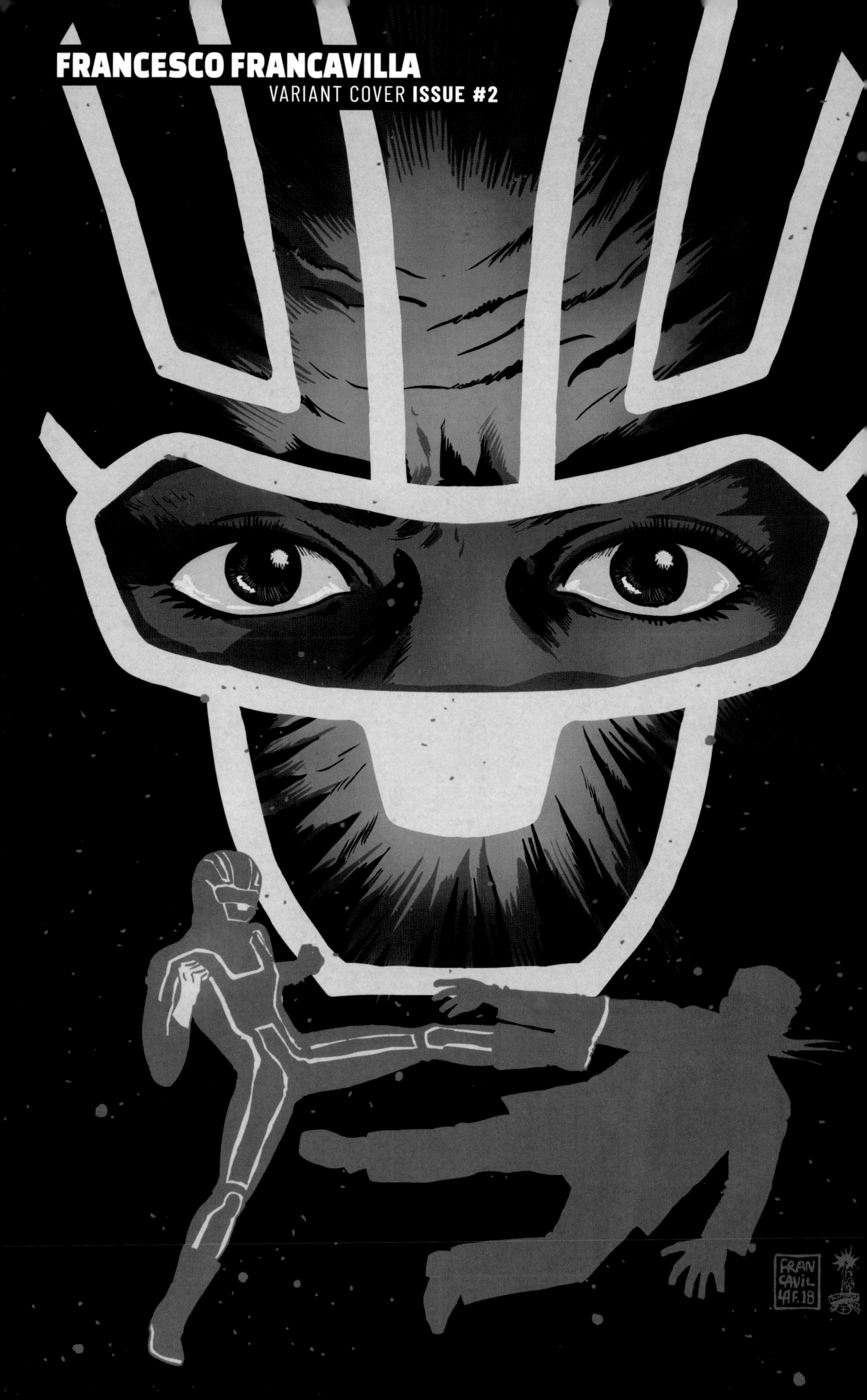
FRANCESCO FRANCAVILLA
VARIANT COVER ISSUE #2

The COMPLETE KICK-ASS and HIT-GIRL

MARK MILLAR • JOHN ROMITA JR.
KICK-ASS
THE DAVE LIZEWSKI YEARS
BOOK ONE

MARK MILLAR • JOHN ROMITA JR.
KICK-ASS
THE DAVE LIZEWSKI YEARS
BOOK TWO

MARK MILLAR • JOHN ROMITA JR.
KICK-ASS
THE DAVE LIZEWSKI YEARS
BOOK THREE

MARK MILLAR • JOHN ROMITA JR.
KICK-ASS
THE DAVE LIZEWSKI YEARS
BOOK FOUR

**KICK-ASS:
THE DAVE LIZEWSKI
YEARS**
Vol 1-4

MARK MILLAR • JOHN ROMITA JR.
KICK-ASS
THE NEW GIRL
BOOK ONE

**KICK-ASS:
THE NEW GIRL**
Vol 1

HIT-GIRL
IN COLOMBIA
MARK MILLAR • RICARDO LOPEZ ORTIZ

HIT-GIRL
IN CANADA
JEFF LEMIRE • EDUARDO RISSO

HIT-GIRL
IN ROME
RAFAEL ALBUQUERQUE • RAFAEL SCAVONE

HIT-GIRL
Vol 1-3

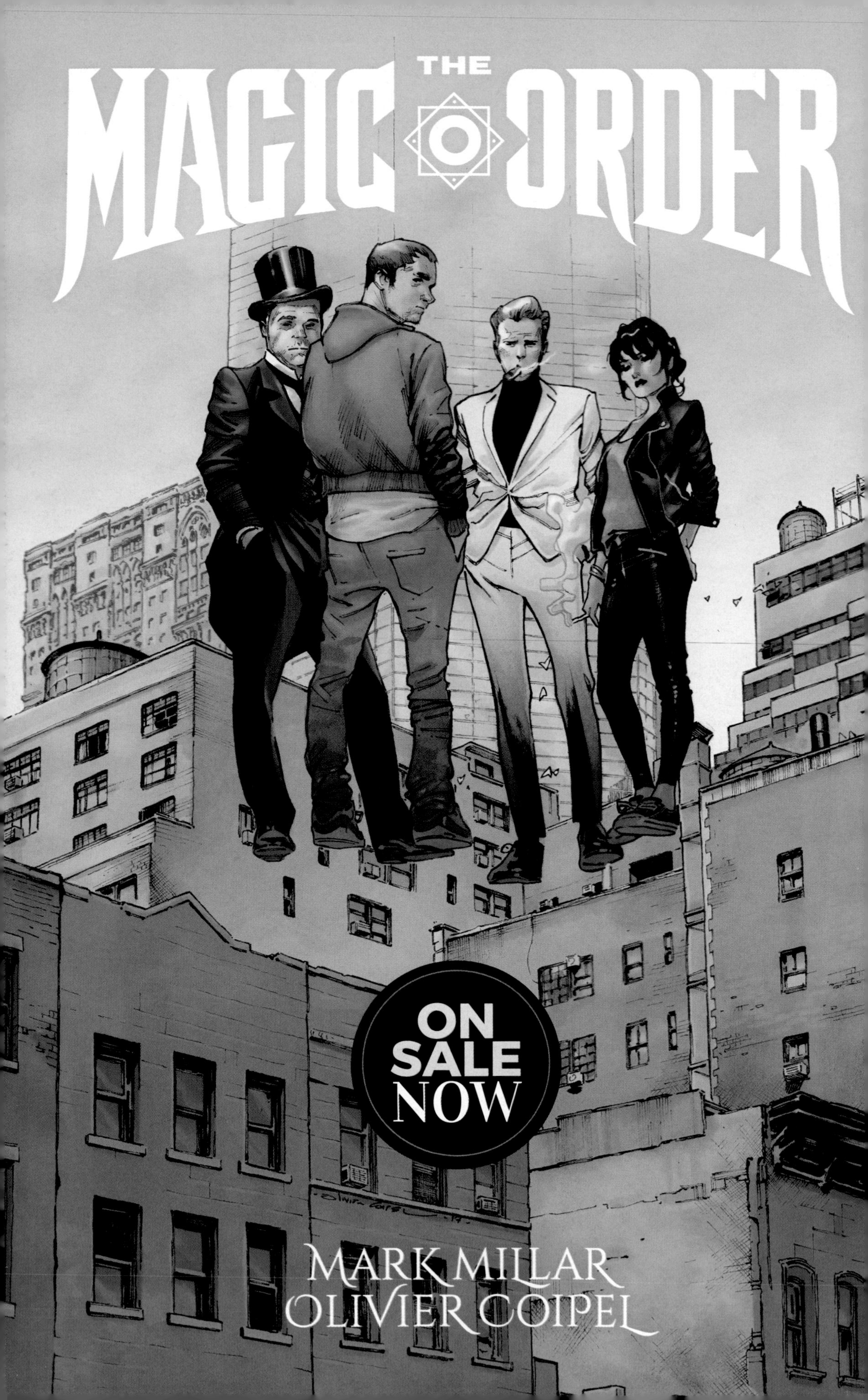
THE
MAGIC ORDER
ON
SALE
NOW
MARK MILLAR
OLIVIER COIPEL

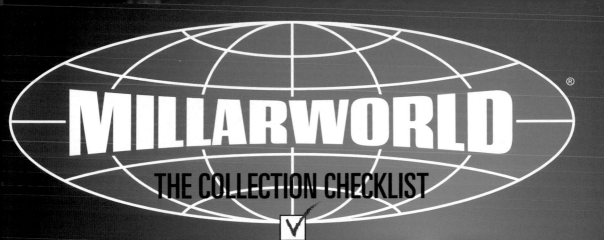

MILLARWORLD®

THE COLLECTION CHECKLIST

EMPRESS
MARK MILLAR STUART IMMONEN

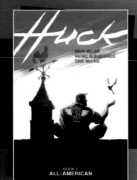

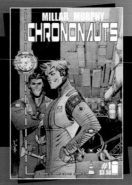

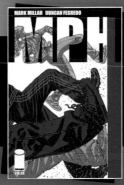

EMPRESS
Art by Stuart Immonen

HUCK
MARK MILLAR
RAFAEL ALBUQUERQUE
DAVE McCAIG
BOOK 1
ALL-AMERICAN

HUCK
Art by Rafael Albuquerque

MILLAR MURPHY
CHRONONAUTS
#1
$3.50

CHRONONAUTS
Art by Sean Gordon Murphy

MARK MILLAR DUNCAN FEGREDO
MPH

MPH
Art by Duncan Fegredo

MARK MILLAR · GORAN PARLOV
STARLIGHT

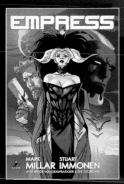

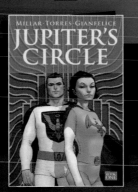

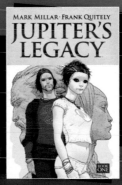

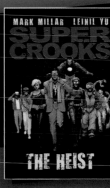

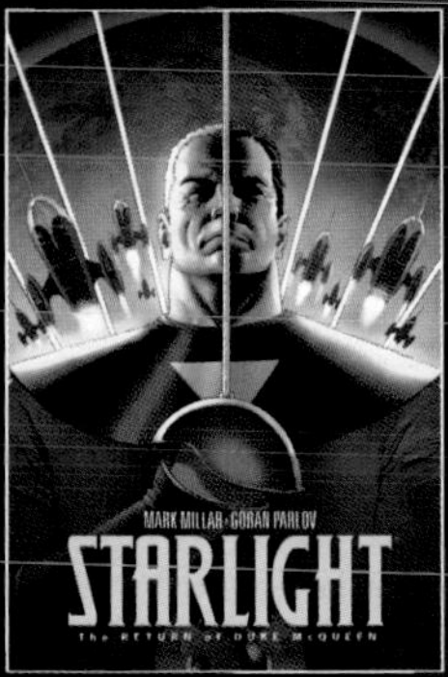

STARLIGHT
Art by Goran Parlov

MILLAR·TORRES·GIANFELICE
JUPITER'S CIRCLE
BOOK ONE

JUPITER'S CIRCLE 1 & 2
Art by Wilfredo Torres

MARK MILLAR · FRANK QUITELY
JUPITER'S LEGACY
BOOK ONE

JUPITER'S LEGACY
Art by Frank Quitely

MARK MILLAR LEINIL YU
SUPER CROOKS
THE HEIST

SUPER CROOKS
Art by Leinil Yu

MARK MILLAR & LEINIL YU
SUPERIOR
FROM THE WRITER OF KICK-ASS

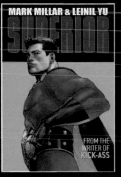

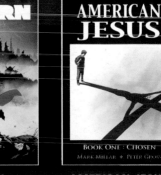

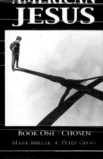

SUPERIOR
Art by Leinil Yu

MILLAR & McNIVEN'S
NEMESIS

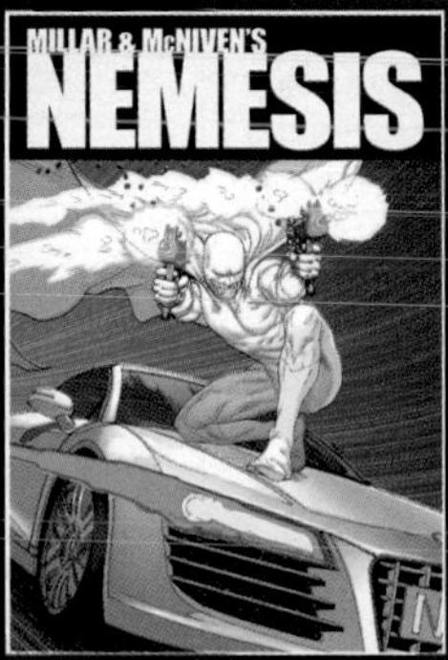

NEMESIS
Art by Steve McNiven

REBORN

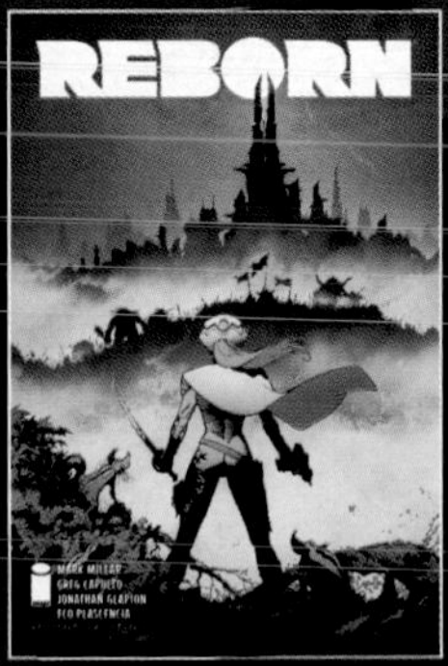

REBORN
Art by Greg Capullo

AMERICAN JESUS
BOOK ONE : CHOSEN
MARK MILLAR ✦ PETER GROSS

AMERICAN JESUS
Art by Peter Gross